JAMES BOWDOIN

AND THE

PATRIOT PHILOSOPHERS

JAMES BOWDOIN

AND THE

PATRIOT PHILOSOPHERS

Frank E. Manuel

AND

Fritzie P. Manuel

American Philosophical Society

PHILADELPHIA

2004

Memoirs of the
American Philosophical Society
Held at Philadelphia
For Promoting Useful Knowledge
Volume 247

Library of Congress Cataloging-in-Publication Data

Manuel, Frank Edward.
    James Bowdoin and the patriot philosophers / Frank E. Manuel, Fritzie P. Manuel
        p.   cm.   — (Memoirs of the American Philosophical Society held at
    Philadelphia for promoting useful knowledge ; v. 247)
    Includes bibliographical references (p.) and index.
    ISBN 0–87169–247–3
    1. Bowdoin, James, 1726–1790. 2. Governors—Massachusetts—Biography.
    3. Revolutionaries—Massachusetts—Biography. 4. Massachusetts—Politics and
    government—To 1775. 5. Massachusetts—Politics and government—1775–1865.
    6. Political culture—Massachusetts—History—18th century. 7. Enlightenment—
    Massachusetts. 8. Massachusetts—Intellectual life—18th century. 9. American
    Academy of Arts and Sciences—History. I. Manuel, Fritzie Prigohzy. II. Title.
    III. Memoirs of the American Philisophical Society ; v. 247.
    F69.B76M36 2003
    974.4'03'092—dc21
    [B]   2003048157

CONTENTS

PREFACE

IN AN essay of the 1760s Edward Gibbon made the point that history reveals itself in little things, *petits traits*, as significantly as in the sonorous public pronouncements of the rulers of states and empires. While the present narrative may be parish history enacted on a small, rickety stage, in retrospect the actors have grown taller, for the major figures of the American revolutionary era in Massachusetts were involved in what they came to consider "their Academy." If preempting the adjective American for the title was presumptuous, it was the act of a creative minority with antennae extending into the future.

Today the American Academy of Arts and Sciences is a society of scientists, scholars, men of letters, executives, administrators, and artists whose number exceeds four thousand. The House of the Academy is located in Cambridge, where the institution was first conceived, but it has broadened geographically to include a midwest and a western center, physical testimony of the valiant efforts to break out of its Cambridge-Boston confines. In annual elections the Academy now chooses representatives of disciplines that were not even a glimmer in the eyes of the original founders, a heterogeneous group of divines, doctors, lawyers, merchants, and public officials mainly from the eastern part of what was still called in the 1780 act of incorporation the State of Massachusetts Bay.

Though the conception of the Academy owes much to John Adams, the pivotal figure around whom its early history revolves is its first president, James Bowdoin, and part of the book is devoted to this descendant of Huguenots who guided the institution in its formative period with a firm hand. Benjamin Franklin, the Philadelphian born in Boston, through his friend Bowdoin kept abreast of what was taking place "in a philosophical way" in his native town, and his image hovers benevolently over the Academy. While he supported the American Philosophical Society, the friendly rival in Philadelphia, his association with the patriot philosophers of Boston helped spread the fame of their Academy among the learned of Europe. The founding of a society for the promotion of knowledge in the midst of the Revolutionary War was a way of joining the comity of nations even before formal independence was achieved. The role of the president and prominent Fellows in suppressing Shays' "unnatural rebellion" — not an official commitment of the Academy itself — discloses the social alignment of the intellectual elite in a dark time and is included in this history.

We confess to an old-fashioned presupposition that somehow the initial stage of an institution bears within it the seed of its full flowering. This story of the establishment of the Academy and the vicissitudes of its first decade aims to preserve the tone of its quaint provincial origins and freely gives itself over to the intrigues and extravagant projects of the early years. After a period of enthusiastic activity the Academy lost its bloom and went into a decline. In the ebb and flow of succeeding centuries it has mirrored the fortunes of the arts and sciences in this country. The beginnings reflect the revolutionary euphoria generated by the prospect of victory. Such moments in the lives of national collectives are always fleeting, but the experience of the first Fellows illuminates the mentality of those who in building a nation imitated their European counterparts and strove to surpass them.

Printed materials on the revolutionary era are accumulating exponentially. We have relied principally upon the unpublished records of the Academy, deposited in the Boston Athenaeum and the Academy, and the personal papers of many of the Fellows, housed in the Massachusetts Historical Society and very kindly made available to us. Other documents are dispersed in the Archives of the Commonwealth of Massachusetts, the Harvard University Archives, the American Antiquarian Society in Worcester, the Essex Historical Institute in Salem, the Longfellow Library in Bowdoin College, Brunswick, Maine, and the Huntington Library in San Marino, California. To the librarians and research staffs of these several institutions, in particular to Stephen Nonack, Head of Reader Services and Curator of Manuscripts at the Athenaeum, and Clark Elliott, Archivist of the Academy, we are greatly indebted for their cordial welcome and their helpfulness. We owe warm thanks to our friend Professor Paul Lucas, who encouraged us to complete our manuscript and played a vital part in its publication.

This study does not presume to be a full-scale biography of James Bowdoin II; nor is it an account of the advancement of science in eighteenth-century America. It is a story of how a group of patriots, moved by their reverence for knowledge and pride in their new country, founded what is now one of its oldest cultural institutions, and of the man who nurtured it in the first decade of its existence. Amid the triumphs of the early Republic, the American Academy of Arts and Sciences deserves an honorable place. It may be well, after more than two hundred years, to remember its origins in a spirit of admiration — though without piety.

JAMES BOWDOIN

AND THE

PATRIOT PHILOSOPHERS

1

ENLIGHTENMENT OVER
MASSACHUSETTS BAY

❦

IN THE course of half a century Massachusetts underwent three very different kinds of revolution. The outpouring of the spirit known as the Great Awakening was called a "strange Revolution, an unexpected, surprising Overturning of Things," by Jonathan Edwards in *Some Thoughts Concerning the Present Revival of Religion in New-England* (1742).[1] The challenge to British sovereignty culminating in the War for American Independence was simply "the Revolution." And, in the mid-eighties, an uprising of debtors and impoverished yeomen against the authority of the newly formed Commonwealth was first labeled an insurrection and then declared officially to be a rebellion; the word revolution had become sacrosanct and reserved. James Bowdoin, the first president of the American Academy of Arts and Sciences, was born in the midst of the religious revolution; was a major (though sometimes neglected) protagonist in the victory of the second or political revolution; and, ousted from the governor's chair by his fellow-citizens, died three years after forcefully quelling the inchoate social revolution in the western counties that has come down in the histories as Shays' Rebellion.

Of the half-dozen Boston patriots honored by posterity as the spearheads of a political break with the British Crown—James Otis, Samuel Adams, John Adams, John Hancock, James Warren, and James Bowdoin—Bowdoin has fared least well, and even the barest facts of his career have been forgotten. He has not been favored with a full-scale biography, though he was eulogized in funeral orations in church and in the Academy, and over the centuries a few appreciative memoirs have appeared. A revisionist portrait is unnecessary because there is no official one to demolish. While recent American history has discovered and endowed with the breath of life populist partisans like Ebenezer Mackintosh and William Molineux, Bowdoin remains lost in the mist. Statues and paintings of other revolutionary leaders have found their way into frequented public places. The best Bowdoin portrait hangs in exile in Maine, in the college that his son established in his memory.

---

1. Jonathan Edwards, *Some Thoughts Concerning the Present Revival of Religion in New-England* (Edinburgh, 1743; ed. pr. Boston, 1742), 1: 47. Though actually published in March of 1743, the work was completed in 1742, the year that appears on the title page.

This history makes no attempt either to follow the intricacies of Bowdoin's business dealings or to treat exhaustively the details of his political career, which spanned almost forty years. It centers on the founding of the American Academy and his presidency, a decade in office during which he molded that institution into an embodiment of his conception of a society for the promotion of knowledge. In the preface to the first volume of Academy memoirs, published in 1785, he defined the duty of what he called a "patriot philosopher": the pursuit of every inquiry that might ultimately promote the security and welfare of his fellow-citizens, the growth of their commerce, and the progress of those arts that enhanced the grace of living. In the 1780s Bowdoin was the first among equals in an assembly of patriot philosophers, most of whom had fought for independence and who, at the same time, gloried in the anticipated triumphs of American arts and sciences.

An Act of Creation

The spring of 1780 following a hard winter was still a grim period of the War for Independence. The Continental army had suffered heavy losses from sickness, desertion, and short enlistments. General Washington, writing to James Bowdoin from his headquarters in Morristown, New Jersey, confessed to his concern that the magnanimity of their French allies might not be seconded by the exertions of the patriots, for nothing was left them but the skeleton of an army, and they were in grave financial straits. At the same time, Lafayette confided to Bowdoin that he had concealed from the French ministry and newly arrived French generals how desperate he had found the military situation, the officers naked, the soldiers starving; he trusted that future efforts by the Americans would eliminate the grounds for so discouraging a report.[2] Not an auspicious moment for the founding of learned societies.

But on 4 May 1780, the Provincial Congress of the State of Massachusetts Bay passed an act creating an American Academy of Arts and Sciences and incorporating sixty-two Massachusetts men by name as its members. The act directed James Bowdoin, former president of the state's Council and of its Constitutional Convention and a Fellow-designate of the new society, to convene the first meeting of the corporate body, which was endowed with the right to receive property if its annual income did not exceed £500. The members of the corporation, listed in the act, were also given authority to expel Fellows for cause and to elect new members under statutes

---

2. George Washington, *The Writings . . . from the Original Manuscript Sources, 1745–1799*, ed. John C. Fitzpatrick (Washington, D.C.: GPO), 18 (1937), 366–67, Washington to Bowdoin, Morristown, 15 May 1780; Massachusetts Historical Society (hereinafter designated as MHS), *Proceedings* 5 (1860–62), 348–50, Lafayette to Bowdoin, Morristown, 30 May 1780. Bowdoin's reply, 12 June, is printed on 350–51.

of their own devising, thus constituting a body in perpetuity. Since the constitution of the Commonwealth of Massachusetts was not formally and finally ratified until 16 June 1780, the Academy was a creation of that twilight period between the divestment of colonial status and the proclamation of an independent Commonwealth.

The broad comprehensive purposes to which the Academy was to devote its efforts were set forth in one long, stem-winding sentence:

> And be it further Enacted by the Authority aforesaid, that the end and design of the institution of the said Academy is, to promote & encourage the Knowledge of Antiquities of America, and of the natural History of the Country, & to determine the uses to which the various natural productions of the Country may be applied: to promote and encourage medical discoveries; mathematical disquisitions; philosophical enquiries and experiments; astronomical, meteorological, and geographical observations; and improvements in agriculture, Arts, Manufactures and commerce; and, in fine, to cultivate every art and science, which may tend to advance the Interest, Honor, dignity and Happiness of a free, independent, and virtuous people.

The punctuation in the manner of the period was excessive, but the estimable activities enumerated covered many aspects of secular existence.

The Academy was not to be a forum for political debates, which were conducted in town meetings, legislatures, and conventions; and mention of the book of Scripture and theological disciplines was avoided in principle (though not in fact), an omission that a more indifferent, irreligious age has rectified—today theology is coupled with philosophy in the same academic class. There was not much discussion about the name of the new institution, nor about the pretentious application of the adjective "American" to what was a company incorporated in Massachusetts, though the historian Ebenezer Hazard, surveyor-general of the postal system and an early Fellow, found the title neither modest nor appropriate.[3]

Twice-Blessed Science

The idea of an academy of arts and sciences did not spring full-blown from the imaginative brain of the Boston patriots in 1780. The scientific revolution, obeying a tempo of its own, had come over to America with the first settlers and no one doubted its authority, though perforce it long remained dependent on the works of European genius. From the time the Massachusetts Bay Colony was established, New England

---

3. Boston Athenaeum, Records of the American Academy of Arts and Sciences (MS), 1:1–4, copy of the act establishing the Academy. The bound volume of manuscripts is hereinafter referred to as "Academy Records." See also MHS, *Collections*, ser. 5.2 (Belknap Papers, 1 [1877]), 63, Ebenezer Hazard to Jeremy Belknap, Jamaica Plain, 27 June 1780.

leaders were committed to the pursuit of secular studies and what today would be vaguely recognized as physical science. A mere six years after the founding of Boston (1630)—the site was chosen for its freedom from wolves, rattlesnakes, and mosquitoes—a college was established in Newton (later Cambridge). Cotton Mather, the magnificent chronicler of the early years, went beyond a mere detailing of the facts of the endowment to leave a description of the intellectual position Harvard fostered: rigorous Dissenter religion combined with pronounced anti-Aristotelianism and acceptance of the Baconian ideals of science. John Winthrop the Younger (1606–1676), son of the first governor of the colony, was honored as a Fellow of the Royal Society of London at the time of its founding—he was to be its western outpost—and the "new philosophy" did not have to fight its way into the curriculum of Harvard College, as it had to in many Protestant and Catholic universities of the Old World.[4] By the time his son, also named John Winthrop (1638–1707), reached maturity and was elected to fellowship in the Royal Society, New England was firmly identified with science. The 1650 charter of the College (the first was granted in 1642) formulated its purpose as "the advancement of all good literature artes and Sciences." There was no conflict in New England between the cultivation of science and the study of classical literature and history in the original Greek and Latin, along with a smattering of Hebrew. Both were essential components of a Harvard education at a time when it was possible to leave the universities of Oxford and Cambridge without any knowledge of the "book of nature."

Harvard was rocked by the scandals of its initial two presidencies—the first officer had been fined for mercilessly beating a student with a cudgel, was excommunicated, left the country, and turned to the Anglican church; the second knew an even more deplorable fate—he became an Anabaptist. But even in those times of trouble, Harvard students were trained to make fresh inquiries into the workings of nature. The science taught at Harvard in the seventeenth century may have been primitive in some respects, but by 1672 the College owned a telescope, the gift of John Winthrop the Younger, with which Thomas Brattle made observations of the comet of 1680 that Newton used in the *Principia*. Three years after Galileo recanted in a terrifying ceremony in Santa Maria sopra Minerva in Rome, and four decades after Bruno was burned at the stake in its Campo dei Fiori, a college of Dissenters in a tiny haven in the wilderness that bordered on Massachusetts Bay was open to a new philosophy of nature. The burning of witches and the hanging of Quakers involved theological, not scientific, questions.

In 1659, even before a charter was granted to the Royal Society of London, John Winthrop the Younger had written to the head of the English Pansophists, Samuel

---

4. See Frederick E. Brasch, "The Royal Society of London and its influence upon scientific thought in the American Colonies," *The Scientific Monthly* 33 (Oct. 1931), 338–41.

Hartlib, begging for information about the activities of his scientific circle, about Cornelis Drebbel (already dead some twenty-five years), about Galileo and discoveries in the celestial bodies, about perpetual motion, and about Sir Edward Kelley's alchemy. Winthrop was especially eager to know whether the "learned mr. Comenius" was still alive and what remarkable inventions had been devised by him. "I am full of more quaeries but I pray excuse me thus-farr, for we are heere as men dead to the world in this wildernesse," he moaned, thirsting for the latest news of European science.[5] Winthrop had once met Comenius, who, the story goes, had been offered the presidency of Harvard College.[6] The Pansophic ideal of invigorating religion with a knowledge of things in the physical universe was taken for granted in Massachusetts.

The Congregationalist ministers who taught at Harvard accepted the logic of the sixteenth-century French anti-Aristotelian theologian Petrus Ramus (Pierre de La Ramée), and they read from a Port Royal textbook at a time when such an innovation would have been considered heretical in English universities. Among the Puritan divines there were acidulous controversies over church governance, Anabaptism, Arminianism, and Socinianism, but no wars over the Copernican theory. The philosophies of Newton and Locke penetrated the intellectual consciousness of Massachusetts clergymen without resistance. When Cotton Mather in the *Magnalia Christi Americana* (1702) reconstructed the philosophical position of his ancestors and predecessors in the New England ministry, he used the term "eclecticism" in a favorable sense, signifying openness to a variety of philosophies about the natural world. Willem Jakob Storm van 's Gravesande's *Mathematical Elements of Natural Philosophy, confirmed by experiments: or an Introduction to Sir Isaac Newton's Philosophy* (1720–21), which in a popular fashion integrated Newtonianism with a religious glorification of divine omniscience and omnipotence, was the standard eighteenth-century Harvard textbook on natural philosophy.[7]

Newtonian thought had first been significantly expounded in America by Isaac Greenwood, the teacher of still another John Winthrop and Hollis Professor at Harvard until his dismissal in 1738 for "gross intemperance." He was succeeded by his disciple, who held the chair for more than forty years. Though Winthrop's writings were not voluminous, he published a letter on the transit of Venus over the sun and on an eclipse of the moon in the *Philosophical Transactions of the Royal Society* (1740), a *Lecture on Earthquakes* (1755), *Two Lectures on Comets* (1759), a

5. G. H. Turnbull, ed., "Some Correspondence of John Winthrop, Jr., and Samuel Hartlib," in MHS, *Proceedings* 72 (1957–60), 39–40, Winthrop to Hartlib, Hartford, 16 Dec. 1659.

6. Albert Matthews, "Comenius and Harvard College," in Colonial Society of Massachusetts, *Publications* 21 (1919), 146–90.

7. The English edition, translated by J. T., was published in London in two volumes. The original was in Latin: *Physices elementa mathematica, experimentis confirmata: sive Introductio ad Philosophiam Newtonianam*, 2 vols. (Leyden, 1720).

"Cogitata de Cometis" in the *Transactions* (1768), and *Two Lectures on the Parallax and Distance from the Sun, as deducible from the transit of Venus* (1769). He led the first American scientific expedition to Newfoundland to observe the transit of Venus in 1761. Recognized as the outstanding American astronomer, he was elected to the Royal Society of London in 1766 and to the American Philosophical Society two years later; honorary degrees were conferred upon him by Edinburgh and Harvard. Benjamin Franklin was a far more original thinker, but Winthrop's training in mathematics and astronomy allowed him to enter areas closed to Franklin, the autodidact genius.[8] Franklin's reflections on his friend's death are a proper measure of the man: "Our excellent Mr. Winthrop, I see, is gone," he wrote wistfully to the Reverend Samuel Cooper from Passy on 27 October, 1779, "He was one of those old Friends, for the sake of whose Society I wish'd to return and spend the small Remnant of my Days in New England. A few more such Deaths will make me a Stranger in my own Country. The loss of Friends is the Tax a man pays for living long himself. I find it a heavy one."[9]

During the early years of the Revolution, these two most eminent men of American science, Franklin and John Winthrop, were high in the councils of the war, along with the merchant James Bowdoin, a Newtonian whose love of science bound him closely to both the Harvard professor and the former Boston boy turned Philadelphian.

Merchants in the seaport towns of New England had an obvious material interest in the perfection of celestial mechanics, in projects for measuring the longitude at sea—for which there had been a long-standing Parliament prize from the time when the aged Newton had reluctantly acquiesced in its offering. The Old World knew, or thought it did, the potentialities of the soil in areas long under cultivation, but the possibilities of the new land were still unexplored. In one of the first *Transactions* of the American Philosophical Society in Philadelphia an adventurous comparison was made between the climates of the east coast of China and the east coast of America, and it was proposed that since they were similar many Chinese products like the silkworm might be successfully introduced—an idea that had already been broached by the English Pansophists in the mid-seventeenth century. As the peril of Indian attacks receded, coastal Americans became ever more curious about their earth and its rocks and minerals. Indian languages had been studied as

---

8. The papers of John Winthrop are in the Harvard University Archives; they include his diaries, 1739–79; meteorological journal, 1742–79; abstracts of sermons, 1728–29; and scientific notes. See F. E. Brasch, *John Winthrop (1714–1779), America's first astronomer, and the science of his period* (San Francisco, 1916; reprinted from *Publications of the Astronomical Society of the Pacific*, no. 165 [Aug.-Oct. 1916]). See also Frederick G. Kilgour, "Professor John Winthrop's notes on sun spot observations (1739)," *Isis* 29. 2 (Nov. 1938), 355–61.

9. Benjamin Franklin, *Writings*, ed. Albert Henry Smyth (New York, 1905–07), 7:407, Franklin to Cooper, Passy, 27 Oct. 1779.

an aid in conversion and commerce from the time of the first encounters between savages and colonists. An Indian college had been established at Harvard, though most of its students failed to survive the course, having fallen victim to physical and psychic disease. The study of Indian artifacts and speech raised serious "scientific" questions about Indian origins and the relations between their tongues and known languages of Europe and Asia. Investigation of American antiquities was early recognized as part of the American Academy's mission.

The idea of an encyclopedia that would order all knowledge was fundamental to Pansophism, and the academies that proliferated throughout the European continent in the eighteenth century considered themselves living, progressing encyclopedias. With American independence, colleges and sodalities for "improvement" sprouted throughout the states. In Massachusetts wealthy merchants like James Bowdoin and clergymen-scientists like John Prince acquired libraries of over a thousand volumes, sizable collections for the period. Bowdoin bequeathed his library to the Academy. Despite the fire of 1764, by the end of the century Harvard had the richest collection on the continent. While Benjamin Franklin dallied with the ladies in Paris, John Adams bought books. Eastern Massachusetts libraries were well stocked with the volumes abandoned by Tory émigrés; and when revolutionary privateering was at its height a whole library, with many scientific works, was captured in the English Channel and ultimately donated to the town of Salem. Private and public catalogues show the holdings to be light on belles-lettres but weighty with theology, history, science, and travel literature. Once the American Academy was founded, it kept alive and gave advertisement to a rationalist tradition that had been imbedded in the New England mind for a century and a half, despite residues of the Puritan terror of hell, and of primitive belief in ghostly existences and the palpable machinations of Satan and his minions.

Among the Boston patriots of the revolutionary period, divergences on political and moral issues were grave, and aggressive rivalry exacted a heavy psychological toll, but it is difficult to find a member of the group who did not give obeisance to science. It was a glory to God and it led to practical inventions that increased prosperity. In 1660, John Winthrop the Younger had worried lest inventions serve the lusts of the wicked, or throw people out of work: "Rich men commonly reape the benefits of invention to make them more rich, and the poore yet more miserable and uncomfortable."[10] A century later such apprehensions had evaporated. Science revealed the secrets of God's book of nature; it engaged men in salutary pursuits; it amused with its curiosities; it directed the mind to higher spiritual things. "The field of science before you has nothing but pleasures and delights ravishing the

10. Turnbull, "Some Correspondence of Winthrop and Hartlib," loc. cit. 60, Winthrop to Hartlib, Hartford, 25 Oct. 1660.

mind," preached the Reverend Phillips Payson in the thirtieth annual Dudleian Lecture at Harvard in 1784.[11]

A wise philosopher like Franklin was not discouraged when Americans failed to profit straightway from his electrical discoveries by putting lightning rods on their steeples; he was aware that such substantive changes were slow to be adopted and he did not despair of the eventual acceptance of new practical inventions.[12] Science would dispel uneasiness and foster the growth of happiness. Three Boston doctors met in secret in the early 1770s to dissect animals in order to refine their art. Individual ministers might preach and write against inoculation for smallpox, but others in rural areas not served by physicians practiced it themselves; and when there were epidemics in Boston throughout the century and one in six died without inoculation—and one in two hundred with—the statistics were too dramatic to be ignored. A clear majority favored this act symbolic of confidence in the new science, and an inoculation hospital was set up in Castle William, situated in what is now South Boston. Rousseau's paradoxical discourse on the evils of the arts and sciences found no significant echo in Boston. The cultivation of science was justified simultaneously on religious and utilitarian grounds, a combination that made it twice-blessed.

Old Lights and New

During the English civil war men had talked about experimental religion, religion actually experienced, and so they did in the colony. Even the enthusiasts established a kinship between religious experience and scientific experiment, and both were validated. They were contrasted with religion by rote embodied in a papist or high-church catechism and knowledge by rote as set out in the books of Aristotle, that darling of the Whore of Babylon and of the two Anglican universities that American divines had repudiated. Scientific doctrines were not subjects of debate between the "old lights" and the "new lights" when the fervor of the Great Awakening stirred the Connecticut Valley. Jonathan Edwards cited Newton on religion, though usually from secondary sources and with notable inaccuracy,[13] and found in Locke's *Essay Concerning Humane Understanding*, which he had read at Yale when he was thirteen and treasured throughout his life, a scientific bulwark for the religious revival.

11. Cambridge, Mass., Harvard University Archives: Phillips Payson, "Sermon at the 30th Annual Dudleian Lecture" (MS), 1 Sept. 1784.

12. Benjamin Franklin, *Papers* 15, ed. W. B. Willcox (New Haven: Yale University Press, 1972), 168, Franklin to John Winthrop, London, 2 July 1768.

13. Edwards relied on George Turnbull, a Scottish philosopher and author of a two-volume work, *The Principles of Moral Philosophy*, published in 1740; the title page of volume two reads *The Principles of Moral and Christian Philosophy*.

Though Harvard was lightly touched by the Great Awakening and a few gentlemen's sons who had been sent there for a polite education were momentarily infused with zeal for the cause of Christ, the enthusiasm passed quickly and the university became a bastion of opposition to Jonathan Edwards and George Whitefield. Under the Reverend William Cooper, revivalist preachers had been allowed to perform at the prosperous Brattle Street Church in Boston, reviling their enemies as men of Arminian, Pelagian, and Deistical principles. By the 1740s, however, the merchants of Boston stood shoulder to shoulder with the scholars of Cambridge in withstanding the gusts from Northampton, that enthusiastical town. In the second half of the eighteenth century a liberal Congregational church could tolerate a variety of religious beliefs in the abstract; but the Great Awakening of Jonathan Edwards had polarized the nature of religious commitment so sharply that respectable Bostonians would not countenance any overt manifestations of zealotry in their midst. There were differences among Congregationalist pastors about whether or not an unrepentant sinner was condemned to everlasting damnation; the arguments adduced in controversy, however, had to be *rational*, based on sober interpretation of Scripture or theological reflections on the nature of God.

Even Edwards represented a lowering of the fanatical pitch of the Mathers. The oscillation of the spirit recorded in Edwards's private diary in late December 1722 and early January 1723 lacks the searing quality of Cotton Mather's confession. Edwards's narration is rather laconic. He was in many ways an observer of the religious experiences of others, a man with a scientific bent who could study a long-drawn-out religious "awakening" and analyze it as if it were a phenomenon of nature. In private Mather shrieked and threw himself on the floor convulsed with anguish. For all the fits and faintings of the auditors before whom he conjured up the gaping jaws of hell, in Edwards himself the wild late-seventeenth-century experience had been tamed.

In pre-revolutionary Massachusetts, atheists—if any existed—did not openly profess their lack of faith, though there were some suspected deists as well as embryonic unitarians. While hell and the devil by the mid-eighteenth century were no longer prominent in the religion of educated Bostonians, the idea of immortality was still generally accepted. And even those who had their doubts about divine intervention in the daily affairs of men—as distinguished from an overall supervision of His creation—would lapse on occasion into a common religious speech that imputed American independence to God's miraculous aid on the side of justice and righteousness. "God has again woonderfuley apeard for his peepel," Robert Pierpont reported to James Bowdoin in 1776;[14] and Bowdoin himself in

14. MHS, *Collections*, ser. 6.9 (Bowdoin and Temple Papers, 1 [1897]), 394, Robert Pierpont to James Bowdoin, Roxbury, 5 Mar. 1776. Some years earlier, in his *Sermon Preached October 25th, 1759* ... (Boston, 1759) at a public thanksgiving on the reduction of Quebec, the pastor of the New North Church (Andrew Eliot) had preached, "In fine, it was God, the great Ruler of the universe, that gave *Quebec* into our hands" (p. 38).

a letter of 20 November 1783, to Thomas Pownall, the former royal governor of Massachusetts who was deeply sympathetic to the American cause, seconded Pownall's perception of the final victory: "I consider it with you, 'as ye visible interposition of divine providence, superceeding the ordinary course of human affairs.'"[15]

The conviction that Americans were a chosen people who had a peculiar relationship to God, conveniently adapted from the image of biblical Israel, was at one time or another entertained even by deists and skeptics. But the methods and laws of science were the normal way of understanding God's creation, and clergymen and gentlemen farmers collected the flora and fauna of God's New World and dug up peculiar specimens of things from the past. As fields were cleared, the strange artifacts that were uncovered provoked inquiry. Old superstitions were tenacious, and cessation of the trials for witchcraft did not signal the end of belief in demonic wiles among the people; but gentleman scientists who could prognosticate an eclipse with precision in the course of their studies were contracting the boundaries of the realm of terror. Some went even further: they treated the dogmas of religion itself in accordance with scientific methodology and measured them by scientific criteria. The Reverend Samuel Williams, later Harvard's Hollis Professor of Mathematicks and of Natural and Experimental Philosophy, divided the manuscript of his "Elements of Theology" (1762) into Axioms and Postulates, Scholia and Corollaries, as though he were a latter-day Newton.[16] And among the papers of the distinguished Salem physician Edward Augustus Holyoke there is a heretical memorandum declaring, "The doctrine of the Trinity appears to be a doctrine of inference. We ought not to admit a doctrine of inference. That three persons can be one person is directly contrary to reason."[17] Both Williams and Holyoke were charter members of the American Academy of Arts and Sciences. George Richards Minot, who became a member in 1789, and distinguished himself both as a historian and a judge, eloquently represented the new religious outlook of many New England intellectuals in the last decades of the century. His diary entry for Sunday, 12 December 1784, is a scornful denunciation of those who spent themselves in professing or attacking trinitarian doctrines:

> I verily think that my Salvation does not depend upon my believing the Trinity or the
> Unity of the Godhead; nor am I a better Christian for enlisting under the banners of

15. In a letter to Bowdoin on 28 February 1783, immediately after peace was announced, Pownall had written, "I consider this wonderfull Revolution as the visible interposition of Divine Providence, superceeding the ordinary course of human affaires . . ." (MHS, *Collections*, ser. 7.6 [Bowdoin and Temple Papers, 2 [1907], 3). Bowdoin's reply, 20 November 1783, is printed on page 21. See also Albert West, "Thomas Pownall, the Most Interesting of the Provincial Governors . . . ," reprint from *Massachusetts Law Quarterly*, August 1953.

16. Cambridge, Mass., Harvard University Archives: Samuel Williams, "The Elements of Theology" (MS), 1762.

17. Salem, Mass., Essex Institute: Holyoke Papers, Box 8, Memorandum.

Christ to support his equality with the Father, or for assisting the omnipotence of the Father in maintaining his superiority over the Son, than if I sincerely imitated the example of the one, & reverentially adored the other. But, say our Saints, the whole ceremony of the Church is founded upon one of these doctrines. And what fools were they who made it, to ground this system of worship on the idle speculations of party zealots.[18]

In the revolutionary period, individuals who were slipping away from the theocratic absolutism of their Puritan forebears displaced the adoration of God with the adoration of country, and the defection left scars. The English émigré the Reverend William Gordon, an outsider, in writing to his friend John Adams, assumed the role of guide to a perplexed soul. This clergyman-historian dissected Adams's conflicting emotions and drew pertinent distinctions between the universality of the Christian ideal and exclusive devotion to the *patria*. Gordon was no great intellect, but his letter verbalized a general experience among many of the patriots, the transfer of religious feeling from God to the newborn nation, the substitution of a desire for fame and a readiness to sacrifice oneself for one's country in the place of mortification of the flesh and humbling oneself before God. Mortification—a term that was still much in use—lost its religious intensity and became a secular psychological word describing the anguish consequent upon a worldly event. Gordon differentiated between the Roman ideal of patriotism and the commitment meet for a Christian revolutionary hero. In a rambling way his letter gave utterance to sentiments that sometimes gnawed at Adams and other ambitious Boston patriots who were casting themselves in a Roman mold:

> That impartial heathen Historians, whether malignant or not, would not allow any higher motive to govern men than ambition, is not strange. they had not the means of ascending or being wrought up to a higher. They well knew that tho' it was a maxim—*dulce et decorum est pro patria mori*—yet the deaths occasioned by it were not owing to the *pro patria*, or to the *dulce*, but to the *decorum*—the character, the character that men gained by dying *pro patria*. The name of a *Patriot* fed the spirit of ambition, and wrought wonders: but who of those great *Patriots* that are upon record would have died in *private* to have saved his country, had he despaired of its ever being known and made public. . . . A Patriot has great charms in the esteem of many; but the friend of mankind or the christian has much greater. The first to serve his country will trample upon the rights of the rest of mankind—thus did the Roman patriotism operate. The last, tho' concerned for his country in particular, wishes liberty and happiness to the world, and gives up his own little spot when the benefit of the world requires it.[19]

18. MHS, George Richards Minot, Journal, 1784–1791 (MS), entry for 12 Dec. 1784.

19. Worthington C. Ford, ed., "Letters of the Reverend William Gordon, Historian of the American Revolution, 1770–1799," in MHS, *Proceedings* 63 (1929–30), 444–45, Gordon to John Adams, Jamaica Plain, 19 Oct. 1780.

Many of the patriots had arrived at a form of religious syncretism. Residues from a Calvinist childhood that had early fashioned their credo persisted, while waves of English Enlightenment thought continued to erode the craggy Dissenter Puritan religion of their ancestors. Greek and Roman ideals of *virtus* and *patria* had permeated an educational regimen constructed on classical texts, and there were some signs of a burgeoning romantic religiosity, without benefit of Rousseau's Vicar of Savoy. The eighteenth-century latitudinarian Anglican polemicists that the clergymen and some of their lay parishioners read left their mark, and there are echoes of the humanitarian gospel preached in the Freemasonic lodges to which some of them belonged (without necessarily dropping church membership). John Eliot, pastor of the New North Church in Boston, delivered a sermon before the Society of Antient and Honorable Free and Accepted Masons on 24 June 1782: "No difference of nation or country will prevent [the Freemason's] charity or cool his compassion.—He will not ask his sentiments upon politics or religion,—But let him be high church, or low church, or no church—let him be whig or tory, Pagan or Jew—it is sufficient that he is an object of misery."[20] However ardent their faith, the religious views of the Massachusetts patriots were something of a patchwork.

By the latter part of the eighteenth century, American Congregationalist ministers often took deep draughts of Arminianism (after the Dutch theologian Jacobus Arminius, born in 1560 and spiritual father of the separatist Remonstrant movement), without courting an open break with Calvinism. In revolutionary Massachusetts, a rigid interpretation of the doctrine of predestination set forth in Calvin's *Institutes* could not readily be harmonized with the straightforward affirmation of the Declaration of Independence, which seemed to contradict Calvin's teaching, "For all are not created equal, but some are foreordained to eternal life, others to eternal damnation." The original texts of Arminius, loosely construed, could sustain inferences that everlasting hellfire was extinguished, divine grace might be extended to unbelievers, constraints on freedom of conscience were impermissible, and theological argumentation, which had absorbed the energies of so many worthy clerics, was an exercise far inferior to the drawing of moral lessons

20. John Eliot, *A Sermon Delivered in the Chapel, Boston* . . . (Boston, 1782), 11; see also his address a year later, *Charge to the Grand Lodge of Free and Accepted Masons, June 24, 1783*. His brother Freemason Christopher Gore expressed nearly identical sentiments in his *Oration delivered at the Chapel, in Boston: Before the Ancient and Honourable Society of Free and Accepted Masons, June 24, 1783*: "Whenever and wherever we meet with the good and worthy—be they Turk or Jew,—Christian or Pagan,—of whatsoever party in church or state — of whatever kindred or tongue, let them have the first rank in our esteem. Should the vilest of men, should our own most inveterate enemy, be an object of charity, his afflictions ought to disarm our resentment, and in the hour of his distress, we must give freely and upbraid not" (p. 10).

and obedience to Enlightenment precepts. The austerity of orthodox Calvinism was not replaced overnight by the softness of Enlightenment virtues, but in practice the old doctrines were pushed underground, to be resurrected at critical moments. A traditional Calvinism that stressed the dark side of human nature and the vaguely benevolent spirit of Arminianism cohabited in the souls of many members of the Academy, not least among them its first president.

None of the prominent patriots was possessed by his sinfulness as Cotton Mather had been. There was no manifest dread of the tortures of hell except in moments of psychic illness. While most worshiped in Congregational churches and formally subscribed to the doctrines of John Calvin, few among them, with the exception of Samuel, son of Cotton Mather, and perhaps Peter Thacher,[21] openly professed a belief in eternal damnation for the wicked. The Brattle Street Church allowed for doctrinal latitude, and charges that it harbored Arminians, Deists, and worse were not without foundation. Men like John Adams and James Bowdoin, though they read bales of theological tracts by English and American divines, did not formulate theological positions to which they adhered unswervingly with the passion and tenacity of their ancestors. As he grew older, John Adams devoted much effort to studying the origins of religion, pagan and Christian, in all times and places, but he did not arrive at unalterable conclusions. He probably ended up as a believer, troubled by the enigmatic nature of religion, but revering Christ as a moral teacher. In Braintree, Adams belonged to a Congregational church; but when he was in Philadelphia he indifferently attended Sunday services of Baptists to judge of the quality of the preaching. He could admire the Catholic martyr Thomas More, calling his *Utopia* "elegant and ingenious — the fruit of a benevolent and candid Heart, a learned and strong Mind."[22] Though John Hancock's uncle, Thomas Hancock, had established a professorship of Hebrew and Oriental languages at Harvard, his nephew ignored abstruse religious questions; he donated books to the university for others to read. On state occasions he made perfunctory declarations of the virtues of religion, and he gave it lip-service in proclamations of thanksgiving. Far removed from Hancock's casual obeisance was the obsessional fervor of Joseph Hawley, the eminent Northampton lawyer and revolutionary patriot.

All the Massachusetts patriots were Christians, even those who, like James Warren, were not formal members of a church; there were no Catholics among them; and they were all buried in churchyards. Papists were actively abominated, and the loose moral ways associated with "southerners" were censured. Jews were too few

21. See Peter Thacher, *That the punishment of the finally impenitent shall be eternal; or that all men shall not be saved; three sermons, October 1782* (Salem, 1783).

22. John Adams, *Diary and Autobiography* (Adams Papers, ser. 1), ed. L. H. Butterfield (Cambridge, Mass.: Belknap Press of Harvard University Press, 1961), 2:51–52, entry for 10 Nov. 1771.

in number to impinge upon their consciousness, except in occasional isolated instances: James Bowdoin's son traded warily with a "Jew-merchant" in Philadelphia; Professor John Winthrop shortly before his death dined with a Jew of Newport; the scholarly concerns of the Reverend Ezra Stiles of Newport and later New Haven brought him into converse with rabbis and "chuzans" (cantors) and prompted his attendance at synagogue services. The mystery, in a theological sense, with which Increase Mather in his sermons of 1666 had endowed the survival of the Jews was gone. Though the characters of the New Englanders had been molded by the ethical practices associated with Calvinism, theological controversies had lost their hold or interest. The intellectual exercises of religion were deflected to science, while disputatiousness over church governance was transferred to the broader expanses of the countryside and the problems of running a state and a nation. On gravestones the urn and the weeping willow replaced the skull and bones of the seventeenth century.

Boston Patriots and the Late Enlightenment

The idea of the neutrality of science was by this time a dogma in the English-speaking world, though in reality even an autonomous body like the Academy was not as divorced from politics as the Boston patriots who established it may have assumed in their rhetorical pronouncements. European academies had been founded by kings and dukes; the American Academy was self-created, one of the first acts of the patriots marking their entry into adulthood. Four years later, in 1784, Immanuel Kant in distant Königsberg, attempting to answer the query "What is Enlightenment?" would write, "Enlightenment is the liberation of man from his self-imposed state of minority. Minority is the incapacity to use one's understanding without the direction of another. The state of minority is self-caused when its source lies not in lack of understanding, but in lack of determination and courage to apply it without the assistance of another. *Sapere aude*! Dare to use your own understanding! is then the motto of the Enlightenment." The Boston patriots offered no reasoned philosophical apology for what they were doing in their Academy; in their own homely way they merely set about institutionalizing the Enlightenment. But theirs was rather different from that of the philosophers in Paris, London, Amsterdam, and Berlin. It was a native adaptation of English ideas, spiced with a few French and Dutch notions. Deeply colored by the Calvinism of the founding fathers, it remained antimetaphysical though not anticlerical, matter-of-fact, and practical; it never became antireligious. The leaders were the professionals of the society, who formed a relatively undifferentiated upper stratum. They represented no separatist philosophical clique and almost all of them were sometime politicians.

The Americans who were active in promoting the arts and sciences in their new land proudly accepted the title "philosopher." In the course of the century it had assumed ever broader meaning both in Europe and in America, as it tended to devour the terms "curiosi" and "virtuosi" and such professional epithets as "mathematicus" and "philologus." The new designation did not necessarily imply specialized knowledge, but denoted a generally positive attitude toward free inquiry and rational argument and experimentation in the Baconian sense. The philosophy under whose standard the Americans were enlisted was not animated by the spirit of the French *philosophes*, with their emphasis on moral philosophy; nor did it suggest secularization of morals after the manner of David Hume. Though the American patriots had immediate political and religious concerns, as philosophers they were not interested in addressing them through integrated systems like those of Descartes and Leibniz, or through ethical propositions worked out with the rigor of geometric proofs. Nor was the solving of technical problems of epistemology and metaphysics a valid intellectual exercise for Americans faced with prosecuting a war and framing the instruments of government for a newly independent country. For them philosophy, intimately related to their sense of *patria*, required the furthering of arts and sciences that would enhance the stature of the nation as a civilized and cultivated entity, while increasing its fire-power in war and prosperity in peace. The operations of their learned society, the composition and character of its membership, their politics and religion, their conceptions of science, are fair reflections of intellectual life among the upper classes of the Commonwealth in the first decade or so of its independence.

James Bowdoin was a Boston patriot with a distinguished revolutionary pedigree whose ties with many of the Academy members had been forged long years before they draped themselves in philosophers' gowns. His choice as first president of the Academy at once recognized him as the epitome of the late Enlightenment in Massachusetts and made him the notable who gave shape to its second most important cultural institution. Politics, religion, and the spread of science were intertwined, and the lineaments of Bowdoin the businessman and politician are visible in any authentic portrait of the Academy during its formative years. Its initial organization is identified with his person, and the character of the man was a heightened expression of its virtues and its deficiencies. Shays' Rebellion represented a challenge to a whole generation of eastern patriot philosophers, members of the Academy, who were cut off from the rural counties of western Massachusetts. Governor Bowdoin was at the same time commander-in-chief of the Massachusetts militia and president of the Academy, and its Fellows, once revolutionary heroes, led troops against the new insurgents.

Bowdoin the stoical descendant of a Huguenot refugee was in one sense a stranger among the Boston patriots, a man of stature who did not belong to one of the old colonial families; but in most respects he shared their beliefs in the absolute right of property, the pursuit of virtue, a diluted Calvinist religion, and

a faith in science as a way of glorifying God. Throughout a life devoted to business, speculating in land, venturing his capital on the high seas, lending money
at exorbitant interest, serving as an opposition leader on the Governor's Council
under the British and as the second governor of the independent Commonwealth
of Massachusetts, James Bowdoin continued in his fashion to keep abreast of new
scientific developments. He was something of a provincial and Lilliputian replica
of Francis Bacon. In 1780, when defeated by John Hancock in politics, he turned
in earnest to his scientific and humanitarian enterprises, foremost among them
the structuring of the American Academy. His austere presence added a measure
of dignity—sometimes pomposity—to the institution.

In a wistful letter, written the year of his death to his life-long friend Benjamin
Franklin, James Bowdoin fantasied an ethereal voyage in his company: as they flew
through the planetary spaces of a world-to-come, they would at leisure discuss the
many scientific queries that Franklin had raised. Both of these men—of unequal
talents, but with callings to explore God's universe—had spent most of their lives
in mundane business and in politics. Franklin, by far the greater man, has been
written about for two hundred years; his friend's earthly progress to the ethereal
voyage he hoped would be awarded by his Calvinist, though enlightened, God has
been largely ignored. But to the patriot philosophers who were gathered around
him, he was the undisputed head of a local academy that strove to emulate the
stateliest of the European learned societies.

2

MYSTERIUM TREMENDUM
Birth of the Academy

⟨❦⟩

ANECDOTAGE has grown up around the initial conception of the American Academy and the passage of the Act of Incorporation, much of it derived from the recollections a quarter of a century later of that brilliant lawyer, statesman, diplomat, theorist, and political manipulator John Adams, an enigmatic figure not wholly revealed by the voluminous papers he left behind, a man strangely unfulfilled despite his election to the presidency of the United States. In the first decade of the nineteenth century, the aging John Adams began to plead his case before posterity and to vindicate himself from the insinuations of a host of maligners who had belittled his role in the forgotten revolutionary era and besmirched his name. He was outraged by the portrait of him drawn by the eminent woman of letters Mercy Otis Warren in her *History of the Rise, Progress and Termination of the American Revolution. Interspersed with Biographical, Political and Moral Observations* (1805). Though she credited Adams with keen intelligence and ability, in her relentlessly candid manner she concluded that "his prejudices and his passions were sometimes too strong for his sagacity and judgment," and — unkindest cut of all — she accused him of a partiality toward monarchy.[1]

Adams composed autobiographical fragments, wrote autobiographical letters, and then published parts of his old correspondence in the *Boston Patriot*, where he introduced notes that were intended to amplify the accounts in the documents. Viewed in a favorable light, this material is a magnificent apology. Looked at with a jaundiced eye, it is an attempt to prove that the important initiatives of the revolutionary period were primarily his, often undertaken at great sacrifice to himself and to his family. From Adams's highly charged historical revision no great figure except George Washington escapes unscathed — Samuel Adams, John Hancock, Thomas Jefferson, Benjamin Franklin, Alexander Hamilton all suffer under his angry pen. The major contests of revolutionary politics for over three decades are rehearsed and John Adams emerges as the hero without blemish. Often he is right; but on more than one occasion his extraordinary memory fails him, sicklied

---

1. Mercy Otis Warren, *History of the Rise, Progress and Termination of the American Revolution* (Boston, 1805), 3: 392, 394.

over with an excess of bile. The wise counsel proffered by his friend the Reverend William Gordon in October of 1780 had been ignored: "[S]hould you turn Historiographer to tell the world what a huge Patriot you are, let me tell you that the more you write in your own praise, the less they will believe you; that the louder you sound your trumpet the deafer they will grow."[2]

Claims to Paternity

The chartering of the American Academy was hardly the most momentous event of the age, but Adams was nevertheless intent upon claiming the original idea as his. He told the story of the founding in a letter of 7 August 1805, to his friend Benjamin Waterhouse, a Harvard professor of medicine, philosopher, and member of the Academy, and then repeated it almost verbatim in the columns of the *Boston Patriot* four years later. According to his witness, the idea was born at a dinner party held in the Philosophical Chamber of Harvard College on 24 August 1779, when Adams was back in Boston during a brief interval in his protracted diplomatic missions abroad.[3] The Philosophical Chamber was the room in which John Winthrop, Hollis Professor of Mathematicks and Natural Philosophy from 1738 to 1779, had unveiled before two generations of Harvard undergraduates the mysteries of Newtonian science made consonant with Protestant religion. He died on 3 May 1779, after a severe pulmonary attack, and the Harvard men dining in the Philosophical Chamber in August must still have felt his presence. They had been students or colleagues of the recently deceased professor, and most of them became incorporators of the American Academy. If there is a spiritual father of the Academy, it is Winthrop.

The dinner party described by Adams in 1805 was given by the Harvard Corporation in honor of the first French ambassador to the new nation, Anne-César, Chevalier de La Luzerne, who had been a fellow-passenger on *Le Sensible* when Adams returned from France. Contemporary Boston newspapers printed an exuberant account of the progress through Harvard of La Luzerne and a retinue of gentlemen of distinction, American and French. They detailed the formalities of his welcome and his grandiloquent Latin oration in reply, in the course of which he voiced the hope that the learned societies of France and America cultivating the

---

2. Ford, ed., "Letters of the Reverend Gordon," loc. cit., 444, Gordon to John Adams, Jamaica Plain, 19 Oct. 1780.

3. Worthington Chauncey Ford, ed., *Statesman and Friend. Correspondence of John Adams and Benjamin Waterhouse* (Boston, 1927), 22–29. A similar account was published in John Adams, *Correspondence of the Late President Adams Originally Published in the Boston Patriot in a Series of Letters* (Boston, 1809), 163–65, Letter 29, Quincy, 31 July 1809.

arts and sciences would further strengthen the bonds of the new alliance, to their mutual improvement and to the benefit of all mankind. The Boston *Independent Chronicle* reported that the company was entertained with Harvard's rich collection of books, its scientific curiosities and equipment, and a fine dinner. "Every countenance indicated pleasure, and every circumstance of the day testified the joy that was diffused through the whole university, upon this agreeable occasion."[4] At this ecumenical meeting between republican Puritans and aristocratic papists, drawn together by the exigencies of war, science was the cementing element. Among the many founding fathers of the American Academy, the Chevalier de La Luzerne deserves a place.

In his letter to Benjamin Waterhouse, Adams recalled that during the dinner he sat next to the Reverend Samuel Cooper, pastor of the Brattle Street Church in Boston, chaplain of the House of Representatives of Massachusetts, and member of the Harvard Corporation. When during their conversation Adams broached the subject of an academy in Boston, Cooper at first demurred, giving as his reasons that few interested men could be recruited for such an enterprise, and that it might deflect needed public support from Harvard. (Enrollment dropped precipitously at the college during the war.) Adams assured Cooper that many of the patriots would respond enthusiastically to the proposal and that an academy would in no way rival or compete with Harvard. The president and principal professors would always be members of the new society, and meetings held within the college precincts would reinforce the ties between the two institutions, whose activities would complement each other. His objections dispelled, Cooper assumed an active role in promoting the idea of an academy.

While it may have been John Adams's conversation with Cooper that gave momentum to patriot philosophers in the Boston area who wanted an academy as the ornament of their new commonwealth, Adams himself had little understanding even of the popular science that was fairly widespread among divines and men of independent means with time on their hands. As an undergraduate at Harvard he too had attended John Winthrop's lectures; but his notes show that he had no special aptitude for the Newtonian physics Winthrop taught, and he conceived of science in a simplistic manner primarily as the collection and arrangement of specimens of flora and fauna. In the end, such repetitive work seemed far less exciting than engagement with the moral and political issues to which a study of jurisprudence would lead him. In a youthful autobiographical fragment, not discovered until 1965, Adams catalogued and described the various types of "genius," a sign

---

4. Boston, *Independent Chronicle*, 2 Sept. 1779, p. 1, cols. 1–2, quoted in *Adams Family Correspondence* (Adams Papers, ser. 2), 3, ed. L. H. Butterfield and Marc Friedlaender (Cambridge, Mass.: The Belknap Press of Harvard University Press, 1973), 225–33, n. 3.

that he was seeking to identify his own, and a commitment to the pursuit of excellence in some field of knowledge. Here again his reflections betray only a limited appreciation of what was coming to be known as science in the mid-eighteenth century. His self-conscious quest for his own particular vocation was a carryover of the Puritan search for a calling, touched by the nascent conception of secular genius. Though aware of his extraordinary gifts, Adams, full of doubt, never wholly succeeded in finding his place in the divine order of things.

The establishment of academies had been on Adams's mind ever since he first went to Philadelphia as a Massachusetts delegate to the Continental Congress. He had even persuaded his fellow delegates to pass a resolution calling upon the several states to found societies for the encouragement of practical arts. The existence since 1769 of the American Philosophical Society in Philadelphia aroused his competitive spirit, as a long letter to his wife, Abigail, on 3–4 August 1776, testifies. Adams, lonely in Philadelphia, had gone to the Baptist meeting with the expectation of hearing the Reverend Samuel Stillman, but he was disappointed that someone else was preaching. The substitute was violent to a degree bordering on fury, with gestures unnatural and distorted, and a tone that was vociferous and boisterous. His motions lacked grace; his style, elegance. The composition was almost wholly without ingenuity. Adams was led to wonder why in the world people up north had such a fondness for scholars educated in the south and for southern preachers. In his judgment the people of Boston clearly surpassed the southerners in the excellence of their university, the erudition of their scholars, and the eloquence of their preachers. Admittedly there were a few southern gentlemen, educated by travel abroad, who dazzled their auditors, but in general old Massachusetts still outshone her younger sisters.

Adams conceded that in some instances the southerners had more wit, and they had societies, above all the Philosophical Society, that excited emulation and spread their fame. He wrote Abigail that if ever he was through with politics and war he would spend the rest of his days trying to induce his countrymen back home to make the most of their solid abilities and virtues. Throughout his life John Adams was given to odious comparisons among individuals, but he loved New Englanders although they were awkward and bashful, pert, ostentatious, and vain, "a Mixture which excites Ridicule and gives Disgust." Adams thrust his own self-image onto the whole region of his birth: "They have not the faculty of shewing themselves to the best Advantage, nor the Art of concealing this faculty. An Art and Faculty which some People possess in the highest degree. Our Deficiencies in these Respects, are owing wholly to the little Intercourse We have had with strangers, and to our Inexperience in the World. These Imperfections must be remedied, for New England must produce the Heroes, the statesmen, the Philosophers, or America will make no great Figure for some Time." Adams prophesied that a philosophical society would be established at Boston, "if I have Wit and Address enough to accomplish it, sometime or other." Abigail had a brother-in-law named Richard Cranch, an immigrant from England and watchmaker by trade, of whom John was very fond. Cranch was forever trying new businesses and failing at them, but Adams thought he had a philosophical head and told Abigail to set him "plodding" about a philosophical society. If they had such a club, many of Brother Cranch's lucubrations would be published.[5]

The plan to found a Boston academy was thus long germinating in John Adams's fertile brain. His conceptions were naive and ill-defined, but passionate. Seemingly insignificant incidents kept the idea alive. An element of hostility to the southerners, who included Philadelphians, and the activities of French learned societies, stimulated his interest, as much as his pleasure at the sight of a botanical garden or a collection of birds and insects in America or abroad. This gloomy and suspicious man who doubted the virtue of everyone he met — with the rarest exceptions — had never questioned the merits of physical science. It represented the kind of truth that could not be denied, especially when it yielded practical fruits. Among the patriots there continued to be a greater consensus about the moral worth of plain scientific fact — not mixed up with metaphysics — than about any political propositions to which they might subscribe in a declaration.

Adams was so full of these thoughts that, according to his own account, in the fall of 1779 he deliberately introduced into the draft of the new constitution for Massachusetts a whole section affirming it the duty of the state to cherish the interests of literature and the sciences and to support the University of Cambridge, as Harvard was called, and other learned institutions, as well as to cultivate among the people virtuous conduct and "good humor," a quality in which he was remarkably deficient. Adams was worried, he admits, that these suggestions would meet with opposition; but though other articles of the constitution were amended, the unique cultural article — which exists in no previous state constitution — survived intact, albeit a few towns with Baptist churches objected to the requirement that the Board of Overseers of the University include the ministers of the Congregational churches of Cambridge, Watertown, Charlestown, Boston, Roxbury, and Dorchester. Critics were apprehensive also lest the accumulation of vast endowments by the university and the power deriving from them endanger the liberties of the Commonwealth.[6] There is no indication, however, in summaries of the town meetings to which the constitution was submitted — a remarkable collective expression of the popular will — that the article encouraging the creation of new cultural institutions was much debated.

5. Ibid., 2:75, John Adams to Abigail, 3–4 Aug. 1776.

6. Ibid., 3:226. The section entitled "The University at Cambridge, and Encouragement of Literature, etc" is chapter 5 of the Massachusetts constitution. See Oscar and Mary Handlin, eds., *The popular sources of political authority; documents on the Massachusetts constitution of 1780* (Cambridge, Mass.: The Belknap Press of Harvard University Press, 1966), introd., 29:465–67.

After approval by the full convention and consideration by the towns, the constitution was declared ratified on 16 June, to go into effect on 25 October. By that time Congress had sent John Adams back to Europe on diplomatic business that involved gaining recognition on the Continent for the new nation and joining the delegates in the negotiation of a peace treaty with Britain, each article of which caused him extreme anguish as he battled with his fellow commissioners more violently than with the British. On the morrow of the signing of the treaty he collapsed —one of a series of similar breakdowns that followed a triumph. Back home there had been only 181 returns from a total number of 290 towns to which the Massachusetts constitution had been sent for review, and doubt remains about their actual approval of all parts of the proposed document.[7] Adams, far away, was under the misapprehension that the act creating the Academy had been passed under the authority of the new instrument of government. Fortunately, the act has an independent existence rooted in the solid rock of the Provincial Congress and not in the shifting sands of the Commonwealth constitution.

By the time the Academy bill had been introduced into the legislature in mid-December of 1779, Adams had sailed off to face Franklin and the French again in his private war. News from America was sporadic and Massachusetts politics had to be left behind. While marking time during long lulls in diplomatic activity, Adams grew ever prouder of his recent single-handed (he came to believe) achievements, the founding of the Academy and the drafting of the Massachusetts constitution. Desperate for activity, he called upon a few sympathetic European journalists who were willing to accept his copy to fill up the pages of their newspapers. One of them was Jean Luzac, publisher of the *Gazette de Leyde*; at Adams's behest he printed the Massachusetts constitution and a notice of the founding of the American Academy.[8] Adams thought he could use what he called the "revival" of the American Philosophical Society in Philadelphia —once a private society, in March of 1780 it was incorporated by the independent state of Pennsylvania —and the establishment of the American Academy in Boston as evidence that, contrary to British reports disseminated on the Continent, the position of the revolutionaries was strong and self-confident. They were civilized and mighty enough in the midst of a barbarous war to dedicate themselves to the arts of peace. The patriots were philosopher-rebels, not the riff-raff of British propaganda. Adams sent to Charles-Guillaume-Frédéric Dumas, the learned agent in Paris charged with planting information favorable to the colonials, similar notices describing American cultural endeavors that were meant to encourage the alignment of the *philosophes* and other literate Frenchmen with the patriots' cause. He lectured Dumas on the especial significance of academies for young countries,

7. Ibid., introd., 25.

8. Adams, *Correspondence in the Boston Patriot*, 154–55, Letter 28, Quincy, 27 July 1809, quoting letter to Jean Luzac, Amsterdam, 22 Aug. 1780.

and hinted that it would be well if correspondence could be established between the scientific and literary companies of Europe and the infant societies of America.[9]

For months on end, while Adams had little to do but chafe, he deluged the Continental Congress with dispatches that were read only by committee secretaries. A new brainchild that he himself called whimsical was submitted in the fall of 1780: he proposed that the Congress found a national academy charged with fixing the English language in a dictionary, which would serve to improve eloquence, a necessary and salutary attribute of democracies, as the history of the ancient Greeks and Romans demonstrated. Adams hoped that there would be a mutual interplay between excellence in eloquence and burgeoning American institutions, and that a standardized language would solidify the union among the states. His model was probably the French Academy, though his scheme may also have echoed the many seventeenth-century projects for a universal language. When Adams had been in Paris in 1778, the dying Voltaire appeared before the French Academy and summoned its members to resume work on their neglected dictionary. In a memorable session, Voltaire allocated individual letters among the various members, and when they had all committed themselves to work diligently, he solemnly arose to thank the body on behalf of the alphabet. This was not Adams's style of humor and he was no friend of the "atheist" Voltaire, who in another dramatic scene kissed Franklin at a session of the Academy of Sciences; but recollections of both events lingered. In memoranda to the Congress, Adams foretold the predominance of English throughout the world in the coming century, and saw an opportunity for his native land to fill a serious gap left by the British. He tried to convince the lawmakers in Philadelphia, preoccupied with the prosecution of the war, that they could win glory for themselves and the new nation by espousing his project: "The honor of forming the first public institution for refining, correcting, ascertaining and improving the English language, I hope is reserved for Congress. They have every motive that can possibly influence a public assembly to undertake it."[10]

Since the paternity of the American Academy has rival claimants, the Adams story should not be accepted without some touching up.

In the first volume of its *Memoirs*, published in 1785, there is a brief preface presenting the official account of the origins of the Academy that does not mention Adams's name. The text was surely supervised, if not written, by James Bowdoin: "In this Commonwealth, a society for promoting useful knowledge was, for many years,

9. Ibid., 159, Letter 29, Quincy, 31 July 1809, quoting letter to C.-G.-F. Dumas, Amsterdam, 5 Sept. 1780.

10. Ibid., 160–62, quoting letter to Congress, 5 Sept. 1780. John Adams's claim to have originated the proposal for an Academy was accepted by Walter Muir Whitehill in his "Learned Societies in Boston and Vicinity," in Alexandra Oleson and Sanborn C. Brown, eds., *The Pursuit of Knowledge in the Early American Republic* (Baltimore: Johns Hopkins University Press, 1976), 151.

in contemplation; but the design was never vigorously engaged in and pursued, 'till the end of the year 1779, when many gentlemen, persuaded of the utility of such an institution, determined, without delay, to use their endeavors, to have one formed upon a liberal and extensive plan, and at the same time, to have it established upon a firm basis, by obtaining the sanction of the Legislature."[11] Three European societies are listed to illustrate the beneficent effects of academies upon the nations in which they have been established: the Academy of Sciences in Paris, the Royal Society of London, and the Society for the Encouragement of Arts, Manufactures and Commerce in London, of which Bowdoin had been a member since 1761.

The brief statement is not incompatible with Adams's anecdote about his proposal, but the assertion that in 1779 "many gentlemen" had been "persuaded of the utility of such an institution," that the design had been in contemplation "for many years," and that its implementation began at the "end of the year 1779," when Adams was abroad, diminishes Adams's contention that he was the sole initiator. Clearly, his monogenetic theory of the Academy's origins was not shared by James Bowdoin. After 1776 all manner of local societies were proliferating in the various states and in European provincial cities, so that the idea had really become commonplace. And there is evidence that as early as 1760 Thomas Hollis, the Englishman who was Harvard's great benefactor, had tried to organize an academy, but it was thought America was not yet ripe enough.[12] Professor John Winthrop had proposed and then dropped a similar idea. By 1785 Bowdoin was well aware of Adams's propensity to claim priority of invention for crucial decisions — turning-points in the Revolution such as the Declaration of Independence, the appointment of Washington as commander-in-chief, and the drafting of a constitution for the Commonwealth of Massachusetts. The preface to the first volume of the *Memoirs* appears to stress the collective initiative of the Boston patriot philosophers in the establishment of the Academy.

The diary of another original Fellow of the Academy, Benjamin Guild, for October and early November 1779, provides a bit of additional evidence about the society when it was still *in ovo*, before the Academy bill was introduced in the legislature. Guild (b. 1749), one of the youngest to be chosen a Fellow, was a Harvard tutor in classics who resigned his post in April 1780, on the eve of the Academy's incorporation. After graduation he had been a schoolmaster, had studied theology, and was often engaged in supplying pulpits in Essex County, without ever assuming the duties of a regular pastor. Upon his appointment to a tutorship in 1776, the effective management of the College devolved upon him and the Reverend Caleb Gannett for a time. Guild, not much of a scholar, was fond of parties, books, and

11. American Academy of Arts and Sciences, *Memoirs: To the End of the Year MDCCLXXXIII* (Boston, 1785), preface, iv.

12. MHS, *Proceedings* 43 (1909–10), 612–13, T. B. Hollis to Secretary Willard, The Hide, 15 Aug. 1783, and 3 Sept. 1783.

conversation, and his unpublished diaries afford intimate glimpses of college life during the revolutionary years. To buy books for the university he would attend auctions of confiscated Loyalist libraries and call upon the widows of parsons.

Guild was restless and frequently absented himself from Cambridge. On 18 October 1779, during a sojourn in Philadelphia, he visited Dr. Thomas Bond, vice-president of the Philosophical Society, to get some pointers about its experience. Bond dilated on how serviceable the foreign members had been to the Society: the Grand Duke of Tuscany offered them anything "that Italy could afford." After inspecting Bond's collection of natural history mounts, worth fifty guineas, Guild gave expression in his diary to the same New England competitive spirit that had moved John Adams. He felt that the Philadelphia Society, by taking the lead, would "reap many advantages, for foreigners, are very desirous of being acquainted with the natural history of America." The next day he was allowed to peruse a copy of the Society's *Transactions* and to make abstracts of its rules.[13]

As Guild moved from one army encampment to another en route home to Cambridge, he remarked upon the paucity of literate Massachusetts men among the Continental forces: "I am told that not more than four or five in the whole line ever had a liberal education. This is not because a superior number to any other state upon the Continent cannot be found but because it so happened that they did not engage in the army: & as our character will in some measure be formed by the appearance and conduct of those we had in the field, I wish they could in general be as justly celebrated for their literary as their martial accomplishments."[14] On the final leg of his journey he stopped to dine with Yale president Ezra Stiles at New Haven. After a tour of the College and conversation abut literary matters, their talk turned to the proposal for an academy that was being discussed in Massachusetts. "He [Stiles] was exceedingly pleased with the plan of having an Academy in this state; said he would immediately after its incorporation, attempt the same thing in that state. We both hoped that after a number may have been formed upon the continent, a grand one, selected from the whole, may be instituted and regularly attended. We had many pleasing conjectures respecting the increasing knowledge and rising grandeur of America."[15] The ambitious scheme for a national academy that Adams submitted to the Continental Congress in the fall of 1780 had been prefigured in the speculations of other New England patriots.

Since Guild was off to France in the spring of 1780, the Academy plan to which he was privy and which he favored apparently was not his prime concern. The object of his European mission is hazy; a book-buying expedition does not seem a likely explanation for risking the hazardous wartime transatlantic crossing. We

13. MHS, Diary of Benjamin Guild (MS), entries for 18 and 19 Oct. 1779.

14. Ibid., entry for 29 Oct. 1779.

15. Ibid., entry for 1 Nov. 1779; see also Ezra Stiles, *Literary Diary*, ed. F. B. Dexter (New York, 1901), 2:385.

know that, whatever other functions he may have performed, he discharged the role of courier, carrying letters and packages between the Boston patriots and their emissaries abroad. He clearly did not leave the College with ill-feeling, though his private diary records his contempt for President Langdon. The Harvard Corporation issued him an elaborate Latin testimonial that served as a passport and Bowdoin gave him a letter of introduction to Benjamin Franklin in Paris.[16] He moved from Nantes, where he landed, through the French capital, to Holland, was received by John Adams, and returned in November 1781 with a public message from the Boston patriot abroad that was published in the newspapers.

When Guild came home he opened a circulating library at the Boston Book Store, 59 Cornhill. A catalogue of the shop's holdings, published in 1790, is a record of the rich repository of books on science, philosophy, and belles-lettres made available to cultivated Bostonians. The works were generally in English, but the collection included a large number of translations from the French, and books by Voltaire, Rousseau, and David Hume that would have been considered too far-out by most New England clergymen. Guild later handled subscriptions for the Academy *Memoirs* and was on the editorial board of *The Boston Magazine*. Among members of the Academy he is a rare example of what might be considered a free-floating intellectual, curious about many things but without much scholarly substance. He married a daughter of Colonel Josiah Quincy, joined the Brattle Street Church, and acquired property in the North End. His health was poor and he died of tuberculosis in 1792. Though he played no significant part in the Academy during its early years, his diary entries may, with a little straining, qualify him as still another founding father of the many-sired institution.

Saved by the Alphabet

Initially, passage of the bill to establish the Academy was in the hands of the Reverend Samuel Cooper, "silver-tongued Sam" of the Brattle Street Church, who had managed to survive the decades of protest against the British Crown and the factional disputes among the patriot leaders without running afoul of any of them. A quatrain on Cooper ran:

> In Brattle street we seldom meet
> With Silver-tongued SAM,
> Who smoothly glides between both sides,
> And so escapes a JAM![17]

16. Harvard University Archives: Corporation Records, 3 (1778–95; an 1855 copy, in MS, of College Book 8), 76, Latin testimonial for Guild, 11 Apr. 1780; MHS, *Proceedings*, ser. 2, 8:290, Bowdoin to Benjamin Franklin, 1 May 1780, introducing Guild.

17. Ezra Stiles, *Literary Diary* 1:492. Benjamin Guild paid Cooper a left-handed compliment: "Heard Dr. Cooper at the Lecture, whose softness of diction and ease of expression are, at least, equal

Cooper appears to have been the moving spirit of a group that compiled the original list of Fellows of the American Academy. A traveling man who loved to go visiting, he knew all the clergymen, doctors, merchants, and lawyers in the eastern part of the state as well as the faculty of Harvard, whose presidency he had declined in February of 1774. While the Tory Peter Oliver's judgment of Cooper placed him on the level of a clerical Machiavelli — "No Man could, with a better Grace, utter the Word of *God* from his Mouth, & at the same Time keep a two edged Dagger concealed in his Hand. His Tongue was Butter & Oil, but under it was the Poison of Asps"[18] — a wide circle of confidants, including Franklin and Bowdoin, Hancock and Sam Adams, admired him.[19] Not among them was Bowdoin's friend Samuel Dexter who, when Cooper lay dying at the end of 1783, observed with his usual acerbity that recovery would give the "Prime Minister" a chance to be more of a spiritual man and less of a politician.[20] In any event, it is unlikely that the astute pastor would have gone about the business of selecting suitable members for the Academy without consulting the leading political and mercantile figures in Boston. Since all recognizable factions were represented, it was to be expected that the Academy bill would sail through the committees of the House and the Council of the Provincial Congress of the Massachusetts Bay without mishap. But even the wily Cooper came near to foundering between Scylla and Charybdis and losing at least one prominent supporter, John Hancock.

The attentiveness of the Boston patriot philosophers to the niceties of balance and position was worthy of the court of Louis XIV; their sensitivity to slight and insult merited a memorialist with the caustic pen of a Duc de Saint-Simon. Unfortunately, in his stead, the chronicler of the local intrigues was the English immigrant William Gordon, pastor of the church at Roxbury, who had managed to ingratiate himself with most of the Massachusetts leaders and with George Washington. The Reverend William Gordon was a John Adams man, and on occasion a James Bowdoin man, but he could not tolerate John Hancock, whom he labeled "John Puff,"

---

to the importance of his ideas" (Harvard University Archives: Diary of Benjamin Guild, 1776, 1778 [MS], entry for 29 Oct. 1778).

18. Cambridge, Mass., Fogg Art Museum, *Harvard Divided*; catalogue of an exhibition, 3 June–10 October 1976, by Linda Ayres, 31. Cf. *Peter Oliver's Origin & Progress of the American Rebellion. A Tory View (1781)*, ed. Douglass Adair and John A. Schutz (San Marino, Cal.: The Huntington Library, 1961), 44. Oliver added that Cooper's manners made him acceptable "to the politest Company, who were unacquainted with his real Character; & he could descend from them to mix privately with the Rabble, in their nightly seditious Associations" (45).

19. Franklin had used his influence to secure an honorary degree from Edinburgh for Cooper in 1767 (Franklin, *Papers* 4, ed. L. W. Labaree [1961], 70 n. 3).

20. MHS, *Collections*, ser. 7, 6 (Bowdoin and Temple Papers, 2), 29, Samuel Dexter to John Temple, Dedham, 13 Dec. 1783.

among other scornful sobriquets. Gordon usually operated on a quid pro quo basis with the American notables who were his correspondents, sending along news with the understanding that they would reciprocate in kind. He even fixed rules for the interchange, advising his informants to distinguish between what they communicated in confidence and what was to be bruited about.

Gordon wrote to John Adams in Paris hoping to be kept abreast of the peace negotiations and extending bits of Boston gossip as enticement. In passing, he told of Cooper's getting into trouble with the Academy bill. The story is related with a certain malicious satisfaction, since Gordon disliked silver-tongued Sam and hinted that he was in the pay of the French. It was a reasonable surmise on his part, borne out by the tone of Cooper's correspondence with the French Ambassador La Luzerne, to whom he regularly transmitted information, writing as though he were reporting to a superior officer.[21] And according to a communication from the minister to the United States, Conrad Alexandre Gérard, to the French foreign minister, the Comte de Vergennes, Cooper was "acheté" in 1779 with an annual stipend of £200 sterling that continued until his death at the end of 1783.[22] At one point Gordon described Cooper as the "pink of complaisance to the French Admirals, Generals and Officers," and warned that he was "Franklified and Frenchified."[23] Francophobia and Franklophobia, however manifested, dovetailed neatly with John Adams's inclinations. In 1786 Gordon went back to England, where he published his *History of the Rise, Progress, and Establishment of the Independence of the United States of America* (1788), and he never returned. He spent his last years ministering to a small parish, and died in poverty. The voluminous work failed to live up to the promise of its title, turning out to be something of a hodge-podge that mixed occasional psychological insights into the behavior of the revolutionaries with passages lifted from a standard history of Europe. His correspondence is far more revealing.

In his letter to John Adams on 19 October 1780, the Reverend William Gordon recounted that Hancock was so annoyed at the sight of Cooper's haphazardly arranged list of Fellows slated for incorporation as the new Academy, with Samuel

---

21. See San Marino, Cal., Huntington Library: Cooper's letters to La Luzerne, 6 Oct. 1779, 1 May, 14 June, 21 June, 13 July 1780. It was at Cooper's instance that both La Luzerne and Marbois were elected to the Academy on 31 January 1781 (Academy Records, 1:25, 120).

22. Charles W. Akers, *The Divine Politician. Samuel Cooper and the American Revolution in Boston* (Boston: Northeastern University Press, 1982), 279.

23. Ford, "Letters of the Reverend Gordon," loc. cit., 470–71, Gordon to John Adams, Jamaica Plain, 9 and 19 Sept. 1782. Gordon was succeeded by Cooper in 1777 as chaplain to the General Court (Cooper had also been chaplain from 1758 to 1770), whence some of the enmity may have derived. The Reverend Jeremy Belknap judged Gordon's work "jejune, stiff, and unanimated"; see MHS, *Collections*, ser. 5, 3 (Belknap Papers, 2 [1877]), 105, Belknap to Hazard, Boston, 12 Feb. 1789.

Adams — now estranged from Hancock — at its head, taking spatial precedence over Hancock, that the first bill was rejected, while Hancock let word drop that he was leaving the Brattle Street Church and joining the Hollis Street congregation in the South End. Dismayed deacons reported this threat to Cooper, who hastened to make amends lest he lose his most generous benefactor. Their friendship dated a long way back, to Madeira-soaked evenings when, along with Samuel Adams, they had planned the great days and nights of the American Revolution in Boston. Hancock was finally mollified when a diplomatic formula was devised: the list of Academy Fellows would be presented to the legislature in alphabetical order. Samuel Adams still appeared first, however.[24]

Apparently it was an ingenious young lawyer from Essex County, Theophilus Parsons, who had broken the legislative deadlock. From Newburyport on 3 August 1780, Parsons sent Francis Dana in Amsterdam a long circumstantial report on family matters and on the naval success of Essex County privateers. He also announced, rather sardonically, the ratification of the new state constitution, despite a few attempted alterations "not from conviction but through fear that the constitution would be too perfect for the acceptance of the People." As for the forthcoming gubernatorial election, he felt that Mr H would win over Mr B; his reason: "We have too many militia officers for a wise unbiased election" (a reference to Hancock's command of the Massachusetts militia). In recounting the final steps in the enactment of the Academy bill he indulged in a bit of self-praise and took a sideswipe at Hancock. With obvious satisfaction he confided to Dana, a charter member:

> I got the Academy of Arts and Sciences erected after much difficulty from very trifling causes — The placing the names had nearly overthrown the Bill until I obviated the objection by proposing the alphabet as a rule — By the bye I wish some of our *great little folkes* understood the alphabet, but a man devoted to popularity cannot have a greatness of mind which will preserve him from meanness & folly — The alphabet also gave some disgust. Mr. H — K said (as I was informed) it was a contrivance of myne to place Mr. A — s above him.

The learned Parsons concluded with a quotation from Horace: *Risum teneatis amici* (Can you refrain from laughing, my friends?).[25]

The Academy bill also got pulled into the ongoing squabbles of John Adams and Benjamin Franklin over the appropriate titles they should bear during the peace negotiations in Paris. Elbridge Gerry suggested to Abigail on 17 April 1780,

24. Ford, "Letters of the Reverend Gordon," loc. cit., 445–46, Gordon to John Adams, Jamaica Plain, 19 Oct. 1780.

25. MHS, Dana Papers, Parsons to Dana, Newburyport, 3 Aug. 1780.

that the passage and printing of the bill might create an opportunity to publicize a fitting honorific designation for her husband, who was sensitive on this point: "It may also be proper to have Mr. A—s appointed a Member of the 'American Academy of Arts and Sciences,' for the Institution whereof I have been lately informed a Bill is depending in the Legislature of the State of Massachusetts; and should You think it expedient to consult our Friend General Warren on the Occasion, he will undoubtedly promote the Appointment, and see that it is properly communicated to the publick."[26]

When a fortnight later the act was passed, with the names of the incorporated Fellows included, John Adams was listed simply as "Hon. John Adams, Esq," like other non-clerical and non-medical notables. Though the family names on the list were alphabetically arranged, the sequence of first names was random, and Samuel Adams took precedence over John.

Despite the offense to his inflated ego, Hancock's pique finally subsided. The absurd tale of intrigue reported by the Reverend William Gordon and, with some variation, by lawyer Parsons is buttressed by the meager official records of the legislative history of the Academy bill that have survived in the State Archives of Massachusetts. On 15 December 1779, it had been ordered in the House of Representatives of the General Court of the State of Massachusetts-Bay, then known as the Provincial Congress, that a Mr. Davis of Boston, Parsons, and William Tudor, a college chum of Parsons who had studied law under John Adams, constitute a committee to bring in a bill for establishing a "society for the promotion of the arts and sciences."[27] Either the bill had been previously prepared or the designated representatives moved with great celerity, for the journal of the House records among the actions taken the same day that a bill entitled "An Act to Incorporate and Establish a Society for the Cultivation and Promotion of the Arts and Sciences" was read a first time and ordered to be read again at ten on the morning of the 16th. This having been duly carried out and a third reading given on the next morning, the bill was passed and sent up to the Council for concurrence.[28]

The Council was dilatory; it appeared to have some reservations about the bill, which was brought back to the House with the Council vote noted upon it: on 17 December it had been read a first time and on 31 December—a long hiatus—a second time, on which occasion, instead of passing the bill, the Council ordered that Thomas Cushing and Timothy Danielson, both of them staunch Hancock men, in addition to those the House might see fit to add, form a committee to re-

26. *Adams Family Correspondence* 3:324, Elbridge Gerry to Abigail Adams, Philadelphia, 17 Apr. 1780.

27. Commonwealth of Massachusetts: Journal of the House of Representatives for Nov.–Dec. 1779, p. 2.

28. Ibid., 2–3, 6.

view the bill and report their recommendations at the next sitting of the General Court. An unseen power had clearly thrown a monkey-wrench into the legislative machinery. The Council's wishes were honored by the House, which named three of its members to the joint committee.[29]

Though the new session of the legislature did not dash precipitately to a consideration of the bill, the idea of a Massachusetts academy formed after the pattern of Philadelphia's Philosophical Society was kept alive by "some gentlemen," Ebenezer Hazard told his friend Jeremy Belknap in February of the new year. Both men heartily approved of such establishments, despite apprehension that jealousy or local pride might impede the free exchange of scientific research and information. As late as 1 April, Hazard, who kept his ear close to the ground, noted impatiently that the proposal was at a standstill, though unlikely to be dropped.[30] Spring was already well advanced when at last, on Monday, 24 April 1780, a so-called new draft was introduced in the House of Representatives. Perhaps the flagging interest of its sponsors had been reawakened by the recent incorporation of the Philosophical Society in Philadelphia. The draft was read a first time and ordered to be read again on the following Thursday morning. By this session, it was anticipated, according to a note written and signed by Hancock that accompanied the bill to the Council, a new joint committee would have reported a "List of Names proper to be inserted in the Bill for establishing a Society for the cultivation of the Arts & Sciences — to be arranged in alphabetical Order."[31] John Hancock had been appeased. (Never again was the alphabet to be slighted when membership lists were at stake: at the meeting of 31 January 1781, it was resolved that the names of the members "belonging at any time to the Academy shall ever be arranged in an alphabetical manner.")[32]

In the original draft of the bill, names of Fellows had not been included, though space had been left for their interpolation. On the manuscript order accompanying the new draft and mandating the list, there is a note signed by John Avery, deputy secretary, that on 25 April the Council added Timothy Danielson and Timothy Edwards to the joint committee charged with naming names; the members who had been designated by the House were Parsons, Major Samuel Osgood, and Tudor. The committee report, signed by Danielson, and the annexed list were then presented to the Council, read, and sent

29. Ibid., 25.

30. MHS, *Collections*, ser. 5, 2 (Belknap Papers, 1), 34, Hazard to Belknap, Jamaica Plain, 18 Feb. 1780; 40, Belknap to Hazard, Dover, N.H., 13 Mar. 1780; 46, Hazard to Belknap, Jamaica Plain, 1 Apr. 1780.

31. Boston, Archives of the Commonwealth of Massachusetts: Manuscript Journals of the House of Representatives, 2 (June 24, 1776-Apr. 25, 1780), 286, entry for Monday, 24 Apr. 1780; Archives of the Commonwealth: "Original Papers of Chapter 46 of the Acts of 1779" (Legislative Packet, 24 Apr.).

32. Academy Records, 1:42.

down to the House by John Avery, all on 27 April,[33] the day scheduled for the second reading in the House. The list of names submitted by the joint committee had been incorporated without change in the Academy bill. John Pitts and Artemas Ward, both of them Council members, had initially been included, but their names were stricken prior to the committee's presentation. An earlier, penciled list—not wholly legible—shorter and unalphabetized, had contained, in addition to the names of Pitts and Ward, that of Timothy Danielson.[34] The reasons for their exclusion remain among the arcana of the Academy's history. A likely supposition respecting Timothy Danielson is that, as he was the signer of the joint committee report, modesty forbade him to confer the distinction of Fellowhood upon himself. The omission was rectified at the first official meeting of the Academy, when he was elected to its ranks.[35]

Though described as a "new draught," the Academy bill was almost identical with the one introduced at the close of 1779. Squeezed in at the head of the manuscript draft, in fresher ink than the rest of the text, are the words "State of Massachusetts Bay." The date preceding the title was altered by scribbling out the word "seventy-nine" and inserting "eighty." The minimum number of Massachusetts Fellows required by the act was reduced from eighty to forty—a short step toward cosmopolitanism—and the words authorizing the major part of the Council to grant a charter of incorporation were deleted. The name of James Bowdoin as the Fellow charged with summoning the first meeting replaced a not completely eradicated, but nonetheless indecipherable, original name. It is plain that the draft of 1779, slightly amended, was resubmitted in the following year as the "new draught." Notes on the last page of the folio on which the bill was written indicate that on 2 May it was read three times in the House of Representatives, passed, and sent up for concurrence, with the signature of John Hancock, Speaker. After readings on 2 and 3 May, it was passed unchanged by the Council and became law on 4 May 1780. There was no executive signature. The final act, which constitutes the charter of incorporation, was published as a broadside.[36]

When on 25 July 1780, Dr. Cotton Tufts announced the founding of the new Academy to his friend John Adams in Paris, he expressed some anxiety about the practical side of its operations: "What shall we do for want of Funds! Can we hope for Benefactions from abroad. I hope the tender Plant will somehow or other be

33. Archives of the Commonwealth: "Original Papers of Chapter 46 of the Acts of 1779" (Legislative Packet, 27 Apr.).

34. Ibid., Annex to Committee Report, folios 1 and 4. In the same packet, on folio 4 of a quarto containing the bill itself, is the penciled list of names.

35. American Academy of Arts and Sciences, *Memoirs* 1:xxi; Academy Records, 1:32 (31 Jan. 1781).

36. Archives of the Commonwealth: Legislative Packet, original MS draft of the bill, folio 3, and Annex to Committee Report, folio 4 (notes on the passing of the bill into law on 4 May). See also Academy Records, 1:1–4, and MHS, Broadside, Boston, 4 May 1780.

nourished but I am sure it must be watered." Four and a half months later John Adams responded from Amsterdam in a proud, xenophobic outburst that frowned on the very notion of reliance on foreign lands for succor. Benefactors like the Hollises, who had supported Harvard, would probably not be found:

> The Institution of an Accademy of Arts and Sciences, does you much honour in Europe, and it will after a little Time be incouraged, many Ways. But dont set your Hearts upon Benefactions from abroad. It is a shame that We should beg for Benefactions. . . .
>
> Indeed America will never derive any good from Europe of any Kind. I wish We were wise enough to depend upon ourselves for every Thing, and upon them for nothing. Ours is the richest and most independent Country under Heaven, and We are continually looking up to Europe for Help! Our Riches and Independence grow annually out of the Ground.[37]

Heroes and Academicians

The first-hand testimony of participants and the gossip of rumor-mongers supplementing the legislative scraps still leave unclear how the original roster of patriot philosophers was drawn up and what criteria were adopted for inclusion or exclusion. Perhaps selection was a free act of God's grace. As for the undistinguished and unsymbolic number 62, since it had reference neither to the membership of the holy Sanhedrin nor to the wise men who translated the Septuagint, it is reasonable to suppose that it was arrived at by happenstance and was simply the total of all the local patriots with pretensions to philosophy (except James Otis, who was considered mad) —and a few without —that came to the minds of the list's compilers. In harmony with a tradition going back to the Renaissance Accademia dei Lincei in Rome and kept alive in the Royal Society of London and the American Philosophical Society, membership was not limited to men who had published scientific discoveries or even to those learned in science; in virtually all European academies there was a close intermingling of the bearers of scientific culture and eminent citizens who aspired to be its protectors and patrons. The same pattern was followed in the early years of the American Academy.

The men named in the Academy's charter of incorporation had not been asked explicitly whether they agreed to be Fellows, so signal an honor that a refusal was inconceivable; no true American patriot could be opposed to the cultivation and promotion of the arts and sciences in the new land. Many Fellows were informed of their selection

---

37. *Adams Family Correspondence* 3:383, Cotton Tufts to John Adams, Weymouth, 25 July 1780; ibid. 4 (ed. L. H. Butterfield and Marc Friedlaender [1973]), 29, John Adams to Cotton Tufts, Amsterdam, 9 Dec. 1780.

for the first time when James Bowdoin had a notice inserted in the newspapers summoning them to a meeting on 30 May 1780.[38] In the early years of the Academy it was not always certain who was actually a member, since certificates of election were not regularly issued. Attempts were made to clarify the status of Fellows by having them sign a document accepting the honor or send in letters of acknowledgment; but there were delinquents, and some had died or were indisposed. Problems of identification are complicated by a fluid orthography and family penchants for retaining the same forenames in successive generations. Members from "abroad"—that is, outside of Massachusetts—and foreign members responded to their election with appropriate compliments and expressions of gratitude. It was not until 1785 that a comprehensive list, which had been compiled earlier, was published in the first volume of the *Memoirs*. In imitation of the Royal Society "FRS," the names of Academy members were dignified with an "FAA." When foreign members wished to present themselves in print in full regalia they included "membre de l'Académie de Boston" among their titles. At home, to the associations and activities that bestowed prestige upon a man— connection with Harvard College and its governing bodies, a pew in the Brattle Street Church, political office as local selectman, town meeting moderator, state representative or councillor—another was added, membership in the American Academy.

Who had been tapped for the new society, and why, had become a topic of local gossip, conjecture, and even cattiness. In a letter to the Reverend Jeremy Belknap on 11 September 1780, the Reverend John Eliot wrote with ill-concealed annoyance, "You asked me why I was not a member of the Academy, as Mr. C. was enrolled in the number. I answer, that I had rather it should be said, Why was *not* Mr. E.? than Why was Mr. C.?. (These things only *inter nos*. To speak seriously, it was meerly accidental that Mr. C. was in the Society, according to what he says. I suppose it was owing to his connection with Mr. Parsons, the lawyer, who made out the list)." After nearly a decade, when the Academy belatedly attempted to make amends for this initial slight by electing Eliot, he declined in an overly polite letter "for a variety of reasons," unspecified, and offered the spurned Fellows an ancient coin from his collection to evidence his good will.[39] Since Theophilus Parsons in fact played a major role in drafting the Academy bill and reporting the alphabetized list of names for insertion in the text, he very likely influenced the selection of Fellows. "Mr. C." was probably Eliot's fellow-clergyman John Clarke, protégé of

38. *The Continental Journal and Weekly Advertiser* for 18 May 1780 (Boston, no. 220) and the 22 May issue of the *Boston Gazette and Country Journal* carried Bowdoin's letter to the Fellows-elect.

39. MHS, *Collections*, ser. 6, 4 (Belknap Papers, 3), 197, John Eliot to Jeremy Belknap, Boston, 11 Sept. 1780; Academy Records, 1:127, meeting of 26 May 1789; Boston Athenaeum, Letters to the American Academy of Arts and Sciences (MS; hereinafter referred to as Academy Letters), 1:79, Eliot to Eliphalet Pearson, Boston, 21 June 1789.

the distinguished Reverend Charles Chauncy, whose granddaughter was Parsons's wife. Family ties bonded many members of the early Academy.

Most of the Fellows named in the Academy Act as incorporators were heroes of the Revolution who had either served as patriot legislators in the political skirmishes with British governors that were the prelude to independence, or fought in the field, or roused their parishioners with fiery sermons from the pulpit. On the whole the men of Massachusetts were more illustrious as politicians than as soldiers, though there were a few general officers from the Commonwealth. Many of the Academicians already met together in other philanthropic and cultural institutions — the Humane Society of Massachusetts, of which James Bowdoin was president, the Massachusetts Charitable Society, the Massachusetts Society for the Promoting of Agriculture, the Society for Propagating the Gospel among the Indians in North America. They had run grave risks in the revolutionary cause: some had endangered their lives, others their property. The leaders who had fled Boston in 1775 to avoid being arrested and transported to England for trial now added their strength to those who had once been under siege in the city and had endured the insults hurled at them by the occupying British troops.

Notables who had sat in legislatures of the Crown, the Continental Congress, and the Provincial Congress — men such as the two Adams cousins, James Bowdoin, John Hancock, Thomas Cushing, James Warren, and Robert Treat Paine — were chosen to be among the first Fellows of the Academy. While ardor for the Revolution was demanded of those in public life, a political test for admission to the Academy was not strictly enforced. Two who kept out of politics, Andrew Oliver, son of the Tory lieutenant-governor and an assiduous observer of the heavens, and the eminent Salem doctor Edward Augustus Holyoke, were among the charter members, though they were indifferent patriots. All of the incorporated Fellows were men with callings: with rare exceptions they belonged to one or more of the four professions — the clerisy, law, medicine, business — that dominated society. A line of exclusion was at first drawn at artists and artisans.

Of the judges, elected state officials, lawyers, clergymen, doctors of medicine, Harvard professors, and merchants who comprised the original Academy membership — in uneven parts, with some overlapping of the categories — the overwhelming number, fifty-six out of sixty-two, had Harvard degrees, only five of which were honorary. Apart from a few physicians, professional scientists were not conspicuous. Dr. Joseph Warren, Samuel Adams's cherished friend who would surely have been among the first Fellows, had been killed at Bunker Hill. The two most eminent scientists born in the Boston area were absent from the original list for opposite reasons. Benjamin Thompson, later Count Rumford, having served as a British spy in the early years of the war, was now ravaging Long Island with his dragoons. Benjamin Franklin, turned a Philadelphian, was in Paris being worshiped as a cult hero, the natural man and *philosophe*. In both instances the omissions were later rectified—Franklin's promptly, at the beginning of 1781, Thompson's nine years later when he had become rich and famous and his old compatriots were ready to forgive, if not forget, his earlier transgressions. In turn the Academy received a handsome bequest from the once-poor Woburn boy whose adventures had brought him fortune, women, and a measure of political power in a petty German principality.[40] The most distinguished Harvard scientist of the eighteenth century, John Winthrop, was dead.

Though there were no great scientists among the charter members, a sizable number had scientific avocations. Bowdoin's accomplishments in that area were more impressive than those of most of the Fellows: he had advanced beyond an antiquarian preoccupation with curious objects and instruments, and an interest in the practical application of new discoveries, to devote himself to the theoretical problems of Newtonian science. The Royal Society had appointed a decorative viscount as its first president, and the American Philosophical Society had divided its headship between a patron and a president. When the Boston Academy elected Bowdoin, he was the best that the men of Massachusetts then had to offer to the Republic of Science.

The leading revolutionary patriots brought together by the Academy in 1780 had had frequent fallings-out with one another. No love was lost at this stage in their lives between Hancock and Bowdoin, Samuel Adams and Hancock, John and Samuel Adams, Benjamin Franklin and John Adams. James Warren took a superior view of the whole lot and found no great virtue in any of them. It required a man adept at insinuation to maintain amicable relations with all the patriots, a feat accomplished with agility by the Reverend Samuel Cooper, first vice-president of the Academy. By the 1780s the fiery revolutionaries of the sixties and seventies had become dignitaries of the new republic whose conspiratorial days were virtually over; they had acquired political dependents, and many ultimately attained high office — Hancock, Bowdoin, and Samuel Adams, the governorship of Massachusetts; John Adams, the presidency of the United States. As the patriots grew older, their political rancor was often intensified, but the Academy of Arts and Sciences was relatively neutral ground. Its rewards were not significant, and the scientific passions, though they burned steadily in Massachusetts, rarely erupted into violence.

In its early years the Academy was a rather placid learned society with none of the vituperative outbursts that marked Newton's Royal Society in its halcyon days and late into the eighteenth century. There were discernible factions in the Academy, but during the first decade of its existence neither religion nor politics intruded into the formal sessions of this private club, and the rules of decorum

40. Academy Records, 1:25, 127: election of Sir Benjamin Thompson, Knight, on 29 May 1789. A year later, on 24 May 1790, he sent from Munich a flowery letter of acceptance for the flattering mark of their esteem (see Academy Letters, 1:90).

were respected. By contrast, Dr. Richard Price had occasion to comment on the unseemly doings at the Royal Society when he wrote to the corresponding secretary of the Academy in March of 1784, "The greatest part of our time this winter has been spent in a manner very unsuitable to the design of our institution; I mean, in violent altercations and disputes occasioned by complaints of misconduct in Sr. Joseph Banks our President and attempts to oblige him to resign."[41]

With twenty clergymen among the incorporated Fellows, the Academy at its very inception had an aura of sanctity, even if by tacit consent theological discourse was excluded. While the religious positions of the members extended over the spectrum from orthodox Calvinism to unitarianism, their beliefs did not disturb the deliberations of the Academy. The Royal Society of London had fixed the pattern of complete separation between inquiries into the book of nature and inquiries into the book of Scripture. In the early sessions of the American Academy there is not a hint of any warfare between science and religion; if anything, the marvels revealed by science were considered cogent proofs for the existence of an omniscient and omnipotent Providence. Religion, science, and patriotism in harmony with one another defined the temper of the Academy.

In the summer of 1780 John Hancock and James Bowdoin vied for the first governorship of the Commonwealth of Massachusetts. The contest was bitter and uneven, but Bowdoin was stunned by the magnitude of Hancock's victory, 90 percent of the votes. The results for lieutenant governor were inconclusive—nobody won a majority—and the new Massachusetts House of Representatives and Senate offered Bowdoin a consolation prize, the lieutenant governorship, or, if he chose, a senatorship. Bowdoin refused both, pleading the state of his health, but adding that even if he were well he would not accept office against the manifest will of the people. The seat was then offered to James Warren of Plymouth, who could no more than Bowdoin endure serving under the flashy Hancock, though Warren stoutly denied an allegation to that effect published in the newspapers.[42] And so it was that Hancock's man Thomas Cushing, a Boston merchant who had sat in many revolutionary assemblies, was awarded the post. James Bowdoin had to content himself with the presidency of the Academy, to which he had been elected pro tem on 30 May and permanently on 30 August.

The selection of Bowdoin placed at the head of the Academy a unique personality: a merchant and Christian gentleman with a penchant for Newtonian science, and a political figure whose life had been bound up with the fortunes of Massachusetts Bay for three decades. Bowdoin had the gift of making tidy separations among

41. MHS, *Proceedings* 43:617, Richard Price to Joseph Willard, Newington-Green, 14 Mar. 1784.

42. *Boston Gazette and Country Journal*, 31 Oct. 1780; MHS, *Collections*, ser. 6, 9 (Bowdoin and Temple Papers, 1), 444–45, Bowdoin to the Senate and House of Representatives; *Boston Gazette and Country Journal*, 16 Nov. 1780.

personal affections, business, science, politics, and religion, without seepage from one aspect of existence to another. That, at least, was the well-ordered personality presented to the world. Some men were chilled by the mechanical economy that allowed him to fulfill the duties of each activity in accordance with its particular rules. Others admired his capacity to so organize a multiplicity of occupations that he never appeared harried or pressed, and left himself time for family converse and social pleasures. This scion of Huguenots who had been hounded from their native France a century earlier rose steadily to a position of eminence in the Boston establishment and was welcomed into its loftiest ranks. But he retained to the end a degree of aloofness from his fellows that may well have been linked to consciousness of a singular ancestral history.

3

THE MERCHANT OF BOSTON

꧁⟨E⟩꧂

T HE prominent role Huguenots played in colonial America was far out of proportion to their numbers. In Massachusetts, after remaining a fairly cohesive group for about four decades following their first settlement in the late 1680s, they were gradually absorbed into the English population. A few of the Huguenot families joined the Anglican King's Chapel after 1690, but the allegiance of the bulk of the immigrants was divided between the French Church that Laurent Van den Bosch had organized in 1685 and one of the Congregational churches. Sometimes individuals supported two religious establishments at the same time. The fusion of Huguenot families with the dominant English population is evident in the marriage records of the city of Boston. During the half-century from 1700 to 1749 only 17 Huguenots wed within their own group, while 305 were exogamous. At first it was principally Huguenot men who married English women, but intermarriage soon involved Huguenot women as well. Though in the second half of the eighteenth century Huguenots were rarely remarked upon as a distinctive alien element, they are identifiable by their French names, sometimes Anglicized, which appear frequently on the roster of Boston revolutionary figures—James Boutineau, Andrew Johonnot, James Pitts, Paul Revere, James Bowdoin. (A descendant of the Huguenot whose name is associated with the most renowned Boston landmark of the period—Faneuil Hall—was a Tory.)[1] Huguenots outside of New England were also distinguished patriots: Henry Laurens and Elias Boudinot were both presidents of the Continental Congress.

Assimilation of the Huguenots

The first Huguenot minister who left a mark on his Boston congregation—though he returned to England in 1691—was Ezéchiel Carré, author of an attack on a Jesuit who had expounded the principal points of religion in twenty-four chapters written in the "Onneiout" (Oneniute, or Iroquois) language. In his *Echantillon*

---

1. Jon Butler, *The Huguenots in America* (Cambridge, Mass.: Harvard University Press, 1983), 82; Gregory Palmer, *Biographical Sketches of Loyalists of the American Revolution* (Westport, Conn.: Meckler, 1984), 261.

de la doctrine que les Jésuites enségnent aus Sauvages du Nouveau Monde (1690), the earliest French book to be printed in Boston, with apologies from the typesetter because he lacked the appropriate accent marks, Carré denounced the Jesuit catechism used in converting the Indians — especially its materialistic description of paradise — as a work of Satan welling up from the depths of hell. Carré, formally identified on the title page as the Ministre de l'Église Française de Boston, was orthodox enough to be honored by an introductory preface from Cotton Mather himself.[2] In the *Magnalia Christi Americana*, Mather records the existence of a congregation of French Protestant refugees, under the pastoral care of Monsieur Pierre Daillé, who used the Latin Schoolhouse to hold their religious services.[3] Later, in 1715, a church was built and André Le Mercier of Caen, graduate of the Protestant Academy of Geneva, was brought over to be installed as its first pastor at the munificent salary of £100 per annum New England money. In 1730 Le Mercier, turned Andrew Mercy, became an Englishman by naturalization. He was a learned man and prolific writer, author of *The Church History of Geneva* (1732), *A Treatise Against Detraction* (1733), and *The Christian Rapture, a Poem* (1747). In his *Treatise Against Detraction* the backbiting of a rigid Calvinist had given way to an urbane condemnation of the vice of slander.

At a time when evangelicalism was posing a serious threat to the older established Protestant sects, Mercy was more intent upon the size of his emoluments and upon preening himself with the feathers of scholarship than concerned with the pouring out of the spirit. There was a widespread complaint that he had alienated the young people and driven them away to other churches. The French congregation diminished so rapidly as the Huguenots intermarried that by 1748, when their brick meetinghouse on School Street was sold and the congregation was dissolved, the male communicants had dwindled to seven and Stephen Boutineau was the only surviving elder. Though family and personal ties among the Huguenots remained strong, by the second half of the century they had ceased to be an organized community. Doctrinally united in Calvin, the Huguenots and the Congregationalists were separated by some minor differences in religious practice. The Huguenots were accustomed to the celebration of Christmas and Easter, which devout Puritans avoided as pagan festivals, recognizing only the Sabbath as the holy day of the Lord. Huguenots observed a less rigid Sabbath rule, and enjoyed a certain ease of living.

2. Worthington C. Ford, "Ezekiel Carré and the French Church in Boston," in MHS, *Proceedings* 52 (1918–19), 121–32.

3. Cotton Mather, *Magnalia Christi Americana; or the Ecclesiastical History of New England, from its first planting in the year 1620 unto the year of our Lord 1698, in seven books* (Hartford, 1820; first American ed. from London ed. of 1702), 1:80.

A measure of favor was shown the Huguenots as refugees, Protestant victims of Louis XIV, the French antichrist. And if Pastor Mercy faithfully voiced their sentiments, the Huguenots of Boston were grateful to God and their English neighbors for undeserved blessings:

> Let us never forget . . . how we have happily fled from Persecution, found acceptance before the People of this Land; how, when we were Strangers, they have taken us in; how several have contributed towards the building of our Place of Worship; how the pious and reverend Ministers have readily joined with us on our Fast Days, to implore for and with us, GOD's Forgiveness and Peace for the remainders of the faithful in *France*; how the honourable the General Court have chearfully admitted us into the great and valuable Privileges which they enjoy themselves as *Englishmen*, by their Act of *Naturalization of Protestant Foreigners*, and their favourable Answer to our Petition; how God has not only fed and cloathed you, but even granted to some of you considerable Estates. . . .[4]

The pastor hoped his flock would dedicate their riches to the glory of God, the relief of the poor, and the service of His church, and he urged that they reciprocate the kindness of those who had entertained them so that they would not repent of their generosity. Rich Huguenots zealously supported the war against the French in Canada: as merchants they prospered by supplying the expedition, which pious Calvinists saw as a crusade; there were chaplains who brought along hatchets with which to demolish the saints in Canadian churches. James Bowdoin II joyously reported to his brother-in-law James Erving in London that on the fall of Quebec, Boston put on "the most general & most brilliant illumination that was ever seen in America."[5] Pastor Mercy displayed his gift for epigram in an exhortation to his readers: eschew the way of Roman Catholics, he admonished them, for they have religious zeal without knowledge, and the way of most Protestants, who have knowledge without zeal; both knowledge and zeal are essential to acquiring virtue and happiness.[6] For James Bowdoin, the precept was a lifelong rule of conduct.

Rise of the House of Bowdoin

The Huguenot process of assimilation and rapid upward mobility is exemplified in the history of the Bowdoin family.[7] James Bowdoin II's émigré grandfather, Pierre

4. Andrew Le Mercier, *Treatise Against Detraction, in Ten Sections* (Boston, 1733), iii. Le Mercier's papers are in the Massachusetts Historical Society and the Boston Public Library.

5. MHS, *Collections*, ser. 6.9 (Bowdoin and Temple Papers, 1), 4, James Bowdoin to James Erving, Boston, 17 Oct. 1759.

6. Le Mercier, *Treatise Against Detraction*, iv.

7. Gerard J. Brault, "Pierre Baudouin and the Bowdoin coat of arms," in *New England Historical and Genealogical Register* 104 (1960), 243–68. Biographical details about Pierre derive from James III's

Baudouin, is listed on 1 April 1683 as a member of a French colony in Dublin. (He has never been traced back to La Rochelle, where legend had him originate, though in family papers La Rochelle is mentioned as the birthplace of his son James; Pierre had a brother, James, who was born in Nîmes, migrated to England, and was buried in a Huguenot cemetery outside London.) Pierre owned a barque, *John of Dublin*, that was engaged in the colonial trade, and on that vessel he and his family sailed to Salem. From there they migrated to Casco Bay, and finally in 1690 to Boston, where they thrived among their fellow Calvinists from England. When he died in 1706 Pierre left a small estate of £1,344 to his wife, Elizabeth, who in turn divided it among four children—James, John, who settled in Virginia, as did his sister Elizabeth, and Mary.[8] Pierre had been a pillar of the early Huguenot community in Boston, and his daughter Mary married fellow Huguenot Stephen Boutineau. Though Pierre contributed funds for the construction of King's Chapel, apparently he did not join its Anglican congregation, and his daughter Elizabeth became a member of Cotton Mather's Second Church.[9] His son James Bowdoin I took as wives successively Sarah Campbell, Hannah Pordage, and the widow Mehetabel Lillie, all of English colonial families. He joined the Brattle Street Church in 1711, when his first son, William, was baptized; James Bowdoin II, the future president of the American Academy and governor of Massachusetts, was born of the second marriage, in Boston on 7 August 1726.

The daughters of James Bowdoin I married a Pitts, a Bayard, and a Flucker, all Huguenots, but his son James II was wed in 1748 to Elizabeth Erving, the beautiful seventeen-year-old sister of his Harvard roommate and offspring of the prosperous and distinguished English settler Captain John Erving, an Episcopalian. Of that union a daughter, Elizabeth, born in 1750, married John Temple (1767), who after many trials succeeded to an English baronetcy; one of their daughters in 1786 married a Winthrop, an Episcopalian. The son of James II and Elizabeth Erving, James III, born in 1752, wed his cousin Sarah (1781), daughter of his father's half-brother William. Pierre Baudouin's son James Bowdoin I had increased the wealth of the family through shipping and land purchases so that at his death in 1747 he was one of the richest men in the colony—his fortune was estimated at

---

information to obituary writers upon the death of his father. For provisions of Pierre's will and those of his son and grandson, see Robert L. Volz, *Governor Bowdoin & His Family. A Guide to an Exhibition and a Catalogue*. Bowdoin College (Brunswick, Maine: Bowdoin College, 1969), 7–9. Brault (250–51) gives the provisions of Pierre's will, dated 16 June 1704, probated 6 July 1719. See also MHS, *Proceedings* 14 (1875–76), 198–99.

8. MHS, Bowdoin and Temple Papers (MSS), Inventory of Mrs. Elizabeth Baudouin's Estate by James Baudouin & Stephen Boutineau, Executors, 18 Aug. 1720.

9. Jon Butler, *The Huguenots in America*, 78, 80.

more than £82,000—and had risen to be a member of the Governor's Council.[10] His portrait, which now hangs in the Bowdoin College Museum of Art, reveals a powerful, corpulent man with a strong, prominent nose and firm chin. In the background, a schooner is making its way across the waters, symbol of the source of his great wealth. The artist has left the impression of a domineering man whose authority was not often questioned. Apart from this and another cruder portrait and some documents respecting his far-flung activities, no personal papers of James Bowdoin I appear to have survived. The younger of his two sons, James II, on the death of his half-brother inherited the main body of their father's estate, consisting of stores, factories (later sold), land, houses, and farms.

After graduating from South Grammar School (later Boston Latin) and Harvard College, James Bowdoin II devoted himself for decades to public service, first in the colonial House of Representatives and on the Royal Governor's Council, and then as a leader of the revolutionary insurgents and governor of the new Commonwealth of Massachusetts. As good Calvinists the Bowdoins found in their phenomenal prosperity presumptive evidence, if not certainty, that they were of the elect of God. Though Huguenot exiles, by their own industry they had reached the pinnacle of wealth, and whatever they touched turned to gold. James Bowdoin III became the American minister to France and Spain during the Napoleonic period, a gentleman agriculturist of refined literary and artistic tastes. With his death the direct male line ended. His property went to the founding of a "seminary" that honored his father, Bowdoin College in Brunswick, Maine.

When James Bowdoin II married into the Erving family, he adopted a style of life that was similar to that of the wealthy English merchants with whom he and his father-in-law, John Erving, did business. Portraits of James and Elizabeth by Robert Feke at the time of their marriage show them opulently clad in satin and velvet. In 1756 Bowdoin acquired Erving's Boston mansion at what is now the area around Beacon and Bowdoin Streets, and spent considerable sums remodeling its exterior and adorning it with the furnishings and silver appropriate to his station. In the midst of political and business affairs, he occupied himself with ordering from his English agents rich fabrics, fashionable head-dresses, and jewelry for his wife and daughter, and for his table pipes of the best-quality Madeira, "light Amber & nut flavor." Entertainments were often lavish and merry, though elegance had its hazards: the Bowdoin mansion, set well back from the road, boasted a long flight of stone steps leading to the main entrance; after a convivial dinner party one winter's night guests, a trifle unsteady on their feet and confronted by the icy

10. On the Bowdoins and Ervings, see the not wholly accurate work by Temple Prime, *Some Account of the Bowdoin Family with a notice of the Erving Family*, 3d ed. (New York, 1900; ed. pr. 1887).

stairs, flung decorum to the chilly winds and sat their way down to the bottom.[11] Though opposed to the extension of slavery, Bowdoin owned a few black household servants, and commissioned a relative, in language appropriate to commodity trading, to purchase for him a "light-timber'd Negro boy" who could serve as a coachman and a barber.[12] There was nothing priggish or sanctimonious about James Bowdoin when he was in his thirties; the figure of the staid upright man took a few decades to be set in place. When one of his slaves, Caesar, got into trouble for his amours with white ladies of the town and Mrs. Bowdoin barred the door to him, her husband interceded in his behalf and had him deported to the Caribbean to escape a harsher fate.[13]

In a funeral sermon for the widowed Elizabeth Bowdoin half a century after her marriage, the Reverend William Emerson attempted to open a window on the Bowdoins' private life and its religious foundation:

> They were christians from inquiry and principle; and though remote from ostentation in religion, yet they felt themselves obligated publickly to manifest that reverence, which they felt for its forms and institutions. To their faith in the saviour, they joined an open profession of his gospel, and maintained a steady adherence to their professional character, as protestant dissenters. . . . In the midst of affluence they were not luxurious; surrounded by dependents, they were not oppressive. Their mansion was the seat of wealth, politeness, and connubial bliss; containing within its walls the rare association of magnificence with contentment, and of publick care with private repose.[14]

Clearly a touched-up portrait, the eulogy nevertheless reveals something of the manner and position of the Bowdoins.

While no expressions of affection among Bowdoin, his father, and his half-brother William have survived, Bowdoin found compensation for any lack of warmth in his early family life in relationships with the Ervings and their English connections. To his brother-in-law George Erving he was "my most dear and inestimable friend,"[15] and they carried on a lifelong correspondence ranging widely

11. See, for example, MHS, Bowdoin and Temple Papers, Letter Book of James Bowdoin II, 35, Bowdoin to Lane & Booth, 15 Oct. 1762; 218, Bowdoin to Henry Lloyd, 10 June 1771; also, Justin Winsor, ed., *The Memorial History of Boston* (Boston, 1880–83, 4 vols.), 2 (1881), 522.

12. MHS, Bowdoin and Temple Papers, Letter Book, 28, James Bowdoin II to Col. George Scott, 14 Apr. 1762. Five years later, Bowdoin drafted an act to discourage the further importation of slaves into Massachusetts by imposing a £40 head tax on them (see Bowdoin and Temple Papers, James Bowdoin, "Draft of an act for an import duty on Negroes," 1767). For a discussion of slavery in Boston see Akers, *The Divine Politician*, 123–24.

13. MHS, Bowdoin and Temple Papers, Letter Book, 56, Bowdoin to George Scott, 14 Oct. 1763.

14. William Emerson, *A Sermon Delivered in Brattlestreet Church, May 5, 1803* (Boston, 1803), 16.

15. MHS, Bowdoin and Temple Papers, George Erving to Elizabeth Bowdoin, Froyle, 26 Dec. 1790.

over personal, political, business, and scientific matters. That they were on opposing sides during the War for Independence and that Bowdoin permitted himself
an occasional jab at British policy after peace had been declared never forced a
breach between the two men. And with George Scott, whose wife, Abigail, was
sister to Bowdoin's wife, Elizabeth, bonds of intimate friendship were forged. They
were of the same generation, and when Bowdoin wrote Colonel Scott on 1 March
1763, congratulating him on his appointment as governor of Grenada, the tone of
the letter evokes excellent dinners and merry drinking parties. The prospects of
wealth open before the new governor are discussed without reticence. Bowdoin
thought the post would net ten thousand pounds a year, "no foolish thing," and
Scott would have the whole power of legislation vested in himself without the annoyance of an assembly: "This is a Situation I should like mighty well, thô (I think)
in a latitude rather more northerly." With a gift for unfortunate analogies that he
displayed on more than one occasion, Bowdoin likened Mrs. Scott's longing for
her husband to Matthew Prior's turtle-widow Turturella moaning for her Colum-
bo, quoted verse, and announced Scott's imminent repossession of his fair nymph.
Bowdoin recalled the affectionate parting of the four of them in Roxbury: "At the
same time it fill'd me with regret, it gave me great pleasure.—pleasure, at seeing
the warm affection you discover'd for your other self, and those connected with
her.—regret, that we must part with so valuable a friend. The affection (I assure
you) was mutual & equally strong; thô exprest, my dear friend! with most warmth
on your part. Such generous passion, if it characterizes, it does at the same time do
honor to the country that produced the subject of it.", In passing, Bowdoin offered
Scott a portion in a new trading enterprise that would run vessels between Boston
and Grenada—a venture organized by a few Boston Huguenots.[16] The chance for
honest gain was never far from this Huguenot's reckoning.

In his frequent letters to Scott, Bowdoin struck the attitude of a man of the
world and something of a bon vivant. At times he sounded remarkably spontaneous; he would indulge in an occasional witticism, even a faint suggestion of rib-
aldry. Gifts traveled between the two households — cheese from Bowdoin's island
estates, oranges and a turtle from Grenada. For the latter Bowdoin sent thanks,
and described the dinner at which friends feasted on the delicacy, afterward toasting the governor of Grenada with "full bumpers." Bowdoin rejoiced in the beneficent effect of Abigail's arrival in Grenada —"water gruel from her hand is more
salubrious than all the physic in nature"—and reported jubilantly on the cure of a
tenacious head rash: "I am more obliged to an old woman (upward of 80) than to

16. Ibid., Letter Book, 43–49, Bowdoin to George Scott, 1 Mar. 1763; among those involved in
the undertaking was James Pitts, Bowdoin's brother-in-law. The reference to "The Turtle and Spar-
row" by Matthew Prior (1664–1721) was prophetic: Abigail Scott was widowed four years later.

all the medical gentry I have consulted. . . . In short my Pericranium is as clear as any baby's: all capital defects (external ones I mean) are perfectly removed." When his little son was about to be inoculated against the smallpox, he informed Scott and conveyed to him the child's happy recollections of the "fine fun" they had had playing marbles when Scott was in Boston. Bowdoin comforted his brother-in-law over his transfer to Dominica, and actively seconded his attempts to effect an exchange of offices with the Massachusetts royal governor Bernard. There were many references to the rumored pregnancy of Abigail Scott, though the Scotts died childless a few years later. At one point Bowdoin congratulated Scott prematurely and jestingly attributed Abigail's condition to the tropical climate: "I begin to have a good opinion of the air of Grenada, at least with respect to its prolific quality. I shall recommend it to my neighbours Hancock and Lloyed; thô I believe their Doxies are rather too far advanced to receive any benefit from it in that way."[17] In later years Bowdoin was not wont to joke about the Hancocks.

When Scott died in 1767, Bowdoin wrote to his bereaved sister-in-law in the accepted idiom of the day: "This melancholy event must give you as it does us great distress: but take consolation from the proper source of it, a source from which your mind is formed to receive it, and the only true one from whence, notwithstanding the general sentiments and practice of mankind, it can spring. I mean religion—which teaches us that all events are under the direction and superintendence of infinite wisdom; and that whatever happens, though for the present it may sadden the heart, yet to the virtuous shall in the end be promotive of their best good." It comes as something of a shock that Bowdoin ended the draft of this letter of condolence with a reference to his "Negro fellow Caesar" and an arrangement for his disposition. The sentence was then crossed out—he had caught the impropriety—and twelve days later the subject was resumed in a separate letter: Caesar was to be sold and what he fetched shipped home in coffee and sugar loaves.[18]

Bowdoin's extant correspondence reveals a doting father; the family was the foundation and center of his life. His father's advice flowed copiously when James III, or Jemmy as the family called him, set sail for England in the winter of 1771 on a voyage undertaken partly for his health. A pithy send-off note of 2 January, on the eve of his departure, promised Jemmy that adherence to the principles explored in their recent lengthy conversation would redound to his "credit, honour

17. Ibid., Letter Book, 43, Bowdoin to Scott, 1 Mar. 1763; 51: 30 May 1763; 60: 3 Dec. 1763; 75: 9 Mar. 1764; 167: 27 Jan. 1767; 176: 8 May 1767.

18. Ibid., Letter Book, 185, Bowdoin to Abigail Scott, 14 Dec. 1767; 186, Bowdoin to Abigail Scott, 26 Dec. 1767. For years Bowdoin tried to collect the twenty guineas and the gold ring commemorating the relationship between himself and Colonel Scott, which his brother Michael Scott owed Bowdoin by the terms of the colonel's will.

& Interest." This was the desiccated conventional formula; but a new emotionality in family relationships broke through in the signature, "most affectionately your best friend"—not the mode of the previous century, when patriarchal authority had been more awesome. A fortnight later, while Jemmy was still on the high seas, Bowdoin addressed to him in London an expanded version that was an admixture of Polonian, Calvinist, and aristocratic precepts. Jemmy was to seek both improvement and entertainment during his stay abroad, always uniting the useful with the agreeable. Only the cultivation of virtue in all aspects of life and a "supreme regard to ye benevolent author of our Being" could insure the self-approbation that was the foundation of lasting happiness. Turning from such sublime preachments to practical affairs, Bowdoin recommended that his son attend courses of experimental lectures in natural philosophy, as well as a good school for training in the French language and in handling mercantile accounts. But he instructed him to acquire the graces of conversing fluently in his own language without becoming loquacious—incessant gabblers were a nuisance in society. Like any solicitous father who had sent a sickly son away from home rather earlier than he would have wished, albeit under the tutelage of Uncle John Erving, Bowdoin closed with a parting word from the youth's grandfather: "*Take care of yourself.*"[19]

Liberal arrangements had been made for Jemmy's expenses while abroad, but the youth frequently exceeded his allowance; on his own for the first time, he had fancies of acquiring body servants and a string of thoroughbred horses. Though Jemmy could on occasion sound like a paragon of righteousness, he was not always a conscientious student. In later years he claimed that no circumstance of his life had caused him greater uneasiness than his negligence during his early college career.[20] Bowdoin was discontented with his son's design to study law at Oxford, but tried to make the best of it—it might be useful in preparing for the mercantile profession. Jemmy had been given leave from Harvard, where he had enrolled in 1767, before taking his degree, and Bowdoin assured him that he would be sent a diploma from the president of the college, "by means of which you will probably be able to procure a degree at Oxford, or perhaps you may obtain it without such a Diploma. If you should be at Cambridge or Edinburg you may possibly obtain Degrees at those universities also: in which case you must not forget to procure their Diplomas."[21] Bowdoin prized public testimonials of worth from universities and loved to join cultural and philanthropic societies, especially to preside over

19. Ibid., Letter Book, 214, Bowdoin to James III, 2 Jan. 1771; ibid., Bowdoin to James III, 17 Jan. 1771.

20. MHS, *Collections*, ser. 7.6 (Bowdoin and Temple Papers, 2), 208, James Bowdoin III to his sister, Lady Temple, Dorchester, 31 Oct. 1793.

21. MHS, Bowdoin and Temple Papers, Bowdoin to James III, 12 June 1771.

them. The documents and offices were further evidence that he was of the elect of God. Bowdoin gave his son free rein up to a point and then firmly called a halt. When in November Jemmy blithely announced that he had quit Oxford to devote himself to French, dancing, and fencing, and as usual asked for more money, Bowdoin made no effort to conceal his annoyance. He regretted that his son had abandoned his university studies, and repeatedly demanded a specific accounting of how he had spent his time and money.[22]

Bowdoin was still considering a proposal to extend Jemmy's stay, when a tiff with another uncle, George Erving, under whose protection he would have been placed, induced an abrupt change of heart in the young man. After some fifteen months abroad, he returned home, his health much improved,[23] to resume his travels in the fall of 1773. His letters passed over in silence the monuments of the Continent, which drew from his father a gentle chiding softened with a jest: on the basis of his son's letters he had concluded that Italy, France, and England were falsely renowned for their curiosities, that reports of their grand works of art were all fictions and inventions.[24] Jemmy's European sojourn was terminated when his father became doubly dismayed by the youth's extravagance and the threat of war. Intimating in deceptive language that a crisis was imminent "in consequence of the wise measures of Ministry & Parliament," Bowdoin hastily ordered his son, who seemed oblivious to the political conflict between England and the colonies, to return without delay to any part of the American continent he thought proper.[25] To his father's chagrin, Jemmy tarried until September 1775, well after hostilities had begun. Since Boston was under siege, he had to make a detour to Philadelphia before continuing on to Middleborough, to which the family had repaired the previous summer during an episode of the recurrent pulmonary illness to which Bowdoin was subject.

In Philadelphia, James III met with Samuel Adams, who sent a letter to Bowdoin Sr. via his son. Rejoicing at the renewal of the young man's vigor, he added, "I dare say it will be still more satisfactory to you to find, that he is warmly attached to the Rights of his Country & of mankind."[26] James was thenceforward associated not only with his father's commercial interests but with his political sentiments and activities as well. Though only in his early twenties, he had begun to be regarded as a patriot and public figure in his own right. He reported to his father on the

22. Ibid., James III to Bowdoin, London, 6 Nov. 1771; ibid., Bowdoin to James III, 28 Jan. 1772.

23. MHS, *Collections*, ser. 6.9 (Bowdoin and Temple Papers, 1), 294, Bowdoin to Samuel Hood, 2 Sept. 1772.

24. Ibid., 359, Bowdoin to James III, 15 Mar. 1774.

25. MHS, Bowdoin and Temple Papers, Bowdoin to James III, 30 Mar. 1775.

26. MHS, *Proceedings* 12 (1871–73), 226, Samuel Adams to Bowdoin, Philadelphia, 16 Nov. 1775.

unyielding disposition of the British ministry, an observation that the elder Bowdoin transmitted to his revolutionary friends, and during periods of his father's indisposition served as an intermediary between him and the Massachusetts Board of War. He accompanied George Washington on his entry into Boston after the evacuation of the British troops, and took him to dine at Grandfather Erving's mansion. When hostilities finally ended in the spring of 1783, a Boston broadside celebrated the young Bowdoin's arrival from New York on 31 March with the "Glorious Intelligence" of peace.[27] He was a member of the General Court during his father's tenure as governor, and both Bowdoins sat as delegates to the Massachusetts convention that ratified the federal constitution.

The strong ties that united them were not severed even with the death of James Bowdoin II, and an old-fashioned filial piety survived in James III until he himself died of tuberculosis in 1811. While outsiders may have seen only the reserve and austerity of the intellectual merchant who was his father, a deep love bound the two, and within the confines of the family circle signs of tenderness were not inhibited.

James was not the sole object of Bowdoin's paternal affections. Though his daughter does not figure prominently in his correspondence, her future was a perennial concern, manifested particularly through Bowdoin's interventions in behalf of John Temple, the British colonial official, her senior by eighteen years, to whom she was married at the age of seventeen. While Temple was in England seeking an appointment, his wife and children lived in Boston with the Bowdoins. In the spring of 1772, when Elizabeth left with her small son to rejoin her husband in London, where he had secured the post of surveyor general of customs, her father sent her a present of £100, along with a letter that invoked the blessing of Heaven on her passage and reunion with her husband, and was signed "I am, my dear child, yr most affectionate father." And to Temple he wrote that Elizabeth and the children had so enhanced his happiness, their leave-taking filled him with sorrow. He could not bear to part with little Betsy, who remained with her grandparents and was raised by them.[28] In the following November, a loving grandfather reported, "Yr little girl is as plump as a partridge & makes us all happy."[29] Bowdoin's guidance of his daughter's moral education did not cease when she left his home. She was already the mother of two children and living abroad when he urged upon

27. Ibid., 227, Bowdoin to Samuel Adams, 9 Dec. 1775; ser. 2.8 (1892, 1894), 289, Bowdoin to Thomas Cushing, 9 Dec. 1775; 14:232; MHS, *Collections* 75 (Broadsides, Ballads, &c Printed in Massachusetts 1639–1800, compiled by W. C. Ford, 1922), 323, no. 2349.

28. MHS, Bowdoin and Temple Papers, Letter Book, 222, Bowdoin to Elizabeth Temple, 9 May 1772; MHS, *Collections*, ser. 6.9 (Bowdoin and Temple Papers, 1), 293, Bowdoin to John Temple, 9 May 1772.

29. Ibid., 302, Bowdoin to Temple, 2 Nov. 1772.

her an ardent religious devotion that in times of adversity would strengthen her composure of mind and complete the victory over her passions.[30]

To Temple himself, whose political difficulties were attended by financial straits, Bowdoin was ever a "bountiful friend,"[31] a protector of this incautious man who got into all manner of political scrapes. His conduct was sometimes politically costly to James Bowdoin; to this day it is difficult to know whether Temple was always candid with his father-in-law about his affiliations.

Elizabeth's love for her father was tinged with awe, and the tone she adopted toward him was self-deprecating, almost abjectly dutiful. She corresponded principally with her mother, apprehensive that her father would be annoyed with the repetition of her ideas and would find her letters tiresome. But she tried desperately to please him. From London she sent him political news she hoped would be of interest; and she planned to inspect an air balloon so that she could give him a detailed description of it. Shortly before the Temples left England in March of 1785 to take up residence in New York, they bought him an elegant little writing table that had belonged to the Earl of Chatham — a gift, Elizabeth surmised, that would be especially welcome to him.[32]

James Bowdoin II had been born to riches, and the assumption of a political position that accorded with his wealth was a duty. But throughout his long career in public office he never allowed his business to go to rack and ruin, though perhaps he slackened in the aggressive amassing of worldly goods if compared with his ancestors. Whatever value he attached to other objects and pursuits, he maintained a consistent regard for money. In responding to his brother-in-law George Scott's proposal of a future bride for Jemmy, then fourteen, Bowdoin conceded that there were many grounds for compatibility between the two children, but he was explicit about a principal concern: "Thus far they are tolerably equal: I wish there was no disparity in another respect. The money — thô for my own part I think it by no means a very essential thing beyond a decent competency — the money, my dear Scott, you know is the *primum mobile* of most matches; and you perfectly understand on which side the disparity in this respect lies."[33] (Bowdoin's cosmological vocabulary cropped up in his conduct of everyday affairs and must have bewildered his less learned interlocutors, increasing the pathos of distance between them.) In the third generation of the House of Bowdoin in America, the pioneer acquisitive

30. MHS, Bowdoin and Temple Papers, Bowdoin to Elizabeth Temple, 15 Nov. 1774.

31. MHS, *Collections*, ser. 6.9 (Bowdoin and Temple Papers, 1), 463, Temple to Benjamin Franklin, Amsterdam, 26 July 1781 (draft).

32. MHS, Bowdoin and Temple Papers, Elizabeth Temple to her mother, London, 23 Jan. 1784; MHS, *Collections*, ser. 7.6 (Bowdoin and Temple Papers, 2), 43, Elizabeth Temple to Bowdoin, London, 7 Mar. 1785.

33. MHS, Bowdoin and Temple Papers, Letter Book, 176, Bowdoin to Scott, 8 May 1767.

ambition of Pierre Baudouin and James Bowdoin I was softened by the graces of literary and scientific culture. The comforts and appurtenances of wealth were always there, but not carried to the point of ostentation or profligacy. No dissipation or debauchery besmirched the good name of the Bowdoins.

Despite his sense of duty and intimate involvement in the patriotic cause, throughout the Revolution James Bowdoin kept close to home base. In addition to his own precarious health and his son's frailty, there were other, more private troubles in his family that had to be endured. Mrs. Bowdoin suffered from nervous diseases graver than the customary women's vapors; she was addicted to the taking of a snuff tobacco whose precise components remain unknown. Their daughter, Elizabeth, at one time tried to comfort her mother, reminding her that weak nerves ran in the family and happily betokened longevity; but in the end she scolded her. It was her duty to her husband and children at least to reduce the quantity of snuff she took, if she was unable to abstain from it entirely. Elizabeth warned her mother that her habit was constantly worsening, and recommended as a cure a Spartan regimen that included cold water showers daily.[34] Bowdoin himself was not always sympathetic. When he had heard from the governor of Grenada about the virtues of the island springs, he voiced a desire to douse his wife in one of them. With some impatience he wrote Scott, "She knows the occasion of her ill state, and the means of removing it. She has nothing to do but to disuse Tea and Snuff, and in a few months she would again be the finest girl in Christendom. A few trials of this sort have had an excellent effect, but the force of habit is too strong for her resolution."[35] Yet he tended her. He journeyed about the countryside with her—long rides were reputed to be good for the nerves, and in the course of one summer they covered seven or eight hundred miles[36]—or remained at home, closeted with his microscopes and telescopes and other instruments of science, some genuine, others the inventions of charlatans.

A Versatile Christian Gentleman

Though science remained a personal passion, the inherited calling of James Bowdoin II was business. He was an entrepreneur with diversified and wide-ranging interests: in addition to shipping and smuggling, he invested in real estate in the Boston area, and was the first president of the Massachusetts Bank.[37] He played a role in the

---

34. Ibid., Elizabeth Temple to her mother, London, 6 Sept. 1775; ibid., Elizabeth Temple to her mother, New York, 30 May 1787.

35. Ibid., Letter Book, 59, Bowdoin to Scott, 3 Dec. 1763.

36. Ibid., Bowdoin to Elizabeth Temple, 15 Nov. 1774.

37. Bowdoin was elected president in 1784; see N.S.B. Gras, *The Massachusetts First National Bank of Boston 1784–1934* (Cambridge, Mass.: Harvard University Press, 1937), 26.

development of lands owned by the Plymouth Company and the Kennebeck Purchase Company, which had substantial holdings along the Kennebec River; and he owned vast properties on the Elizabeth Islands off the shore of southern Massachusetts that he rented out to tenant-farmers, providing meat and grain for his own table. The lots along the Kennebec were occupied by settlers who had been there for decades, and Bowdoin pressed the legality of his claims, driving out squatters and preventing trespassers from logging. For years the Kennebeck Company was in litigation with the Crown over its claims —John Adams was Bowdoin's lawyer.

Bowdoin was a punctilious, not always generous, businessman. The monies he loaned on interest had to be repaid on time or the collateral was forfeited. And when he was on the point of seizing a mortgaged house, he instructed his agent to observe elaborate and ceremonial procedures: "Roundy, who lives upon the premises, must with his family go out of the house and shut the door, then delivering you the key you are to enter and take possession in my name. When that is done you'll be pleased to allow Mr. Roundy & family to become tenants."[38] In a letter-book Bowdoin kept copies of his correspondence with reasonable regularity from 1759 until his death, except for a hiatus during the revolutionary period 1776–81, when his clandestine activities had to be surrounded with precautions. The normal record deals principally with business transactions, intricate legal matters connected with family bequests, and orders for his London agents. But the book is only a dim reflection of his extensive investments in shipping and of the intricacies of trade during the pre-revolutionary period.

Bowdoin's orderly and methodical business practices carried over into other aspects of his daily life. When he contemplated the remodeling of his house, his first move appears to have been the purchase of works on architecture from a Boston bookseller.[39] And he involved himself in the details of designing and carrying out the renovation, ordering the materials and supervising their use. This same application to the task at hand was displayed when he chaired a committee to rebuild the Brattle Street Church, and not only kept himself informed about the projected expenditures but discoursed knowingly with the architect about such matters as entablatures, pilasters, and the number, dimensions, and placement of pews. And he asked his brother-in-law George Erving, who was in London, to make inquiries about a warming machine sold by "Buraglo, or some such name," for installation in the new meetinghouse.[40]

38. MHS, Bowdoin and Temple Papers, Letter Book, 14, Bowdoin to Simon Orne in Marblehead, 13 Dec. 1760.

39. Gordon E. Kershaw, *James Bowdoin II, Patriot and Man of the Enlightenment* (Lonham, Md.: University Press of America, 1991), 123, 142 n. 65. (A briefer version was published by the Bowdoin College Museum of Art in 1976.)

40. See MHS, *Collections* 71 (Letters and Papers of John Singleton Copley and Henry Pelham, 1914), 185–86; MHS, Bowdoin and Temple Papers, Bowdoin to George Erving, 22 Apr. 1772.

Unlike John Hancock, who left his affairs to agents, in war and peace Bowdoin supervised his own business and trained his son to assist and ultimately succeed him by sending him on missions. At the height of the Revolution, James III was in Virginia exchanging paper currency of dubious value for as much tobacco as he could obtain, to be shipped to France in boats that had to run the blockade. In Bowdoin's letter-book there is a dispatch from Middleborough, 25 May 1776, to his London agents Lane, Son, & Fraser complaining of his protracted illness and expressing dismay that the war made it impossible to send them remittances; instead he urged them to collect from his brother-in-law's brother and executor the bond and interest owed him, which should leave them a "surplusage."[41] A second letter nearly five years afterward, on 6 January 1781, acknowledged a notification from the agents that the payment had been made, leaving Bowdoin a credit of £997.6 sterling.[42] Despite the war, Bowdoin was exact in discharging his financial obligations and in demanding what was his due, no more and no less. Business dealings dependent on trust were absolutes that had to be honored despite political vicissitudes.

Even a New Englander's distaste for southern living was suppressed in the interests of making money. Though Bowdoin's uncle and an aunt had settled in Virginia, the family's wealth was concentrated in New England, and the Bowdoins had become generally identified with Puritan control and reserve of manner. Like John Adams, Bowdoin tended to disapprove of southerners, an attitude echoed by his son James when he was obliged to spend some time among Virginia gentlemen in 1778. In January he wrote his father from Alexandria, requesting his recipe for a special water against "the itch," not further defined, which was so widespread that it was perilous to shake hands with anybody in the area. And on 26 February, anxious because he had received no replies to previous letters and no instructions as to how to proceed with his business transactions, he confessed, "You may believe me Sir when I tell you that I wd. not live in Virginia for its yearly produce of Tobacco. Inhabitants, Manners, Customs, Climate &c.ᵃ &c.ᵃ &c.ᵃ all conspire to make me abhorr it. although I am continually obliged to disguise my sentiments upon this head, being every day ask'd if I did not think Virginia the finest country in ye world, or that I had ever seen. being willing to have an easy passport thro' this country, & looking upon it but a small sacrifice to honesty, have always declared it what the Virginians think it."[43] Undaunted by the rigors of a Boston winter and his own weak constitution, James was eager to expedite his business

41. Ibid., Letter Book, 230, Bowdoin to Lane, Son, and Fraser, 25 May 1776.

42. Ibid., Letter Book, 230, Bowdoin to Lane, Son, and Fraser, 6 Jan. 1781.

43. Ibid., James Bowdoin III to his father, Alexandria, 27 Jan. 1778; ibid., James Bowdoin III to his father, Alexandria, 26 Feb. 1778.

and return to his native place—the only hope that bolstered his flagging spirits. His candid letter, written at a period when the inviolability of the mails could not be assumed, brought a recommendation from his father that he observe greater caution. From his retreat in Middleborough, on 14 July 1778, James Bowdoin issued a mild admonition that in letters to other persons (at least) his son let nothing indelicate escape him, "lest it should occasion a reflection on your character as a Gent^n, and in other respects operate to y^r disadvantage."[44] Back in Boston later in the year and hearing that his father was suffering a recurrence of his illness while at Middleborough, James tried to allay his apprehensions by observing that the intemperate heat had bred fevers and fluxes throughout the whole country—the role of the comforting parent was now assumed by the son—and anticipated the pleasure of embracing him the "first moment I am released from Business."[45] The senior Bowdoin would not have been displeased by the order of priority.

While John Adams, with the acquiescence of Abigail, subordinated the needs of his family to the cause, and prodigal John Hancock, once he was caught up in the revolutionary whirlwind, let the House of Hancock suffer great financial losses from neglect, the existence of James Bowdoin II was carefully organized around the interests of his family. Though his sympathies and his fortune were committed to the Revolution and he was prepared to make sacrifices, preserving the legacy of the Bowdoins was an abiding concern. Throughout the war, even at critical junctures, he continued to occupy himself with his own business affairs and those of his in-laws, including George Erving, the somewhat reluctant Tory who emigrated to England.[46] At a time when the French were deciding whether to raise the siege of Newport, Bowdoin, convalescing at his Middleborough refuge, was writing his son somewhat testily about the rising price of tobacco and intimating that he showed a lack of business acumen when he failed to invest in it at the low rate and sell it at a profit.[47] James Bowdoin lent money on interest, numbering among his debtors Thomas Jefferson (who eleven years later hesitated to pay the note given for a debt of his brother's).[48] Nor did Bowdoin refrain from requesting, on 28 August 1779, an abatement of at least five-sixths of his tax bill of £942, on grounds that his properties were in disrepair, his money tied up in loans, his Elizabeth Island holdings ravaged by the enemy,

44. Ibid., Bowdoin to James III, Middleborough, 14 July 1778.

45. Ibid., James Bowdoin III to his father, Boston, 6 Aug. 1778.

46. See, for example, ibid., Letter Book, 234, Bowdoin to John Hodshon, 30 Apr., 3 May 1782; MHS, *Collections*, ser. 6.9 (Bowdoin and Temple Papers, 1), 472–75, Bowdoin to George Erving, 4 May 1782.

47. MHS, Bowdoin and Temple Papers, Bowdoin to James III, Middleborough, 22 Aug. 1778.

48. Thomas Jefferson, *Papers*, ed. Julian P. Boyd, 16 (Princeton: Princeton University Press, 1961), 307, Jefferson to Philip Mazzei, New York, 5 Apr. 1790; 17 (1965), 422, Jefferson to William Short, New York, 25 Aug. 1790.

and his son's investments in a trading company, which Bowdoin Sr. had financially assisted, entirely lost, "every vessel having been taken or cast away."[49]

Not a great theoretician, James Bowdoin II early in his life had formulated simple economic principles that embodied what has since become known as the Protestant ethic. Had Max Weber been aware of his existence, he might have found in him an even more convincing archetypal figure for his thesis than Benjamin Franklin. For half a century Bowdoin glorified the trinity of honesty, industry, and frugality, while he denounced as the parents of poverty and ruin the luxurious tastes that were nourished by paper money, the demon he sought to banish from the world. The servant was worthy of his hire, but only the easy availability of cheap labor would allow for economic expansion in the colonies, and he composed a lengthy memorandum on the advisability of encouraging the immigration of foreign workers. "Let [us] but introduce industrious People among us," the young Harvard graduate had written sententiously in 1748, "& we shall find our Riches increase in proportion to their numbers. The Price of Labour, on which every Improvement must depend, will then be reduced, & the Reduction of it, an Encouragement to our Improvements."[50] Thirty years later Bowdoin equated a depreciated currency with the forces of Satan and elevated hard currency to the highest moral principle, but he was in a dark mood about its prospect. "It is in vain to expect ye revival of the moral principle in any tolerable degree of vigour, while the great corrupter of it, ye more than Daemon, a depreciating medium, exists. Before this can take place, nature must change, and effects cease to flow from their proper necessary causes."[51] He translated the forces of evil, no longer embodied in devils, into satanic economic principles. His friend Samuel Dexter, who served with him on the revolutionary Council, was in full accord; he denounced paper money as the "wampum of the savages" and "vile trash."[52]

James Bowdoin was no ordinary businessman. In his own eyes he was a Christian gentleman and a man of reason, a civilized and educated Bostonian. While science was his principal avocation, there was also a hidden poet in his soul. Bowdoin chose to render into verse part of a didactic prose work, *The Oeconomy of Human Life*, supposedly written by Robert Dodsley but now assigned to the Earl of Chesterfield and John Hill. This collection of worn-out dicta, exotically disguised as the

49. MHS, Bowdoin and Temple Papers, James Bowdoin, Request for tax abatement, 28 Aug. 1779 (an addendum to his memorandum on his rateable estate, Feb. 1779).

50. Ibid., James Bowdoin, "Some Thoughts on the Importation of foreigners: to encourage it" (ca. 1748, on the back of a letter from Josiah Quincy). Kershaw, *Bowdoin, Patriot and Man of the Enlightenment*, 39, notes that for his master's degree in 1748 Bowdoin defended the proposition that commutative justice required equality of work and wages.

51. MHS, Miscellaneous bound papers, Bowdoin to Governor Trumbull of Connecticut, 25 Mar. 1780.

52. MHS, *Proceedings* 6 (1862, 1863), 359–60, Samuel Dexter to Bowdoin, Woodstock, 26 Jan. 1779.

translation of an Indian manuscript transmitted from Peking to an unidentified earl, evidently impressed Bowdoin with its precepts on how to lead a good life and the eulogy of science as a gloria to God and a benefaction to mankind.[53]

The topics Bowdoin selected to versify—his doggerel appeared anonymously in Boston in 1759—covered a variety of human emotions and relationships: anger, desire and love, woman, husband, father, son, brothers, wise and ignorant, magistrates and subjects, and religion. Often Bowdoin's paraphrase had only a tenuous connection to the prose original. Though much of the *Oeconomy* dealt with the duties and obligations attaching to one's ordained social role and had a moralizing tone, some of Bowdoin's poetry struck an alien note. The lines describing the virtuous maiden, which may well have been inspired by the charms of Elizabeth Bowdoin, are startlingly erotic:

> See down her neck the charming locks descend;
> And, black as jet, in waving ringlets end:
> The jetty locks, as down her neck they flow,
> The lovely white to great advantage show:
>
> . . . .
>
> Her tempting breasts in whiteness far outgo
> The op'ning lilly, and the new faln snow:
> Her tempting breasts the eyes of all command,
> And gently rising court the am'rous hand.[54]

The saccharine verses instructing SON were essentially a commandment to honor and love his parents, so that he would prove a model for his own progeny, who in turn would bestow affection upon him. The brief notice of FATHER in the pseudo-Dodsley ballooned in Bowdoin's version into a dithyramb on the glories of a scientific career, a destiny he was denied:

> Observe the bent and genius of his mind;
> To what it's equal, and to what inclin'd:
> To arts and science if his genius bend,
> And all their depths attempt to comprehend:
> Betimes implant the scientific seed;
> And, what you plant, with streams refreshing feed:
> If shoot th' implanted seed, manure the soil;
> And on the tender shoot vouchsafe a smile:

53. Philip Dormer Stanhope, Fourth Earl of Chesterfield, and John Hill, *The oeconomy of human life; tr. from an Indian manuscript . . . ; prefixed, an account of the manner in which the said ms. was discovered, in a letter from an English gentleman now residing in China to the Earl of E.* (London, 1750).

54. Bowdoin, *A Paraphrase on part of the Oeconomy of Human Life. Inscribed to his Excellency Thomas Pownall, Esq; Governor of the Province of the Massachusetts Bay* (Boston, 1759), 17.

> A smile from thee will emulation fire;
> And in his breast an ardent love inspire —
> A love of science, — which can joys dispense,
> Superior far to those perceiv'd by sense;
> A love of science, — which improves the mind,
> And elevates the heart with truths refin'd:
> A love of science, and each sister art —
> Which growing pleasures to the mind impart:
> A love of thee — whose smiles inspir'd his breast,
> And set on work th'ambition there impress'd.[55]

Perhaps the poem reflects Bowdoin's cares and hopes for his own son, then a little boy of seven. Or he may have been musing about his father, the first James Bowdoin, sketching a portrait of what he was, or the ideal he failed to realize. In that event, it would be the only personal reference to him in Bowdoin's extant papers, published or manuscript.

Though his critical opinions of their work were occasionally sought by lady poets,[56] Bowdoin's talents as a versifier were not widely appreciated. He commanded far greater attention in the realm of political and scientific discourse.

The moral core of the man is perhaps best revealed in attitudes he expressed during the Revolution. Letters he wrote in the midst of the war bear witness that he abided by an old-fashioned military code — he was a merchant with an aristocratic concept of honor — and that he subscribed to a rule of conduct toward civilians that made no exception, even for dire military necessity. An imprisoned British lieutenant-colonel, Sir Archibald Campbell, petitioned the Massachusetts Council's Board of War that while waiting to be exchanged he be allowed to return from Concord jail to his rented house at Reading, where he would be attended by a complement of servants — his clerk, his cook (with wife and children), his groom, and two body servants. Though the letter was rather pompous, even exigent, Bowdoin, presiding member of the Board of War, treated him with elaborate courtesy, presenting his request to the Council through another member (because of his own illness) and regretting their inability to comply with it: "It would have given me great pleasure, if they had seen the way clear to have gratified you."[57] Noblesse

55. Ibid., 42–43.

56. See, for example, a letter from Mercy Warren to James Bowdoin seeking his opinion about the proposed publication of her poems, in MHS, *Collections*, ser. 7.6 (Bowdoin and Temple Papers, 2), 197–98, Mercy Warren to Bowdoin, 28 June 1790.

57. MHS, Bowdoin and Temple Papers, Bowdoin to Lt. Col. Sir Archibald Campbell, 14 Apr. 1777. See also Washington, *Writings* 7 (1932), 207–09, Washington to Massachusetts Council, Morristown, 28 Feb. 1777, and 214, to Lt. Col. Archibald Campbell, Morristown, 1 Mar. 1777.

oblige. And he was plainly bewildered when General Gage broke the word he had given Bowdoin during the occupation of Boston that citizens would be permitted to leave town with their goods if they turned in their arms; gentlemen kept their promises. Nor could he support Lafayette's proposal that if the troops were in need of provisions they be requisitioned from the countryside. Such acts might be perpetrated by pagan conquerors, not by Christians fighting according to the rules. The towns could adopt measures encouraging re-enlistment, but American soldiers should not be retained without their consent. On 10 July 1780, in a letter to Lafayette, Bowdoin spelled out his convictions with respect to the laws of war and the immutable principles of private property:

> I wish my dear Marquis we were intitled to the Compliment, which your goodness and politeness have bestowed upon us; and that we could emulate the military character, (the worthy part of it I mean) of Caesar & Alexander. Perhaps we might have made some approaches towards it in the instance alluded to, if like opportunities of obtaining money, the main sinew of war, had offered, and we had not been under ye restraint of moral principles. But "heroism, patriotic spirit and public virtue," though they may effect great things at home, or within ye verge of personal influence, yet at a distance where that influence does not extend, and nothing can be had without money, they must be in a great measure inoperative, unless they should inspire their possessors, in the true Caesarian and Alexandrian stile, to take what they wanted without the consent of ye owner, which you know does not comport with American ideas of liberty nor with the modern ones of civilization. . . .[58]

The merchant of Boston could teach the British and French officers a thing or two about civility.

Huguenot Memories

Among the books collected by James Bowdoin there remain numerous fine editions of the Old and the New Testaments; but what distinguished his library from that of other patriot philosophers was the inclusion of a French Bible, with elaborate commentaries, in David Martin's grand Amsterdam 1707 edition. Bowdoin's culture was English, but he was never completely cut off from his Huguenot roots; for all the English stamp on his breeding, there was an alien element in him. He read French, and while there are no direct references to his ancestry in the family correspondence, he advised his beloved son, James, to learn the language well. From the time he was a child of seven, his father ordered French textbooks for him, and when he was older and away from home encouraged him to write letters in both French and English. The ostensible reason for this insistence was that

58. MHS, *Proceedings*, 5:352, Bowdoin to Lafayette, 10 July 1780.

French would be useful in commerce, but it was a matter not likely to have concerned a Boston colonial of English descent. During the Revolution there was not much talk of James Bowdoin II's French origins, but French diplomats often reverted to earlier spellings of the name, such as "Baudouin," and when d'Estaing's fleet landed in Boston the officers gravitated to Bowdoin for direction; he could understand their conversation. Though he did not provide the lavish entertainments that his rival Hancock put on, they paid closer attention to his information and advice. Claude Blanchard, quartermaster under Rochambeau, commented in his journal on Bowdoin's "noble demeanor," and was flattered when his host remarked upon his resemblance to Franklin as a young man.[59] Like his Anglo-Saxon counterparts, Bowdoin illuminated his mansion when the dauphin was born in June of 1782. Despite this wartime friendship, however, when hostilities ceased Bowdoin had to face recurrent charges that his sympathies were pro-British. An informant wrote Vergennes in 1786 that Bowdoin's implacable hatred of France had its source in the revocation of the Edict of Nantes, which had compelled his Huguenot forebears to flee their native land.[60]

After the Huguenots intermarried with the English colonists, allegiance to Massachusetts, a new kind of loyalty, solved or masked the problem of their identity. Yet the intensity of some of their reactions to the behavior of King George III stems from the collective memory of Huguenot persecution as well as from their consciousness of the rights of Englishmen. Three historical events were branded into Bowdoin's Huguenot soul: the Saint Bartholomew Massacre, Louis XIV's tyrannical revocation of the Edict of Nantes, and the quartering of royal troops on French Protestant communities in order to force them, through calculated molestation, to abjure their religion. The translation of these experiences of his ancestors into American terms created a Boston patriot who resembled his English colonial friends and relatives in the harboring of grievances against the Crown, while his style preserved distinct French Huguenot overtones. The Boston Massacre was conflated with the Saint Bartholomew Massacre, George III with Louis XIV, British troops quartered in Boston with the French troops in La Rochelle. In a letter written to his son-in-law John Temple on 10 September 1774, Bowdoin alluded with bitter sarcasm to the presence of the troops, including Canadians and Irishmen, who had been foisted upon the town "for ye purpose of enlightning our intellects, and convincing us that our lives, liberty, & property are safer in ye hands of foreigners than our own."[61]

59. Claude Blanchard, *Guerre d'Amérique 1780–1783, Journal de Campagne* (Paris, 1881), 42.

60. Jefferson, *Papers* 14 (1958), 78, editorial note summarizing a dispatch from Otto, chargé d'affaires, to Vergennes, 1 Aug. 1786.

61. MHS, *Collections*, ser. 6.9 (Bowdoin and Temple Papers, 1), 374.

When the French-speaking General Burgoyne took over Bowdoin's elegant mansion on King Street in May of 1775, remaining until the general evacuation of troops in March of the following year, deep-rooted animosities came to the surface in this third-generation Huguenot. In the place of Louis XIV's dragoons, who had been imposed on his ancestors in La Rochelle—that, at least, was the family legend—a new tyrant, George III, had sent a general to evict Bowdoin from his house. It did not help that Burgoyne was a dandified intellectual and a playwright (the Marquis of Buckingham later alluded to him as "that scribbling general")[62] and that George Erving, Bowdoin's brother-in-law and a Tory who later emigrated, was allowed to draw up a thorough inventory of the books Bowdoin left behind. Burgoyne's installation was quartering, a violation of the rights of an Englishman, and the Bowdoins were now Englishmen. The Huguenot memories evoked by this act were not spelled out in words, but the emotional associations were powerful. It was no solace that another brother-in-law, William Erving, a fellow-officer of Burgoyne's, had recommended him in a letter and expressed the confident hope that Bowdoin's conversation would give proof of the civilized and cultivated men to be found among the colonials.[63]

That the story of their Huguenot past remained with the Bowdoins is attested by references to Louis XIV in James II's poetry and by documents among the family papers. In their files there is a carefully penned copy of the Royal Proclamation of 18 July 1790, following verbatim the decree of the French National Assembly, that provided for the restoration of Huguenot properties seized in the seventeenth century.[64] James Bowdoin III apparently made an effort to recover what was his due. Unfortunately, he could offer only family recollections as evidence, since, he said, the requisite papers had been lost when General Burgoyne occupied his father's house during the billeting of British troops in Boston.

62. MHS, *Proceedings* 9 (1866–67), 79, Marquis of Buckingham to Sir John Temple, London, 4 Oct. 1787.

63. Ibid., 14:232, William Erving to Bowdoin, 4 Feb. 1775.

64. MHS, Bowdoin and Temple Papers, "Proclamation du Roi Concernant les biens des Religionnaires fugitifs. . . ." The files contain as well the National Assembly decree and rules related to its execution.

4

THE HONOUR OF THE
AMERICAN PHILOSOPHY

ᑐᑕ

INQUIRERS into the origins of the Royal Society of London have discovered an "invisible college" of virtuosi with roots in the civil war period as one of the many antecedents of the formal establishment of the institution under the Restoration. Similarly, a primordium of the American Academy can be found in correspondence between Benjamin Franklin and James Bowdoin beginning as far back as the 1750s, an exchange of letters that often involved other American men of science. Franklin and Bowdoin were brought together by a common commitment to advance what they called "the American philosophy." Long before an institution dedicated to that purpose was incorporated by the state of Massachusetts, they sought to achieve its ends by conducting experiments, making practical inventions, and communicating their results and hypotheses to each other and to like-minded friends of science.

Education of a Philosopher, Class of 1745

Nothing has survived to afford an insight into the relationship between the masterful James Bowdoin I and his cultivated son. Nor are there any facts or tales about the boyhood of James Bowdoin II, apart from a few vital statistics. He appears to have emerged full-grown from the loins of a formidable father. There is not even an inkling of what his mother was like, and both parents had died by the time their son married—his mother, when he was a child of eight. His maternal grandmother, Elizabeth Pordage, included him in a deed of gift to her grandchildren dated 1 June 1742, in gratitude for their dutiful affection; no other papers remain that might have bearing on her position in the family. A stepmother, who joined the household when young James was nine or ten, lived until 1748, but remains without voice. The seeker after psychological understanding of the formative years of James Bowdoin II comes away almost empty-handed, except for a few conjectures and anecdotes about his college career.

Like his counterparts the sons of well-to-do British colonial families, James Bowdoin went to Harvard, where his experience and education followed the usual course, as did those of others who later became founders of the Academy. As a freshman he lived at the home of the theology professor Dr. Edward Wigglesworth; thereafter, he shared quarters in Massachusetts Hall with fellow students. In June of 1742 he was ranked second among his two dozen classmates, but the order was determined by social status and had nothing to do with scholastic achievement. He was not caught playing cards, stealing, or behaving contumaciously to ministers of the gospel (as was the miscreant charged with calling a preacher a "dumb dog"). But Bowdoin stopped short of saintly perfection: he was fined ten shillings for absence after vacation was over, and was punished along with other senior sophisters for making indecent noises and consuming an excessive quantity of strong drink on the night they met to choose their officers. The class of '45 was no exception to the rambunctiousness of Harvard students at this period, and reports of their disorderly conduct, intoxication, and insolence relieve the pomposity of Corporation and faculty records.

High jinks apart, Bowdoin was educated according to the set curriculum of his day. For purposes of recitation it stressed Horace, Cicero, Caesar's *Commentaries*, Homer, Xenophon's *Cyropaedia*, Demosthenes' select orations, and the New Testament in Greek. In September of 1743 the college made an effort to enforce its rules with respect to Hebrew after the instructor, a converted Jew named Judah Monis, complained that class-cutting and insubordination were rife; but there is little evidence that the admonitions of the college were heeded, and the unruly students, if they showed up at all, continued to disrupt classroom procedures with their pranks. Small wonder that Bowdoin does not appear to have acquired even a nodding acquaintance with Hebrew. Nor is there any sign of his having retained much from his Greek studies. When as a mature man he began to collect a library, he bought translations of the classics, more Latin authors than Greek.

In one area, the bailiwick of John Winthrop, the mathematics professor, Bowdoin had thorough schooling: the elements of the physical sciences, logic, and John Locke's philosophy. On 2 March 1742/3, the president and tutors, in one of their intermittent reforms of the Harvard curriculum, decreed that, in addition to the classics and the Greek Testament, books to be recited should include a "Compendium Logica extracted from Le Grand, Lock—of Humane Understanding, Gordons Geographical Grammar, Euclides Elements, Gravesande's Natural Philosophy & Dr. Watt's Astronomy."[1] In eighteenth-century Massachusetts the sciences were sapping interest in Hebrew studies and in the classics. The number of amateur scientists who came out of Harvard in Bowdoin's generation and in the decades that followed is impressive. Massachusetts lawyers, pastors, businessmen, and independent gentlemen — not least among them James Bowdoin II — dabbled in science and, after the American Academy was established, filled the pages of its memoirs with their researches and their sometimes extravagant theories.

1. Harvard University Archives: Faculty Records (MS), 1:219–21; A Book for Recording the Acts & Agreements of the President and Tutors in Harvard College, 1725–1752 (MS), 178, 188, 222.

The intellectual horizons of James Bowdoin broadened after his graduation. An extant catalogue of his library dated 1775 shows a substantial and diversified collection, which continued to expand despite the impediments of war and serious illness. Bowdoin bequeathed more than 1,200 books to the American Academy of Arts and Sciences (which after World War II deposited on long-term loan those still in its possession in Bowdoin College, Brunswick, Maine).[2] In the sixties, when he began to acquire books in earnest, he sent orders in hasty succession to his London agent George Keith for the works of the pansophist Gabriel Plattes, Adam Ferguson, Richard Price, David Hume; for Rousseau's "Principles of Politic Law" [sic] at a time when he was not widely read in the colonies;[3] for Latin classics, often in translation, as well as translations of Anacreon, Bion, Moschus, and Musaeus; for D'Arnay's *Private Life of the Romans*. Earlier he had imposed on his brother-in-law James Erving, asking for Justinian's *Institutes* in the George Harris translation for himself, and for a number of French and Latin textbooks for his "little boy." He also purchased books locally, from Boston booksellers or at auction. He owned Newton's *Principia* and Whiston's *New Theory of the Earth*, as well as many works on mathematics, astronomy, and the practical applications of science. As a devout Newtonian, he collected his master's theological and chronological works, which he read with the same meticulous care that he devoted to the *Principia*. The histories in Bowdoin's library included Herodotus, Polybius, and Cotton Mather's *Magnalia*. On the lighter side were travel literature, the *Satyricon* of Petronius with lascivious illustrations, More's *Utopia* and Fénelon's *Télémaque*, and the novels of Henry Fielding and Laurence Sterne. From a numbered catalogue he selected theological disquisitions, including Michaelis's introductory lectures on the New Testament, legal treatises by Grotius and Pufendorf, medical books, and, inexplicably, such esoterica as legal casebooks on impotency, polygamy, concubinage, adultery, and divorce, which may have answered to occasional fleshly needs. Bowdoin was not an undiscriminating or naive purchaser. On 18 August 1763, he wrote to Keith complaining that the plates of a treatise on anatomy adapted to the art of designing that had been shipped to him lacked relevant texts: "The persons you have the books of, seem inclined to dispose

2. MHS, Bowdoin and Temple Papers, "Catalogue of Books left in the Library of James Bowdoin Esqr—in the possession of Major Genl. Burgoyne Boston Sept. 9th. 1775" (signed George Erving). Some 565 volumes (357 titles) still in the possession of the Academy at the end of World War II were identified at the time of the long-term loan to Bowdoin College as having belonged to Bowdoin (Kershaw, *Bowdoin, Patriot and Man of the Enlightenment*, 124); for a detailed account of his library, see Kershaw, 121–33, and MHS, *Proceedings* 51 (1917–18), 362–68, where Erving's catalogue is published, with Bowdoin's endorsement that it represented "Part of my Books."

3. James Truslow Adams, *Revolutionary New England 1691–1776* (Boston: Atlantic Monthly Press, 1923), 288 n. 3: "Rousseau's *Treatise on the Social Compact or the Principles of political Law* made its first appearance, so far as I have found, in *Boston Gazette*, Dec. 17, 1764."

of the defective ones first. I should be glad to have no more of them."[4] No one could cheat James Bowdoin with impunity in a business transaction.

There are hardly any manuscript marginalia in the books preserved from the original library, though occasional underlinings in the writings of philosophers like Montesquieu indicate Bowdoin's political predilections. Passages in a 1759 translation of Montesquieu's work on Roman decadence, *Reflexions on the Causes of the Rise and Fall of the Roman Empire*, are marked up to reveal Bowdoin's belief in the importance of a strong bond of social union buttressed by strict observance of the laws: "Nothing is so powerful as a commonwealth, in which the laws are exactly observed; and this is not from fear nor from reason, but from a passionate impulse, as in Rome and Lacedaemon; for then the wisdom of a good legislature is united to all the strength a faction could possibly possess" (p. 30). The sentiments expressed in this book accorded with Bowdoin's political orientation: faith in cohesiveness, accompanied by the pessimistic view that all societies contained within them the elements of their own corruption.

The Religion of James Bowdoin II

By the time Pierre's grandson James Bowdoin II matriculated at Harvard in 1741, new currents of thought had penetrated Puritan Boston. It was no longer a Theopolis, a theocratic city set upon a hill, a New Jerusalem, but a flourishing seaport town engaged in accumulating wealth. Official historiography has it that the Bible Commonwealth simply vanished after the Charter of 1691 formally separated religion and politics. The franchise was made dependent upon a relatively loose property qualification, not a confirmed religious conversion, and the necessary forty pounds were easy to come by in a land where labor was scarce. As the hegemony of the minister gave way to the rule of the merchant, or perhaps the merchant and the lawyer in tandem, public attention was diverted from rival pastors and their theological disputations over infant baptism to the activities of men of business vying for the conspicuous adornments of wealth and political office.

For a time some of the intellectual novelties that accompanied riches were accepted and coexisted with the old ways as if nothing fundamental had changed. New and old ideas occupied different compartments of the mind, and men could be unaware that flagrantly contradictory beliefs and feelings resided within them, that they were no longer integrated wholes. The original Puritan spirit of a century before had dissipated, but not without leaving stubborn residues. The officers of Harvard College remained Calvinists, while they admitted to the library works of outrageous Arians

---

4. MHS, Bowdoin and Temple Papers, Letter Book, 5, Bowdoin to James Erving, 25 Dec. 1759; 12, Bowdoin to George Keith, 2 Oct. 1760; 16: 6 Apr. 1761; 17: 18 Aug. 1761; 26: 3 Mar. 1762; 34: 9 Oct. 1762; 38: 28 Oct. 1762; 55: 18 Aug. 1763.

whose doctrines were anathema to earnest Protestants. There was little room for Jesus Christ in that world, though He regularly reappeared at the annual Dudleian Lecture at Harvard. The astronomy course Bowdoin took with John Winthrop used a text by a heterogeneous group of scientists, all of them heretical in the eyes of an orthodox Calvinist: the Flamsteed Tables were composed by an Anglican, the notes by the reputed atheist Edmond Halley and the Arian William Whiston, a scandalous figure in English religious life.[5] As a student of the classics, Bowdoin read and underlined Cicero's *De Natura Deorum*, whose spirit, though hardly subversive, did not harmonize too closely with an orthodox belief in predestination. On a deep layer of James Bowdoin II's consciousness there dwelt a strict Calvinism, but his college education had opened the floodgates to heterodox thought.

At Harvard in his late teens Bowdoin was unmoved by the Great Awakening, resisting the threat of contagion from a converted roommate, Joshua Prentiss.[6] Bowdoin was one of the "old lights," without the taint of religious ecstasy in his sober, rationalist Calvinism. There is no record that he (or his father or son) ever underwent a proper conversion as Cotton Mather or Jonathan Edwards would have understood it. No enthusiasm, no millenarian expectations came from his lips. The new handmaiden of religion was science; the Newtonian system, not the believer's sudden awakening to Christ in an emotional conversion, was the bulwark of religion. The Reverend Charles Chauncy was the spokesman of Boston enlightenment, and Bowdoin could not have missed his work published in 1743: *The Late Religious Commotions in New England Considered: An Answer to the Reverend Mr. Jonathan Edwards's Sermon, Entitled, The Distinguishing Mark of a Work of the Spirit of God; and Seasonable Thoughts on the State of Religion in New England.*

Bowdoin, his last pastor testified, had matured to religious conviction through inquiry and reading — on his deathbed he recalled the crucial significance of his perusal of the Anglican Bishop Butler's *Analogy of Religion Natural and Revealed, to the Constitution and Course of Nature, to which are added two brief dissertations: I. Of Personal Identity, II. Of the Nature of Virtue* (1736), one of the most widely read works of religious apology in the English-speaking world of the eighteenth century.[7] Bowdoin owned a copy of Calvin's *Institutes* and he collected scores of religious polemics and

---

5. In the opening sentence of his manuscript "The return of the comet of 1532 and 1661 in the year 1789," now in the Harvard University Archives, the Reverend Samuel Williams could ignore Halley's reputation and refer to the "singular sagacity and penetration of that great man"; Bowdoin owned Whiston's *Astronomical Lectures* while he was a college student (Volz, *Bowdoin & His Family*, 56).

6. On Prentiss see Kershaw, *Bowdoin, Patriot and Man of the Enlightenment*, 38, 39, and Clifford K. Shipton, *Sibley's Harvard Graduates* 10 (Boston, 1958), 312–14.

7. By 1776 there were seven editions. Joseph Butler (1692–1752), after a Presbyterian upbringing, had conformed and joined the Anglican Church. He was successively bishop of Bristol and bishop of Durham.

justifications of faith, mostly Anglican, but he himself never exercised his dialectical skills on the niceties of theology. Metaphysics was for him a term with the same pejorative connotations it had for most enlightened gentlemen. He relied on methodical demonstrations of the existence of a God whose infinite wisdom had arranged a perfect physical order and who, through Christian teachings in the Gospel, had set forth the guiding principles of moral conduct. The evidence for Christ provided by men, women, and children in seizures and fits was unworthy of a rational creature made in God's image. Those who spoke with tongues might imagine that they were divinely inspired, but there was no cause to believe them.

Though later in life Bowdoin was able to avert his eyes from the deism of his English friend Dr. Joseph Priestley, he could never tolerate the emotionalism of an Edwards and his pietist evangelicals. A new Huguenot rationalism could even expose itself to the spirit of Pierre Bayle, while turning away with distaste from the prophetic vapors of Pierre Jurieu, the pastor who had once ruled the Huguenot émigrés in Holland with an iron hand. In a manner wholly consonant with Newton's explicit purpose in the General Scholium of the *Principia* — and the thousands of manuscript folios on theology that Bowdoin never saw — Bowdoin exalted the study of natural and experimental science as a gloria to God. He might adopt the precepts of Lockian psychology and political theory, but he would not use them in the manner of Jonathan Edwards as an underpinning for a religion of feeling. Religion was a matter of rationalist conviction sustained by proofs such as those formulated by Bishop Butler.

The marvels of the lawful universe being revealed by science sustained Bowdoin's faith in the beneficence and omniscience of God. Calvin and his early followers like Lambert Daneau had sanctioned research into the movements of the heavens as knowledge leading to the glorification of God. Adoration of the Creator through the study of nature had never been forbidden (Servetus was burned for theological, not scientific, heresy). In his religion Bowdoin harked back to the world of Woodward, Burnet, Whiston, and Newton himself. They had demonstrated through convoluted arguments that there was a sacred physics hidden in the Bible, that many biblical events considered miracles could be explained scientifically, that the book of nature and the book of Scripture were harmonious with each other. And an eighteenth-century member of a Congregational church who read Anglican apologists could give new relative weights to the two books. Science, the book of nature, was outbalancing the book of Scripture, though the moral truth of a biblical text was in no sense challenged and the reverence accorded it was undiminished.

James Bowdoin's pastors at the Brattle Street Church where he was baptized and married, Samuel Cooper and Peter Thacher, bore witness to his private devotions and regular attendance at public worship. A question remains as to how far he strayed in the direction of fashionable deism. He would never go all the way with Priestley, though he was prepared to entrust the darling of his heart, his young son Jemmy, to the doctor's academy in Warrington, for instruction in accordance with his *Essay on a Course of Liberal Education for Civil and Active Life* (1765).[8] (Unfortunately, Priestley had moved to Leeds and young James passed his sojourns in England and on the Continent in more amusing pursuits.)[9] Bowdoin ordered David Hume's works from his bookseller in England, but it is doubtful that he followed the impious subtleties of *The Natural History of Religion* (he makes no mention of the *Dialogues Concerning Natural Religion*, which had been left in manuscript until after their author's death). Bowdoin's vision is unlikely to have pierced the veil of Hume's Aesopian language in matters of religion. Hume's moral principles, not his religious skepticism, informed Bowdoin's official utterances, and the Humean useful and the pleasant, the pleasing and the instructive, were his commonsense moral criteria.

The last quarter of the eighteenth century has been described as an age of relaxed religious and moral standards in the colonies under the influence of heretical French thinkers. Bowdoin owned Voltaire's *Age of Louis XIV*, his *Letters Concerning the English Nation*, and Montesquieu's *Spirit of the Laws*. At one point in 1776 he praised Paine's *Common Sense*, oblivious of the man's religious views, which approached too near atheism for even Benjamin Franklin to down them.[10] Unexpectedly, the writings of Arminians and Deists such as Bolingbroke and Trenchard filled Bowdoin's library shelves. But in the 1780s an attempt to impugn his Christianity after the publication of his emendation of the *Principia* brought forth as sharp a rejoinder as this gentleman was capable of writing. Bowdoin's friend Robert Treat Paine, a charter member of the Academy and the attorney-general for independent Massachusetts, allowed into his library Voltaire's more skeptical works like the *Philosophical Dictionary*, which Bowdoin avoided, but for the most part their collections duplicated each other. Both were rich in seventeenth-century apologists of rational religion like Hugo Grotius, Newtonian glorifiers of God like John Ray and William Derham, Scottish moralists like Francis Hutcheson (born in Ireland).

More than some of the patriots, James Bowdoin II was a believer in the immortality of the soul in a direct, literal sense. There was a dark side to the man; but even in moments of despair he could evoke the consolations of another world in simple, unequivocal language that can hardly be found in the writings of John Adams, Franklin, or Hancock. Strangely enough, Sam Adams and James Bowdoin, the populist leader and the wealthy merchant, were united in a firm, old-fashioned

---

8. MHS, *Collections*, ser. 6.9 (Bowdoin and Temple Papers, 1), 277, Bowdoin to Benjamin Franklin, 5 Nov. 1771.

9. Franklin, *Papers* 19, ed. W. B. Willcox (1975), 10, Franklin to Bowdoin, London, 13 Jan. 1772.

10. MHS, *Collections* 72 (Warren-Adams Letters, 1 [1917]), 208–09, Bowdoin to Mercy Warren, Middleborough, Feb. 28, 1776.

religious faith, and during Shays' Rebellion their joint condemnation of the sons of Belial who defied the American Mosaic authority had Calvinist overtones that drowned out their social differences.

From time to time in writing to members of his family Bowdoin delivered little sermons on the comforts of religion, as he had to his sister-in-law Abigail Scott when she lost her husband. On 9 May 1772, Bowdoin wrote to his son-in-law John Temple, whose partiality for the American cause had occasioned him political embarrassment, "We have this consolation, that nature, whose operation is not controulable by acts of Parliament, will in time free us from all unreasonable impositions, if Parliament should refuse to do it." He closed with the hope that, if they did not meet again in this world, "in ye next scene, the invisibility of which makes it too little regarded," Temple and his family would be admitted to permanent and uninterrupted joys. Two and a half years later, when the Temples were in trouble once again, Bowdoin praised his daughter for the fortitude with which she bore her misfortunes, and counseled her to place "trust & confidence in the great original Source of happiness. You will then enjoy a tranquillity & contentment to which Tyrant-lordling and the oppressors of mankind are wholly Strangers; and, when the dropt Curtain shall hide from us the present Scene, participate [in] joys ineffable, and be admitted to honours, to which their little souls had not ambition enough to aspire."[11] For Bowdoin this was not merely a manner of speaking.

Contemplating the emotional serenity and intellectual pleasures of the afterlife was a continual solace to Bowdoin. Earthly existence was but a prelude, under the guidance of the Great Preceptor, to that heavenly future he confidently anticipated would be his. In January of 1776, a desperate time for the colonies and for himself personally, when his consumptive illness was seriously exacerbated and he had reason to believe that death was approaching, he wrote in exalted vein to Josiah Quincy about his hopes that the Beneficent Creator, "through the mediation of our blessed Redeemer, will completely beatify the virtuous expectants of his kingdom." In the temporal world, the members of different classes were educated and assigned to different tasks, their performance judged and rewarded by the Almighty. Friendships on earth, which were interrupted by the oppressions of despotism, had an almost sacred quality, for they were a preparation for the eternal friendships to be enjoyed in heaven. Thoughts about the society of kindred spirits that he would savor in a future state and the glories of science that would finally be revealed to him assuaged the bitterness of his Middleborough exile and the physical anguish of tuberculosis.[12]

11. Ibid., ser. 6.9 (Bowdoin and Temple Papers, 1), 293, Bowdoin to Temple, 9 May 1772; MHS, Bowdoin and Temple Papers, Bowdoin to Elizabeth Temple, 15 Nov. 1774.

12. Josiah Quincy, *Memoir of the Life of Josiah Quincy Jun. of Massachusetts* (Boston, 1825), appendix, 484–87, Bowdoin to Josiah Quincy, Middleborough, 29 Jan. 1776.

The possibility of hell does not figure in Bowdoin's conception of his future. The last testaments of four generations of Bowdoins tell of the changing religious convictions in one family, a mirror of the sensibility of members of their station and class. Jesus Christ was slowly disappearing from the final confessions of faith. In 1741 He was still named; in 1790 He was referred to only as the Redeemer; in 1811 He was passed over in silence. Even the formula of belief in immortality was subtly altered. In 1704, Pierre Baudouin (calling himself Peter Boadwin) committed his soul to God and his body to the earth, and hoped to receive full pardon for "all my Sins and Salvation through the alone merrits of Jesus Christ my Redeemer. . . ." James Bowdoin I's will read, "first & principally, I comend my Soul into the hand of Almighty God my Creator in hopes of Eternal Life thro' the Merits and Intercession of Jesus Christ my Redeemer and my Body I Comit to the Dust to be Decently Interred at the Discretion of my Executors in faith of the Resurrection and Re-Union of it with my Soul at the Last Day." In James Bowdoin II's will the traditional hope for the resurrection of the body was omitted. He contented himself with entrusting his soul to his Redeemer, hoping for God's mercy, and enjoining his friends not to wear mourning, an expensive import, when he died, "being desirous from their evil effect upon the community that Mourning Habits should not again come in regard." When his son, James III, died in 1811, he left a plain will covering the distribution of his property without any avowal of his religious faith, though he bequeathed money to the poor of his church and to its minister, as his ancestors had done before him.[13]

Cooper's church, where Bowdoin regularly worshiped, had had an odd history. The stench of burning witches still hung over Salem and Boston when a group of citizens separated themselves from existing Congregational parishes and established a new meetinghouse in 1699. Such biological fission had been common among Boston churches in the seventeenth century and continued well into the nineteenth. The occasion was usually a quarrel over the person of the minister, some refinement of Calvinist theology, church discipline and order of worship, or a combination of the three. The new church on Brattle Street brought a spirit of innovation into the cantankerous ecclesiastical atmosphere of the Boston Puritans when it took the unprecedented step of issuing a *Manifesto*, a flysheet printed in bold type that set forth the reasons for establishing a new body and announced a set of radical precepts by which they would regulate their conduct. They talked of a desire for liberal principles in church governance, and proposed the unheard-of idea of allowing women parishioners to vote in the selection of a minister.

13. For the will of Pierre Baudouin, written 16 June 1704, see Brault, "Pierre Baudouin and the Bowdoin coat of arms," loc. cit., 250; also, MHS, Bowdoin and Temple Papers, Will of James Bowdoin I, 7 Sept. 1747; copies of wills of James Bowdoin II, 23 Mar. 1789, and James Bowdoin III, 4 June 1811.

The first pastor of the Brattle Street Church was Benjamin Coleman, a brilliant young man educated and ordained in England. He was assisted by William Cooper; in 1743, at nineteen and newly graduated from Harvard, Samuel Cooper took over from his father, succeeding to the office of sole pastor in 1747. The church prospered and attracted some of the outstanding merchants of the town, usually men of new money. Among its parishioners was James Bowdoin I, the second-generation Huguenot who had become one of the wealthiest men in the colony and for whom the new church served as a transitional body, furthering his assimilation with the older English families of the original settlement. He still gave donations to the small French Huguenot church on School Street, but he had his son, James Bowdoin II, the future president of the Academy, baptized in the Brattle Street Church in 1726. Another wealthy merchant parishioner was Thomas Hancock, uncle of John, whom he later adopted. In time Cooper's church came to serve as an arena in which Hancock and Bowdoin, perennial rivals in Massachusetts politics, tested their strength.

It has been noted before that Cooper's church and Harvard College were crucial in mobilizing revolutionary sentiment in Massachusetts. Samuel Cooper had been early committed to the Revolution and, along with his older brother, William, who was town clerk of Boston from 1761 until his death in 1809, for thirty years had defended the rights of the colonials, the Americans, the sons of New England, from the intrusions and usurpations of the Excise Bill, the Stamp Act, the Boston Port Bill.[14] Back in 1754, in his pamphlet *The Crisis*, he had denounced British tyranny with a startling rhetoric that would soon become commonplace: "Perhaps it may not be long before we are plunged into the most abject Subjection, and the *unconscious* Mud of Slavery may sleep over us—we will NOW improve the Liberty which GOD and Nature has given us, and our Constitution has not thought proper to restrain."[15] With the hyperbole for which he became famous, Cooper raised the grim image of the Spanish Inquisition probing into every nook and cranny of existence as the ultimate degradation toward which the Excise Laws were inevitably leading: "Besides this destroys the exclusive Right that every Man has to the *innocent Secrets* of his Family. For if an Account of any Part of his innocent Conduct is extorted from him, every other Part may with equal Reason be required, and a *Political Inquisition* severe as that in Catholick Countries may inspect and controul every Step of his private Conduct. And if the Exigencies of the State Increase, and this be the *only* Way of answering them, this State Inquisition may be extended, as much beyond Decency, as it is at present beyond our natural rights."[16]

14. For evidence of Cooper's commitment to the colonial cause, see Frederick Tuckerman, ed., "Letters of Samuel Cooper to Thomas Pownall, 1769–1777," *American Historical Review* 8 (1902, 1903), 301–30.

15. Samuel Cooper, *The Crisis* (n.p., June 1754), 4.

16. Ibid., 5.

When it came to defining the position of the Deity in the conflict, Cooper spoke with the certainty of the anointed. The man who fought the excesses of British power was not only a friend to the best interests of his country, but a "Friend to Mankind, a Friend to the Universal Chorus of Rational Beings. . . . And he shall hereafter BE CALLED THE FRIEND OF GOD."[17] A dozen years later, Cooper published in London another pamphlet entitled *The Crisis*, whose prose was even more frenetic. Unless the Stamp Act were protested, it would be only the first in a long series of onerous duties that would drive Americans to seek refuge with the more merciful savages of the interior wilderness, whom a spark of humanity had taught "involuntary sympathy for the cries of distress."[18]

Cooper was chaplain to the General Court from 1758 to 1770, and again from 1777 to 1783. Following incidents in which his alignment with the patriots led him to tangle with British officers occupying Boston, Cooper left town on 16 April 1775, on the eve of the Battle of Lexington, and took refuge in Weston, from which he made forays on horseback to neighboring towns to visit his parishioners. The siege of Boston delayed his return until almost a year later, after the evacuation of the troops in March of 1776. The British had turned his church into barracks, confident that the patriots would never shell it, and had left it filthy and damaged. When he entered his house in Boston, he was greeted by another desolate scene. Marks of plunder and destruction were everywhere: linens had been pilfered, china, glass, and mirrors smashed. By order of the General Court he was permitted to refurbish his household with the effects of Tories who had taken flight.[19]

The Reverend Samuel Cooper and James Bowdoin were united in the cause of the Revolution, and in moments of distress when Bowdoin was struck down by his disease, Cooper provided him with spiritual comfort, a service for which he repaid his pastor with small presents. They prayed together—though it is difficult to see Cooper as the mentor of Bowdoin's soul. James Bowdoin's mind required strong meat for men of full age, not milk for babes. His intellectual provider was a man of another world, sometimes reputed to be an atheist—Benjamin Franklin.

---

17. Ibid., 13.

18. Cooper, *The Crisis. Or, A full defence of the Colonies; in which it is incontestably proved that the British Constitution has been flagrantly violated in the late Stamp Act* . . . (London, 1766), 8–9.

19. Samuel Kirkland Lothrop, *A History of the Church in Brattle Street* (Boston, 1851), 102–03, 107–08; Akers, *Divine Politician*, 210, 214. A portrait of Cooper hangs in Memorial Hall at Harvard, another in the Massachusetts Historical Society. For a description of the devastation of Boston churches during the British occupation, see MHS, *Collections* 71 (Letters and Papers of John Singleton Copley and Henry Pelham), 368, Pelham to Copley, Boston, 27 Jan. 1776. The plundering of Cooper's house is described in a letter to Franklin: *Papers* 22, ed. W. B. Willcox (1982), 387, Cooper to Franklin, Boston, 21 Mar. 1776.

Franklin, Bowdoin, and the Lost Vocation

However different the religious commitments of Franklin and Bowdoin, belief in empirical science and the rules of scientific evidence as they understood them, as well as their political allegiance, bound them firmly together. For a period of forty years there was a fairly constant interchange of letters and messages between Franklin the self-made son of a candle- and soap-maker and Bowdoin the son of a wealthy Boston merchant. Their correspondence began shortly after Bowdoin's visit to Franklin in Philadelphia in 1750, in the company of the Reverend Samuel Cooper of the Brattle Street Church and Thomas Cushing.[20] The recent Harvard graduate cut a handsome figure, as his portrait by Robert Feke shows; and Bowdoin displayed the benefits of Professor John Winthrop's tutelage in natural science to such good effect that Franklin had copies of his papers on electricity prepared, corrected them with his own hand, and sent them to Bowdoin on 25 October 1750, asking for his criticism.[21] Their acquaintance blossomed into the most enduring friendship of Bowdoin's life, though offhand the relationship seems incongruous. Franklin, twenty years older, was witty, hardly religious, even immoral by Bowdoin's Calvinist standards of sexual behavior.

Franklin occasionally addressed his letters to "James Bowdoin, merchant," but the two men rarely adverted to matters of business; instead, they covered the gamut of intellectual and political affairs in which they were involved. For much of the time science was the substance of their exchange, especially the electrical experiments that had made Franklin world famous. They supplied each other with books and materials — even in the middle of the Revolutionary War, Franklin troubled to send

---

20. Bowdoin may have met Franklin when he was in Boston in 1743 (Kershaw, *Bowdoin, Patriot and Man of the Enlightenment*, 111). At New Haven, the president of Yale awarded the Boston visitors master's degrees (for a fee), admitting them to the same degree they held from Harvard (Akers, *The Divine Politician*, 29).

21. In late summer 1750, at Franklin's behest, Lewis Evans copied all Franklin's reports on electricity for Bowdoin; Franklin corrected the manuscript of 155 pages and sent it to Bowdoin on 25 October. Other marginalia in another hand were perhaps added from printed editions. The manuscript, which belongs to the American Academy of Arts and Sciences and is presently housed in Harvard's Houghton Library, was first used by I. B. Cohen and described in *Benjamin Franklin's Experiments and Observations on Electricity*, edited, with critical and historical introduction, by I. B. Cohen, 1941. Cohen was the first to clarify the relations of Bowdoin and Franklin; see Franklin, *Papers* 3, ed. L. W. Labaree (1961), 116 n.6. Bowdoin continued his studies on astronomy after graduation and in 1749 he purchased his first electrical apparatus. In the 1760s he returned to astronomy and published "An Improvement Proposed for Telescopes" in the *London Magazine* for November 1761. In 1752 Franklin sent to London his correspondence with friends on philosophical subjects, including Bowdoin's letters, which were read to the Royal Society (Kershaw, *Bowdoin, Patriot and Man of the Enlightenment*, 113, 114).

Bowdoin a Russian book on comets for Andrew Oliver, Jr., the Salem astronomer, and Vattel's *Droit des Gens* for Harvard[22] — and Franklin would sometimes announce a new invention to his young friend. Writing from London in December of 1758, he described his sliding plate for keeping rooms warmer with less fire, correctly surmising that it would be of particular interest to Bowdoin, since in frosty Boston "firing" was often costly.[23] The correspondence turned also to homelier sources of heat: at Bowdoin's request Franklin sent him the recipe for a milk punch requiring six quarts of brandy and the rinds of forty-four lemons thinly pared.[24]

The topics discussed extended beyond science to encompass the treatment of Indians, with whom Bowdoin and Franklin both negotiated in an official capacity, relations between the colonies and the Crown, and policies to be pursued during the Revolutionary War. Bowdoin had met with the Indians at the George's and Kennebec rivers and, smug with the success of his mission, in November of 1753 sent Franklin some platitudinous guidelines: "Trade and Commerce between Nation and Nation, especially when carried on to mutual advantage, have a natural Tendency to beget and confirm a mutual and lasting Friendship."[25] The two men freely introduced visitors to each other by letter, and Bowdoin had no hesitancy in asking Franklin to take a look at his son James when he was in London.[26] Franklin expected to be kept informed if anything new "in the Philosophical Way" had occurred in America during his long absence abroad.[27] Bowdoin was one of a small group to receive a print of Mason Chamberlain's portrait of Franklin.

Franklin treated the younger man as a fellow scientist and a person of discretion. On Christmas Day of 1750, the same year in which he had sent Bowdoin his electrical papers, Franklin wrote his brother John in Boston after injuring himself during an experiment in electricity, "You may Communicate this to Mr. Bowdoin As A Caution to

22. Franklin, *Papers* 10, ed. L. W. Labaree (1966), 351–52, Franklin to Bowdoin, Boston, 11 Oct. 1763, regarding a pedestal for Bowdoin's telescope, and books by a Russian electrician that he lent Winthrop, who would later pass them along to Bowdoin. See also Franklin, *Papers* 22, ed. W. B. Willcox (1982), 389–90, Franklin to Bowdoin, Philadelphia, 24 Mar. 1776, and 569, Bowdoin to Franklin, 19 Aug. 1776.

23. Franklin, *Papers* 8, ed. L. W. Labaree (1965), 195–96, Franklin to Bowdoin, London, 2 Dec. 1758. In the same letter, Franklin also wrote of modifications for chimneys that would allow cool air to pass through a house in summertime (196–97).

24. Ibid. 10:352, Franklin to Bowdoin, Boston, 11 Oct. 1763.

25. Ibid. 5, ed. L. W. Labaree (1962), 111, Bowdoin to Franklin, 12 Nov. 1753.

26. Bowdoin wrote Franklin on 2 Jan. 1771, that his son's voyage had been undertaken because of his precarious health (MHS, *Collections*, ser. 6.9 [Bowdoin and Temple Papers, 1], 248). On 5 November 1771, he wrote again, asking Franklin to introduce James III to Priestley and noting his son's interest in studying law (ibid., 277).

27. Franklin, *Papers* 10:177, Franklin to Bowdoin, Philadelphia, 15 Dec. 1762.

him, but do not make it more Publick, for I am Ashamed to have been Guilty of so Notorious A Blunder."[28] Again, on 12 April 1753, when Franklin sent Bowdoin eighteen glass jars for electrical experiments, six for himself and twelve for Harvard College, he advised precautions in an affectionate, fatherly manner: "If you charge more than one or two together, pray take care how you expose your Head to an accidental Stroke; for I can assure you from Experience, one is sufficient to knock a stout Man down; and I believe a Stroke from two or three in the Head, would kill him."[29] Bowdoin took seriously Franklin's invitation to continue their scientific correspondence, and praised the papers on electricity as "very curious and entertaining; and by far the best and most rational that have been written on that subject"—a comment Franklin modestly omitted when he published Bowdoin's letters in the collected papers on electricity.[30]

When Franklin's most original associate, an unemployed Baptist clergyman named Ebenezer Kinnersley, went up to Boston with his electrical apparatus to earn a little money from displaying the wonders of science, Franklin sent Bowdoin a letter of introduction, taking for granted that he would sponsor a performance among his friends. Scientific experiments long remained a form of entertainment, and even the unbending Newton had had his "experimenter" do his act before aristocrats and ambassadors at the Royal Society. In Boston, Kinnersley presided over a popular show in Faneuil Hall. On 21 December 1751, Bowdoin reported to Franklin the success of Kinnersley's lecture-demonstrations, though differing with him on some details and proposing experiments of his own on the "velocity of the electrical fire." In passing he sententiously reiterated the Baconian scientist's credo: "Let us have recourse to Experiments. Experiments will obviate all objections, or confound the Hypothesis."[31] On 2 March 1752, Bowdoin acknowledged a misapprehension he had been under "respecting the polarity given to needles by the electrical fire," and told Franklin of his examination of the curious results of a stroke of lightning on the Dutch Church steeple in New York.[32]

Franklin had been elected to the Pennsylvania Assembly in 1751. Bowdoin congratulated him on his advancement in public life, but at the same time expressed a

28 Ibid., 4, ed. L. W. Labaree (1961), 83, Franklin to John Franklin (?), Philadelphia, 25 Dec. 1750.

29. Ibid., 462, Franklin to Bowdoin, Philadelphia, 12 Apr. 1753.

30. Franklin, *Experiments and Observations on Electricity, Made at Philadelphia in America. To which are added, Letters and Papers on Philosophical Subjects* (London, 1769), 166–72, 178–81, 273–76. Franklin had intended to publish the letters in an earlier edition—he wrote on 30 December 1754, asking permission to do so (*Papers* 5:455)—but they were not included until the fourth edition, along with papers by Kinnersley, Winthrop, and others. For the full text of Bowdoin's letter of 21 December 1751, see Franklin, *Papers* 4:216–21; note especially 217.

31. Ibid., 218, Bowdoin to Franklin, 21 Dec. 1751.

32. Ibid., 270–71, Bowdoin to Franklin, 2 Mar. 1752.

certain foreboding about the direction Franklin's career was taking. Bowdoin was apprehensive that politics would devour the philosopher: "I hope it will not be the means of diverting your tho'ts from philosophical subjects, which would be a real injury (I speak it without flattery) to the philosophical world."[33] From his mid-twenties, Bowdoin thought of himself as part of the republic of science he called "the philosophical world." Being seduced by politics, the danger about which he warned his elder, was his own destiny.

In the 1750s Franklin tried to act as an intellectual clearing house for American scientists. There is an openness in his communications often lacking among the scientific geniuses of the previous century. In a series of letters to Bowdoin he preached the need to promote the disciplines of geography and astronomy as the universal concern of all polite nations. He recognized the handicaps of his status as an autodidact, but it seems not to have overly inhibited him. And he was the complete opposite of the secretive Newton: Franklin was not reticent about sending around his spontaneous jottings, expecting that they might be wrong, ever prepared to rectify errors and withdraw hypotheses. In a letter describing some of his electrical experiments to Peter Collinson, the British naturalist, antiquary, and Royal Society Fellow, Franklin stated his position with clarity and with the generous spirit that was the hallmark of his professional correspondence:

> These Thoughts, my dear Friend, are many of them crude and hasty, and if I were merely ambitious of acquiring some Reputation in Philosophy, I ought to keep them by me 'till corrected and improved by Time and farther Experience. But since even short Hints, and imperfect Experiments in any new Branch of Science, being communicated have often-times a good Effect in exciting the attention of the Ingenious to the Subject, and so becoming the Occasion of more exact disquisitions . . . and more compleat Discoveries, you are at Liberty to communicate this Paper to whom you please; it being of more Importance that Knowledge should increase, than that your Friend should be thought an accurate Philosopher.[34]

It was Franklin's hope that Cadwallader Colden (1688–1776), the surveyor-general for New York and from 1761 until his death its lieutenant-governor, would join Bowdoin and himself to form the nucleus of a sort of invisible college of science. Colden's *Principles of Action in Matter* (1751) brought from Franklin a forthright admission of his own deficiencies in mathematics, which occasioned his reluctance to criticize the work. He confessed that though he had doubts about the principle of *vis inertiae*, his ignorance made him diffident. He did, however, know a young man to whom Colden's work should be sent for a just evaluation. Bowdoin, a gentleman whose great fortune had not spoiled his amiable character, was "a Person of Worth

33. Ibid., 272.
34. Ibid., 5:79, Franklin to Peter Collinson, Philadelphia, Sept. 1753.

and Candour, and of a very philosophic Genius, to whom these abstract Researches are more familiar and more engaging than to me; and who will be, I think, such a Correspondent as you desire. He lives near Boston, and therefore to save Postage to you both, let me be the Medium of your litterary Commerce. I may then with your Permission have an Opportunity of seeing what passes between you, and perhaps assisting now and then with occasional Remarks. I think it behoves us all to join Hands for the Honour of the American Philosophy."[35]

Franklin was as good as his word, and sent Bowdoin the book, as well as a letter from Colden seeking to prove that sea-clouds harbored less electricity than did land-clouds.[36] But not much came of Franklin's efforts to promote the Bowdoin-Colden association. Bowdoin, without judging Colden's conclusion about the electricity in clouds, attacked his reasoning as not supporting the evidence; and though Colden was in "a longing expectation" of seeing Bowdoin's observations on his book, he died in 1776 without benefit of the awaited critical estimate. In any event, Bowdoin would have found uncongenial this obdurate Loyalist inimical to American shippers.[37]

Bowdoin informed Franklin of any chance investigations he happened to conduct. One day while on a boat out of Portsmouth in the company of some friends on business, Bowdoin observed a luminous appearance at the point where the oars dashed the water. Various hypotheses were proposed by the gentlemen on board to explain this phenomenon, all of which Bowdoin rejected. His own theory was that a great number of little animals floated on the surface of the sea, and that on being disturbed they might, by expanding their fins or otherwise moving themselves, expose such parts of their bodies as exhibited luminosity in the manner of a glowworm or firefly. On 12 November 1753, Bowdoin sent Franklin this "idle conjecture for want of something better"; but it appears that Franklin accepted Bowdoin's explanation of marine phosphorescence, for he read it before the Royal Society of London on 16 December 1756, and printed it in the 1769 edition of his *Experiments and Observations on Electricity*.[38] Franklin generously diffused the bits of scientific observation Bowdoin submitted to him.

A lively correspondence was carried on in the 1750s about Franklin's experiments and the polemics to which his theory of electricity gave rise among

35. Ibid., 4:464, Franklin to Cadwallader Colden, Philadelphia, 12 Apr. 1753.

36. Ibid., 277–78, Bowdoin to Franklin, 16 Mar. 1752; 5:80, Franklin to Colden, Philadelphia, 25 Oct. 1753.

37. Ibid., 122, Colden to Franklin, Coldengham, 29 Nov. 1753.

38. Franklin, *Experiments and Observations on Electricity* (1769), includes twenty-five pages of correspondence between Franklin and Bowdoin on chimneys, electricity and lightning, and the luminous quality of the sea at night. For Bowdoin's letter on marine phosphorescence, see Franklin, *Papers* 5:113–15, and n. 4.

European scholars. On 13 December 1753, he noted the death of Georg Wilhelm Reichmann, a Swedish physicist, who was engaged in duplicating Thomas-François Dalibard's confirmation of Franklin's hypotheses on electricity. Franklin asked Bowdoin the favor of "peeping" into his reply to the Abbé Nollet's attack on the theory so that he might correct it by his advice. Dalibard was preparing an answer for Franklin and this pleased him. He was not ashamed to display a little self-love before his younger friend: "And will not one's Vanity be more gratify'd in seeing one's Adversary confuted by a Disciple, than even by one's self?"[39]

When a new edition of Franklin's papers on electricity was published, he received a long letter from Bowdoin (27 January 1755) that expressed his pleasure. Though Bowdoin took exception to certain reflections on heat and cold, he was delighted with the hypothesis that there might be regions of electric fire above the atmosphere and that the aurora borealis could be currents of that fluid visible from their motion. Bowdoin corrected his own conjecture that a point 1,027,709 million times less than 1/10 of an inch afforded light enough to affect the sight at four miles distance; he had previously not employed the right method of calculating. He was already absorbed with the problem that the sun might be diminished greatly by a constant efflux of light, a supposed flaw in the perfection of the universe that a quarter of a century later he attempted to explain away with a controversial hypothesis presented to the American Academy. He questioned Franklin's theory that all the phenomena of light might be more conveniently accounted for by supposing universal space to be filled with a subtle elastic fluid not visible at rest, whose vibrations nevertheless affected that fine sense in the eye, as those of air did the grosser organs. The correspondence between the two men was candid, infused with good humor and even tenderness. Rejecting Franklin's conjecture about the nature of light, Bowdoin wrote with a touch of whimsy, "If no objection lay against your hypothesis, and the sun is not wasted by expense of light, I can easily conceive (in *your* method of accounting for it) that it shall otherwise always retain the same quantity of matter; but at present I cannot give into your 'philosophical heresy'; for which, though you 'are not subject to the Inquisition like poor Galileo,' you are not wholly without punishment, as it has occasioned you the trouble of this epistle."[40]

While Bowdoin was always respectful, even reverential, to Franklin, he was not inhibited from tearing apart with exquisite dialectical skill Franklin's probably casual philosophical reflections on the nature of matter, extension, God, and the creation. He avoided direct criticism of Franklin's dangerous religious posture, and when the subject became too nettlesome they both receded behind common-sense ramparts, relegating their differences to that realm of metaphysics in which

39. Ibid., 155–56, Franklin to Bowdoin, Philadelphia, 13 Dec. 1753.
40. Ibid., 477–90, Bowdoin to Franklin, 27 Jan. 1755; quotation appears on 483.

neither they nor most of their educated contemporaries felt intellectually at ease. They were always happier to discuss concrete experiments.

Franklin inadvertently got himself involved briefly in the thorny problem of God's relationship to space and matter, the same issue that had opened pious Newton's system to Leibniz's strictures at the beginning of the century. Bowdoin quoted from an earlier letter of Franklin's: "If God was before all things, and filled all space; then when he formed what we call matter, he must have done it out of his own thinking immaterial substance. The same, though he had not filled all space; if it be true that *ex nihilo nihil fit*. From hence may we not draw this conclusion, that if any part of matter does not at present act and think, 'tis not from an incapacity in its nature, but from a positive restraint. I know not yet what other consequences may follow the admitting of this position, and therefore I will not be obliged to defend it." Then with a series of theological and scientific arguments Bowdoin ripped into this rather loosely-worded untheological utterance. It was perilously close to the ungodliness of which Franklin was occasionally accused. Bowdoin worried that the use of such language presumed a knowledge of the nature of God that he himself was loath to claim. His Calvinist upbringing made him shrink from pretensions to intimacy with God's purpose and will. His own views, expressed with argumentative virtuosity, were in a more traditional spirit. He made a forthright statement of the limitations of men's knowledge of other beings in the great chain:

> We can judge of things only in proportion to our knowledge of them, and of consequence can form no adequate judgment of a power, whose extent we do not fully know. We cannot determine, then, even in regard to beings in a lower class than ourselves, precisely how far their powers extend; we only know in general that our own powers exceed theirs. . . . If we cannot determine the quantum of our own power, nor that of beings below ourselves much less can we of beings superior to us, and least of all, of the supreme being. In regard to the supreme being we are in some degree acquainted with his power — the more we inquire into it, the higher opinion we conceive of it — those, that know most of it, by being most acquainted with its effects, acknowledge that they know nothing of it in compare with what remains to be known: and they hesitate not to pronounce it infinite. . . .

Bowdoin was especially disturbed by the possibility that in Franklin's philosophy matter might be mixed with the nature of God:

> If God formed matter out of his own thinking immaterial substance, then the substance of God must be diminished, and therefore he cannot be infinite: or if not diminished, the matter formed out of it must be God, or a part of God: in which case he must greatly debase and degrade himself, if matter be less excellent than thinking immaterial substance, and therefore he cannot be unchangeable: in which case he

must be a compound of matter and spirit, and therefore not a pure and simple being: he must be both cause and effect, creator and creature, and therefore holy and unholy, wise and foolish, just and unjust, good and mischievous, eternal and temporal, unchangeable and mutable, almighty and frail, true and a liar, happy and miserable.

The deeper Bowdoin became drawn into the debate about the nature of God, the more uncomfortable he grew. Finally he retired modestly: "For my own part, I am very little versed in metaphysics: but so far as I am able to judge, I am quite of your opinion 'that there is great uncertainty in that science, and that the contradictions and disputes it affords are endless': and it is no wonder that this should be the case, for its object is beyond our ken."[41] Franklin thenceforth stepped warily away from theological quagmires. Bowdoin remained faithful to his unknowable infinite God and Franklin shunned any overt relations with Him in churches.

Franklin was unstinting in his praise of Bowdoin, sometimes laying it on with a trowel. When Bowdoin sent him a copy of the *College Poems* published in honor of George III's accession—Bowdoin was an anonymous contributor—Franklin responded, "I think, and I hope it is not merely my American Vanity that makes me think, some of them exceed in Beauty and Elegance those produced by the Mother Universities of Oxford and Cambridge, on the same Occasion."[42] Writing from London on 13 January 1772, by which time both men were deeply enmeshed in the politics of the coming Revolution, he referred to the new edition of his papers on electricity (1769) that included Bowdoin's communications: "It gives me great Pleasure that my Book afforded any to my Friends. I esteem those Letters of yours among its brightest Ornaments, and have the Satisfaction to find that they add greatly to the Reputation of American Philosophy."[43]

In his turn, Bowdoin could lavish extravagant compliments upon his friend, occasionally fashioning clumsy figures of speech from which he could hardly extricate himself. A letter of 19 August 1776 bears witness to his earnest but infelicitous efforts: "I am glad to find that notwithstanding your Countrymen have had so many good slices of you for those forty years past: there's enough remaining of you to afford them good Picking Still. Notwithstanding the past Regales they still expect

41. Ibid., 486, 487–89.

42. Ibid., 10:176–77, Franklin to Bowdoin, Philadelphia, 15 Dec. 1762. The *College Poems* were published in Boston in 1761 as *Pietas et Gratulatio Collegii Cantabrigiensis apud Novanglos*, and a copy was sent to the Massachusetts agent in England, Jasper Mauduit; four of the poems—two in Latin, two in English—have been attributed to Bowdoin (Kershaw, *Bowdoin, Patriot and Man of the Enlightenment*, 135). In a letter to Mauduit, 25 April 1763, Bowdoin expressed his satisfaction that the "College Verses" had met with approval and his hope that the dedication might win the royal favor for the colonies, especially for the needy university at Cambridge (MHS, *Collections*, ser. 6.9 [Bowdoin and Temple Papers, 1], 17).

43. Franklin, *Papers* 19, ed. W. B. Willcox (1975), 12, Franklin to Bowdoin, London, 13 Jan. 1772.

to feast upon you, and to feast as usual most deliciously. Like Beggars once indulged they ask for more."[44] Bowdoin strove to be whimsical, affectionate, friendly, to imitate the debonair Dr. Franklin, but he could only contrive a cannibalistic metaphor.

Yet Franklin's vitality and high spirits were too infectious not to leave their mark on his reserved friend. Hearing through Lafayette that the seventy-year-old Franklin, then in Paris successfully negotiating French assistance for the colonies, was in splended health, Bowdoin wrote him an almost giddy letter on 1 May 1780. He speculated on the meaning of age, and concluded that if a man felt well and sprightly he would be young even at a hundred. Then, suppressing the memory of wrongs sustained by the Huguenots at the hands of Catholic kings, he deftly moved to the generosity of Louis XVI: "I wish ye continuance of your health and that half a century hence, as well as frequently at times intermediate, we may have ye pleasure of drinking a bottle together and toasting the health, prosperity & long life of our illustrious ally his present most christian majesty. When ye title Most Christian was given to ye Kings of France, it was prophetic of ye present reign; for what can be more Christian than to relieve the oppressed and support & defend ye liberty & happiness of mankind? *Buvons, alors, buvons à la santé du roy!*"[45] This was not the last time Bowdoin cheerfully ruminated—perhaps half-seriously—on the friendly intercourse with Franklin he anticipated in the afterlife.

When Franklin included letters from Bowdoin in the 1769 edition of his essays on electricity, it was a testimonial from the greatest American scientific genius of the age. If a scientific enterprise needed public support, Bowdoin could be relied upon to act as an official spearhead.[46] His possessions inventoried in September of 1774 included half a dozen telescopes, a microscope, globes, and electrical apparatus.[47] He donated instruments to Harvard College —still a part of its collection—and encouraged American participation in international scientific enterprises such as the observation of the transit of Venus. In 1788, two years before his

44. Ibid. 22:571, Bowdoin to Franklin, 19 Aug. 1776 (also MHS, *Collections*, ser. 6.9 [Bowdoin and Temple Papers, 1], 402). The metaphoric language of an earlier draft had been even clumsier, with reference to Franklin's embonpoint and mounting years: "There's enough remaining of you to regale them further and to afford good Picking still and as 'tis said the sweetest meat grows upon old bones, and yours continue well fleshed, they still expect to feast. . . " (Franklin, *Papers* 22:571 and n. 7).

45. MHS, *Proceedings*, ser. 2.8 (1892–94), 290, Bowdoin to Franklin, 1 May 1780.

46. When John Winthrop, at Franklin's instance, sought support for an expedition to Lake Superior to observe the transit of Venus, he enlisted the aid of Bowdoin, then a member of the Governor's Council (after much correspondence, the enterprise was abandoned); see MHS, *Collections*, ser. 6.9 (Bowdoin and Temple Papers, 1), 116–19, Winthrop to Bowdoin, Cambridge, 18 Jan. 1769, and 119, Bowdoin to Gen. Gage, 23 Jan. 1769; also, Harry Woolf, *The Transits of Venus, a Study in Eighteenth-Century American Science* (Princeton: Princeton University Press, 1959), 170–72.

47. MHS, Bowdoin and Temple Papers, "Inventory of goods at present in the house of James Bowdoin Esqr . . . ," 15 Sept. 1774.

death, he attained the high honor of fellowship in the Royal Society of London. Though Bowdoin has not left a mark on the history of thought, his writings are characteristic of the eclectic outlook of an eighteenth-century American colonial with intellectual aspirations. His peculiar admixture of Newtonianism for the merchants, a rather dismal view of human nature, a sense of the immanent presence of God, with a smattering of natural law theory and a gentlemanly concept of honor, was not often replicated in later generations. When in 1780 the patriots were in search of a presiding officer for their newly incorporated Academy, James Bowdoin, the friend of Franklin, was a natural choice.

5

UNION AND DISCORD AMONG
THE BRETHREN

J AMES BOWDOIN II belonged to the "high ones," as his daughter put it
when she feared British reprisals against him during the Revolutionary War.
Though his gifts were not exceptional, his wealth, intellectual attainments,
dignified bearing, and reputation for probity combined to earn him considerable
prestige among his peers. Right-thinking people would choose this sort of man
to sit in the chair at public assemblies and in private committees. He served as
first president not only of the American Academy of Arts and Sciences, but of the
Humane Society and of the Massachusetts Bank; he was the leading member of
the Board of War; he presided over the convention and its three-man committee
that drafted a constitution for the Commonwealth and was its second governor.
Elected to the Massachusetts legislature in 1753 when he was about twenty-
seven, he was not completely freed from the cares of public office until his death in
1790. His personal life was closely intertwined with the politics of the Revolution
from its beginning through the final ratification of the federal Constitution by the
Commonwealth, in which he played a major part. Since he was important enough
to make an appearance in the diaries, papers, and correspondence of most of the
leaders of the Revolution, his activities can be viewed from many angles — there
are spontaneous appraisals from friends and foes alike.

A Colonial Against the Prerogative

From the early years of the dispute with the British Crown, James Bowdoin II
— landowner, merchant, amateur scientist, poetaster—was one of the mainstays of
the opposition. But a forthright demand for the redress of grievances did not necessarily involve advocating a complete divorcement from the mother country at the start.
If colonials can be divided into unquestioning Loyalists who later went into exile,
professional political leaders like Samuel Adams who very early decided that a breach
was inevitable and set about moving the political process in that direction, and a third
group that hoped and worked for an accommodation until the introduction of British troops and the shedding of blood in the Boston Massacre, James Bowdoin should
be counted among the less precipitate ones. As late as 1774, while characterizing the

situation in the colonies as very disagreeable and ripening to a crisis, he still hoped that measures taken by the Continental Congress would bring about the "restoration of tranquillity and mutual confidence."[1] Five years afterward, viewing the separation from the mother country in retrospect, Bowdoin adopted a tone that was at once nostalgic and moralizing. In a letter to Thomas Pownall, who had preceded Bernard and Hutchinson as royal governor and had been consistently favorable to the colonists, Bowdoin reflected on the happiness they had all known under Pownall's regime. England and America could have continued for ages to enjoy peace and trade, "but the demon Avarice has rent them asunder, and thereby deprived Posterity of the sight of the greatest empire, founded on right government, that ever existed."[2]

The path leading to a clear-cut declaration of independence was long and tortuous, especially among the notables of the Massachusetts Bay, as an individual adopted a forward position one day, receded from it the next, then leapt into the darkness of rebellion again. Extant documents written in the same period by the same person bear witness to the inner conflict: they are flagrantly contradictory, changing with the circumstances of their composition and the recipients for whom they were destined. Fluidity rather than unflinching steadfastness characterized most of the prominent colonials, and charges of hypocrisy and double-dealing can be leveled against them all too easily. Many were torn by interest, the protection of a family fortune. At moments some were seized with an elementary fear —not without reason — that they would be apprehended, deported, tried for treason, executed, drawn and quartered.

Party lines of Whig and Tory cannot be marked with finality. What appeared to be see-sawing or equivocation was often a response to the shifts and inconsistencies of British policy. In April of 1765 Bowdoin could write his brother-in-law the governor of Grenada that Bostonians were put out of countenance by a long string of Parliamentary resolutions regarding a stamp tax in the colonies: "We have been treated as the meer property of G Britain; and as if we stood in no other relation to her, than the Blacks of your Island to their respective owners & Taskmasters." But less than a year later, his letter abounded in expressions of joy and loyalty to king and Parliament, as he recounted the preparations of the Sons of Liberty to celebrate the expected repeal of the hated duty.[3] Colonial governors watched the

1. MHS, Bowdoin and Temple Papers, Letter Book, 228, Bowdoin to John Temple, 10 Sept. 1774.

2. MHS, *Proceedings* 5:241–44, Bowdoin to Pownall, 17 May 1779. In a letter to Bowdoin on 14 July 1770, Pownall had noted that he was "marked as an American partizan" (MHS, *Collections*, ser. 6.9 [Bowdoin and Temple Papers, 1], 196). He was so taken with the colonies that in the middle of the war, on 19 April 1778, he wrote to Bowdoin, as he had to Samuel Cooper, inquiring as to his likely reception if after the war he settled in America as a place of retirement, with a "house in town, and a little farm in the country" (*Proceedings* 5:240–41).

3. MHS, Bowdoin and Temple Papers, Letter Book, 108, Bowdoin to George Scott, 9 Apr. 1765; ibid., 144, Bowdoin to Scott, 31 Mar. 1766.

high ones and categorized them in reports to the ministry in London; challenging the government on one issue could invite a political label that might disregard the stand on other royal pronouncements. Men who were still ambivalent or tergiversating were thereby pigeonholed, and accusations sometimes froze hesitant colonials in the posture of insurgency.

James Bowdoin II was regularly elected first to the House of Representatives, from 1753 to 1756, then to the Governor's Council. And as a distraught Thomas Hutchinson tried to enforce the Crown's repressive statutes, Bowdoin became the spokesman for the outraged upper crust of Bostonians on the Council, writing in his cramped little hand their replies to the Governor's addresses, responding with trenchant arguments to affirmations of royal prerogative. He was at once a barometer of the sentiments of the dominant Boston merchants and a crystallizer of their opinions.

On 12 March 1770, at an open town meeting of the freeholders and other inhabitants of Boston in Faneuil Hall, Bowdoin had been chosen member of a committee of three — and became its reporter — to conduct an inquiry into what was called the Massacre, so that the false reports of Governor Bernard and the commissioners might be refuted before they were made public. The committee took long and detailed depositions. Bowdoin's summary of the evidence was embellished with psychological analyses of the conduct of the governor, the commissioners, whose supercilious behavior rendered them "disgustful to people in general," the grenadiers and their damaged amour-propre, the merchants of Boston, and the members of the colonial legislature. Accusations of illegal action on the part of the government were elaborated with evocations of the feelings of indignity suffered by the merchants of Boston, the provincial representatives, and the officers of the law courts, as they were everywhere confronted by troops and ousted from their chambers and from their normal business exchange on the State House lower floor, which Governor Bernard had snatched from them and given over to the British soldiers.

Even before the Massacre on the evening of 5 March, universal uneasiness had been created, general apprehension, Bowdoin charged. A dispute that had erupted between the XXIXth Regiment and the ropemakers, in which the regiment was worsted, had fueled a conspiracy among the soldiers to redeem their honor by striking ruthlessly against the citizens of Boston. The main guard had taken up a position not twelve yards away and pointed two field pieces at the State House. The legislators were deeply offended by this threat. Sentries posted outside the lodgings of British officers provoked quarrels with the people and gravely distressed the merchants. The taunts of the grenadiers were seconded by the coarse malevolence of their wives. One of them had said that the "town was too haughty and too proud; and that many of their arses would be laid low before the morning."[4] The troops were inciting black slaves to take the lives and property of their masters. Writing to the agent of the Council in London, William Bollan, about the "horrid massacre" of the fifth, Bowdoin complained that the soldiers of the XXIXth Regiment had generally behaved "with great insolence and have committed many abuses upon the inhabitants of the town." He urged that Bollan use his influence to counter any intimation that the town had been at fault or that there had been a design to pillage the Custom House; and Bollan was to make strenuous efforts to have the troops permanently removed and not merely exchanged with replacements.[5] In his published report Bowdoin recounted the events immediately following the Massacre in the dramatic mode of the Roman historians of tyranny on whom he had been reared. The soldiers had been "outrageous on the one hand, and the inhabitants justly incensed against them on the other: both parties seeming disposed to come to action. In this case the consequences would have been terrible."[6]

Bowdoin's *Short Narrative of the Horrid Massacre in Boston, Perpetrated in the Evening of the Fifth Day of March, 1770, by Soldiers of the XXIXth Regiment; which with the XIVth Regiment were then quartered there: with some Observations on the State of Things prior to that Catastrophe* went through seven editions, including three published in London, and copies were distributed throughout the colonies and among friendly Englishmen overseas.[7] Benjamin Franklin wrote from London that as the leader of the Boston patriots Bowdoin was regularly toasted by Irishmen, who themselves had old scores to settle with the British Crown and empathized with the Americans.[8] Sixteen years later Bowdoin's position radically changed. As governor of Massachusetts he occupied Bernard's chair, and it was his troops that fired on a disaffected citizenry.

The seizure of the brigantine *Sarah*, which belonged to Bowdoin's father-in-law, John Erving, was one of the first hostile acts committed under the revival of the long dormant Writs of Assistance, an offense neither forgotten nor forgiven by members of the family. Smuggling had become a colonial right, and enforcement of the

4. Bowdoin, *A Short Narrative of the Horrid Massacre in Boston, perpetrated in the Evening of the Fifth Day of March, 1770, by Soldiers of the XXIXth Regiment; which with the XIVth Regiment were then quartered there. With some Observations on the State of Things prior to that Catastrophe* (Boston, 1770), 19.

5. MHS, *Collections*, ser. 6.9 (Bowdoin and Temple Papers, 1), 167–69, Bowdoin to William Bollan, 27 Mar. 1770.

6. Bowdoin, *Short Narrative of the Massacre*, 31.

7. See Kershaw, *Bowdoin, Patriot and Man of the Enlightenment*, 178–82, for the effect of the *Short Narrative* as propaganda.

8. Franklin, *Papers* 19:12, Franklin to Bowdoin, London, 13 Jan. 1772. Dr. Charles Lucas, who proposed the toasts, was often Franklin's dinner companion; a physician and reformer called the "Wilkes of Ireland," he had died the previous November. Franklin's letter was endorsed "Dr. Benja. Franklin's Letter London Jany.13.1772, political and important" (p. 13).

antiquated law, which increased the price of imported goods through the imposi-
tion of duties, united in anger and resentment the country party of Massachusetts
and the Boston merchants, once natural enemies. When ships carrying contraband
were seized and confiscated by the king's customs officers, the royal governor was
awarded a third of the booty.[9] A practice denounced by Bowdoin's son-in-law, John
Temple, it encouraged overzealousness on the part of greedy officials and further
estranged the colonials from the British administration. Temple, though he had just
been appointed surveyor-general of the customs service in England, was so incensed
by the conduct of ex-governor Bernard that he declared him more infamous than
Jonathan Wild, the notorious rogue, executed at Tyburn, who had been a receiver of
stolen goods and the model for the anti-hero of Fielding's novel.[10]

For a number of years the Governor's Council, virtually a family affair of Erving,
Pitts, and Bowdoin, simmered with antagonism to the Crown. Governor Bernard in exasperation called Bowdoin the "perpetual President, Chairman, Secretary & Speaker of
this new Council."[11] Bernard's successor, Governor Hutchinson, described Bowdoin in
the Council and Samuel Adams in the House of Representatives as acting in concert to
bedevil the loyal servants of George III. Though coming from an antagonist, the profile
of Bowdoin drawn by the governor, like most of his thumbnail sketches of the leading
Boston patriots, is a plausible likeness, even if it suffers from a fault frequent in contemporary histories of the Revolution—the tendency to seek out and isolate a single
personal grievance as the cause for a man's defection from allegiance to the king:

> Mr. Bowdoin was without a rival in the council, and, by the good understanding
> and reciprocal communications between him and Mr. Saml. Adams, the measures of
> council and house harmonized also, and were made reciprocally subservient each to
> the other; and when the governor met with opposition from the one, he had reason
> to expect like opposition from the other. Mr. Bowdoin's father, from a very low con-
> dition in life, raised himself, by industry and oeconomy, to a degree of wealth beyond
> that of any other person in the province, and, having always maintained a fair charac-
> ter, the attention of the people was more easily drawn to the son, and he was chosen,
> when very young, a member for Boston, and, after a few years, was removed to the

9. Kershaw, *Bowdoin, Patriot and Man of the Enlightenment*, 154.

10. MHS, *Collections*, ser. 6.9 (Bowdoin and Temple Papers, 1), 281, Temple to William Samuel
Johnson, London, 4 Dec. 1771. Temple was incensed that Bernard had been given the commission-
ership of Ireland, an appointment Temple had coveted for himself. Some years earlier he had complained of Bernard's insatiable avarice (ibid., 27, Temple to Thomas Whately, Boston, 10 Sept. 1764).

11. Kershaw, *Bowdoin, Patriot and Man of the Enlightenment* (1976 version), 76, quoting from the
Bernard Papers, 7.78, Bernard to the Earl of Hillsborough, Boston, 14 Oct. 1768 (Harvard University,
Houghton Library, Sparks MSS). In this connection, see MHS, Bowdoin and Temple Papers, Bowdoin to the Earl of Hillsborough in vindication of the Massachusetts Council "against the calumnies
and misrepresentations of his Excellency Francis Bernard," 15 Apr. 1769.

council. He found more satisfaction in the improvement of his mind by study, and of his estate by oeconomy, than in the common business of the general assembly, and had taken no very active part during the administrations of Mr. Shirley and Mr. Pownal. In general he was, in those times, considered rather as a favourer of the [royal] prerogative, than of the opposition to it. But Mr. Temple, the surveyor-general of the customs, having married Mr. Bowdoin's daughter, and having differed with governor Bernard, and connected himself with Mr. Otis, and others in the opposition, Mr. Bowdoin, from that time, entered into the like connexions. The name of a friend to liberty was enough to make him popular. Being reserved in his temper, he would not have acquired popularity in any other way. His talents for political controversy, especially when engaged in opposition, soon became conspicuous. He had been used to metaphysical distinctions, and his genius was better adapted to entangle and darken, than to unfold and elucidate.[12]

While Governor Hutchinson recognized the stature of this man in the colony, he never fathomed the complexity of his motives: he blamed Bowdoin's defection from the Crown on his relationship to John Temple, the British customs official who was complaisant to the colonial merchants and shipowners. The deep hatred of royal prerogative that had been bred in the descendant of Huguenot émigrés escaped Governor Hutchinson's perception. Both Temple and Bowdoin reciprocated in full measure Hutchinson's enmity toward them. Temple alluded to him as "that most infamous of all villians [sic] . . . whose mallace & revenge (under a cloake of religion) is equal to that of the Devil." And according to Abigail Adams, who visited Bowdoin during one of his severe attacks, despite a racking cough he sputtered at the mention of Hutchinson: "Religious rascal, how I abhor his name!"[13] Hutchinson was an Episcopalian, to be sure, but Bowdoin's antipathy was obviously less sectarian than it was political.

Though Bowdoin was neither a lawyer nor a political theorist by education and training, the statements he drew up for the pre-revolutionary Governor's Council were lucid and forceful, occasionally pungent with bitter sarcasm. And they pushed him into an intellectual position that had its own revolutionary implications. He mingled declarations of self-interest with sturdy proclamations of the rights of self-preservation, liberty, and property, indissolubly linked to the right of representation. Arguments from Jean-Jacques Burlamaqui's *Principles of Natural Law* (1748) and *Principles of Politic Law* (1752)[14] were supplemented by the tenets of English

12. Thomas Hutchinson, *History of the Colony and Province of Massachusetts Bay*, ed. L. S. Mayo (Cambridge, Mass.: Harvard University Press, 1936), 3:210–11.

13. MHS, *Proceedings* 12:210, Temple to Bowdoin, London, 5 Aug. 1772; ibid., ser. 2.8:59, Abigail to John Adams, 15 June 1775.

14. Translations into English of the *Principes du droit naturel* (1748) and *Principes du droit politique* (3 vols., 1751) followed closely upon their original publication.

constitutional law derived from Sir Edward Coke and standard pronouncements on the rights of Englishmen inherited from the English civil war and the Glorious Revolution. In Bowdoin's rhetoric, nourished also with a smattering of Grotius and Pufendorf, the abrogation of traditional liberties was a violation of natural law. To tax without representation, to seize property without consent of the owner, was to tamper with the very conditions of human life and trespass on the fundamental right to self-preservation: "Life, Liberty, Property, and the Disposal of that Property with our own Consent, are natural Rights. . . . Representation: which being necessary to preserve these invaluable Rights of Nature, is itself, for that Reason, a natural Right, coinciding with, and running into, that great Law of Nature, Self-Preservation."[15]

Bowdoin quoted the Magna Charta, the statutes of Edward I, Edward III, and William III, and the Petition of Right under Charles I in support of his argument that an essential part of the English constitution prohibited the levying of any tax without the assent and goodwill of the freemen of the commonalty. Otherwise their property could not really be said to belong to them. The inhabitants of the colony were entitled to all the rights and privileges of English subjects, especially the inviolability of property, rights derived from the common law and confirmed by the charter of the province. Deprivation of these rights "would be Vassalage in the extreme; from which the generous Nature of Englishmen has been so abhorrent, that they have bled with Freedom in the Defence of this Part of their Constitution."[16] Bowdoin shrewdly pointed out that while the colonies had rendered great service to the mother country during the war with France, there had been no quid pro quo, not even protection from Indian incursions that imperiled their existence. The sole benefit accruing to them had been the grant of English liberties; and therefore, "instead of being violated by military Power, or explained away by nice Inferences and Distinctions, [they] ought . . . to be acknowledged by every Minister of the Crown, and preserved sacred from every Species of Violation."[17] Without the right of representation in matters respecting taxation, an essential right of nature, government would degenerate into despotism.

Bowdoin's arguments rested heavily on the historical development of the British constitution — the accretion of events, precedents, customs, and institutions — to

15. John Phillip Reid, ed., *The Briefs of the American Revolution. Constitutional Arguments between Thomas Hutchinson, Governor of Massachusetts Bay, and James Bowdoin for the Council and John Adams for the House of Representatives* (New York: New York University Press, 1981), 43.

16. Ibid., 28, 36, 37.

17. Ibid., 41. For Bowdoin's draft of a letter from the Council and House of Representatives to Lord Dartmouth, 29 June 1773, on the colonies' being deprived of their charter rights , especially the control of officers of the Crown and judges through salary grants from the Assembly, see MHS, *Collections*, ser. 6.9 (Bowdoin and Temple Papers, 1), 302–05.

which he opposed the arbitrary acts of Parliament. The limitations of power once invoked by Parliament to restrain the king were now turned against Parliament itself. In the Council's reply to Governor Hutchinson's address of 6 January 1773, Bowdoin insisted that Parliament was assuming powers only God could possess, that constitutional projection of English liberties was not subject to Parliament's alterations, especially when those affected were not represented. Since supreme, unlimited authority could properly belong only to the Sovereign of the Universe, its usurpation by any earthly institution would make of those subject to it "emphatically Slaves: and equally so whether residing in the Colonies or Great Britain."[18] The perfervid language, so "repugnant" to Governor Hutchinson, was not provoked merely by the passions of the moment. In a business letter written as early as 1767, in which he declined to subscribe to a series of English engravings because he was observing the non-importation agreement, Bowdoin had melodramatically declared, ". . . to slavery we think ourselves now damned."[19] And when two years later his election to the Council had been negatived, he responded with a sarcastic speech addressed to the then governor, Bernard: "Your Excellency has thought proper to confer upon me a Mark of Distinction, which I should think it a Happiness to be intitled to, I say a Happiness, because Your Excellency is such a Judge and Rewarder of Merit, that your Favours of this sort have always been a Consequence of it. . . ."[20] In the Council's reply of 1773, with its insinuation that the highhandedness of Parliament threatened subjects in the home country as well as in the colonies, Bowdoin seemed to be casting his net widely for allies in Britain.

The forthrightness and skill of Bowdoin's draughtmanship were prized by his contemporaries. Inflammatory language was the medium of James Otis, Samuel Adams, John Hancock, and the Reverend Samuel Cooper; but it was in the cogent, if legalistic, prose of James Bowdoin that the merchants of Boston found their voice. He was the spokesman for their interests and grievances. It was he who sought to justify their conduct to British administrators when opposition to the revenue acts exceeded lawful bounds. And at the same time he answered the attacks of intemperate critics like John Temple, who accused the colonials of pusillanimity and dog-like cringing before authority when they abandoned their associations for the non-importation of British goods. Bowdoin responded with eminent reasonableness that it was surprising the agreements had survived for so long, since British agents were stealthily sowing dissension among the merchants, those of other colonies were constrained to follow the defection of New York, and

18. Reid, *Briefs of the American Revolution*, 34.

19. MHS, *Collections*, ser. 6.9 (Bowdoin and Temple Papers, 1), 84–85, Bowdoin to John Lane, 13 Dec. 1767.

20. Kershaw, *Bowdoin, Patriot and Man of the Enlightenment*, 169.

in any event non-importation was rendered ineffectual by heightened demand for British goods from Russia and other sources. While not condoning the merchants' fall from grace, Bowdoin dismissed it as no worse than could have been expected among any other people under the sun.[21]

No ordinary colonial rebels defending their position, the merchants of Massachusetts were godly Calvinists, proud men who saw the history of Europe as a rise from barbarism attributable chiefly to their endeavors. They led well-ordered lives in which the *dulce* and the *utile* — Bowdoin employed the terms[22] — were intermingled, inducing a general state and temper they called ease and happiness. Among the arguments against the punitive Crown laws, Bowdoin in his addresses of the early 1770s repeatedly stressed the "uneasiness" and "unhappiness," touchstones of the new moral psychology, into which the colonials had been flung by the British acts, and pleaded for the restoration of happiness and tranquillity.[23] The absolutism of a religious distinction between good and evil was being modified with new conceptions. The introspective anguish of a Cotton Mather had been muted, and instead of searching their own souls for sin, men ascribed their malaise to external causes. Religious explanations for good and evil were being replaced, or perhaps more accurately, diluted, with ascriptions to secular virtues and vices.

A royal governor could veto with impunity the choice of a John Adams for the Council, not so easily a great Boston merchant — though Bowdoin too was twice negatived. According to Mercy Warren, his "understanding, discernment, and conscientious deportment, rendered him a very unfit instrument for the views of the court, at this extraordinary period."[24] Lacking the mad genius of a James Otis, the obdurate legal tenacity of a John Adams, the populist skills of a Samuel Adams, or the oratorical fire of a John Hancock, Bowdoin was nevertheless a Boston patriot who faithfully represented the merchants and enjoyed the respect of a broad constituency of freeholders. It was only in the mid-1780s that he became anathema to the yeomen of Massachusetts.

The Ailing Revolutionary

On the eve of the 1774 meeting of the Continental Congress, to which he had been elected, Bowdoin suddenly retired from the public scene, though Hancock, Samuel Adams, and Franklin continued to write him at regular intervals about

---

21. MHS, *Collections*, ser. 6.9 (Bowdoin and Temple Papers, 1), 293, Bowdoin to John Temple, 9 May 1772.

22. See MHS, Bowdoin and Temple Papers, Bowdoin to James III, 17 Jan. 1771.

23. Reid, *Briefs of the American Revolution*, 33, 44.

24. Mercy Warren, *History of the American Revolution* 1:131.

the course of events in Philadelphia, and the American agent of Massachusetts in London directed reports to him. The rich and admired merchant was stricken with the plagues of Job. After his wife had recovered from one of her attacks of nerves he took to his bed. (He had never been robust; a letter of 1755 from his brother-in-law, a budding physician, mentions a whole complex of maladies and advises that he remove himself from the care of a physician identified only as the "Chiron of Connecticut.")[25] Though Bowdoin's letters usually make reference to a poor state of health without further specification, the symptoms described by contemporaries suggest tuberculosis. Considered a plebeian disease and frightening because of its high mortality, like cancer a generation ago it was not talked about freely. His son-in-law, John Temple, the native American in the royal service who was sympathetic to the merchants, after much maneuvering had finally obtained in 1771 the lucrative post of surveyor-general of customs and subsequently migrated with his wife to England, leaving behind a child with its maternal grandparents; but in England Temple became embroiled in a duel over American policy. He was implicated in putting into Benjamin Franklin's hands the fateful dispatches of 1767–69 to Thomas Whately, a member of Parliament and protégé of Grenville's, from Governor Hutchinson and his wife's brother-in-law, Lieutenant-Governor Andrew Oliver (at that time respectively lieutenant-governor and secretary of the province). The letters had secretly advised that the British ministry curtail traditional English liberties enjoyed by the colonists, create a patrician order from which the Council would be chosen, and institute repressive measures as the way to end American tumults—a revelation of treachery deftly used by Sam Adams and Samuel Cooper to kindle revolutionary ardor in Boston.

When in December of 1772 Franklin had confidentially forwarded to Thomas Cushing the correspondence incriminating the royal officials, he urged that the letters be shown to selected "Men of Worth in the Province for their Satisfaction only"; they were members of the Committee of Correspondence or of the Council, in particular Bowdoin, his brother-in-law James Pitts, the Reverends Charles Chauncy and Samuel Cooper, and Professor Winthrop.[26] Bowdoin was a thorn in the governor's flesh, and the publication in Boston of the purloined letters, *The Representations of Governor Hutchinson and Others, Contained in Certain Letters Transmitted to England, and Afterwards Returned from Thence, and Laid before the General Assembly of the Massachusetts-Bay* ... (1773), in which Councillor Bowdoin had been tagged as a dissident to the ministry in London, made a Boston hero of him. In

25. Brunswick, Me., Bowdoin College, Hawthorne-Longfellow Library, Bowdoin Family Papers, MS letter (no. 20), William Erving to James Bowdoin II, Scituate, 27 Oct. 1755.

26. Franklin, *Papers* 19:411–12, Franklin to Thomas Cushing, London, 2 Dec. 1772, transmitting "Part of a Correspondence" that had "fallen into" his hands.

June of 1773 he was named to a committee of the Council charged with examining the perfidious correspondence; and the committee concluded that both Hutchinson and Oliver should be summarily removed as advocates of harsh and unjustified British policies—the dispatch of royal troops to Boston and the king's refusal to redress the colony's grievances.

Even after two centuries, the mystery has not been unwrapped from the deeds and motives of the principal actors in the drama. After Thomas Whately's death, Temple, who was related to Grenville and friendly with the Whatelys, apparently had been allowed by William, a banker, to inspect his brother's papers, in which, among other subjects, Temple's conduct had been discussed. It was widely supposed that, during a visit in October of 1772, Temple had stealthily removed a considerable portion of the documents and turned them over to Franklin, and as a consequence suspicion of impropriety fell on both Whately and Temple. Since denials by Whately that anyone except Temple had had access to the papers and assurances by Temple that he had withdrawn only letters he himself had written were mutually inconsistent and left both men with tarnished reputations, they sought to establish their innocence—or at least to assert it—through the ordeal by firearms. On 11 December 1773, they fought a tragicomic duel that was as indecisive in its outcome as other aspects of the case. After a false start with pistols fired into the air, the reluctant combatants resorted to swords. Temple was hard of hearing; when his opponent's plea for surrender literally fell on deaf ears, Temple pressed the attack and wounded him.

At this juncture, when rumors were rife that the duel would be resumed as soon as Whately recovered, Franklin broke his silence, exonerated the two men, and took the blame on himself, saying the letters had never been in William Whately's possession and therefore Temple could not have seized them during his October visit. Franklin left open, of course, the possibility that Temple had procured them at another time and place, or had informed Franklin how he might himself gain possession of them. Later Temple, to prove his sympathy for the American cause, was at great pains to advertise his role in spiriting the papers out of England and across the seas. Franklin's excuse, his intention to show the Massachusetts leaders that their fellow-Americans, royal administrators to be sure, were more careless of colonial interests than were the king's ministers, was unconvincing. At a meeting of the Privy Council he was publicly denounced as a thief and a blackguard, and was stripped of the office of postmaster in America.[27]

---

27. For a full discussion of the affair, see Franklin, *Papers* 19:402–04; 20:513–15; Bernard Bailyn, *The Ordeal of Thomas Hutchinson* (Cambridge, Mass.: Harvard University Press, 1974), 225–38; Ronald Clark, *Benjamin Franklin. A Biography* (New York: Random House, 1983), 224–50. Esmond Wright, *Franklin of Philadelphia* (Cambridge, Mass.: Belknap Press of Harvard University Press, 1986), 224–28; MHS, *Proceedings* 104: 123–47, "The Missing Temple-Whately Papers," ed. Neil R. Stout.

Upon Franklin's dismissal, Bowdoin in the fall of 1774 sent him a vigorous denunciation of the British government and an account of the angry solidarity it had generated among the colonies: "The Several Acts of Parliament relative to this Town and Province will instamp eternal infamy on the present Administration, and tis probable that they themselves will soon See the beginning of it. The Spirit those Acts have raised throughout the Colonies is surprising. It was not propagated from Colony to Colony, but burst forth in all of them spontaneously as soon as the Acts were known, and there is reason to hope it will be productive of a union that will work out the Salvation of the whole."[28] Bowdoin was by this time wholly committed to united colonial action. After noting that his wife's ill-health had prevented him from attending the Congress at Philadelphia to which he had been elected, for a fleeting moment he resumed with Franklin the manner of more tranquil times (they were, after all, philosophers): "I am glad to understand your Retirement is not displeasing to you. In one view of it I am sure it will not be displeasing to the friends of Science: as it will give you a further opportunity of exerting your happy Genius in the walks of Philosophy."[29]

But for the most part the tone of Olympian detachment in the correspondence between Bowdoin and Franklin had given way to one of passionate concern, as relations between the colonies and the Crown reached a breaking point. Philosophical interests were temporarily eclipsed by political matters of the greatest moment, and a stormy decade was to elapse before Franklin would be liberated from his responsibilities as an American official. His wrath had been fired by the scurrilous attack upon him before the Privy Council. Once the advocate of prudence, he now hoped the Massachusetts assembly would pass strongly worded resolutions in retaliation for the hostile acts of the British. On 25 February 1775, he wrote Bowdoin that he had published a part of his letter of 6 September, and he urged the continuation of the non-consumption agreement with respect to British goods, perhaps with compensation to traders who might be injured by it. Franklin had begun to talk the language of open rebellion: "The Eyes of all Christendom are now upon us, and our Honour as a People is become a Matter of the utmost Consequence to be taken Care of. If we tamely give up our rights in this Contest, a Century to come will not restore us in the Opinion of the World. We shall be stamp'd with the Character of Dastards and Poltroons, and Fools, and be despis'd and trampled upon, not by this haughty insolent Nation only, but by all

---

28. Franklin, *Papers* 21, ed. W. B. Willcox (1978), 282, Bowdoin to Franklin, 6 Sept. 1774.

29. Ibid., 284. In a postscript Bowdoin expressed perplexity that Temple was dismissed from his post as surveyor-general of customs, unless it was because of his role in sending to America the "infamous Letters of certain persons," which should have been excluded by Franklin's publicly taking upon himself "that most meritorious Act."

Mankind."[30] Franklin and Bowdoin, already warm friends in the fifties and sixties, were drawn even closer by their commitment to the colonial cause. Whenever Franklin turned up in Boston on a mission for the Continental Congress, he was welcomed at Bowdoin's home. And during the Revolution, Bowdoin and his pastor, Samuel Cooper, would concert with Washington and Franklin at breakfast or dinner over measures to be adopted for prosecuting the war in New England.[31]

In the early seventies, members of the Bowdoin family, especially Elizabeth Temple, were worried that the British would confiscate the goods and properties of those who were "high." On 15 September 1774, two days after his name appeared on a list of patriots circulated among British troops and later published in the *Boston Gazette*, Bowdoin had an inventory made of all the possessions in his Beacon Hill mansion. John Pitts, a fellow Huguenot and Bowdoin's nephew, expressed fear in a letter of 16 October that even the personal safety of the patriots was in jeopardy: they might be apprehended and shipped to England for trial.[32] The Erving-Bowdoin-Pitts-Temple families, all interrelated, were in danger, or so they believed. In 1774–75, when the prominent citizens of Massachusetts stood at the parting of the ways, many of them experienced a bewildering ambivalence about their next course of action that aggravated psychic and physical indispositions.

The severity of Bowdoin's illness in the mid-seventies is attested by matter-of-fact entries in the diary of Samuel Cooper. In May of 1775, with General Burgoyne in occupation of his Beacon Hill mansion, Bowdoin had fled to Dorchester, where his disease was seriously exacerbated. Samuel Cooper's diary charted the onset of the attack and its remission: "May 17. Visited Mr Bowdoin at Mrs Bowman's of Dorchester. found him extremely low with a Lung Fever. He had met with gt

---

30. Ibid., 507, Franklin to Bowdoin, London, 25 Feb. 1775. A year earlier Temple had written to Bowdoin in the same vein: "Prudent, yet manly and resolute Conduct on your parts is what will Carry you through. The Eyes of all Europe are watchfully on you, and will not suffer Tyranny to prevail against you, but their must be firm spirit on your parts." (ibid., 118, Temple to Bowdoin, London, 20 Feb. 1774).

31. See Franklin, *Papers* 22:225–41, Minutes of Conference held at Washington's Headquarters, Cambridge, 18–24 Oct. 1775; ibid., 387, Cooper to Franklin, Boston, 21 Mar. 1776; San Marino, Cal., Huntington Library, Diary of Samuel Cooper, April 19, 1775–May 17, 1776 (MS), entries for 17, 26 Oct. 1775; Frederick Tuckerman, ed., "Letters of Samuel Cooper to Thomas Pownall, 1769–1777," *American Historical Review* 8 (1902, 1903), 301–30.

32. MHS, Bowdoin and Temple Papers, "Inventory of goods at present in the house of James Bowdoin Esqr . . . ," 15 Sept. 1774; ibid., John Pitts to ? , Boston, 16 Oct. 1774. See also MHS, Hutchinson-Watson papers, Jonathan Sewall to Elisha Hutchinson, Bristol, 25 Nov. 1780, hoping that Judge Oliver will once again be on the "Seat of Justice" in Massachusetts and will pass sentence on Bowdoin, Adams, and other "arch rebels & Traitors"; Mercy Warren, *History of the American Revolution* 1:213–14; and MHS, *Proceedings*, ser. 2.17 (1903), 295, Charles Chauncy to Richard Price, Medfield, 18 July 1775, on British orders to "seize our leading men."

Difficulty in getting out of Boston. The Admiral had refus'd a Pass to the Vessel he had provided for himself & some Necessaries to Elizabeth Island. I pray'd with him—went to Mrs Foyes at Milton. Met Mrs Jones; procur'd from her an easy Chair for Mr Bowdoin—Mrs Bowman having remov'd her own Furniture." A day later Cooper found his friend "a little reliev'd but still dangerous." By the end of September Bowdoin, now installed in Middleborough, was visibly improved. Cooper dined with him and rode out with him six miles in his chaise, and the convalescent gave thanks to the Almighty for his survival with a generous gift to His earthly minister: "He put into my hands at parting a Bill of six Pounds Lawful money, & a chicken & Bottle of Wine into our chaise."[33] Nevertheless, some months were to elapse before Bowdoin's health was restored. When Sam Adams congratulated him prematurely, writing with more affection than tact, "For my own part, I had even buried you, though I had not forgot you," Bowdoin replied on 9 December 1775 that he was a little better, but not yet entirely well.[34]

In June Bowdoin had repaired to Braintree, and thence to Middleborough, where he occupied the house formerly belonging to the Tory chief justice Peter Oliver. There he remained, except for interludes on revolutionary business in Watertown, Boston, and Cambridge, until October of 1778. After Abigail Adams visited him in Braintree in the summer of 1775 she reported that he looked "like a mere skeleton," unable to converse because of the severity of his cough.[35] His daughter, Elizabeth, imputed her father's illness to psychic causes, principally his dismay at the conduct of "the General," possibly an allusion to General Gage, governor of the colony until his recall in September 1775. Gage had broken his word that unarmed Bostonians would be allowed to leave the town with their goods and chattels, and Bowdoin was denied permission to depart with his heavily laden ship for the Elizabeth Islands, where he owned property. From London, where she was residing with her husband, Elizabeth wrote indignantly to her mother in September of 1775, marveling at her father's fortitude in the face of his vexations and, in a burst of patriotic fervor, hoping that he would be compensated for his sufferings by seeing America rise "glorious out of her calamities." In passing she alluded to the Loyalist sympathies of the two E—gs (doubtless her Erving uncles),

33. Huntington Library, Diary of Samuel Cooper, entries for 17, 18 May and 27, 28 Sept. 1775. Charles Akers, *The Divine Politician*, 428, notes that most of Cooper's diaries have been lost. The Huntington Library manuscript was published by Frederick Tuckerman in the *American Historical Review* 6 (1901), 301–41. The MHS also has a fragment with brief entries from 10 to 18 April 1775, longer journal entries for 10, 27, 30 April 1775, and scattered accounts for May to August of that same year.

34. MHS, *Proceedings* 12:226, Samuel Adams to Bowdoin, Philadelphia, 16 Nov. 1775; 12:227, Bowdoin to Adams, 9 Dec. 1775; see also ibid., ser. 2.8:289, Bowdoin to Thomas Cushing, 9 Dec. 1775.

35. Ibid., 59, excerpts from a letter of Abigail to John Adams, 15 June 1775.

regretting the part they had taken and warning that it would bring dishonor upon them in their own and all future generations. She worried — for naught — when she heard that her grandfather was walled up in Boston with nothing to sustain him but salt provisions.[36] The aged Captain Erving was made of sterner stuff: he refused to budge from his house during the entire occupation of Boston, and enjoyed the distinction of entertaining Washington at dinner when he entered the town upon the evacuation of the British troops.

By the close of 1775, along with the other Massachusetts leaders, Bowdoin turned into an advocate of the risky radical position. Though at first he had pleaded for conciliation, he came to support independence and open rebellion. Toward the end of 1772 he had already predicted the separation of the colonies from Great Britain as the natural consequence of the ministerial system operating in America. Three years later he sent an explicit — and moralizing — letter to Samuel Adams: "The Independence of America will probably grow out of the present dispute. . . . I perfectly agree with you, that we live in an important age; in which from the increased illumination of the human mind, we might have expected an enlargement of the Empire of Liberty; but luxury has taken so general a spread, has so far counteracted that illumination & destroyed the principle of virtue, that the ruling part of the [British] nation, to support that luxury have not disdained the ministerial bribe, but have in consideration of it bartered away their own & the national liberty, together with the liberty of America."[37] By the end of March 1776 he concluded that the only solution to the untenable position of the colonies was to proclaim their separation from the mother country, before any negotiations with the British were undertaken.[38]

When Bowdoin's "disorder" recurred with great violence in 1775–76, he complained of pains in the chest and aching eyes.[39] Though he could not himself serve in the Continental Congress, his estimate of its members was generally favorable: they had good sense, historical knowledge, and integrity.[40] A similar view of the Massachusetts delegation was not consistently maintained when he recuperated from his attack and returned to political action. Not that he was ever distant from

36. MHS, Bowdoin and Temple Papers, Elizabeth Temple to her mother, 6 Sept. 1775.

37. MHS, *Collections*, ser. 6.9 (Bowdoin and Temple Papers, 1), 302, Bowdoin to Temple, 2 Nov. 1772; MHS, *Proceedings* 12:228, Bowdoin to Samuel Adams, 9 Dec. 1775.

38. MHS, *Collections*, ser. 6.9 (Bowdoin and Temple Papers, 1), 399, Bowdoin to Mercy Warren, Middleborough, 23 Mar. 1776; also ibid. 72 (Warren-Adams Letters, 1), 215.

39. Ibid., ser. 6.9 (Bowdoin and Temple Papers, 1), 392, Bowdoin to Josiah Quincy, Middleborough, 16 Dec. 1775, and Josiah Quincy, *Memoir of Josiah Quincy Jun.*, appendix, 484–87, Bowdoin to Josiah Quincy, Middleborough, 29 Jan. 1776.

40. MHS, *Collections*, ser. 6.9 (Bowdoin and Temple Papers, 1), 398, Bowdoin to Mercy Warren, 23 Mar. 1776.

the conduct of the Revolutionary War. General officers and friends who held less exalted positions sent him circumstantial reports on military setbacks and on victories, often in the midst of battle. His analyses of the changing situation of the American states were always clear-headed and incisive, and he did not hesitate to intervene from his sickbed. Even during his "exile" in Middleborough, he continued to receive intelligence from the delegates in Philadelphia, and to proffer advice both military and economic.

In the spring of 1776, when John Adams and James Warren of Plymouth, the lawyer and the gentleman farmer, consulted with each other about who would be an appropriate choice for the governorship of an independent Massachusetts, they agreed on Bowdoin after a clinical examination of his health and character. They were intent on preventing the rise of factions, that plague of the ancient Roman Republic and contemporary British politics; the choice had to be unanimous, and they were prepared to select the unanimous candidate. On 12 May Adams wrote from Philadelphia:

> Bowdoin's Splendid fortune would be a great Advantage at the Beginning. How are his Nerves and his Heart? If they will do, his Head and Fortune ought to decide in his favour.

> The Office of Governor of the Massachusetts Bay Surrounded as it will be with Difficulties, Perplexities and Dangers of every Kind, and on every Side, will require the clearest and coolest Head and the firmest Steadyest Heart, the most immoveable Temper and the profoundest Judgment, which you can find any where in the Province. He ought to have a Fortune too, and extensive Connections. I hope that Mr. Bowdoins Health is such, that he will do.[41]

James Warren's reply from Watertown was less enthusiastic, even somewhat barbed, but generally favorable: "The nerves of one of the gentlemen you mention are weak, owing perhaps to his state of health. His heart, I believe, is good, tho' not so decisively zealous as I could wish, perhaps owing to his splendid fortune. His head is undoubtedly good."[42] When Bowdoin once again was forced to withdraw from public life in May of 1777 because of his pulmonary disease —he clung to his post on the Board of War for months, transmitting his wishes through his son —Adams was obliged to drop his premature advocacy. But under no circumstances would he support Hancock, an "Idol in the Chair that I cannot and will not worship."[43]

---

41. Ibid., 72 (Warren-Adams Letters, 1), 243, John Adams to James Warren, Philadelphia, 12 May 1776.

42. Ibid., 253, James Warren to John Adams, Watertown, 2 June 1776.

43. Ibid., 340, Adams to James Warren, Philadelphia, 7 July 1777.

In July 1776 James Bowdoin was at the zenith of his revolutionary career. Though once again beginning to have intimations of illness, with the Adams cousins and Hancock engaged in Philadelphia, Bowdoin assumed the public role of revolutionary leader of Massachusetts. While not actually designated head of government, he was recognized as "first member" of a council of twenty-eight that, aided by a house of representatives, was charged with handling the business of government on an interim basis until a constitution could be adopted and put into effect. In this capacity Bowdoin operated as the state's chief executive, especially in the conduct of two affairs that highlighted his position.

The first was a protracted conference, from 10 through 19 July, with delegates of the Saint John's and Micmac Indians of Nova Scotia, during which he recounted examples of British perfidy in language fashioned to appeal to his hearers:

> You have heard that the English people beyond the great water have taken up the Hatchet, and made war against the English united Colonies in America. We once looked upon them as our Brothers, as Children of the same Family with ourselves, and not only loved them as Brothers, but loved and respected them as our older Brothers. But they have grown Old and Covetous: many of their great men have wasted and squandered not only their own money, but the money of the public; and because they cannot obtain in their own country a sufficiency to support the excessive luxury and satiate their avarice they want to take from us our money and our lands for those purposes; and at the same time to deprive us of our Liberties and make us Slaves.[44]

Bowdoin's rhetoric, attuned to the special audience, to be sure, emphasizes the sincerity of his convictions and the bitterness of his resentment against the Crown and its officers.

The second event over which Bowdoin presided took place on 21 July, when the Declaration of Independence was formally celebrated at the State House in Boston. The ceremonies, which included reading the Declaration, firing cannon, and burning symbolic vestiges of the British Crown, were climaxed by Bowdoin's oration hailing the downfall of tyranny, a speech that Abigail Adams praised in glowing terms to her husband. While the conference with the Indians was still in session, its proceedings had been dramatically interrupted by stirring news from Philadelphia that Bowdoin straightway conveyed to the delegates: the Great Council of the Representatives of the United States of America had issued a declaration of independence from Great Britain and proclaimed the former colonies free and independent states. A copy of the full document was exhibited and patiently interpreted by John Prince. Before extending to the Indians a treaty of alliance and friendship, Bowdoin set forth graphically the great might of the newly

44. Archives of the Commonwealth: Archives of Massachusetts, 29:502–29.

born union: "The United States now form a long and strong Chaine; and it is made longer and stronger by our Brethren of the St. John's and Mickmac Tribes joining with us; and may Almighty God never suffer this Chain to be broken."[45] A formal treaty concluded between the governors of the State of Massachusetts Bay and the delegates of the Saint John's and Micmac tribes was signed by members of the Council, Bowdoin's name heading the list.

Feeble attempts to rouse the English Nova Scotians, who included former New Englanders, against the Crown, came to nothing. In the course of time a copy of the treaty with the Micmacs found its way into the hands of the British Foreign Office, but the elaborate military accord was never implemented. Shortly after the conference, Bowdoin was again stricken with a severe pulmonary attack that kept him from the Council chamber, and he virtually vanished from the political scene until the late 1770s. His intermittent bouts of illness made it impossible for him to assume active command of the Massachusetts regiments and in crucial years of the Revolutionary War he was not often in the public eye — a circumstance that gave rise to malicious and damaging rumors about his lack of enthusiasm for the revolutionary cause. Though among Mrs. Bowdoin's family there were some Loyalists, charges in the 1780s that Bowdoin had favored the enemy were slanderous propaganda from the Hancock-Sullivan political machine. The mere fact of Bowdoin's absence from the Continental Congress to which he had been elected and his replacement on the Massachusetts delegation by Hancock fostered these suspicions. The correspondence of the revolutionary period, however, makes it abundantly evident that the great patriot leaders trusted Bowdoin, relied on him, and made him privy to the most secret events of war and peace.[46] When Washington was angry and distressed that Massachusetts men were avoiding army service by hiring as replacements British deserters, who promptly abandoned the Continental army, too, he sought Bowdoin's help in suppressing the "pernicious practice." And Bowdoin was responsive to his constant appeals for money, ammunition, salt provisions, meat, and clothing for his ragged, famished soldiers. On 15 May 1780 Washington wrote Bowdoin in

45. Ibid.

46. Between 18 and 24 October 1775, the Committee of the Continental Congress, composed of Franklin, Thomas Lynch, and Benjamin Harrison, and representatives of Connecticut, Rhode Island, New Hampshire, and a Committee of Council of Massachusetts Bay headed by James Bowdoin met with Washington at Cambridge to examine the conduct of the war in New England. Problems of supply and the discipline of the new army (which involved the right to administer up to thirty-nine lashes) were resolved; Franklin, *Papers* 22:225–41, minutes of conference. For Bowdoin's role in maintaining and providing for the army and in transmitting intelligence, see also Washington, *Writings* 4 (1931), 22, n. 30, Washington to the president of Congress, Cambridge, 12 Oct. 1775; 5 (1932), 403, idem, New York, 8 Aug. 1776; 6 (1932), 312, Washington to Major Gen. Charles Lee, Brunswick, 29 Nov. 1776.

the strictest confidence, requesting intelligence on British military preparations in Halifax, which the French contemplated attacking as a principal source of supply for the enemy's fleet. Within a fortnight Bowdoin replied with full information on fortifications and a map of Halifax Harbor, for which Washington warmly thanked him: "The plan and table of reference are very intelligible and satisfactory, and convey a clear idea of many points, about which I was uninformed before."[47] Though he was a cautious man, Bowdoin's revolutionary credentials were impeccable.

The Temple Episode

In the fall of 1778 Bowdoin began to sound like himself again. On 12 October he wrote his son, James, announcing his impending return and the shipment of three loads of furniture to Boston if the British did not attack; on that point he requested nothing less than authoritative information from General Heath himself. With an eye to his homecoming, he gave James detailed instructions covering everything from the price of carting oats from Middleborough to Boston to ordering wood for the house. In passing, he expressed satisfaction at the arrival of one of his ships and made inquiry about another. And he requested that coach horses and chariot be secured for his son-in-law, John Temple, who had returned to America on a mission that Bowdoin imagined might hold the promise of peace with independence. At the beginning of the new year, his "grumbletonian" friend Samuel Dexter, in a querulous letter about the failings of his compatriots and his devastating financial losses, could at least take pleasure in the restoration of Bowdoin's health.[48]

The clumsy efforts of John Temple to mitigate the harshness of British policy and effect a reconciliation of sorts brought him disgrace in England and aroused suspicion among American patriots and their French allies. Claude Blanchard, Rochambeau's quartermaster, though pleased to be served tea by Bowdoin's daughter, "a very pretty woman," in his diary dismisses her husband as a Tory and an enemy of the Revolution, and Ezra Stiles branded him a political hypocrite.[49] Temple's status at this point, like his involvement in the publication of the Hutchinson-Oliver letters, is still beclouded. During the war his movements back and forth across the Atlantic in an abortive attempt at mediation, with the approval of the British ministry, resulted in charges that he acted as a British spy. Lord North had acquiesced in the

47. Ibid., 11 (1934), 98–99, Washington to Bowdoin, Valley Forge, 17 Mar. 1778, and 180–81 (31 Mar. 1778); 18 (1937), 366–67, Washington to Bowdoin, Morristown, 15 May 1780; see also 361–62, Washington to Major General William Heath, Morristown, 15 May 1780, and 19 (1937), 8–10, Washington to Bowdoin, Springfield, N.J., 14 June 1780.

48. MHS, Bowdoin and Temple Papers, Bowdoin to James III, Middleborough, 12 Oct. 1778; MHS, *Proceedings* 6 (1862, 1863), 360, Samuel Dexter to Bowdoin, Woodstock, 26 Jan. 1779.

49. Blanchard, *Guerre d'Amérique*, 41–42; Ezra Stiles, *Literary Diary* 3:90.

mission with misgivings, as the Temple papers show, and no written instructions had been issued despite John Temple's repeated requests, but the Admiralty had been told to facilitate his passage and he traveled in comfort. Bowdoin defended his son-in-law as a man of honorable principles devoted to the American cause. And in fact, as was generally known, he had been dismissed from his post as surveyor-general of customs in early 1774 because of his complicity in obtaining the Hutchinson-Oliver correspondence for the Boston patriots, even though Benjamin Franklin had publicly taken upon himself the entire blame for the venture.

On 21 September 1778, Bowdoin drafted a letter to his friend Samuel Adams that was level-headed and coolly analytical. After regrets that a severe attack of his old disorder had prevented him from complying with Temple's request to meet the family upon their arrival at Philadelphia (was he also apprehensive that public intimacy with Temple at that point might have been too compromising?), Bowdoin expressed cautious support of the Temple mission. He reasoned on two alternative assumptions: either Temple was in the employ of the British ministry, or he was back in America in a private capacity to settle his family. In any case, Bowdoin believed, it would be prudent for some members of Congress to see him informally. If Temple was in America for personal reasons, he might provide information useful to the United States. If he had been sent to effect a reconciliation, and could do so in a manner consistent with principles of honor, he would "doubtless be glad to have an opportunity for it; and as I think he wd act an open, candid part, a meer conversation with him by some of ye members of Congress in their private capacity might be productive of some good, & possibly bring on a treaty, wch might end in a solid peace, founded on the independence of America, and the mutual interests of both Countries."[50] Bowdoin was himself not averse to negotiating with Britain at this point, especially in the light of a new danger of attack on Boston by land and sea, though his letter is silent on this threat.

Since a request for a hearing sent directly by Temple to the Continental Congress had already been refused on grounds of suspected espionage, Samuel Adams had advised on 3 September that he establish his credentials in Boston before renewing his efforts with the Congress. This was Bowdoin territory, and on 3 November 1778, after removing there with his family, Temple received a passport to go from Boston to Philadelphia, "He having exerted himself greatly in the American Cause, and suffered much in opposing British Tyranny." This certificate of civism granted to a suspect well antedated the French Revolutionary procedure. The document was attested by John Avery, deputy secretary of the Council, and Major General John Sullivan signed the pass in Providence. From the Massachusetts Council Temple also received a recommendation that he be allowed to pay his respects to the Congress.

---

50. MHS, *Collections*, ser. 6.9 (Bowdoin and Temple Papers, 1), 425–26, Bowdoin to Samuel Adams, Middleborough, 21 Sept. 1778.

While Temple was en route to Philadelphia and his family was in Boston, Bowdoin on 7 November wrote again to Samuel Adams, proposing in effect to use his son-in-law as a double agent. Bowdoin shrewdly calculated that if Temple were sent back to England, he would give an authentic account of American vigor and determination to continue the war, and thus strengthen the hand of those in Britain prepared to grant independence as the price for ending a conflict their financial condition could no longer support. Apparently rumors — not wholly without foundation — were circulating in England that the "people of America in general" were tired of the war, disappointed with Congress's rejection of the British commissioners formally dispatched to America, and alarmed by the rapid depreciation of the paper currency.[51] By counteracting these reports (which had appeared in New York newspapers) Temple would serve his native country. Bowdoin openly sought Sam Adams's assistance for his beloved daughter's husband: "Your knowledge of mankind and of Mr Temple in particular enables you to determine . . . whether his being in England at ye time of the approaching session of Parliament might not be of advantage to the American cause. If I did not think so, I should not intimate such a thing to you. But however that may be I have no reason to doubt your knowledge of his character will procure him the happiness of your friendship."[52]

The innocent and discreet backing that he gave Temple redounded to Bowdoin's disadvantage when Hancock's men distorted and exploited what little was known of Temple's activities, in order to tar Bowdoin with the brush of pro-British sympathies. Even Lafayette, with whom Bowdoin was on excellent terms, made adverse comments on the involvement.[53] Bowdoin was pilloried for the Temple connection both by Tories such as Governor Hutchinson, who accused Temple of favoring the colonials, and, on the other side, by populist Hancock supporters who regarded Temple as a British agent. Bowdoin's allegiance was too well established, however, for the charges to be taken seriously by Washington, Franklin, Sam Adams, and other congressional leaders, whose confidence in him was unimpaired. Washington himself in November of 1778 furnished Temple with a letter of introduction to the president of the Continental Congress in which, on the strength of recommendations from Bowdoin and others, he called Temple a "Gentleman of

51. See, for example, ibid., ser. 6.4 (Belknap Papers, 3 [1891]), 177–78, John Eliot to Jeremy Belknap, Boston, 29 Mar. 1780.

52. Ibid., ser. 6.9 (Bowdoin and Temple Papers, 1), 430–31, Bowdoin to Samuel Adams, 7 Nov. 1778. A letter of 7 May 1779, from Temple to General Horatio Gates repeats almost verbatim Bowdoin's letter to Adams. Temple would on his return to England report on America's determination, especially to Englishmen at the German spas, to which he meant to repair as soon as he landed in Holland (ibid., 433).

53. Louis R. Gottschalk, *Lafayette and the Close of the American Revolution* (Chicago: University of Chicago Press, 1942), 344.

sense and merit and of warm attachment to the rights of his Country, for which he appears to have suffered greatly in the present contest."[54]

Nothing came of the Temple mission and of Bowdoin's scheme to turn it to America's advantage. But Temple was allowed to depart in May 1779, making another Atlantic crossing in the middle of the war, and carrying to Lord North the message that the Americans were determined never again to place themselves under the government of the British Crown. A tenacious and persistent man, Temple visited again in October of 1781, with no more fruitful outcome. Though Washington, Franklin, and others were persuaded of his devotion to the American cause, his enemies were numerous and powerful. He had encountered difficulties in leaving England the previous spring, and was well aware of the hostile reception awaiting him when he reached the opposite shore. On 26 July 1781, he wrote to Benjamin Franklin from Amsterdam requesting a testimonial about his part in obtaining the Hutchinson-Oliver letters, and lamenting the "series of trouble & mortification I have had . . . the sacrifices I have made, the losses & persecution I have sustained" because of friendship for America. He denied any secret connection with the English ministry, and, deploring the calumnies on both sides of the water, asked in exasperation, "Do not our affairs begin to wear a Complexion something like the famous Salem *Wichcraft*?"[55] —an analogy certain to have an appeal to the freethinking Franklin. John Hancock, now governor of Massachusetts and no friend to Bowdoin and his relatives, exacted from Temple a bond of £3,000 sterling in December of 1781, on grounds that he had entered the United States without authorization. Despite Temple's repeated protests, the bond was not discharged until after the Treaty of Paris was signed.[56] Temple had to refute recurrent rumors that he was working to destroy the alliance between France and the United States, while Hancock's retainer James Sullivan was "baiting poor Temple, as tho' he was a British Spy."[57]

54. MHS, *Collections*, ser. 6.9 (Bowdoin and Temple Papers, 1), 427, Bowdoin to Washington, 7 Nov. 1778; Washington, *Writings* 13 (1936), 309, Washington to the president of Congress, Fredericksburg, 23 Nov. 1778.

55. Washington, D.C., Library of Congress: Franklin Papers, Temple to Franklin, Amsterdam, 26 July 1781. A rough draft of the letter, with significant variants, was published in MHS, *Collections*, ser. 6.9 (Bowdoin and Temple Papers, 1), 456–63. Temple was appointed consul general in February 1785, but the appointment was not recognized by Congress until the following December; see John Adams, *Diary and Autobiography* 3:174, n. 2.

56. MHS, *Collections*, ser. 7.6 (Bowdoin and Temple Papers, 2), 6, Temple to John Hancock, Boston, 13 Sept. 1783; 10–12, Temple to Tristram Dalton, Boston, 20 Oct. 1783; 12–21, Resolves of the General Court.

57. W. C. Ford, ed., "Letters of the Reverend William Gordon," loc. cit., 470, 477, Gordon to John Adams, Jamaica Plain, 7 Sept. and 30 Nov. 1782; Richard Henry Lee, *Life of Arthur Lee* (Boston, 1829), 2:288, Gordon to Lee, Jamaica Plain, 2 Oct. 1782; MHS, *Collections* 75 (Broadsides, Ballads, &c), 323, no. 2344.

In December 1784, with peace restored, Temple and his family embarked for England, where he shortly succeeded to a baronetcy. But in less than a year and a half, accompanied by Lady Elizabeth, he returned to America and settled in style in New York as His Majesty's Resident and Consul General—an appointment that perhaps throws light on the complexity of his feelings during the Revolutionary War. When John Adams, still in France, heard of Temple's elevation, he sent off a letter to James Warren that was a keen, if not altogether kindly, estimate of the British consul-elect: his personal charm, courtly manners, and thorough knowledge of American commerce had to be balanced against his lack of prudence, confused conceptions of public opinion, ignorance of the wellsprings of political action, and penchant for stormy disputes. Adams understood Temple's wartime ambivalence as a native American attached to his country and as a royal official; but he suggested that Warren, who had defended Temple when he was being hounded by Massachusetts politicians, advise him on how to comport himself in his new position, especially with respect to avoiding equivocal conduct. "He is now an Englishman, and a servant of his King. let him then make no Pretensions as an American, because they will not be admitted and will only expose him."[58]

The Adams Cousins

More than a quarter of a century later, when the events of the revolutionary era hardened into stereotyped tableaux—many of which, like the collective signing of the Declaration of Independence, had never been acted out in reality—John Adams undertook to re-arrange the characters and their respective parts. In one of his autobiographical fragments, he delineated with bold strokes the temper of the outstanding Boston patriots at a critical period of the Revolution, in 1775. Carried away by the vividness of his descriptions, one forgets momentarily that his reflections were those of an old man recording what he remembered of his feelings and observations decades earlier. Adams re-created a small circumscribed world of revolutionaries linked by strong emotional ties—the Boston patriots. Inaccurate in detail and manifestly self-serving, the portrait nonetheless conveys profound psychological truths. Adams evoked the suspicion, fear, and hostility in which the patriots lived and worked. If the autobiography is read for factual information, it is a field mined with booby-traps; but as a picture of the mutual antipathy and apprehensiveness of the Massachusetts patriots, it attains a heightened reality. Adams painted himself as alert to the slightest change of attitude among his fellow insurgents. An alteration in the visage of an actor in the political drama

58. Ibid. 73 (Warren-Adams Letters, 2 [1925]), 250–51, John Adams to James Warren, Auteuil, 26 Apr. 1785. See also a similarly worded letter to Elbridge Gerry, 4 Oct. 1785 (ibid., 264).

was interpreted, often overinterpreted, as the outward sign of an inner reversal of sentiment. Hawk-eyed, the patriots watched one another's faces.

In the course of rehearsing a scene in the Continental Congress, John Adams passed in review the major Massachusetts leaders. On 14 June 1775, or a day or two before, the editors of his autobiography surmise, Adams made a speech on the state of America before the Congress sitting as a committee of the whole. In this account he appears as the astute manipulator of that august but indecisive body. His alone was the spark capable of animating the otherwise inert mass. He had prepared the way for his impending action by taking his cousin Samuel Adams for a walk and confiding his intentions: "I am determined this Morning to make a direct Motion that Congress should adopt the Army before Boston and appoint Colonel George Washington Commander of it." Samuel Adams was noncommittal. As John Adams addressed the Congress about the parlous state of the colonies and began to refer indirectly to the gentleman from Virginia whose excellent character recommended him for the supreme post, he saw Washington, with his usual modesty, dart out of the chamber and into the library. Adams, still orating and watching, then focused his eyes on Hancock, who was in the Chair. So long as he dwelt on general conditions in the land, Adams recalled in his imaginative reconstruction of the past, Hancock listened with "visible pleasure." Then, abruptly, his face was transformed. ". . . When I came to describe Washington for the Commander, I never remarked a more sudden and sinking Change of Countenance. Mortification and resentment were expressed as forcibly as his Face could exhibit them. Mr. Samuel Adams Seconded the Motion, and that did not soften the Presidents Phisiognomy at all."[59]

Adams had not read Lavater, but he fancied himself no mean physiognomist: in a remarkable feat of memory, a quarter of a century later he claimed to have discovered in Hancock's features evidence of a sharp change of feeling while the business of appointing a commander-in-chief was discussed. Adams fashioned a system out of the fleeting emotions of his friends, the kind of structure-building that is often characteristic of a paranoid. He pinned down his nomination of Washington as the immediate cause of a breach with Hancock. Everything in their future dealings stemmed from this one act, as love turned to hate in the bosom of Hancock. The idea rooted itself so deeply in John Adams's mind that none of Hancock's later blandishments ever affected him. "Mr. Hancock however never loved me so well after this Event as he had done before, and he made me feel at times the Effects of his resentment and of his Jealousy in many Ways and at diverse times, as long as he lived, though at other times according to his variable feelings, he even overacted his part in professing his regard and respect to me."[60]

---

59. John Adams, *Diary and Autobiography* 3:322–23.

60. Ibid., 324. Adams quoted Samuel Cooper to the effect that Hancock felt so aggrieved "his friends had the utmost difficulty to appease him" (325).

That the rich merchant John Hancock, colonel of a regiment of Boston militia, whom he costumed in resplendent red uniforms and called out to parade on ceremonial occasions, should have fancied himself capable of leading the Continental army against the British staggers the imagination. If Hancock felt any pique at being passed over by the Continental Congress, it was not long-lived: in 1778 his newborn son was presented for baptism to the Reverend Samuel Cooper with the forenames John George Washington. And Adams himself speculated that Hancock may have coveted only the honor of being named commander-in-chief and had the intention of declining the post.[61] But the possibility of Hancock's ambitious illusion cannot be entirely excluded, nor can Adams's malicious delight in catching Hancock in a fantastic act of presumption be dismissed. This was the atmosphere in which the Boston patriots fought their way to victory. Whatever Hancock's subterranean resentment, Bowdoin, at least, welcomed the news of Washington's appointment with enthusiasm. He warmly praised him as a patriot and military leader, and thought it fortunate that he was a Virginian, as a closer bond might thus be forged between the southern and northern colonies.[62]

Adams's autobiographical fragment has a remarkable stream-of-consciousness flow, and recollection of the silent psychological interplay with Hancock was straightway associated in his reflective imagination with similar isolated events that had brought him into conflict with eminent Boston patriots. He digressed from the chronology of his recital to settle his account with another Massachusetts man, a favorite of the artisans, his cousin Samuel Adams (with whom he was sometimes confused by the French), an instance of friendliness superseded by jealousy and envy. If the testimony of Governor Hutchinson can be credited, John Adams's ambition was boundless, and "he could not look with complacency upon any man who was in possession of more wealth, more honours, or more knowledge than himself." Comparing the two cousins, the royal governor concluded that John Adams "may be said to have been of stronger resentment upon any real or supposed personal neglect or injury than the other." As with James Bowdoin, Hutchinson simplistically attributed John Adams's alignment with the patriots to his anger at Governor Bernard's failure to name him a justice of the peace.[63]

In recapitulating the wrongs dealt him by his old comrades, John Adams turned from Hancock to his cousin Samuel. "Many Years had not passed away before some Symptoms of it [jealousy] appeared in him, particularly when I was first chosen to go to Europe, a distinction that neither he nor Mr. Hancock could bear."[64] When

61. Ibid., 321.

62. MHS, *Proceedings*, ser. 2.8:289, Bowdoin to Thomas Cushing, 9 Dec. 1775.

63. Hutchinson, *History of Massachusetts Bay*, ed. Mayo, 3:213–14.

64. John Adams, *Diary and Autobiography* 3:324.

John Adams was sent to Paris as a representative of the new American government, he was teamed with Franklin, and there Adams's hatred and jealousy overflowed, as he was neglected and Franklin was worshiped by the French. "To be sure," Franklin wrote from Passy, "the excessive Respect shown me here by all Ranks of People, and the little notice taken of them [Adams and his son], was a mortifying Circumstance."[65] The impression grows that it was John Adams who was consumed with envy and projected his own emotions into others. He imagined that antagonists were always concealing their true sentiments. Samuel Adams, John believed, had disguised his envy under the pretense that his cousin could not be spared from the Congress and from the state.

The envy was exacerbated, John Adams claimed, when at Bowdoin's and Samuel Adams's behest, he had drawn up a constitution for Massachusetts and it was about to be reported in his handwriting to the Constitutional Convention (of which Bowdoin had been elected president when it met on 1 September 1779). For the normal functioning of the convention a committee of thirty had been selected, but the real work was left to a subcommittee composed of Bowdoin, Samuel Adams, and John Adams, who had returned from Europe a month before. John Hancock, gouty, had for the moment retired to the shadows. On the authority of John Adams himself, who declared that he was the "principal Engineer," he is credited with being the true author of the final document, and Charles Francis Adams published it among his grandfather's collected writings.[66] In his autobiography Adams charged that Samuel Adams never forgave him for his authorship of the draft, though Samuel and Bowdoin had themselves asked him to prepare it. After the coalition between Samuel Adams and Hancock in 1788, so runs the narrative, they defamed him: "these Gentlemen indulged their Jealousy so far as to cooperate in dissiminating Prejudices against me, as a Monarchy Man and a Friend to England, for which I hope they have been forgiven, in Heaven as I have constantly forgiven them on Earth, though they both knew the insinuations were groundless."[67] Such acidulous charges were common among the Boston politicians. The accuser was the soul of virtue, while all about him were hypocrites, dissemblers, liars, and falsifiers, the stock-in-trade of the self-proclaimed victim of persecution.

65. Franklin, *Writings*, ed. Smyth, 8:236–37, Franklin to William Carmichael, Passy, 12 Apr. 1781. A letter to Samuel Cooper from Passy, 26 December 1783, refers to Adams's "Calumnies" against Franklin (ibid., 9:146).

66. John Adams, *Diary and Autobiography* 2:401, n., Adams to Edmund Jenings, Paris, 7 June 1780; Adams, *Works*, ed. Charles Francis Adams, 4 (Boston, 1851), 213–67. Adams also told Richard Price that he had drawn up the plan of the Massachusetts constitution (MHS, *Proceedings*, ser. 2.17 [1903], 365, Adams to Price, London, 4 Feb. 1787). For a full discussion of Adams's authorship, see ibid. 13 (1873–75), 300–01.

67. Adams, *Diary and Autobiography* 3:324.

No manuscript text of the Massachusetts constitution has been found, but there is no reason to doubt that John Adams —the constitution-monger, as he dubbed himself —was responsible for the preliminary form of the document. All the same, it is difficult to envisage either Sam Adams or James Bowdoin as completely silent partners on a drafting committee; men of their intellectual calibre and forthright opinions are likely to have contributed in a significant manner to the final result. Some of the ideas and phraseology are standard Bowdoin formulations, found in his earlier writings; and his signature is affixed to a copy of the section on the encouragement of literature preserved among the papers of the Harvard Corporation.[68] Bowdoin was clearly the author of the *Address* that accompanied the draft of the constitution when it was submitted to the various towns of the Massachusetts Bay for their consideration and ratification. His justification of the religious and educational provisions is wholly in the Bowdoin spirit. It was Bowdoin who as president of the Constitutional Convention received praise for its achievements: a personal letter from George Washington extolled the balance of this new instrument of government and expressed the hope that it would become a model for other states since it appeared to "possess all the requisites towards securing the liberty and happiness of individuals, and at the same time giving energy to the administration."[69] Bowdoin never underestimated John Adams's part in the framing of the constitution and later wrote to him in Paris regretting his absence during the discussion of amendments: "I wish we could have had more of your assistance in compleating the plan of Government. Some of the alterations made in it after you left us were by no means for the better."[70]

The friendship between Bowdoin and Sam Adams was warm and constant. These two men, of grossly unequal financial status —one the heir to a great fortune, the other a maltster's son —had worked together since the days when, as respective leaders of the Council and the House, they had acted in concert against Governor Hutchinson. At first glance they seemed to operate at opposite ends of the revolutionary spectrum, Sam Adams among the artisans, Bowdoin among the rich merchants. But both were honest, reasonably self-revealed, religious men, somewhat inflexible in character, and they could be relied upon to hold to a course once it was set. The flamboyant John Hancock was not their type, and neither was John Adams, the self-tortured, self-deluded man who was devoured by envy. In middle life James Bowdoin had the reputation of being formal and stiff, a man of rectitude who tended to exhibit humorless self-righteousness. He was surely not

---

68. See Volz, *Governor Bowdoin & His Family*, 19-20; Harvard University Archives: Corporation Papers (MS), 1:5, 120.

69. Washington, *Writings* 18:298, Washington to Bowdoin, Morristown, 26 Apr. 1780.

70. MHS, Bowdoin and Temple Papers, Bowdoin to John Adams, 11 Jan. 1781.

one to curry popularity through the strategies that Hancock cultivated. Though Bowdoin stood up to the British governors and collaborated with other patriots from lower levels of society, it is hard to imagine his having direct personal contact with the likes of Mackintosh or delivering a rousing speech to electrify a boisterous audience in the Old South Church on the eve of the Boston Tea Party. He was wholeheartedly committed to the American cause, but he was the quiet gatherer of intelligence, the sage counselor, the skillful financial manipulator, not the revolutionary firebrand.

Bowdoin's assisting behind the scenes with secret funds was remembered by Sam Adams and revealed publicly when rumors were spread by the Hancock party that Bowdoin had been wanting in patriotic zeal. The Hancock henchman James Sullivan, in a sycophantic letter congratulating his patron on the gubernatorial victory of 1780, took occasion to impugn Bowdoin's revolutionary courage: "As I ever supposed your Excellency would have no Rival . . . my Surprize was beyond Description when I found that you had a Competitor for the Chief Magistracy; who in times of publick Danger feared to venture upon the Stage, and whose after Conduct seems rather to have proceeded from fortunate Successes on our Side, than from the Result of Choice and Deliberation."[71] When the letter was published a month later in the New York *Royal Gazette* of 18 December 1780, Sam Adams was incensed and rushed to Bowdoin's defense, summarizing his revolutionary career:

The Gentleman whom he [Sullivan] has attacked, was long before he paddled out of obscurity one of the Helmsmen of the Ship of the State; was marked by Bernard and Hutchinson as a Champion for American Liberty, was negatived by them repeatedly, by express Order of the British Ministry, when he had the full Voice of his Country for a Councillor; continued in the high Esteem of his fellow Citizens, till the Royal Government was dissolved by Common Consent, when the opportunity offerd, for him to take a Seat which had so long been prevented by the Governor. This he did, at Watertown, while the Enemy were in Boston. . . . He remained a Member of that Board, till every Body saw his Health was in so bad a State as no longer to allow of it. He therefore resigned his Seat; a Circumstance, which, though all judgd necessary, was regretted by all. He has since however sustained the honorable Place of President of that much revered Body who formed the constitution, and President of the Council of the State and he is at this time President of the American Society of Arts and Sciences in Massachusetts. How little are the Great Characters in this Revolution known, to those who were not the earliest in the virtuous Conflict![72]

71. MHS, *Collections* 73 (Warren-Adams Letters, 2), 161–62. The Sullivan letter, dated 18 November 1780, was enclosed in a letter from Samuel Adams, signed Aristides, to James Warren, Philadelphia, 1 January 1781.

72. Ibid., 163. See also James Warren's letter to his son Winslow, Boston, 3 June 1781, calling Sullivan's charge "not only ridiculous but contemptible" (MHS, Mercy Warren Papers).

Letters written by the wives and daughters of the patriots contain some of the most astute reflections on the personalities of the Boston leaders. The colonial women, though not as well educated as the ladies of the French salons and English drawing-rooms, watched their menfolk attentively and often developed acute psychological perceptiveness as they ruminated in the privacy of their homes with no outlet in the political arena. Their eyes penetrated through any outward composure to the weaknesses and vulnerable spots of their husbands and fathers and of the political enemies with whom they contended. Before they became estranged, John Adams himself had written to Mercy Warren, "You ladies are the most infallible judges of Character, I think."[73] And his wife, Abigail, though a model of devotion, had a telling way of teasing him. When she disliked his offhand response to a "list of female grievances" she had sent him in Philadelphia, with a proposal for laws to restrain the natural propensity of men to dominate their womenfolk, she threatened to foment a rebellion. To her friend Mercy she wrote that she had tested the disinterestedness of his virtue and found it wanting.[74] While the men resorted to acerb classical allusions in their correspondence, the women used a vitriol compounded of close and intimate observations. Bowdoin was esteemed as a philosopher and treated respectfully by the ladies, but he was too remote a figure to excite their enthusiasm; nevertheless they much preferred to see him, rather than the ostentatious Hancock, in public office. Of Hancock, Mercy Warren later wrote that his abilities were less impressive than his superficial accomplishments: "He scattered largesses without discretion, and purchased favors by the waste of wealth, until he reached the ultimatum of his wishes, which centered in the focus of popular applause."[75]

Psychic Scars of Rebellion

On the eve of the Revolution, Mrs. Mercy Warren's overheated prose illuminated the relations of Britain and America with a family analogy, a metaphor that reappeared often among the literate classes. It is also the key to the psychic ambivalence that accompanied colonial actions. "But tho' America stands armed with resolution & virtue, she still recoils at the thought of drawing the sword against the state from whence she derived her origin, tho' that state like an unnatural parent has plunged the dagger into the bosom of her offspring."

Mercy Warren conjured up a dreadful vision: "I behold the civil sword brandished over our heads & an innocent land drenched in blood. I see the inhabitants

---

73. MHS, *Collections* 72 (Warren-Adams Letters, 1), 201, John Adams to Mercy Warren, Braintree, 8 Jan. 1776.

74. Ibid., 235–36, Abigail Adams to Mercy Warren, Braintree, 27 Apr. 1776.

75. Mercy Warren, *History of the American Revolution* 1:212.

of our plundered cities quitting the elegancies of life, possessing nothing but their freedom—taking refuge in the forests—I behold faction & discord tearing up an Island we once held dear as our own inheritance and a mighty Empire long the dread of distant nations, tott'ring to the very foundation."[76]

The reality of the Revolution was perhaps less bloody than the awful reveries of Mrs. Warren; but beneath the surface of a relatively civilized war, a psychic battle raged in the bosoms of the patriots. In their relationships with one another, they were acting out an ancient drama that has continued to be rehearsed in the twentieth and twenty-first centuries in newly liberated nations achieving independence. But the eighteenth-century protagonists, symbolically leaping at one another with murderous intent, shed no blood in their fratricidal wars, an extraordinary circumstance that still arouses a measure of wonderment.

By the time the Battle of Lexington was fought, Boston patriots had become rebels with a price on their heads. The majority of those later chosen to be incorporated Fellows of the Academy were political activists. They either headed factions or were partisans of those who did. Leaders in a war for independence were joined in fear of retaliation for betrayal of their king, and at the same time were engaged in a covert contest with one another. As allies they were brothers bound by a sacred oath; as conspirators they were united in their resolve to destroy a sovereign father; but they were also rivals full of mistrust and resentment, for many years apprehensive that one of the brothers would defect and leave them in the lurch. There is a manifest tension in their relationships, a labile love-hate among brothers implicated in a heinous crime. All of them were vying for the headship they had deposed, and this entailed finding favor with the people, the formless mass they courted, despised, idealized, and diabolized in turn.

The interests of social classes, sometimes dichotomized as the "mob" and the "high ones"—at least in private—criss-crossed with ancient personal feuds, the memory of slights once administered, and the vengefulness born of a green-eyed goddess they called Envy or Jealousy. The stage on which the drama was enacted was a small one, and the protagonists understood one another's vices, if they overlooked their virtues. The resentment that consumed them had a complex etiology, but if one had to single out the psychologist who guided their thoughts onto set paths it was no mean knower of men, William Shakespeare —"that great Master of every Affection of the Heart and every Sentiment of the Mind as well as of all the Powers of Expression . . . ," Adams wrote in the *Diary*.[77] They read his works over and over again, and

---

76. MHS, Mercy Warren Papers, Mercy Warren to Mrs. Macaulay Graham, Plymouth, 29 Dec. 1774 (?). On the reliability of Mercy Warren's so-called Letter Book, see *Adams Family Correspondence* 1, ed. L. H. Butterfield (1963), 93–94, n. 1.

77. John Adams, *Diary and Autobiography* 2:53, entry for 9 Feb. 1772.

perceived through his eyes the heroes and villains of republican Rome, their ideal image for the newborn nation. Their world was populated with Iagos, Timons, Cassiuses, Brutuses, Richard IIIs, Coriolanuses, and Caesars, for even though Massachusetts law prohibited the performance of plays, the tragedies had been declaimed in Harvard clubs. For their more theological moments, there was always the subtle personality of Milton's Lucifer to serve as a model of evil. And the Roman historians, above all Tacitus, contributed their portion to any diagnosis of individual treachery. The patriots had inherited a formal literary psychology that fixed rules of interpretation for behavior as explicit as those of a modern scientific psychology.

Early in the century Cotton Mather had commented at length on the frequency of melancholy indispositions among even the pious in New England, "a country where *splenetic* maladies are prevailing and pernicious."[78] In Mather's *Magnalia Christi Americana* religious experience was already infiltrated with the scientific analogy: the time of Satan's reign over a man obeyed a law of deviltry and was finite; a physical disposition, an acerbic acid in a victim's blood, made him more susceptible to evil as demons readily insinuated themselves into the impaired organism. "There are many men, who in the very constitution of their *bodies*, do afford a *bed*, wherein busy and bloody *devils*, have a sort of a lodging provided for them. The *mass of blood* in them, is disordered with some fiery *acid*, and their *brains* or *bowels* have some juices or ferments, or vapours about them, which are most unhappy *engines* for *devils* to work upon their souls withal." For a critical but limited duration of time the devil would be given free rein, but once the hour of temptation had passed, by inexorable law he would be routed. The disease had run its course. It was "a *law* in the *invisible world* strictly kept unto, that if the *resistance* be carried on to such a period, though perhaps with many intervening foyle, the *devil* will be gone; yea, whether he will or no, he *must* be gone. There is a *law* for it, which obliges him to a *flight*, and a *flight* that carries a *fright* in it; a *fear* from an apprehension that God, with his *good angels*, will come in, with terrible chastisements upon him, if he presume to continue his *temptations* one moment longer, than the *time* that had been allowed unto him."[79]

Melancholy was the general term Mather had used to describe the anguish of the suicidal; the revolutionary sons of Mather's contemporaries had a more complex nosology of nervous and mental diseases.

It has been noticed before that an impressive number of the Massachusetts leaders were subject to intermittent physical and psychological disorders. Outbreaks occurred when they were faced with crucial decisions or when the republic was in mortal danger. At once wary of their fellow revolutionaries and dependent upon them for their very lives, some of the Boston patriots found temporary surcease from the anguish of

78. Cotton Mather, *Magnalia Christi Americana* 1:396.
79. Ibid., 396–97.

their dilemmas in illness. Others weathered the most harrowing political confrontations, even appeared for a time to thrive on them, and then collapsed shortly after a major crisis had been resolved. Many feigned sickness as a political instrument. Drawing the line between the refuge of a psychological breakdown with physical symptoms and an actual physical disability is often impossible. The tight group of Boston patriots got to know one another's weaknesses, subterfuges, even unconscious dodges, and frequently associated physical ill-health with psychological unease or anxiety. Constantly suspicious of one another's motives, they were quick to label a rival's physical ailment as malingering. A crippling attack of anxiety was sometimes called cowardice.

The clearest case of what today would be perceived as psychotic disorder was James Otis. He had lost his mental balance even before he was beaten up in the British Tavern; but he continued to be re-elected to office by the patriots through 1771, though his active role in politics was much diminished. Perhaps the most brilliant of the band, he died a lunatic, contemned and mocked by a new generation who had not known him in his prime. After Benjamin Guild, the empty-headed, gossipy Harvard tutor, encountered Otis at the home of Stephen Sewall, the first Hancock Professor of Hebrew and other Oriental Languages, he drew a brief sketch of the once celebrated patriot: "He now appears among the lowest ranks and whenever he can have an unrestrained access to his glass he appears perfectly delirious. He is a terror to the young and defenceless, and altho he discovers the ruins of a great mind; yet he is rather a nuisance than a benefit to society."[80] Sewall himself in 1785, at the age of fifty, was removed from his professorship because of "physical and mental debility."

John Adams has left in his letters the most circumstantial accounts of his own breakdowns; this master of introspection was even able to recognize the symptoms of an oncoming attack. His behavior was not sufficiently controlled to escape the notice of Benjamin Franklin, who, in a famous character sketch, touched with malice, that he sent to the president of the Congress, spelled out his concern over Adams's offensive conduct toward the French court.[81] At other times Franklin called his colleague a "mischievous madman," and though he conceded that Adams was always honest and often wise, in exasperation he declared him "absolutely out of his senses" on occasion.[82] In a letter of 21 November 1776 to her husband, Mercy Warren drew a convincing portrait of John Adams during one of his attacks of nerves: ". . . I can make allowances for a thousand neglects, apprehensions, & inconsistencies in

80. Harvard University Archives: Diary of Benjamin Guild, 1776, 1778 (MS), entry for 4 Dec. 1778.

81. Franklin, *Writings*, ed. Smyth, 8:126–28, Franklin to Samuel Huntington, Passy, 9 Aug. 1780.

82. On 7 March 1783, Franklin wrote Robert Morris, with clear reference to John Adams, "I hope the ravings of a certain mischievous madman here against France and its ministers, which I hear of every day, will not be regarded in America, so as to diminish in the least the happy union that has hitherto subsisted between the two nations" (ibid. 9:17). See also ibid., 62, Franklin to Robert R. Livingston, Passy, 22 July 1783.

a man whose nerves at times are a little touched: & the system rendered somewhat variable—we have seen him at times draw frightful pictures: we have seen him also wraped in silence —or breaking out into epithets of despair—and you have seen me laugh off his chagrin: and bring him back to a social companiable creature."[83]

It was in a period of frantic exasperation over his neglect by the Congress that Adams wrote a raving letter from The Hague to his longtime adversary Benjamin Franklin: "It is now near two years that I have led the life of a spider, after having led that of a toad under a harrow for four years before." He announced, almost threatened, that he would invade Franklin's domain of science and begin a course of experiments in physics or mechanics, of telescopic or microscopic observations: "Bertholon [Berthollet] and Spalanzini [Spallanzani] and Needham have so entertained me of late, that I think to devote myself to similar researches."[84] A clinician might observe that Adams was identifying with his putative aggressor. He too would be a scientific genius and win the plaudits of the world. Franklin apparently passed over the outburst in discreet silence.

Hancock vanished from the scene from time to time, covering his periods of nervous exhaustion with an official history of the gout, a respectable illness that was known to generate irascibility, providing an explanation for his violent outbursts. His attacks were probably real enough—a life of excessive drinking of heavy Madeira made him look like an old man by the time he was in his early fifties; but James Warren, not famed for his charitableness, wrote in the fall of 1785, after Hancock's candidate for governor of Massachusetts had been defeated, "H— has got the Gout; whether it is a political or natural fit, I dont know."[85] The Reverend Peter Thacher was free enough with Thomas Cushing to jest about the convenience of the gout whenever there were awkward political decisions to be evaded, though the onset of such ailments was not always easily regulated: "You are certainly one of the most fortunate men in the world. If there are any difficultys by your conduct in which you might forfeit your popularity, either a friendly fit of the gout or a journey on public affairs extricates you from them."[86] Samuel Cooper, Otis's Harvard classmate, died mad, tormented by suicidal fantasies.[87] The re-

83. MHS, Mercy Warren Papers, Mercy Warren to James Warren, Plymouth, 21 Nov. 1776.

84. Franklin, *Complete Works*, ed. John Bigelow, 9 (New York, 1888), 11, John Adams to Franklin, The Hague, 19 July 1784.

85. MHS, *Collections* 73 (Warren-Adams Letters, 2), 265, James Warren to Elbridge Gerry, Milton, 14 Oct. 1785.

86. MHS, Cushing Papers, Peter Thacher to Thomas Cushing, 15 Sept. 1786.

87. Akers (*The Divine Politician*, 355) maintains that Cooper died of some kind of viral infection of the nervous system, others claim that his addiction to Scotch snuff and a mental disorder were related to his death. The several causes to which his final illness has been attributed are not mutually exclusive. S. K. Lothrop (*A History of the Church in Brattle Street*, 117) with Victorian reticence states only that the malady "was of a nature which precluded much conversation."

vered science professor John Winthrop, during one of the convulsive fits to which he was subject, fell into the fire and scorched his leg so severely that he was for some time confined to his chamber.[88]

Organic and psychosomatic diseases at critical times were not limited to the colonial insurgents. Thomas Hutchinson, born a colonial and, as governor, bearing the burden of enforcing the royal acts that culminated in the Revolution, at one point took to his bed, where he lay stricken with paralysis, an affliction from which he recovered after a number of months; the symptoms are those of a classical case of male hysteria, though he may have had a minor stroke. Hutchinson himself remarked in letters that his friends linked his ailment to the mortification he suffered.[89] And Benjamin Rush of Philadelphia, patriot and pioneer psychiatrist, author of an "Account of the Influence of the Military and Political Events of the American Revolution upon the Human Body," was so impressed with the symptomatology of Tory sympathizers who had developed an obsessional concern for their persons and their most trivial possessions that he coined a name for their fixation, "Revolutiana."[90]

In the closed society of Massachusetts patriot philosophers who became founding fathers of the American Academy, a nexus of complicated interrelationships was formed. The hostility of Hancock and Bowdoin, the friendship of Bowdoin and Samuel Adams, the mutual respect of John Adams and Bowdoin were constants. Samuel and John Adams approached each other with alternate coolness and warmth, though at a nostalgic moment John could talk of their uninterrupted friendship of thirty years and insist that they were "not so far asunder in sentiment as some people pretend."[91] Samuel Cooper and Thomas Cushing accommodated themselves to virtually everybody's foibles, while James Warren tended to stand aloof and criticize all his associates with more or less asperity. Of course, after a fellow-patriot had long been dead, an aging enemy could regard him with generous benevolence. In 1817

88. On Winthrop, see Harvard University Archives: Diary of Benjamin Guild, 1776, 1778 (MS), final entry for December 1778.

89. Archives of the Commonwealth: Massachusetts Archives, 25:185, Hutchinson to Israel Mauduit, Boston, 6 June 1767 (MS draft); ibid. 26:276, Hutchinson to Richard Jackson, and 238, Hutchinson to William Bollan, Boston, 2 June 1767.

90. George Rosen, "Emotion and Sensibility in Ages of Anxiety: A Comparative Historical Review," *American Journal of Psychiatry* 124.6 (Dec. 1967), 774, quoting Benjamin Rush, "Account of the Influence of the Military and Political Events of the American Revolution upon the Human Body," in his *Medical Inquiries and Observations*, 2d American ed. (Philadelphia, 1794), 1:263–78.

91. John Adams, Samuel Adams, *Four Letters. Being an Interesting Correspondence between those Eminently Distinguished Characters, John Adams, Late President of the United States; and Samuel Adams, Late Governor of Massachusetts, on the Important Subject of Government* (Boston, 1802), 21, John Adams to Samuel Adams, New York, 18 Oct. 1790.

John Adams wrote of Hancock, "I can say with truth that I profoundly admired him, and more profoundly loved him. If he had vanity and caprice, so had I. . . . Nor were his talents or attainments inconsiderable. They were far superior to many who have been more celebrated. He had a great deal of political sagacity and penetration into men. He was by no means a contemptible scholar or orator. Compared with Washington, [Benjamin] Lincoln, or Knox, he was learned." Adams could not praise one fellow revolutionary without demeaning others. But he acknowledged that the War of Independence had been set in motion by three men — Otis, Hancock, and Cousin Samuel.[92]

Washington and Franklin, with their relative equipoise and calm, stand out as men of good sense and fortitude, stalwarts alongside both the patriots and the Tories of Massachusetts Bay. (Though Franklin was born in Boston, he escaped at an early age.) Mercy Warren with her usual incisiveness and more than a little condescension, described Washington as a gentleman of a polite, though not learned, education and a considerable knowledge of mankind, who "supported the reserve of a statesman, with the occasional affabillity of the courtier."[93] Franklin's superior genius, Mercy declared, made it painful for her to record his foibles; nevertheless, she observed without flinching that Franklin, intoxicated by the flattery of the French, allied himself with the interests of the Count de Vergennes — a man she claimed had ambivalent feelings, at best, toward the United States — and thus became "susceptible of a court influence."[94]

James Bowdoin II was a trusted friend of both Franklin and Washington; and though outbreaks and remissions of his pulmonary disease sometimes appear to harmonize with the rhythm of his political anxieties, successes, and defeats, he was among the steadier breed of Boston patriot philosophers. The reins of psychic control were taut in the inner life of this Christian gentleman. Bowdoin came to his conclusions through cool and careful reasoning, whether business, politics, war, or religion was involved. He was chosen as the presiding officer of assemblies and committees — the Boston Town Meeting, the Board of War, the Massachusetts Constitutional Convention — but he never stirred the people. He was a man who often worked behind the scenes, leaving few traces of his activities. Like Warren, he was a man of virtue, but there was perhaps more reverence for religious law than for Roman law in his world-outlook. The aristocratic gentleman whose word was his bond, the man of honor and character — that was his self-image. Of course, raking through Bowdoin's financial dealings might well uncover a trace of hypoc-

92. John Adams, *Works*, ed. C. F. Adams, 10 (1856), 259–61, John Adams to William Tudor, Quincy, 1 and 5 June 1817.

93. Mercy Warren, *History of the American Revolution* 1:233.

94. Ibid. 2:132–33.

risy in the upright man; but by the standards of the times he generally practiced what he preached. Character to Bowdoin meant constancy in behavior, and the capacity to arrive at a decision and adhere to it. A decent merchant's compromise was not excluded—and this was his hope during the early years of difficulties with the Crown. But once the die was cast there was no tergiversation.

Bowdoin was held in high regard by some of his most critical and exigent contemporaries. He was considered to be intelligent, brainy. The Reverend John Eliot, predicting that Bowdoin would be the next governor of Massachusetts and commenting on the New Hampshire election of 1785, wrote in a jocular vein to the Reverend Jeremy Belknap of Dover, "I think you will not excel Mr. B. if you extract the sense of all your candidates & put it into any one head." [95] Bowdoin's crusty old friend Samuel Dexter singled him out as a patriot uniquely worthy of his trust and respect, declaring that he had no good opinion of anyone except "your Honor." [96] Bowdoin was never caught by his contemporaries in acts that betrayed a loss of control. The hard shell of a stoical Calvinist encased him. He believed that if misfortune befell a man he could win new merit by preserving his equanimity in the midst of painful circumstances. To persevere, not to succumb to despair, was a religious and a moral imperative. Though some Bostonians were put off by his show of uprightness, he was not wholly without humor, as an occasional labored witticism in his private correspondence bears witness. But while he was respected, he was not popular, and when the voices of ordinary people designated "the elect," he was in trouble, politically and theologically. The presidency of the American Academy had been awarded him without a contest, and he fulfilled the duties of his office as though it were a sacred calling. If science was his lost vocation, the grace of an academic presidency was at least a partial recompense.

95. MHS, *Collections*, ser. 6.4 (Belknap Papers, 3), 293, John Eliot to Jeremy Belknap, Boston, 12 Apr. 1785.

96. MHS, *Proceedings* 6:360, Samuel Dexter to Bowdoin, Woodstock, 26 Jan. 1779.

6

GROUP PORTRAIT OF THE FOUNDING FELLOWS

❦

THE PATRIOT philosophers convened by James Bowdoin in the late spring of 1780 might be aligned by age, profession, religion, ethnic origin, political allegiance, or scientific knowledge; situated geographically; studied for manifest physical and psychological diseases. Reliable statistics on their weight and height are not available, and examination of their skeletal structure is precluded by state and local laws. A good number kept diaries and journals that are extant, and their letters and papers have been preserved. Many had their portraits painted by artists of greater or lesser skill. Almost all attained sufficient eminence, at least in their own towns, to merit lengthy obituary notices, and some have been favored with biographies. About half the Academy charter members were descendants of the original seventeenth-century settlers of the area in which they lived. A few were immigrants from Connecticut, Vermont, or New Hampshire. Virtually all were of English stock; Bowdoin, the only Huguenot, and two sons of Ireland were sports. With the exception of one or two Episcopalians and a stray Presbyterian, the Fellows belonged to Congregational churches, though of different degrees of orthodoxy. Riches were respected, and envied—Bowdoin's lot. While others, too, had inherited their wealth, on the whole the first Fellows were self-made men who had knocked about before settling into a calling and had experienced many stations in life; often they were the sons of artisans or country parsons dependent upon the bounty of parishioners. The clergy were still learned, but the mantle of prestige and power was passing from them to the lawyers, a transfer that started early in the life of the new society and long persisted.

The hagiography of the early Fellows has left us a posed assemblage of liberal educators, preachers, lawyers careful not to overcharge their clients, judges tirelessly riding circuit, and doctors indefatigable in ministering to their patients—when they were not serving in the militia, the Continental army, and the numerous legislative bodies that the new society brought forth. Of course the half-dozen major political figures have too voluminous a record to be fitted into the stereotypes without straining, and their biographies are more human, revealing frailties and blemishes; but the lesser lights depicted in funeral orations were outstanding in virtue and benevolence. In the course of time a few members were found guilty of peculation, and one was a notorious drunkard, but no great scandals erupted involving marital infidelity or sexual deviation. While the number who fell victim to nervous and mental diseases was substantial, it was perhaps no greater than the proportion of such sufferers in the rest of the population.

Though there was a certain randomness to the selection of the incorporated Fellows, a prosopographical analysis presents a group portrait of the leadership of Massachusetts society after the Loyalists had left. The members later divided along Federalist and Republican lines, but in the beginning common devotion to the ideals of the Revolution gave them a measure of cohesion despite their internecine quarrels. They were the new aristocracy, conscious of their intellectual superiority, and prepared to distribute the accolades of their Academy to citizens of the world who had earned the honor of membership.

The occupational grouping of the Fellows is a revealing way to initiate an overview of the body, for profession of a calling had become more significant than profession of faith, though the difficulties of maintaining rigid professional categories are patent. Movement from divinity to the bench and the bar was frequent, and almost all the Fellows were sometime officials and legislators on the local, state, or national level.

Godliness without Hellfire

About a third of the Fellows incorporated were ministers of Congregational meetinghouses or ordained ministers connected with Harvard College, with a median age of about fifty. It would be difficult to discover religious enthusiasts among them, and the strictness of their adherence to Calvinist teachings varied. Few openly threatened sinners with the everlasting fires of hell, and they numbered at least one outspoken Arminian. A theologian who examined their convictions would detect a veering toward unitarian beliefs. Though before independence many Congregational ministers feared that the British Crown intended to impose an episcopacy in the colonies, in matters of Christian doctrine—if they can be separated from the order and discipline of the church—there was little to differentiate a latitudinarian English Episcopalian from a Boston Congregationalist of 1780.

The American patriots who were philosophers no longer felt the presence of God in their daily lives with the intensity of seventeenth-century Puritan ministers. Their diaries deal with their conduct, their comings and goings, not with soul searching, the hope of attaining salvation, or the fear of being cast into hell. The Devil had spent himself in his witchcraft exertions in Salem; Jonathan Edwards's attempt to revive the diabolical existence in Northampton was a dismal failure, and he had turned to the Indians, who might better comprehend such avatars. The ritual of the Congregational churches was not seriously altered, but novelties such as organ-playing, group singing, and Bible reading in churches, which would previously have been frowned upon, were introduced. Though not full-fledged Deists, many of the ministers were no longer trinitarians in the traditional sense.

The oldest of the incorporated Fellows of the Academy was Charles Chauncy (1705–1787) of the First Church of Boston, who had spearheaded the battle against Jonathan Edwards' Great Awakening. Close on his heels was Samuel Mather, aged seventy-four, last of the family dynasty of preachers, who had been dismissed from the Second Church of Boston and now led a newly formed Bennet Street Church in Boston's North End. He owned a fine library and was respected as a scholar by some, though more frequently considered a piddling antiquarian. Son of the formidable Cotton Mather, he had been co-opted to fill the ranks of Academy members, but while he was touched by the honor, he was too advanced in years to attend meetings. If only he had been thirty or forty years younger! he mused ruefully in a note to Bowdoin.[1] He decided all the same to contribute his mite, assembling a few facts about the duties of Fellows in two foreign academies, the Accademia degl'Intronati in Siena and the Académie française. He sent in a proposal, written in a shaky hand, to set up one committee for the collection of curiosities in Massachusetts and throughout America, another committee to communicate what might be serviceable to commerce and agriculture, and a third that would draft rules to make the society more useful, which would redound to its credit. The fervid Calvinist spirit of Cotton Mather had been tamed in a generation—though not completely. In the early eighties the two senior pastors in the Academy, Chauncy and Mather, confronted each other from opposite sides of Calvinist doctrine, and outside the precincts of the Academy engaged in violent controversy over eternal damnation. Not many Academy members cared.

Chauncy, descendant of the second president of Harvard and son of a prominent Boston merchant, was married to the daughter of a supreme court judge. After ordination in the First Church of Boston, he served there for sixty years, a vigorous mind in a frail body. His active life spanned the major political and theological battles of eighteenth-century New England. He was an ardent defender of the rights of the colonists against the Crown, and the veritable embodiment of an enlightened rational theology. As the Revolution approached, in *Letter to a Friend* (1774), Chauncy dramatically described the sufferings of the people of Boston after the British had closed the port: "Few, comparatively very few in Boston, are men of independent fortunes. . . . You will readily perceive that vast numbers [of workmen and their dependents], not less, I suppose . . . than fifteen thousand at the lowest computation, are reduced to a starving condition."[2]

---

1. Academy Letters, 1:7, Samuel Mather to Bowdoin, Boston, 6 Nov. 1780.

2. Charles Chauncy, *A letter to a friend, giving a concise but just representation of the hardships and sufferings the town of Boston is exposed to . . . in consequence of the late act of the British-Parliament . . . shutting up its port* (Boston, 1774), 5–6.

During his long ministry, Chauncy was engaged in three major religious wars. First he opposed Edwards and Whitefield during the Great Awakening, for he distrusted the religious enthusiasm of the Revival as befogging the mind, and had contempt for oratorical display. When there was talk of an attempt by the English bishops to introduce episcopacy into America, he fought them with weighty historical arguments going back to the church fathers, from whom he cited long excerpts in *A Compleat View of Episcopacy* (1771). Apprehension about the coming of the bishops fired his commitment to the Revolution as much as the economic restrictions imposed by the British Crown had stiffened the opposition of the colonial merchants. His third religious war grew out of the position assumed in the first, which involved the doctrines of depravity and eternal damnation. Two years after the founding of the Academy, he published anonymously his *Salvation for all Men, Illustrated and Vindicated as a Scripture Doctrine*, followed in 1784 by *The Benevolence of the Deity fairly and impartially Considered*, and in 1785 by *The Mystery Hid from Ages . . . or the Salvation of All Men and Five Dissertations on the Fall and Its Consequences.*

Back in the 1740s Chauncy had greeted one of the "new lights" from Long Island, the Reverend James Davenport, with an admonition against the "wilds of a heated imagination" and a shower of sardonic barbs: "I doubt not, you verily think, GOD sent you hither; and that your preaching here is by *immediate* commission from *him*: But others must be excus'd, if they han't the same tho't of the matter."[3] Davenport had been proceeding through the town of Boston, openly interrogating one minister after another about his religious experiences. Rumor had it that he had addressed a prayer to God implying that the greatest part of the Boston ministers were unconverted and in a carnal state. Davenport's presumption to judge from men's hearts was derided by the rationalist Chauncy: "We have no way of judging but by what is *outward* and visible."[4] Generations of Puritan censors were being denied.

The post-civil war Anglican suspicion of enthusiastic tinkers who spoke with tongues was being rehearsed by a pastor who carried the torch of an old enlightenment. Chauncy refused to judge—he left to God the decision as to how far Davenport was under the power of a disturbed imagination; but in the body of his sermon *Enthusiasm describ'd and caution'd against* (1742) Chauncy resorted to a medical diagnosis of religious fanaticism or imaginary inspiration that recalls Burton's *Anatomy of Melancholy*: "The cause of this *enthusiasm* is a bad temperament of the blood and spirits; 'tis properly a disease, a sort of madness: And there are few; perhaps, none at all, but are subject to it; tho' none are so much in danger of it as those, in whom *melancholy* is the prevailing ingredient in their constitution."[5] Chauncy analyzed the symptoms of

3. Chauncy, *Enthusiasm describ'd and caution'd against. A Sermon . . . With a letter to the Reverend Mr. James Davenport* (Boston, 1742), ii.

4. Ibid., v.

5. Ibid., 3.

the disease, the wild look of the victims, the looseness of their tongues, their convulsions, quakings, and tremblings, but above all their disregard of the dictates of reason. His ideas were skillfully expanded in the five-part treatise *Seasonable Thoughts on the State of Religion in New-England* (1743), which linked the Great Awakening with the Antinomians, Familists, and Libertines of the seventeenth century and urged pastors to suppress the prevailing disorders. The work enjoyed the support (through subscriptions) of Governor William Shirley, Edward Holyoke, president of Harvard, and the merchant Thomas Hancock (who took six copies).

Samuel Mather denounced Chauncy's arguments on universal salvation as "insidious,"[6] and in 1782 John Clarke, who was Chauncy's colleague in the First Church and at twenty-five the Benjamin of the American Academy, counterattacked wickedly in *A Letter to Doctor Mather. Occasioned by his disingenuous Reflexions upon a certain Pamphlet, entitled, Salvation for all Men*: "You know, a scheme that makes all men happy at the day of judgment, cannot be confounded with one, which consigns *numbers* of the human race to *ages of* suffering. Your reason is not so impaired by years as to be incapable of seeing these things."[7] The redoubtable Mathers had clearly lost their authority for Boston preachers, when a minister in his twenties could dress down the elderly Samuel in this fashion.

Three of the ministers in the Academy were presidents of Harvard: the Reverend Samuel Langdon, who had been helped into the presidency by Hancock and who resigned under student fire in August 1780, the Reverend Joseph Willard, who was to succeed him, and the Reverend Edward Wigglesworth, Hollis Professor of Divinity, who served as an interim president between Langdon and Willard. Though Willard had been lampooned as a tyrant by a Harvard student with a talent for doggerel,[8] his Dudleian Lecture of 1785 delivered in the college chapel, "Persecution opposite to the genius of the Gospel," ranged him unequivocally on the side of religious latitudinarianism. "Never endeavor to control," he admonished the students, "never even dispute the right of private judgment; but consider that others have the same claim to search the Scriptures, determine their sense for themselves, and form their own creed from them. . . ." To those preparing for the ministry he added a special note of exhortation: "Thus will you be charitable and candid: — thus will you be gentle to all men, will recommend, by your own lives, the excellent Religion you will preach, and will shine as lights in the world."[9]

6. Samuel Mather, *All men will not be saved forever: or, an attempt to prove, That this is a Scriptural Doctrine: and to give a sufficient Answer to the Publisher of Extracts in favor of the Salvation of all men* (Boston, 1782).

7. John Clarke, *A Letter to Doctor Mather* (Boston, 1782), 6.

8. Harvard University Archives: Clementiae amator, "Poem giving a true Description of a number of tyrannical Pedagogues. Dedicated to the Sons of Harvard" (1769), photostat.

9. Harvard University Archives: Reverend Joseph Willard, "Persecution opposite to the genius of

The Academy boasted three Williamses bearing the title Reverend. Abraham had a reputation for heresy; he was pastor of the First Congregational Parish of Sandwich, and was known for his capacities as a surveyor and a drafter of business and probate papers. Nehemiah hailed from Brimfield. And Samuel was the recently chosen successor to John Winthrop in the Hollis Chair of Mathematicks and of Natural and Experimental Philosophy. He had accompanied Winthrop to Newfoundland to view the transit of Venus in 1761, and he published a report on the eclipse of 27 October 1780, after a scientific expedition of his own that proved to be a fiasco.[10] His mathematical papers printed in the Academy *Memoirs* were notorious for their errors. He resigned from Harvard under a cloud in 1788, when charges of forgery were leveled against him, and took refuge in Rutland, Vermont, where he continued to compose treatises on natural theology.[11]

Other clerical Fellows, though less controversial than some of their brethren, were not wholly without distinction. The Reverend Samuel Deane (1733–1814), born in Dedham the son of a blacksmith, was for fifty years pastor of a Congregational parish in the town of Portland, Maine, After the British fleet bombarded Falmouth (of which Portland was then a part), in 1775 he moved to Gorham and began a series of agricultural experiments. A magnum opus published in 1790, an encyclopedic collection of data on agriculture unique for the period, fulfilled at least one significant mission for which the Academy was originally organized, the advancement of husbandry; *The New England Farmer or Georgical Dictionary, Containing a Compendious Account of the Ways and Methods in which the Most Important Art of Husbandry in all its Various Branches is or may be practiced to the Greatest Advantage in this Country* was reprinted and revised a number of times. Deane proudly announced his authorship: "By a Fellow of the American Academy of Arts and Sciences." He was also a poet who had participated with Bowdoin in the collection honoring George III in 1761 and was the author of a long piece in hexameters celebrating his homestead, known as Pitchwood Hill.[12]

---

the Gospel," Dudleian Lecture given in the Chapel of Harvard College, 7 Sept. 1785 (MS), 52, 53–54. Other Willard manuscripts in the archives include a letter to his brother, 4 August 1800; sermons, 1768–92; a commencement address, 1799; and a poem, "On the Power of Love," 1764.

10. Robert F. Rothschild, "What went wrong in 1780?" *Harvard Magazine* 83.3 (Jan.–Feb. 1981), 20–27.

11. The Reverend Samuel Williams's lectures on astronomy, electricity, theology, and other subjects, in manuscript, are in the Harvard University Archives. See also Williams's *Daybook from the Office of the Rutland Herald, 1798–1802*, ed. Marcus A. McCorison (Worcester, Mass., 1967; reprinted from *Proceedings of the American Antiquarian Society*, Oct. 1966: 293–395).

12. On Deane, see William Willis, ed., *Journals of the Rev. Thomas Smith and the Rev. Samuel Deane, Pastors of the First Church in Portland*, 2d ed. (Portland, Me., 1849).

The Reverend Daniel Little had studied languages at Harvard with the Hebraist Stephen Sewall and theology with Samuel Moody. As a clergyman at Wells he appears to have turned the church in a unitarian direction. At the age of sixty this doughty pastor climbed Mount Washington. His learned interests embraced chemistry, natural history, and the collection of minerals and Indian relics. A clergyman with a similar theological bent was Samuel West (1730–1807) of Yarmouth. He simultaneously ministered to congregations in Dartmouth and in Fairhaven, where he so resolutely led his parishioners down the Arminian path that he has been considered a unitarian. His *Essays on Liberty and Necessity* (1793) was an outspoken reply to Jonathan Edwards's *Freedom of the Will.* He was one of the early pulpit preachers against British tyranny and for a time served as a chaplain with the revolutionary army. During the war his decipherment for Washington of a treasonable letter in code was evidence of his versatility, which found further expression in alchemical studies as well as in the discovery of the course of the Revolution in the biblical books of prophecy. In December of 1785, he asked the Academy's help in applying to the powers of Europe for a bounty, in exchange for which he would communicate to them his secret for extracting fresh water from salt. The machine invented by his partner, Jethro Allen III, only required perfecting before it could be put to practical use. A few years later this penurious cleric, whose small salary was paid principally in kind and whose devotion to science had further impoverished him, was obliged to resign from the Academy because his dues were in arrears.[13] While he believed that New England had been signaled by the Deity as a place of refuge for the persecuted of other nations, he disliked individuals who claimed to be in special communion with God. As his mind failed, he became intemperate in his food and drink and in denunciations of the French Revolution.

The Reverend Peres Fobes was pastor of the First Church of Raynham and active in the fostering of arts and sciences in the local schools. His scientific curiosity, already in evidence when he was a boy of fifteen, extended to astronomy and botanical classification. Like Samuel West a chaplain in the revolutionary army, he ultimately became Professor of Natural History at Brown, commuting from Raynham to his lectures. He was an important property-holder and money-lender in the area of Raynham and Taunton, which did not deter him from pleading poverty and complaining bitterly when his name was erased from the membership rolls for delinquency in paying his dues. Fobes was an apostle of progress under the aegis of a beneficent Deity. He saw a swamp in the neighborhood of his home as the residue of a large pond once teeming with fish and fowl to sustain the Indian

13. Academy Letters, 1:36, Samuel West to Bowdoin, Dartmouth, 7 Dec. 1785; ibid., 120, West to Ebenezer Storer, New Bedford, 17 Oct. 1791; W. B. Sprague, *Annals of the American Unitarian Pulpit* (New York, 1865), 39, 43. James T. Austin, *The Life of Elbridge Gerry* (Boston, 1828), 1:32–33, contends that it was Gerry, not Dr. West, who originally deciphered the letter. In any event, the honor belongs to an Academician.

inhabitants nearby—testimony to the wisdom and goodness of divine Providence supplying the wants of man, even as He often changed uncivilized nature to a state of cultivation and refinement.[14]

Another minister with a scientific bent of mind was the Reverend Phillips Payson, pastor at Chelsea, who had a talent for natural philosophy and astronomy and published "Some Select Astronomical Observations" in the first volume of the Academy *Memoirs*. Like other academic clergymen, voices of an Enlightenment theology, Payson eschewed both deism and enthusiasm, but his abhorrence of enthusiasm had a passion that was lacking in his reasoned refutation of deism. In his Dudleian Lecture at Harvard in 1784, he excoriated the fanatics: "To suppose a scheme of mad and wild enthusiasts should be abetted by the greatest and wisest men in their senses and that in matters of their highest interest, their greatest hopes, and most important concerns, is repugnant to every dictate of common sense."[15] Payson was touched with the family epilepsy, but seems nevertheless to have discharged his ministerial responsibilities until his death.

Some of the clergymen distinguished themselves more as educators than as religious leaders. Samuel Moody of Newbury, whose career as a minister was cut short by his susceptibility to violent tremors whenever he was agitated, was far better known as the first master of Dummer Academy, from which a substantial number of students regularly went to Harvard. Described as "sociable & romantic," he openly condemned orthodox Calvinism as self-righteous and intolerant.[16] He was well versed in the classics and Hebrew, and had a lively interest in science. In old age his eccentricities became exacerbated to the point where he had to be removed from the headship of the school. The Reverend Caleb Gannett had preached in Nova Scotia for a number of years before he was appointed a tutor of natural philosophy at Harvard. There he served as "pulpit supply" on Sundays during the war, supervised the transfer of the college to Concord when Cambridge was threatened by the enemy, selected books for Harvard from sequestered Loyalist libraries, and was finally named steward of the college. He was a member of the Society for Promoting Christian Knowledge and later of the Massachusetts Historical Society. Though he discharged his chief service to the Academy in the office of corresponding secretary, he also contributed papers on eclipses and the aurora borealis. Edward Wigglesworth,

14. Fobes's Diary and Commonplace Book, 1759–1760, in manuscript, is in the Harvard University Archives; it has been edited by E. H. Dewey and reprinted from the *New England Quarterly* 2.4 (1929); see especially p. 654. See also MHS, *Collection for the year 1794*, 3 (Boston, 1794; reprinted in 1810), 172, Peres Fobes, "A Topographical Description of the Town of Raynham in the County of Bristol, Feb. 6, 1793," and Academy Letters, 1:125, Peres Fobes to Ebenezer Storer, Raynham, 20 Dec. 1791.

15. Harvard University Archives: Phillips Payson, 30th Annual Dudleian Lecture, 1 Sept. 1784 (MS).

16. Harvard University Archives: Benjamin Guild, Diary, 1776, 1778, entry for 27 Nov. 1778.

a descendant of original Massachusetts Bay settlers, was first a tutor, then Hollis Professor of Divinity at Harvard; but his writings suggest greater preoccupation with statistics of American population growth than with matters theological. His *Calculations on American Population* propounded the thesis that the simple living and early marriage of British Americans would double their number every twenty-five years until it reached a billion and a half by the end of the twentieth century.

The Reverend Elijah Lothrop of Boston remains a cipher. While Lothrops and Lathrops abound in the records of Harvard and the American Academy, a search has failed to unearth anything about Elijah except his inclusion in the first list of appointed Fellows. Yet there is negative evidence of his existence, for his name was crossed off the official list of "Home Members" drawn up in 1785 (where he appears as a resident of Springfield), and was marked by an asterisk indicating "deceased."[17] An Elijah *La*throp of Barnstable, who was ordained in Connecticut and resided there from 1752 until his death in 1797, was not an Academy member. John Lathrop, pastor of the Second (Old North) Church, became a Fellow, but not until 1790.[18] Of the Reverend Zedekiah Sanger it is known that he came from Duxbury. Benjamin Guild was listed as "Mr." in the Academy charter, though he was an ordained minister and preached occasionally in the surrounding towns, accepting, as he noted in his diary, whatever he could gather in contributions. John Bacon was one of the sometime ministers who moved into other occupations. As a migrant from Connecticut, a graduate of Princeton, and a Presbyterian by upbringing, he was a triple mutation in the ranks of Academy Fellows. When he was ousted as pastor of the Old South Church for his unpopular views on the doctrine of atonement and the practice of the halfway Covenant, he abandoned Boston for western Massachusetts, established himself as a farmer in Stockbridge, and served the state and the nation in many offices as judge and legislator.

Stephen Sewall was one of two Sewalls from York, Maine, who became Fellows incorporated. While not ordained, he was probably the most learned biblical scholar in the Academy assemblage. Though his father was a poor tanner, young Sewall got his Harvard degree in 1761 and succeeded Judah Monis as the Hebrew instructor. Three years later he was the first scholar to be appointed Hancock Professor of Hebrew and other Oriental Languages, a post he held for twenty years. Like many seventeenth-century Christian Hebraists and scholars of Near Eastern languages, he was largely self-taught, a man with a natural linguistic genius. He published a Hebrew grammar

17. Elijah Lothrop's name was included in the original penciled list; see Appendix 2. See also American Academy of Arts and Sciences, *Memoirs* 1:xxi, where his name is prefixed by an asterisk noting deceased, and Academy Records, 1:31–32, 35, where his name is crossed from the "List of Fellows Incorporated." For biographies of Elijah Lathrop and several Lothrops, see Frederick Lewis Weis, *The Colonial Clergy and the Colonial Churches of New England* (Lancaster, Mass., 1936).

18. Academy Records, 1:25, 138: election of the Reverend John Lathrop, 25 Aug. 1790; Academy Letters, 1:99, John Lathrop to Eliphalet Pearson accepting election, Boston, 15 Sept. 1790.

in 1763 that was widely used, replacing the awkward compendium Judah Monis had compiled and enjoined his students to purchase. Sewall exercised his very considerable talents in a number of different areas. During the Revolution he was an elected representative to the General Court. His publications included "Magnetical Observations Made at Cambridge," which appeared in the Academy *Memoirs*, and a Latin translation of Young's *Night Thoughts*. Two works of biblical commentary were based upon his Harvard lectures: *The Scripture Account of the Schechinah* (1794) and *The Scripture History Relating to the Overthrow of Sodom and Gomorrah* (1796). The lectures on Hebrew and oriental literature, a Greek lexicon, and a lexicon of Aramaic words in the Old Testament are preserved in manuscript in the Harvard Archives.[19]

Sewall's Harvard lectures, centering on the Old Testament, show a reasonable acquaintance with seventeenth- and eighteenth-century English and German scholarship, which used new critical methods in the reading of the text and treated parts of the Bible as literature. He had to steer his way through waters perturbed by the challenges of the nascent biblical higher criticism, and he tried to hold to a middling position in his teaching. His reading of Scripture involved, among a host of other problems, the controversial matter of miracle narratives. He was leery of overplaying the miraculous element in biblical events, lest someone plausibly interpret the miracle as a natural occurrence, a deflation of a religious assumption that would breed incredulity. When natural causes could be demonstrated without straining he reported them, but only after a careful examination of the scientific facts. He rejected as based on inadequate evidence, however, the naturalistic tidal theory of the Mosaic Red Sea crossing. Special lectures were devoted to such prickly subjects as the borrowings of the Israelites from the Egyptians, hypotheses about the Book of Job, and the meaning of circumcision. Though not an innovator in scholarship, he kept abreast of the most advanced thinking on the nature of Hebrew poetry, the distribution of the first men throughout the globe, the rules for ascertaining the true meaning of a biblical text, and the introduction of error into texts through transcription. Sewall's teaching career came to a tragic end when he was in his early fifties: physical and mental debility that proved irreversible occasioned the removal from his professorship. Harvard awarded him a gift of thirty pounds upon his departure.

The Bench and the Bar

The lawyers, who were the orators of the Revolution, were represented on the Academy roster by some fifteen men, almost all of them in their thirties and

---

19. In the Harvard University Archives, in addition to the seven manuscript volumes of Sewall's lectures on Hebrew and oriental literature delivered from 1765 to 1782, are his published funeral orations for Edward Holyoke and John Winthrop.

forties. Samuel Adams of Boston, who had once studied law but turned exclusively to politics, at fifty-eight was an exception among them. In the early years of independence they occupied prominent posts in the judiciary and in the executive, and one of their number, John Adams, rose to be president of the United States, while his cousin Samuel became governor of the Commonwealth. William Cushing of Scituate was a member of the Supreme Judicial Court of the state at the time of his election to the Academy, the only important holdover from the previous royal judicial system. He was a descendant of an old Massachusetts family that boasted a long line of pastors and office-holders, a man who weathered the stormy pre-revolutionary period by maintaining a discreet judicial silence during times of crisis. Later he became the first associate justice to be appointed to the United States Supreme Court. A hardworking circuit-rider in Massachusetts, Maine, and in the federal system, he was renowned for his dignity, his terse decisions, and his insistence on wearing a full-bottomed English judicial wig long after the fashion had died out. During Shays' Rebellion he refused to shut down his court and walked undaunted through the ranks of the protesters to discharge his official duties. The high point of his career came when, as acting chief justice, he administered the oath to George Washington at his second inauguration. James Sullivan, born in Maine and brother of General John Sullivan, was a Hancock supporter who sometimes wrote under the pen name Cassius. A successful lawyer, he became a justice of the Massachusetts Supreme Court, and later a member of Congress and attorney-general of Massachusetts. Francis Dana, independently wealthy, had entered the country's diplomatic service as secretary to John Adams, was unofficial minister to Russia from 1781 to 1783, and eventually became chief justice of the Massachusetts Supreme Court.

Dana was succeeded on the court by Theophilus Parsons, the able young lawyer who had played a part in drafting the Massachusetts constitution and the bill establishing the Academy. Theophilus's brother Theodore was in fact the Parsons whose name was included in the Academy Act and in the initial summons to the Fellows-elect; but Theodore, a ship's surgeon on a revolutionary privateer, was missing in action—in April of 1780 Francis Dana had written Theophilus from Paris, "No intelligence of poor Theodore"—and he was finally presumed dead. His older brother was substituted in January of 1781.[20] Theophilus Parsons was a man of broad culture with a passionate interest in Greek studies, as well as in mathematics and astronomy; he contributed a paper, "Astronomical Problems," to the second volume of Academy *Memoirs*, and at his death left an unpublished

---

20. MHS, Dana Papers, Francis Dana to Theophilus Parsons, Paris, 29 Apr. 1780; Academy Records, 1:32: election of Theophilus Parsons, 31 Jan. 1781. See also Walter Muir Whitehill, "Learned Societies in Boston and Vicinity," loc. cit., 156.

Greek grammar and several mathematical essays. Like Bowdoin an avid collector of scientific instruments, he was given to conducting experiments that produced thunderous explosions and set his servants fleeing through the house in terror. In politics he was a conservative, a member of what Hancock had disparagingly named the Essex Junto; and in Massachusetts feuds he sided with Bowdoin. Parsons had not joined in the early struggles of the Revolution, but after recovering from a bout with consumption and melancholia, he became an active patriot and a leading member of the Essex County Convention, where he was an advocate of strong executive power. Parsons emerged as a behind-the-scenes manipulator of no small talent. He succeeded in elevating his pastor, John Thornton Kirkland, to the presidency of Harvard, calling down upon himself the fulminations of the enraged Dr. Benjamin Waterhouse, fellow-Academician and Harvard professor, who wrote to President Thomas Jefferson, "Our college at Cambridge is under the absolute direction of the Essex Junto, at the head of which stands Chief Justice Parsons . . . a man as cunning as Lucifer and about half as good."[21]

Levi Lincoln of Worcester held several Massachusetts legislative offices and crowned his career as attorney general under President Jefferson. During the Revolution he performed only a brief tour of duty in the militia, concentrating his energies on the civil offices of the new society. As a trial lawyer he appeared, along with Academician Caleb Strong, for John and Seth Caldwell in a suit that challenged the legality of holding a black man in slavery under the Massachusetts Constitution of 1780, and won a landmark decision. Strong of Northampton represented his area in revolutionary councils and, after victory, in the United States Senate. He became famous during the War of 1812, when as governor of Massachusetts he refused to order part of the militia into federal service. The contest led to the calling of the Hartford Convention and a demand for reshaping the federal compact, a project that was aborted by the end of the war.

Another Northamptonite was Joseph Hawley, one of the few Yale graduates among the founding members. A descendant of the eminent Reverend Solomon Stoddard, he was himself a minister until his conversion to Arminianism, after which he forsook the ministry for the law. He retained his interest in church affairs, however, and during the religious dispute in Northampton in 1749–50 he was instrumental in the ousting of Jonathan Edwards, a role he later regretted. Hawley was a perennial representative from Northampton to the legislature in Boston from 1747 to his death in 1788, was an early opponent of the royal prerogative, and was one of the most vociferous enemies of Governor Hutchinson. As a leader

---

21. Quoted from S. E. Morison, "The Great Rebellion in Harvard College, and the resignation of President Kirkland," *Publications of the Colonial Society of Massachusetts* 27 (1932), 59. There is a portrait of Parsons by Gilbert Stuart, and a memoir of him by his son Theophilus (1859).

of the revolutionary party in western Massachusetts, he worked closely with Samuel Adams, except when he was incapacitated by attacks of "the glooms," the family curse, which Governor Hutchinson duly noted. Hutchinson observed of Hawley that he had "a very fair character as a practitioner, and some instances have been mentioned of *singular* scrupulosity, and of his refusing and returning fees when they appeared to him greater than the cause deserved."[22] Hawley declined election to the Continental Congress because of ill health, but like Bowdoin continued his revolutionary activity from his home base in the Connecticut Valley, until he was overcome by spells of insanity in 1776. The melancholy that struck him down at intervals assumed traditional forms, terror at the prospect of his own damnation accompanied by strange fantasies. Hawley is another Massachusetts patriot whose inherited Calvinism did not always mesh with his new Enlightenment views. The spiritual tensions of the revolutionary leaders who were scions of Congregationalist notables may not have initially generated their mental disequilibrium, but they doubtless contributed to it.

John Lowell, the son of a clergyman and originally from Newburyport, moved to Boston in 1777. He represented the town in the General Court, was a delegate to the state constitutional convention and to the Continental Congress, and from 1784 until his death in 1802 served as a member of the Harvard Corporation. He reached the zenith of his career as chief judge of the First Circuit Court. In addition to his public duties, the thrice-married Lowell devoted himself to his botanical interests: he was for many years president of the Massachusetts Agricultural Society, and contributed to the establishment of the Botanic Garden at Cambridge. A cultivated gentleman and on occasion a versifier, he ran a well-respected law office. At the Academy he was a mainstay of support for Bowdoin. To him fell the honor of delivering the formal eulogy at the Academy meeting memorializing Bowdoin's death.

Robert Treat Paine, a signer of the Declaration of Independence and an ex-preacher, was the first elected attorney general of Massachusetts. After graduation from Harvard he had knocked about for a time, joining the crew of a whaling expedition, teaching school, preaching as a supply pastor, before his acceptance at the bar. He experimented with the manufacture of gunpowder and saltpeter, was active in the quelling of Shays' Rebellion, and tended toward unitarianism in religion. He was an exemplar of the new Puritan tradition that accepted jurisprudence as a holy calling, which slowly spelled the supersession of the minister by the lawyer in the public esteem of Congregationalist Massachusetts. His fame as a patriot dated from the time he acted as an associate prosecuting attorney in the trial that grew out of the Boston Massacre, in which he argued against the right of

22. Hutchinson, *History of Massachusetts Bay*, ed. Mayo, 3:212–13.

Parliament to quarter a standing army in a town without its consent. During this same period close ties with James Bowdoin were forged, and Paine became one of the Academicians who could be relied upon to show up at scheduled meetings. His laconic diary bears witness to his regular appearance and his frequent dinners with Bowdoin when a quorum failed to be assembled.[23]

Theodore Sedgwick, a Connecticut man educated at Yale, moved north to establish himself in Berkshire County. There he shifted from divinity to law and, after some tergiversation, joined the insurgents in the Continental army and in the Massachusetts legislature. From his home in Stockbridge he was repeatedly elected to the Congress and later the Senate of the United States, and in 1802, after his retirement, he was appointed to the Supreme Judicial Court of Massachusetts. Along with many other Fellows of the Academy, he actively opposed the Shaysites, ignoring their threats against his life and courageously fighting off attacks in their stronghold of Berkshire County. Nathaniel Peaslee Sargeant of Haverhill combined law practice and service in the legislature and on the bench of the Superior Court with financial investment in a distillery that netted him hard cash.

Samuel Phillips, Jr., served in various revolutionary legislative bodies, presided over the legislature at the time of Shays' Rebellion, and for a while was justice of the Court of Common Pleas for Essex County—he was commonly addressed as "Judge Phillips." His repute derived from the construction of a powder mill on the Shawsheen River that supplied the revolutionary troops with ammunition, and from the founding of Phillips Academy, an endowed non-conformist secondary school under pronounced Lockian influence that opened in 1778 with the objective of inculcating true piety and virtue in young men. Finally there was David Sewall of York, Maine, the biblical scholar's brother, who filled public and private offices in Harvard, the state, and the federal judiciary. He was appointed to the Supreme Judicial Court of Massachusetts in 1781, and in 1789 was named judge of the United States District Court for Maine. With few exceptions the gentlemen of the robe, who formed a solid phalanx in the Academy, were prefigurations of the aspiring lawyer in American politics.

Scientists and Doctors of Physic

On the final roster of incorporated members of the Academy there were few who today would be recognized as "men of science," though many had scientific interests. In addition to the clerisy and the lawyers, there was room in the Academy for a serious cosmologist, a talented eccentric with appropriate family connections and some knowledge of mathematics, and of course the doctors of physic.

Among the first members, Andrew Oliver probably approached nearest to what

23. MHS, Robert Treat Paine, Diary (MS).

would today be called a scientist, though he was trained as a lawyer and before the Revolution had served on the bench for many years. The odium borne by a father who had been lieutenant-governor to the hated Hutchinson hung over him—when Andrew Oliver, Sr., died in 1774 his funeral cortège was attacked and the Sons of Liberty cheered as the coffin was lowered into the grave. Andrew, Jr., chose not to go into exile, but to retire to Salem, where, unmolested, he occupied himself with his instruments and papers. Mindful of the brutal treatment meted out to his father, Oliver was careful not to give offense to his fellow townsmen, and when officers of the militia summoned the citizens to a muster in full military accoutrement, he was in a quandary. Though he feared an attack of the gout if the weather should prove inclement, he prepared his equipment for inspection and made a formal protestation of loyalty to America: "These are now, and ever have been ready for use in the service of my native Country and for the Support and Vindication of the constitutional Rights, Liberties, and Privileges of british Americans." Timothy Pickering, the officer to whom his letter was addressed, responded in the rhetoric of the moment that Andrew Oliver had shown his true allegiance by refusing the "justly odious office of a Mandamus Counsellor," informed him that the order was not a requisition, and assured him that his appearance would not be required. If he was not one of the heroes of the War for Independence, he kept his military equipment in good order and was welcomed into the Academy. Though the American insurgents were zealous in prosecuting their cause, there was a sort of "benefit of scientists" that protected men like Andrew Oliver and his fellow Salemite the clergyman-scientist John Prince. A few years later, the Academy even cordially admitted Count Rumford, who had fought savagely against the patriots.

Andrew Oliver's extant commonplace books reveal a sad, often self-tortured man; thoughts of suicide obtrude. He tries to set strict moral rules for himself. He makes an effort to fix workable principles of natural religion and to define evil; but he also reads Voltaire's *Philosophy of History*. Oliver was one of those introspective philosophers upon whom the Revolution left deep scars; and he found his solace in the contemplation of the heavens. He combined a knowledge of astronomy with a broad humanistic culture, and was a reader of divines, deists, Fontenelle, and Shakespeare.[24]

Surprisingly, it was not Oliver's superior officer, Timothy Pickering, who was chosen an original incorporator, but his brother John, of Salem. While Timothy

24. MHS, Pickering Papers, Andrew Oliver to Timothy Pickering, Salem, 11 Mar. 1775; Timothy Pickering to Andrew Oliver, draft of reply written on the back of Oliver's letter; MHS, A. Oliver, Historical Notes, 1781–99. For the career of John Prince, see Sara J. Schechner, "John Prince and Early American Scientific Instrument Making," in *Sibley's Heir, A Volume in Memory of Clifford Kenyon Shipton* (Boston: The Colonial Society of Massachusetts, 1982), 431–503.

became quartermaster general on Washington's staff and after the Revolution had a tumultuous career as a pioneer in Pennsylvania, a politician, and a polemist noted for his acerbity, John stayed home to farm and serve in minor offices. On 28 April 1781, John wrote Timothy at the headquarters of the American army, in reply to his inquiries about the "Academy of Sciences," that he had been to but one meeting, though he hoped to attend more often in the future. "I have been told there were several speculations exhibited by members relative to the late great eclipse of the sun. I know nothing more particular at present but will endeavour from time to time to notice any transactions worth mentioning in my correspondence with you." Since his farming did not leave him much leisure, he had little to report, nor did he quite know what he was doing in the Academy. "The Society is instituted upon the designs of other such societies. I was without my seeking made a member by the Bill of their incorporation." Timothy's curiosity suggests that he may have been piqued at being passed over in favor of his less distinguished brother. John may have profited from being confused with another John Pickering, no relation, who was known to James Bowdoin and was one of the few learned lawyers in New Hampshire, but whose career as a judge was ended in 1803 by what appears to have been an unfair impeachment.[25]

James Winthrop was the son of Professor John Winthrop, to whom virtually all the founding members of the Academy owed their early scientific education. James Winthrop's post as librarian of Harvard automatically entitled him to Fellowship. Although he was once considered a likely successor to his father, his contributions to learning turned out to be problematic. His solutions to trisecting the angle and duplicating the cube, published in the Academy *Memoirs* (1793), were fallacious, and his outlandish interpretations of Daniel and Revelation further tarnished his reputation. He was perhaps better equipped temperamentally to lead an active life than the contemplative life of scholarship. He fought at Bunker Hill, joined in rousing the Harvard students against President Langdon, served as a judge in minor offices; surveyed proposals for canals and bridges; and took up arms against the insurgents during Shays' Rebellion. But neither his historical nor his scientific contributions allow placing him comfortably under a professional rubric. Regarded as an intriguer, drunkard, and cynic, he was the misfit son of a gifted father, and was tolerated out of respect for his ancestors.

The physicians in the first contingent of Fellows, with the outstanding exception of Dr. Edward Augustus Holyoke of Salem, were dedicated patriots from the eastern towns. They had been members of the committees of safety, had been elected to revolutionary legislative bodies, and had served as surgeons with the Massachusetts regiment. Many of them were to participate in the founding of

25. MHS, Pickering Papers, John Pickering to Timothy Pickering, Salem, 28 Apr., 13 June 1781.

the Massachusetts Medical Society, and in their communities they were highly respected for their cure of bodies, as the ministers were for the cure of souls. John Sprague of Lancaster, Micajah Sawyer of Newburyport, David Cobb of Taunton, Charles Jarvis of Boston, Joseph Orne of Salem, Oliver Prescott of Groton, John Bernard Sweat (or Swett) of Marblehead, and Cotton Tufts of Weymouth were among the active members of the Academy, assiduous in presenting statistics on morbidity and mortality and reporting their bizarre medical experiences.

The longevity of Dr. Holyoke, as well as his personality and skills as a physician, gave him an edge over the rest of his colleagues. He was an incorporator and first president of the Massachusetts Medical Society, and in 1814 became president of the American Academy. Short and wiry, of agreeable mien and placid temperament, he passed the great age of one hundred, surviving two wives and ten of his dozen children. The orderliness of his life was proverbial. He was said to have deliberately adopted a regimen of retiring and rising late, so as to prevent interruption of his sleep by the nocturnal demands of his patients.

Holyoke kept methodical shorthand records of his extensive family practice and of his meteorological observations (even when he was ninety-nine), was well read in the medical literature of his day, and diligently instructed some three dozen medical students. In the last decades of his life scientific interests were rivaled, and to some degree supplanted, by his absorption with heterodox theological inquiries.[26] The draft of a letter of 1762, apparently sent to a budding physician who sought his advice on a course of study, underscores the importance Holyoke attached to a firm grounding in general physical science as a foundation for the practice of medicine: "Some of ye Best Writers in Natural & Experimental (or what is otherwise call.d ye Newtonian) Philosophy almost every Branch of which you will in ye End find to contribute to ye Advancing You in a firm & Rational Theory of Physick: Gravesand's, Desaguiliers [*sic*] & Martin's Philosophical writings are I believe as well suited as any to this Purpose and ye first of these You will find particularly adapted to recall to Your mind ye Experimental Lectures you heard from Mr. Winthrop while at College."[27]

His colleague Cotton Tufts was born in Medford. After a brief stint at teaching school, he studied medicine with an older brother, established a practice at Weymouth, and became an active organizer of the Massachusetts Medical Society, over which he presided in 1787. An assiduous attendant at its sessions even in rough winter weather, a local church deacon, and president of the Society for the Reforma-

---

26. Holyoke's *An Ethical Essay or an Attempt to Enumerate the Several Duties which we owe to God, our Saviour, our Neighbour and ourselves, and the Virtues and Graces of the Christian Life* was published posthumously in Salem, 1830.

27. Salem, Mass., Essex Institute: Holyoke Papers, Box 6, Folder 1, E. A. Holyoke to Mr. A., undated draft; final copy sent 25 Oct. 1762.

tion of Morals, he was one of the local revolutionaries who voted regularly with the colonial insurgents and later with the federalists, consistently following the lead of his friend John Adams. (Tufts was married to Lucy Quincy, Abigail Adams's aunt.)

David Cobb of Attleborough had a motley career not unusual for the period: a doctor by training, he exchanged his role as an army surgeon for that of a general officer on Washington's staff; subsequently he became a judge and a legislator, whose political activities were interspersed with attempts at farming in Maine. The memoranda to be found among his papers, now in the Massachusetts Historical Society, give evidence of his versatility: they dealt with subjects such as the effects of opium use and pickling salmon. Doctors turned successively soldiers, judges, legislators, and gentlemen farmers testify to the professional fluidity of the new leadership. The Academy received them all under its canopy, though some of its councillors had misgivings about members not wholeheartedly committed to the promotion of arts and sciences.

Cobb was brother-in-law to Dr. Ebenezer Hunt. In this small society the marital alliances among the notables were frequent and their meetings in the Academy were reunions of old Harvard classmates, fellow revolutionaries, brother parishioners, and family relations. Dr. Hunt belonged to one of the first families that had settled along the Connecticut River. His practice covered a large territory around Northampton, and he was famous for his devotion to his patients in all seasons, tending them with gentleness and good humor irrespective of their station in life. Descriptions of his manner as a doctor note that he was adept at relieving his patients' anxiety and depression, though sparing in the use of medicines. In 1789 his brother-in-law Cobb prevailed upon him to have an operation performed on his head, where a cancer was forming. The fortitude with which he bore excruciating pain during the procedure became legendary. After the retirement of the lawyer Major Hawley, Hunt became the perennial moderator at Northampton town meetings and from time to time was elected to the Senate, though citizens of the district were uneasy about his absenting himself from their midst.

Oliver Prescott, who practiced medicine at Groton before the Revolution, joined the militia like a number of other doctors, and rose to the rank of major-general. At the time of Shays' Rebellion his law-and-order stance was akin to that of his fellow soldier-doctors in the Academy: he undertook to enlist recruits and to collect intelligence of the insurgents' movements. One of the incorporators of the Massachusetts Medical Society, Prescott was awarded an honorary M.D. by Harvard in 1791, the university's way of compensating for the lack of a medical school before President Willard filled the vacuum.

John Barnard Swett was a rarity among the incorporating members. Born in Marblehead of a family who had introduced foreign commerce into the town and a graduate of Harvard like almost everybody else, he received his medical education abroad, in Edinburgh, where he made the acquaintance of the leading intellectuals, including David Hume. Thereafter he attended hospitals both in England and in France. He served with the revolutionary army in Rhode Island under General Sullivan and survived the disastrous Penobscot expedition, escaping with his surgical instruments. Like his fellow-physician Dr. Joseph Warren he rose to the highest degrees of the Freemasonic order, though it has been vehemently denied that he was an initiate into the German sect of Illuminati. In 1796, while attending the sick of Newburyport during a yellow fever plague, he was infected and died a martyr to his profession. Charles Jarvis of Boston had also studied in England and was acquainted as well with French medical practice. In politics he was a maverick. After the War of Independence he favored pardoning the Loyalists; and he supported France through all her revolutionary permutations. The formation of the Massachusetts Medical Society does not seem to have alienated the allegiance of the doctors of physic from the Academy—their sociability encompassed both institutions.

Businessmen Virtuous and Reprobate

A significant segment of the original incorporated members was composed of merchants and men of independent wealth not identified with the three principal civilian callings. Of the three Cushings, Thomas was the best known in his lifetime. After twenty years as a Boston merchant, in the 1760s he was elected to the General Court, the beginning of his career as a professional politician. He was one of the merchants who helped organize opposition to the successive regulatory innovations of the Crown, while at the same time working for an amicable settlement of the colony's differences with the mother country. Cushing accepted membership on the Committee of Correspondence (1773) and the Committee of Safety (1774), and was elected to the various revolutionary bodies, provincial congresses of Massachusetts, and continental congresses. But for a time he followed the insurgents only up to—not inclusive of—the fire, and when he was averse to joining with other patriots in declaring independence from the mother country, the General Court of Massachusetts replaced him with Elbridge Gerry as a delegate to Congress. Once the die was cast, he sat on the Council that acted as the supreme executive power in Massachusetts, and after the state constitution was adopted he became the perennial lieutenant-governor. As a Hancock man he was no intimate of James Bowdoin's, but he managed to get on tolerably well with all parties. His minister Peter Thacher knew his changeling soul and on occasion was censorious of his capacity for accommodation. On the day of Bowdoin's inauguration as president of the Academy, Cushing was conveniently missing.

Nathaniel Tracy of Newburyport was one of the richest and most adventuresome of the charter members. During the Revolution he and his brother-in-law Jonathan

Jackson, also a charter member, outfitted a fleet of privateers that captured scores of British vessels carrying ammunition and supplies. Tracy also launched 110 merchant vessels, all but 12 of which were seized by the enemy. His meteoric financial rise was followed by reverses that plunged him into virtual bankruptcy. Being named to the Academy was probably a reward for his devotion to the cause, though, as with other honored entrepreneurs, his qualifications also included a Harvard degree. Jackson, after a period as aide-de-camp to General Benjamin Lincoln when he was engaged in suppressing Shays' Rebellion, became a federal tax official as well as treasurer of Massachusetts and of Harvard College. These varied activities did not exhaust his intellectual curiosity, and in his old age, perhaps stimulated by the scientific interests of his colleagues in the Academy, he took up the study of chemistry. Tristram Dalton, also of Newburyport, supplied the revolutionary army with rum, oatmeal, and clothing, and held offices in the legislature and at Harvard. He was a religious anomaly among the Academicians, an Episcopalian active in the organization of his church. Though generally considered a Hancock man, he supported Bowdoin during Shays' Rebellion. In the nineties he left Massachusetts for Washington, to take up his duties as treasurer of the mint and director of the Bank of the United States.

Among the first Fellows chosen to be the earliest members of the council of the Academy were two men of means renowned for their zeal during the crucial revolutionary years, James Warren of Plymouth and John Hancock turned Bostonian, one a friend and collaborator of James Bowdoin, the other his bitter political rival.

The Stoical Warrens

James Warren was a descendant of Richard Warren of the *Mayflower*. Perhaps it was family pride that in part accounted for the occasionally superior attitude he manifested toward the new leaders. With roots in Plymouth, he was reluctant to move out of the Massachusetts sphere, where he occupied a prominent political position in successive legislative assemblies from 1766 on. He participated in the Revolution in a military capacity as well, and was variously known as "Colonel" or "General" (he was paymaster general of the Continental army), until his resignation over a matter of rank. Warren was a loner who never won great popular acclaim; nor did he remain friends with any of the old patriots in his later years. Sour and querulous, he was captiously critical of all of them, while complaining that they neglected him. In some respects his political career paralleled Bowdoin's; both were outshone by John Hancock and John Adams.

Women were not candidates for the American Academy of Arts and Sciences —the question never arose—but a Plymouth matron as formidable as any of the Massachusetts leaders whose names appeared on the original list was Warren's wife, Mercy, sister of the mad patriot James Otis. Though Mercy terrified others, in her relations with James Warren she was the obedient wife, adopting a Stoic posture, guiding her sons along the path of virtue, religion, honor, and patriotism. The hardiest of men dreaded her sharp tongue; but in her affectionate letters to her husband, enlisted in his country's defense and fighting for its rights, she purred. While her correspondence with English friends was fiery, defiant, often exploding into purple passages with contrived and overheated imagery, the letters to her absent husband had a touching simplicity. She confided to him her fears, told of her nightmares, worried about his safety, reported on her training of their sons with meticulous care, and sought his counsel. And the loving trust was returned.

Ultimately the Warrens recoiled before the realities of Massachusetts politics, which besmirched their Roman ideal. In the nature of things their bête noire was John Hancock, who was deficient in every virtue they expected in a republican. Mercy called him a wealthy flagitious villain and a man of straw.[28] The extravagance and luxury that were invading their American idyl outraged them. They were appalled by the frequent balls and assemblies, appurtenances of courts; the issuance of paper money spelled the end of virtue; and they deplored the spirit of debauchery that was spreading through the countryside. On 18 December 1780, James Warren wrote to his son Winslow from Plymouth, "Could we agree to Level to the Ground all Ball & Assembly rooms, to Abolish all Extravagant Living & Equipage, & again recur to our antient Living, & simple Manners, to bring into Countenance again Patriotism Virtue & religion, we might soon regard Britain with all her Fleets & Armies as an Insignificant Nation."[29]

Warren's God was the God of nature, but He also provided for immortality and commanded upright living. Both Mercy and James Otis had learned to emulate their classical models, and in their writings Romans were invoked far more often than Christ. But the Calvinist spirit was sufficiently alive in them to make them abhor Baptists, Quakers, Deists, and Catholic priests. In their souls Calvinism had turned into a Roman civic religion in which duty and obligation were writ large. Their estimates of human conduct were not graced with any conceptions of the natural goodness of humankind. Men being what they were, the Warrens were not surprised by political treachery, infamy, contemptible behavior. But their own course was clear: they walked uprightly in the shadow of their Roman heroes.

Bowdoin was Warren's friend during the revolutionary years, when they sat in councils together, but after the fighting was over Warren grew estranged from his old comrades-in-arms.[30] He got to dislike Bowdoin, with his chilly aspect, on political and personal grounds: he believed that Bowdoin had violated the Mas-

---

28. MHS, *Collections* 73 (Warren-Adams Letters, 2), 253, Mercy Warren to John Adams, Milton Hill, 27 Apr. 1785.

29. MHS, Mercy Warren Papers, James Warren to Winslow Warren, Plymouth, 18 Dec. 1780.

30. MHS, *Collections* 73 (Warren-Adams Letters, 2), 325, Mercy Warren to John Adams, Plymouth, 14 Jan. 1791.

sachusetts constitution in holding the Shaysites in prison, and he was under the misapprehension that Bowdoin had refused to write a letter in behalf of Warren's son Winslow, the apple of Mercy's eye, when he tried to obtain the consulship in Lisbon.[31] Even Roman virtue had its weaknesses.

Of the revolutionary leaders in Massachusetts, both James Warren and James Bowdoin were tied to their native soil and businesses with strong bonds that gave them reason to avoid service outside their own territory. There were doubtless supporting motives—their state of health, the anxieties and sickness of their wives. They disliked having to compete for office—the humiliation of a possible rejection at times outweighed the ambition for power and the dignities of position, to which they were far from indifferent. James Warren was a worthy merchant-farmer of Plymouth, and in his own locality office was bestowed upon him by right of his person. To travel as far as Boston was a burden to him, and though he was often chosen as the speaker of the General Court it meant being uprooted from the soil that he owned and the town that he usually dominated by his mere presence. He thought of himself as a man of character, full of republican virtue, and he was quick to castigate his compatriots for their avarice and peculations. He and Mercy often repeated the identical charges simultaneously in their letters to friends. With continual disappointment he would discover that neither his austerity nor his virtue were universally appreciated. One of his constant worries, when he was paymaster-general of the Continental army while it was at Cambridge and Boston, was that there might be some conflict between his private interest as a merchant and the public interest. Incorruptible as he was, however, Warren was exceedingly touchy about the recognition and honor due his station. In September of 1776 the General Court had designated him, as one of the three major generals of the provincial militia, to lead a force into Rhode Island; but, unwilling to be subordinate to a Continental army officer of lower rank, he pled illness, and the next year resigned his commission in order to avoid further embarrassment. Both Warren and Bowdoin were respected for their integrity and good sense on the Massachusetts Board of War during the Revolution, but outside their own bailiwicks they were not loved or known by the people.

Hancock, the Perennial Adversary

In the surviving papers of James Bowdoin there are few explicit attacks on revolutionary colleagues, and he in turn usually got off rather lightly at the hands of

31. Bowdoin had warmly recommended Winslow to Jefferson; see Jefferson, *Papers* 8 (1953), 601, Bowdoin to Jefferson, 10 Oct. 1785; see also Jefferson to John Adams, Paris, 27 Dec. 1785, referring to letters from Bowdoin, Adams, and Cushing in favor of the young man (ibid. 9 [1954], 127) and Jefferson to Bowdoin, Paris, 8 Feb. 1786 (ibid., 263).

his contemporaries. But there was one exception to Bowdoin's forbearance: he expressed enduring animosity toward John Hancock, with whom he battled for the top of the hill—Beacon Hill—where both had come to own mansions.

The governing boards of Harvard College and of Cooper's church were normally the places where Hancock and Bowdoin, like two billy-goats, locked horns. If personality differences generated antagonism from the very beginning, a series of encounters deepened the enmity. Grievous wounds were inflicted, and though many shifts in political alignments occurred during the revolutionary era, deadly hostility between Hancock and Bowdoin in Boston civic affairs was perennial. They were divided over everything. When Cooper's death left the Brattle Street pulpit vacant, as the Reverend John Eliot related with clerical murmuring to the Reverend Jeremy Belknap, "The Bowdoin interest have set up John Bradford [of the Second Church in Roxbury] & are determined to push for him. . . . The Hancock party, which I believe are ye most numerous, are determined to crush him."[32] In the end, the Reverend Peter Thacher won, and he buried Bowdoin and Hancock in sequence with appropriate funeral orations.

In any sodality where they met, these two powerful men challenged each other. A duel would have been the inevitable consequence in an aristocratic society, or at least a bloody skirmish between their respective "toughs." In the newborn peace-loving world of Christian businessmen, they had to vent their spleen by bidding for the most prominent pews in Samuel Cooper's church, by fighting over the location of the new church structure in 1772,[33] by vying for the role of chief patron of Harvard College, by competing for the governorship of the Commonwealth of Massachusetts. Except for an initial foray, John Hancock abandoned the swampy fields of the American Academy to James Bowdoin. Once Hancock won the governorship in 1780, he held it until his death except for Bowdoin's ill-fated terms in 1785 to 1787. Though scenes of combat between them were open and bitter, the tilting of lances at Harvard was kept relatively quiet—but nothing was effectively concealed for long in this small, backbiting, cantankerous society.

Hancock was simultaneously treasurer of Harvard College, an office to which he had been appointed in July 1773, and president of the Continental Congress. In 1776 an Overseers' committee chaired by Bowdoin reported a resolution declaring it inexpedient and unsafe that the obligations and securities belonging to Harvard should remain in Philadelphia in Hancock's hands. Since the enemy was occupying New York, it could cut off communications between the southern and northern colonies, with di-

---

32. MHS, *Collections*, ser. 6.4 (Belknap Papers, 3), 271, John Eliot to Jeremy Belknap, Boston, 6 Feb. 1784.

33. Lothrop, *History of the Church in Brattle Street*, 95–99. Charles W. Akers, Cooper's recent biographer, doubts that Hancock and Bowdoin disputed over the new building for the church (*The Divine Politician*, 129).

sastrous consequences for the existence of the university. A committee was appointed on 18 November to wait upon Hancock in Philadelphia and receive the securities from him.[34] Harvard was in a most embarrassing position: in the midst of a war it had to importune Hancock, heroically preoccupied with the service of his countrymen, for an accounting of funds. Hancock, who continued his customary style of elegant living even in benighted Philadelphia and was often short of cash to pay his debts, was offended by the persistence and presumption of Harvard, and retaliated by striking a defiant, spiteful, hurt, and sometimes downright insolent pose in his dealings with the college. Once the Hancockian feathers had been ruffled, this arrogant man made no attempt to mask his profound contempt for the professors and clergymen with whom he occasionally had to consort. Nathaniel Balch the hatter was his preferred crony on tavern-hopping expeditions. Hancock could appear at a meeting of the Corporation and face down his most daring adversary. He bullied Harvard's officers as he would insistent business creditors for whom he had scant regard.

On 8 January 1777, Stephen Hall, a tutor at the college, was instructed to get at least a list of the securities that had been changed since Hancock's appointment as treasurer, along with an account of the time to which the interest on all the securities in his hands had been paid. In a private letter from President Samuel Langdon, Hall was advised to consult with John Adams, Hancock's fellow delegate from Massachusetts to the Continental Congress, and have the list attested by a notary public. At that point the Congress, fearing a British attack, had removed briefly to Baltimore. Hancock and his family were residing in wretched quarters, and the treasurer was in no mood to treat with Hall. He sent him off with some of the money, but no interest and only a few records. On 12 March 1777, Hancock's attorney forwarded to the Corporation bonds, mortgages, and notes to the nominal value of £16,000, but without the accounting that was to have accompanied the securities. For the rest of Hancock's life, Harvard made repeated attempts to obtain a full record of his stewardship. Responding to Hancock's complaint at being dunned, on 22 April the President and Fellows substituted verbosity for peremptory action and sent him a letter of twenty-eight pages that endeavored to explain their conduct toward him. When the windy memorandum made no stronger impression than earlier efforts, the Corporation on the advice of the Board of Overseers elected Ebenezer Storer to replace Hancock as treasurer. Though they felt his letters to them had been harshly worded, they professed great esteem for him and explained his removal on the ground that his employment in the American Congress unavoidably prevented the discharge of his duties toward the college.[35]

---

34. Ford, ed., "Letters of the Reverend Gordon," loc. cit., 338, William Gordon to John Adams, Jamaica Plain, 27 Mar. 1777.

35. Harvard University Archives: Corporation Records, II F.

To celebrate the landing of the French in Boston in October 1778, "General" Hancock—general of militia—gave lavish entertainments that became legendary. Of one ball Benjamin Guild cattily recounted in his diary that it "was attended by Count D'Estaing and about 70 of his officers, on whose more immediate account it was made. About 130 or 140 ladies appeared with all their brilliance. They danced &c till morning. Many of the few gentlemen of the town that were invited were aged and married. The expences of the entertainment were estimated at about 1500£."[36] But Harvard still received no settlement.

In its dealings with Hancock the university blew hot and cold, threatening him at one moment, at another timorously seeking to mollify him. At the invitation and expense of the Corporation he had consented to be painted by Copley, and as a quid pro quo offered Harvard a new fence, but still neglected to furnish a reckoning of his years as treasurer. The Reverend William Gordon, an overseer, commented sardonically that though this "egregious trifler" would probably never honor his commitments, the Corporation and Board of Overseers had no reason to feel affronted, since he treated everyone in the same manner.[37] Clearly, Hancock was practiced in the art of stalling creditors. Copley's half brother, Henry Pelham, trying in vain to collect money owed the artist, complained angrily at the transparent pretexts Hancock resorted to in order to avoid paying his bill: he was forever lying down, suffering with headache, absent, or without access to his papers when Pelham sought an audience with him.[38] Upon Hancock's election as governor of the Commonwealth the university warmly congratulated him; yet they talked of filing suit against him even while he occupied the highest office in the state. At ceremonial functions during Lafayette's visit to the college acrimonious disputes involving the deference due or not due Hancock arose over seating precedence.

After Bowdoin became a Fellow and member of the Corporation, he used his influence in person or through intermediaries to have Hancock censured. An Overseers' committee headed by General Artemas Ward had made valiant and persistent efforts to bring Hancock to terms, but quit in frustration when the great patriot seemed im-

36. Harvard University Archives: Benjamin Guild, Diary, 1776, 1778 (MS), entry for Thursday, 29 Oct. 1778. For a detailed description of the ball that corroborates Guild's account, see the Boston *Independent Chronicle*, 5 Nov. 1778, quoted in *Adams Family Correspondence* 3:118, n. 3. Though his remarks appear under the date 29 October, Guild clearly wrote them later, for on that day he had tea with acquaintances who *were to attend* the ball in the evening. See also MHS, Miscellaneous Bound, Hancock, fragment of a letter, 28 Oct. 1778, where plans for the ball are said to be "secret and confidential."

37. Ford, ed., "Letters of the Reverend Gordon," loc. cit., 436, William Gordon to John Adams, Jamaica Plain, 22 July 1780.

38. MHS, *Collections* 71 (Letters and Papers of John Singleton Copley and Henry Pelham), 232, Pelham to Copley, Boston, 17 July 1774, and 268, Pelham to Copley, Philadelphia, 2 Nov. 1774.

pervious to their petty molestation. Thereupon Bowdoin, along with Mr. Lothrop and Mr. Howard—businessmen were being introduced into the governing board to deal with financial matters—notified His Excellency that they had been constituted a committee to report on the status of Harvard's funds at the forthcoming Overseers' meeting; and in May of 1783, with Hancock in the Chair, the Overseers after a presentation of the facts finally voted that they would advise the Corporation to sue if their presiding officer continued his dilatory tactics. Though more than the usual pressure was now being exerted on Hancock to put his accounts in order, William Gordon shrewdly observed that the ex-treasurer would likely contrive still another postponement.[39] Nevertheless, the meeting embarrassed Hancock and he saw it as a grave offense to his person. Evasive or brash when confronted with his unconscionable indifference toward meeting financial obligations, he resented any measures taken by Harvard to protect its interests. In the summer of 1785 he wrote a curt note to the newly elected Governor Bowdoin declining to attend Harvard's commencement because of the indignity he had suffered at the Overseers' meeting two years earlier, when he had presided while the record of his derelictions as treasurer was read aloud.[40]

On 23 September 1785, the President and Fellows, including Bowdoin, now governor of Massachusetts, voted that the sum due the Corporation from Hancock be settled by payment or security before the fifteenth day of October, and that the new treasurer be directed, in case of Hancock's failure to comply, to bring an action for recovery. Hancock admitted he owed more than £1,300, but, unabashed, made no move to discharge the debt. A month after the deadline, since the money was not forthcoming, the President and Fellows again voted that Lowell, the treasurer, and Howard constitute a committee to seek proper means for securing the balance due from Hancock, but whatever steps they took were ineffectual. The spectacle of Harvard suing its former treasurer and ex-governor of the state, however, was denied the groundlings of Boston. And in 1792, when Bowdoin was dead and Hancock once again governor, the university bowed to political expediency and awarded him the degree of Doctor of Laws (an honor he had rejected in 1782, probably because Bowdoin was then an influential figure in the Corporation).

Since Hancock died intestate, his heirs were left with the problem of finally closing his accounts with the university, which took what it could get: the principal of the debt along with simple interest, but without the compound interest that had accrued through the years. Hancock's signature as the symbol of financial integrity is one of the little ironies in the history of the Boston patriots. Great revolutions often spawn Hancock types: the people love their panache, revel in their prodigality,

39. Ford, ed., "Letters of the Reverend Gordon," loc. cit., 494–95, William Gordon to John Adams, Jamaica Plain, 28 June 1783.

40. MHS, *Proceedings*, ser. 2.8:63–64, Hancock to Bowdoin, Dorchester, 18 July 1785.

drink their kegs of rum, and ultimately enshrine them in the temple of virtue. As Mercy Warren observed, after Hancock's death "a mantle of love was thrown over his foibles by his countrymen."[41]

Hancock contributed no scientific memoirs to the American Academy of Arts and Sciences, but he stayed on its council for five years. He was usually reluctant to surrender office — any office; when re-elected president of the Continental Congress, he held onto the post for months without ever putting in an appearance. The soul of John Adams was a battleground for conflicting political and moral philosophies; Samuel Adams had plain but firm conceptions of liberty and government that he clutched with the religious enthusiasm of a believer from another age; Hancock, without giving a hoot about philosophical abstractions, for which he had no stomach, moved from one popular triumph to another, a manipulator with no known vices more grave than drunkenness. He was given to outbursts of generosity, to sentimentality, even to occasional assumptions of responsibility. To our knowledge, his megalomania was free of the self-doubt and self-persecution that tormented John Adams. Hancock was surely deficient in the Calvinist sense of duty, the obsessive orderliness, the refusal to court popularity openly, and the capacity for cool analysis that distinguished James Bowdoin. Despite its partisan nature, Thomas Hutchinson's character of Hancock is not far from the mark: "[His] ruling passion was a fondness for popular applause . . . but he was fickle, and inconstant in the means of pursuing it."[42] Another hostile witness, the Tory chief justice Peter Oliver, expressed the contempt of a shrewd investor for Hancock's overweening political ambition and the consequent neglect of business that had reduced his finances to a low ebb: "His Mind was a meer *Tabula Rasa*," Oliver snarled.[43]

Under British rule neither Bowdoin nor Hancock had been strangers to the world of the smugglers, but their personalities were poles apart. James Warren caught the contrast of temperaments in a letter of 11 July 1780, written during their first contest for the governorship: "I dont envy either of them their feelings. the Vanity of one of them will Sting like an Adder if it is disappointed, and the Advancements made by the other if they dont succeed will hurt his *Modest* pride."[44] After the election Warren wrote with penetrating hindsight that Bowdoin had never stood a chance. Hancock's "frequent and brilliant Entertainments strengthen his popularity, and whether it will end in Absolute Adoration, or in the Exhaustion of the Sources of profusion I cant say."[45] When John Adams was in-

41. Mercy Warren, *History of the American Revolution* 1:431.

42. Hutchinson, *History of Massachusetts Bay*, ed. Mayo, 3:214–15.

43. *Peter Oliver's Origin & Progress of the American Rebellion*, ed. Adair and Schutz, 40.

44. MHS, *Collections* 73 (Warren-Adams Letters, 2), 135, James Warren to John Adams, Boston, 11 July 1780.

45. Ibid., 141, James Warren to John Adams, Boston, 12 Oct. 1780.

formed by Samuel Cooper about the election results, he replied from Amsterdam avoiding congratulations to the new governor and expressing his hopes—and obvious misgivings—for the Commonwealth: "Much will depend upon the wisdom and firmness of the first governor; and much upon the impartiality and liberality with which he hearkens to the advice of such as have abilities and dispositions to give the best. There are characters in the Massachusetts, very able, if they draw together, to conduct the state through every perplexity and danger; but if any little or great animosities, should estrange them from each other, the consequences will be very disagreeable. They may be very pernicious."[46]

After his initial intervention over the unalphabetized list of incorporated Fellows when the Academy Act was still in the legislature, Hancock never again played a significant role in the history of the society. While in his own eyes he was the greatest patriot, philanthropist, man of affairs, friend of the people, orator, strategist, even military commander of the Revolution, he had no pretensions to being a scholar. With James Bowdoin in the chair, there was small likelihood of his assisting at academic exercises. But popular versifiers continued to feature Hancock as the Hero of the Academy. The peroration of a poem by one "Philotechnus" immortalizes his name alone among the members:

> This New Academy, the World shall bless.
> The source of future Nations's Happiness.
> May all its noble Patron's—*Hancock*, with the reste
> With growing Glories here,—with Endless Life,—be blest.[47]

---

46. John Adams, *Correspondence Published in the Boston Patriot*, 290, Letter 38, Quincy, 25 Aug. 1809, quoting letter to Samuel Cooper, Amsterdam, 6 Dec. 1780.

47. Academy Letters, 1:14, poem by "Philotechnus."

7

TEN YEARS IN THE CHAIR

❦

IN THE early fall of 1780 the war with Britain was far from resolution, and many of those in attendance at the inauguration of the Academy on 8 November were proscribed men. The Harvard student body, its numbers much reduced, was back in Cambridge from its Babylonian Captivity in Concord, but it had been infected with a rebellious spirit, manifested in the public humiliation and forced resignation of President Langdon. Though the port of Boston was relatively secure again, anxieties were not completely dissipated even when the French expedition landed in Newport to aid the patriots. Boston was only beginning to recuperate from the depredations of the British occupation, during which many hallowed Congregational churches had been desecrated, turned into barracks or practice grounds for the cavalry. The Second Church, known as the Old North, had been demolished by order of General Howe. The interior of the Old South Church had been entirely destroyed by British dragoons, and its library of ancient books and manuscripts deposited in the steeple had been vandalized. The Peace of 1783 would find the "Venice of New England" shorn of many of the attributes that had made it pre-eminent among the towns. Before the war its population had reached nearly twenty thousand; at the time of the siege in 1775 it had sunk to six thousand, consisting of those who were unable to move or refused to leave their homes. By the early 1780s the inhabitants numbered a little over twelve thousand. British occupation, pestilence, and the flight of the Tories had devastated Boston; a decade was to pass before it returned to its former size.

There had been a strong Tory contingent that played at forming an aristocratic court around the British governor. Now country squires who had resisted the British came to settle in the capital and filled the gap left by the expatriates. Many upper-class families had been divided by the war: three of James Bowdoin's brothers-in-law, two the sons of Captain John Erving and one his sister's husband, Thomas Flucker, were Loyalists, and so was the elder son of the Reverend Samuel Mather. Merchants who stayed behind during the siege were open to accusations of conniving with the enemy. After the evacuation of the British troops, those suspected of Loyalist sympathies suffered harassment at the hands of their demonstrably patriotic fellow citizens. John Rowe, the owner of Rowe's Wharf, created such a fracas in the council chamber when he was about to attend the funeral of his fellow Freemason Dr. Joseph Warren, who had died in the battle of Bunker Hill and was to be re-interred in Boston to the accompaniment of Samuel Cooper's prayers, that he prudently withdrew. When Harvard chose a new steward whose political opinions were questionable, public clamor in the newspapers forced the Corporation to rescind the appointment.[1] Even the most dedicated patriots, like James Bowdoin himself, during election contests were charged by their opponents with lukewarmness. Denunciations of Loyalist sympathizers did not reach the later frenzy of the hunt for suspects during the French Revolution, but neutrality toward the cause was not often tolerated.

The Inaugural Lecture

During the summer months of 1780, while Hancock, Bowdoin, Sam Adams, and James Warren—or their partisans—busied themselves spreading false rumors about one another, the work of the newborn Academy was carried forward. Articles for its governance were drafted by a committee, and minor offices filled by careful voting procedures. Only after the heat of the state election had subsided was the American Academy of Arts and Sciences formally inaugurated in a ceremonial performance in the Brattle Street Church. In the early 1780s political leadership of the state and control of the American Academy were vested in the same heterogeneous group of patriots, an amalgam of rival factions. The headship was clearly divided, Governor Hancock wielding the temporal sword, President Bowdoin girded with a spiritual sword in a sheath of science. John Adams continued his intermittent correspondence from afar with the American Academy in Boston, and may be credited with some, though not all, of the peculiar choices of foreign Fellows in the early years, for example his publicist friends Luzac and Dumas, and two obscure Spanish noblemen who had befriended him. Upon the death of Bowdoin in 1790 Adams would succeed to the presidency of the Academy. But in 1780, with Adams absent, James Bowdoin grasped the reins of office and put his personal stamp upon the institution, an imprint not completely faded after two centuries.

The eighth of November 1780 was a great day in the history of the Academy, full of contrarieties to the observer from another age. It had been voted on 30 August that the oath prescribed by the statutes would be administered to the new president by the Honorable Thomas Cushing Esquire, lieutenant-governor of the Commonwealth; but since for reasons unrevealed he was absent from the county courthouse in Boston where the meeting of the Academy was held, the Fellows decided that the

1. MHS, *Proceedings*, ser. 2.10 (1895–96), 99, Diary of John Rowe, entry for 8 Apr. 1776; Harvard University Archives: Diary of Benjamin Guild, 1776, 1778 (MS), entries for 16 Nov., 7, 15 Dec. 1778.

oath would be given to Bowdoin by His Excellency Governor Hancock, who had recently beaten him in a hotly contested election.[2] The swearing-in brought together these two inveterate enemies against a new background. The spectacle of Governor Hancock administering the oath of office to James Bowdoin as first president of the American Academy of Arts and Sciences is one of the minor comic episodes of Massachusetts political life, which has so often bordered on the theater of the absurd.

After the ceremony in the courthouse, the Fellows repaired to Dr. Cooper's church, where, the records show, "a learned and elegant oration adapted to the nature of the institution was delivered by the Honorable, the President, to the members of the Academy and a numerous and respectable auditory."[3] After introductory remarks extolling learned societies, the fountainheads of science whose delicious waters might be imbibed in deep draughts without danger of intoxication, Bowdoin launched into the principal themes of the discourse. He first dilated upon the evils of luxury, the fatal disease that had ever led to the decay of states and empires. A philosophical memento mori was a peculiar subject for the initiation of the new order of the centuries, but it was an authentic mirror of the president's soul, which never overflowed with easy optimism. Bowdoin reflected on the world *sub specie aeternitatis*: "It is very pleasing and instructive — to recur back to the early ages of mankind, and trace the progressive state of nations and empires, from infancy to maturity, to old age, and dissolution." It was at the summit of greatness that the inevitable principle of mortality was set in motion by affluence and luxury. With the neutrality of a Newtonian observing the revolutions of the planets, Bowdoin foresaw after the final catastrophe of a civilization "new kingdoms and empires rising upon the ruins of the old; all to undergo like changes, and to suffer a similar dissolution."[4] Coming from the wealthy merchant and landowner with a well-stocked cellar of wines addressing his equals, this was a moral homily in which a historico-philosophical lesson replaced the traditional sermon on the vice of ostentation. It was reasonable and abstract, distant from the realities of everyday life and the hardships of the war endured by many insurgent patriots, perhaps a Calvinist residue embroidered with the thoughts of an American *philosophe* who had delved into the volumes of his own rich library. Six years later, during Shays' Rebellion, the new barbarians appeared within the city and harangued against the Bowdoin style of life. In half-literate scribbles they berated the eastern merchants for covering their women's backs with shining silks while the people starved and shivered, their farms seized for debt.

2. Academy Records, 1:37–38.

3. James Bowdoin, *A philosophical discourse, addressed to the American Academy of Arts and Sciences, in the presence of a respectable audience, assembled at the Meeting-House in Brattle-street, in Boston, on the Eighth of November 1780, After the inauguration of the President into Office* (Boston, 1780).

4. Ibid., 10–11.

With a creaky shifting of gears, Bowdoin moved from the rise and fall of ancient empires to the promotion of a knowledge of American antiquities, one of
the stated purposes of the Academy. Antiquities could serve to verify history, rectify its errors, and fill in its interstices, even as, reciprocally, history could explain
and illustrate the inarticulate objects. Typically Europocentric, Bowdoin in passing denigrated the culture of the American Indians, which he concluded had been
static through the ages because of their contemporary lack of civilization and, in
particular, literature. But he appealed to the descendants of early settlers to report
to the Academy remains or records that might in any way correct history or otherwise benefit the public.

In treating the importance of natural history, the next subject mentioned in the
charter of the Academy, Bowdoin noted that elementary arts had been communicated by the Creator to early, necessitous men, and that further skills and accomplishments were consequent upon exercising the capacities with which they had
been endowed. At this point Bowdoin found himself in something of a quandary.
How to reconcile the declaratory "All men are created equal" with the striking
differences in state of civilization between Europe and Africa, between the most
advanced nations and the Hottentots? Was there a greater or lesser exertion of
equal capacities or better use of them? Or were those faculties unequal, "collectively taken, as probably is the case?"[5] In grappling with the troublesome question,
Bowdoin resorted to Montesquieu's climatic explanations of racial and national
characteristics—but not without emendation. Inequalities were fostered also by
human and social factors such as education, religion, government, or the "appearance of some happy genius" to instruct and direct the people.

This observation heralded the interpolation of a spirited denunciation of British
tyranny. Would the people of the United States, in the same temperate climate
and with the same natural capacities, have exerted themselves so vigorously, if at
all, against Britain's "inslaving domination, if they had not been educated in the
principles of liberty; if their religion, like that of some sectaries among them, had
not allowed them to make use of carnal weapons in the defence of their liberty;
or if they had lived under a despotic government, and believed in the doctrine of
passive obedience and non resistance? Or, lastly, if some among them, well situated to observe the course and tendency of British policy, had not alarmed them
of their danger?"[6]

Having disposed of antiquities and natural history with various ramifications
according to his best lights, Bowdoin turned to a panegyric of Harvard, as though
he had exhausted his rather meager philosophical treasury. He saw the Academy as

5. Ibid., 15.
6. Ibid., 17.

intimately connected with Harvard so long as science remained in the world and nature endured. He expressed gratitude to the founders of the college, which had suckled the members of the new society with the "nectareous milk of science" and prepared them for the serious inquiries they were now expected to undertake.[7] In the most extravagant terms he thanked by name John Harvard and a half-dozen of the early benefactors of the college, and, anonymously, its contemporary supporters, in the hope that others would be inspired to imitate their generous example.

Bowdoin donned the mantle of the soothsayer. "Rapt into future times," he imagined the pages of some American Livy or Thucydides a century hence narrating the events of war "made peculiarly calamitous by *British humanity*" and singing the praises of those broad-visioned ancestors now foregathered in the Reverend Samuel Cooper's meetinghouse. Who would have thought that amid the anguish of civil strife they could have given heed to matters of the intellect? Yet "superior to their distresses and animated by the generous principles which liberty and independency inspire, they instituted the excellent society, called THE AMERICAN ACADEMY OF ARTS AND SCIENCES."[8] It was an invitation to bask in the admiration of posterity. Bowdoin prophesied that the Academy would flourish by adhering to the tenets of Baconian experimental science, practiced by men to be chosen from every country, class, and profession on no other basis than their personal characters and professional skills.

The peroration of the president's address was a gloria to God in an idiom that had become familiar in the course of more than a century:

> When we contemplate the works of nature, animate and inanimate, connected with our earth . . . when we raise our view to the heavens, and behold the beauteous and astonishing scenes they present to us—unnumber'd worlds revolving in the immeasurable expanse; systems beyond systems composing one boundless universe: and all of them, if we may argue from analogy, peopled with an endless variety of inhabitants:—When we contemplate these works of nature, which no human eloquence can adequately describe, they force upon us the idea of a SUPREME MIND, the consummately perfect author of them.[9]

James Bowdoin II saw the dark side of human events, and speculated about the decline of nations, the end of the world, the absorption of eternity itself in the existence of the Deity. But he was not a pessimist in the spirit of Schopenhauer's nineteenth-century neologism. In his lecture-sermon before the Academy, Bowdoin discoursed on the evils of luxury and the catastrophes to which they inevitably led. But his address was more celebratory than admonitory, dedicated to a predic-

7. Ibid., 23.
8. Ibid., 26–27.
9. Ibid., 30.

tion of America's political and intellectual triumphs rather than its ultimate fated dissolution. To the extent that his auditors could pierce the haze of his infelicitous rhetoric, they probably ignored his general moral strictures and responded to the evocation of America's magnificent challenge to an obstinate and unjust Britain, already on the downgrade—though later, in December 1784, when his brother-in-law George Erving in London proposed to republish the oration, Bowdoin saw fit to delete a few harsh observations on Britain "wch may now be improper to be repeated"—among them the biting reference to "British humanity."[10]

Bowdoin's belief in the cyclical course of empires was a conception he held in common with John Adams, whose later marginalia on the works of Condorcet and other prophets of progress betray skepticism of any universal linear development of mankind. In the 1780s only a few of the surviving French *philosophes*, notably Turgot and Condorcet, and the English dissidents Price and Priestley firmly embraced the idea of infinite perfectibility without reservations. Such questions were being actively discussed among *philosophes* in the Anglo-French world, and American men of affairs had at least heard of their debates. John Adams read and cited Edward Gibbon. James Bowdoin's library did not include Gibbon's recently published work on the decline and fall of the Roman Empire, but they shared a certain similarity of viewpoint—though alas not of style. Speculative world philosophical history was becoming modish, and European fascination with the subject was dimly reflected in Bowdoin's provincial speech.

Though the American Revolution bred utopian and millennial expectations about the future—a *novus ordo seclorum*—and there were still some echoes of the seventeenth-century conviction that the Massachusetts Bay Colony was a New Jerusalem, a more traditional cyclical view of history persisted. The Boston patriots fancied themselves down-to-earth, practical men—John Adams made fun of millenarian and utopian thought.[11] Yet Adams read Thomas More, and Bowdoin, Fénelon; a translation of Sébastien Mercier's *Memoirs of the Year Two Thousand Five Hundred*, a progressionist manifesto, had an American edition (it was listed in the catalogue of Benjamin Guild's bookshop); and Washington's library included popular eighteenth-century utopias. The coexistence of two such incompatible conceptions, linear progress and the circular course of history, is another example of the intellectual and religious conflict in the breasts of the more philosophical New England revolutionaries. On the one hand Puritan millenarianism, fortified by a providential victory over the most powerful empire in the world, strengthened

10. MHS, Bowdoin and Temple Papers, Letter Book, 255, Bowdoin to George Erving, 15 Dec. 1784. Phrases were silently dropped from the version of the inaugural lecture printed in the first volume of the Academy *Memoirs*.

11. John Adams, *Works*, ed. Charles Francis Adams, 4:97.

their confidence that America was ushering in a new age. On the other hand, they could not free themselves of the normative cyclism they had imbibed from reading the classical historians. On alternate pages an American writer or orator advanced contradictory arguments. The dissonance was blaring.

When a conciliation was attempted, it was troubled. All societies were doomed because of the vice of *luxuria* that accompanied prosperity; but the patriot philosopher could try to stem the tide of evil and delay the end by teaching his fellow-countrymen the ways of virtue and continence. Sometimes it was supposed that wise laws would restrain the propagation of evil, the wicked propensities that a Calvinist knew resided in the soul of Everyman. Beneath the veneer of an ideal of worldly happiness and comfort lay the Puritan suspicion that any excess of material goods would lead to damnation. Yet these same men exerted themselves to found academies for the promotion of arts and sciences that would bring a life of ease, which would inevitably encourage vice and corruption. One catches the thoughtful ones, who knew the warring elements in their own natures, pleading on both sides of the contest without resolution. There were, of course, the heedless activists like Hancock, who plunged into their enterprises oblivious of the antinomies of any philosophical position.

An exchange of letters between the two Adams cousins—both members of the Academy—in the fall of 1790, when news of the revolution in France began to disturb the old Massachusetts firebrands, now grown mellow, honored, and skeptical, exemplifies the different admixtures of disenchantment and stubborn faith. On 12 September 1790, Vice-President John Adams wrote from New York to Samuel Adams, lieutenant-governor of Massachusetts:

> What, my old Friend, is this world about to become? Is the millennium commencing? Are the kingdoms of it about to be governed by reason? Your Boston town-meetings, and our Harvard College, have set the universe in motion. Every thing will be pulled down. So much seems certain. But what will be built up? Are there any principles of political architecture? What are they? Were Voltaire and Rousseau masters of them? Are their disciples acquainted with them? Locke taught them principles of liberty; but I doubt whether they have not yet to learn principles of government. Will the struggle in Europe, be anything more than a change of impostors and impositions?[12]

Burke's *Reflections on the Revolution in France* had not yet been published, but John Adams shared his misgivings about the idea of progress in action.

In his reply of 4 October, Samuel repeated John's forebodings, but tenaciously clung to his trust in the triumph of reason through education:

---

12. John Adams, Samuel Adams, *Four Letters*, 6, John Adams to Samuel Adams, New York, 12 Sept. 1790.

Has mankind seen the happy age? No, my Friend. The same tragedies have been acted on the theatre of the world, the same arts of tormenting have been studied and practised to this day; and even religion and reason united have never succeeded to establish the permanent foundations of political freedom and happiness, in the most enlightened countries on the earth. . . .

What then is to be done? Let divines and philosophers, statesmen and patriots, unite their endeavors to renovate the age,—by impressing the minds of men with the importance of educating their *little boys* and *girls* —of inculcating in the minds of youth, the fear and love of the Deity, and universal philanthropy. . . .[13]

The two Adamses expressed the differing moods of many literate Bostonians as they sought their way to a tenable moral position.

For James Bowdoin III the direction civilization would take had been foretold in the inaugural address by his father, from whom he inherited a few platitudinous analogies between the laws of politics and those of science that he sententiously imparted to his correspondents during the period of the French Revolution: "The Commotions in Europe seem at present to engage the attention of the world: and as Monarchies had their Origin in the ruin of Republics; so Republicks may be restored in the ruin of Monarchies; the counter operation of Extremes like the Vibrations of the Pendulum are influenced by Principales perhaps as powerful & certain in the political, as in the natural World."[14] As philosophical historians the Bowdoins were beyond their depth.

After the lecture, the Fellows repaired to the president's house, where they were regaled with a sumptuous dinner. In the afternoon it was the president's turn to administer the oaths to the other elected officers, beginning with Samuel Cooper, vice-president, and proceeding to His Excellency Governor Hancock, a councillor, before the rest—Henry Gardner, Esq., the Reverend Phillips Payson, the Honorable James Warren, Mr. Caleb Gannett, the Reverend Joseph Willard, future president of Harvard, and Ebenezer Storer. The august officers and councillors, at least nominally Calvinists and scions of Calvinists, full of dinner and of one another's oaths—which might have been anathema to many of their ancestors, for whom taking the name of God in vain was a sin of sins—then proceeded to serious business.

The Fellows voted thanks to Bowdoin for his oration and generous efforts to encourage and promote the arts and sciences, and begged the president for a copy of his speech in order to have it published. The next order of business was the

13. Ibid., 7–10, Samuel Adams to John Adams, Boston, 4 Oct. 1790.

14. MHS, Bowdoin and Temple Papers, Letter Book, 323, James Bowdoin III to John Elliott [*sic*], 1792(?).

nomination of a raft of new members, Massachusetts citizens who had not been named in the original act of incorporation, along with a number of men who in the future would be classified as either "abroad" (Americans from outside Massachusetts) or foreign: Benjamin Franklin, Ebenezer Hazard, surveyor-general of the post offices and roads of the Eastern District, the Chevalier de La Luzerne, minister plenipotentiary from His Most Christian Majesty to Congress, François, Marquis de Barbé Marbois, councillor of the Parlement of Paris, George Washington, the Reverend Ezra Stiles, president of Yale, Benjamin West of Providence, and General John Sullivan, the fiery-tempered soldier who was an older brother of Hancock's hanger-on. Eager to become known to their counterparts elsewhere, the Fellows voted to have the act of incorporation sent around to the various philosophical societies of Europe. Since they had no money, they appointed a committee to raise by subscription the funds needed to pay for expenses already incurred and for future outlays—purchasing instruments, offering prizes, and printing the president's address. The Fellows were then entertained with scientific papers: James Warren read an essay by Timothy Matlock of Philadelphia on the growth of vegetables; Vice-President Cooper read Samuel Mather's proposals for enhancing the reputation of the Academy; President Bowdoin communicated an essay by J. Palmer on converting iron into steel and rendering cast-iron malleable.[15]

Though it has little appeal to present-day tastes and was totally derivative, the presidential sermon won some attention at the time.[16] Bowdoin was not displeased even when he poked fun at it—a ritual defense against criticism—and he saw to it that it reached an elite audience at home and abroad who had not had the good fortune to hear it from the lips of its author. He cast his bread upon the waters on 11 January 1781. A letter to John Adams in Paris was accompanied by copies of the speech for himself and Francis Dana. To James Lovell in Philadelphia Bowdoin sent thanks for a French piece on the art of making a durable cement and enclosed the inaugural address. Another copy was dispatched with a witty letter to General Artemas Ward, who was indisposed: "I would recommend the reading a page of the enclosed pamphlet: which from my own experience I have found to be an excellent soporific. A page is a sufficient dose, to be taken as there shall be occasion, toties quoties."[17] Bowdoin requested that Samuel Adams, who was in Philadelphia, present the talk, with the compliments of the American Academy, to the French ambassador, the president of Congress, Governor Joseph Reed of Pennsylvania, Dr. Arthur Lee, the president of the American Philosophical Society, and the president of the college. In time of war, Bowdoin would not neglect the

15. Academy Records, 1:39, meeting of 8 Nov. 1780.

16. MHS, *Collections*, ser. 6.4 (Belknap Papers, 3), 207, Reverend John Eliot to Reverend Jeremy Belknap, Boston, Feb. 1781; 215, 31 July 1781.

17. MHS, Bowdoin and Temple Papers, Bowdoin to Artemas Ward, 11 Jan. 1781.

officers gallantly defending the nation against the British enemy: Count Rochambeau at Newport and General George Washington were among those to whom the little pamphlet was presented.[18] Benjamin Franklin, ambassador at Paris, was the recipient whose opinion Bowdoin valued most, and his gift accompanied the announcement that Franklin had been nominated to membership in the Academy and would surely be elected. Bowdoin's letter affected the self-deprecatory tone of epistolary convention: "In the mean time give me leave to present to you a specimen of its first fruit, which though it be unripe and imperfect and shews but an inferior power of vegetation in the particular stock from whence it fell, it is hoped will be the harbinger of maturer and better flavoured fruits from other stocks in ye same plantation."[19]

The establishment of the Academy aroused interest beyond the confines of the Commonwealth. Connecticut érudits were inspired and galvanized into action. Ezra Stiles of Yale, a newly elected Fellow, in a letter of 22 November 1780, congratulated Bowdoin on the inauguration of an academy that did honor to the republic of letters, and added that for some time Connecticut people had contemplated the founding of a similar society: "Could we have seen your Charter, I believe [we] might have obtained one from the Asembly in [this] session last month. We could wish to have a draught prepared for this Session in December."[20]

But Bowdoin, with his eye for prestige, was more interested in impressing the Royal Society, his model of organization. Richard Price was asked to communicate the act and list of Fellows, with the expectation that the Society, governed by the concept of the neutrality of philosophy, would favor the American Academy with its encouragement. In his reply Price rejoiced that in the midst of war and the most important struggle in which a people was ever engaged a new academy had been founded for promoting arts and sciences; but the president of the Royal Society, Sir Joseph Banks, had sent him a chilly response that it was not customary to lay before the membership notices of any society whatsoever. As for the dissemination of Bowdoin's inaugural address, issued separately and earlier, Price had to step cautiously. There were castigations of the British in the speech that, even though Price agreed they were deserved, made it obviously unfit for communication in an England at war with the colonies.[21] The idea of science in the heavens transcending earthly wars was being eroded.

18. Ibid., Bowdoin to Samuel Adams, John Adams, Count de Rochambeau, James Lovell, George Washington, 11 Jan. 1781. Washington's copy is still extant and forms part of his collection now in the Boston Athenaeum.

19. MHS, *Collections*, ser. 6.9 (Bowdoin and Temple Papers, 1), 449, Bowdoin to Franklin, 11 Jan. 1781.

20. Academy Letters, 1:8, Ezra Stiles to Bowdoin, Yale College (New Haven), 22 Nov. 1780. In fact, a Connecticut academy was not established until 1799, though in 1786 Stiles had formed a voluntary association, the Connecticut Society of Arts and Sciences, which published only one paper, a study by Jonathan Edwards on the analogies between the Hebrew and Mohican tongues.

21. MHS, *Proceedings* 43:609–10, Richard Price to Joseph Willard, Newington-Green, 21 July 1781.

Rules of Governance

Bowdoin had served as president pro-tem from 30 May to 30 August 1780, through the long summer months when, under his direction, a committee composed of Caleb Gannett, Samuel Langdon, John Pickering, Stephen Sewall, Edward Wigglesworth, and Samuel Williams, almost all of them members of Harvard College, were engaged in framing the statutes and nominating the officers of the Academy.[22] All the while, the gubernatorial contest between Hancock and Bowdoin was being fought with more than the customary abusiveness. At the 30 August Academy meeting the drafted statutes were accepted, with changes, by the Fellows, and Bowdoin was formally elected president, the Reverend Samuel Cooper vice-president, and the Reverend Joseph Willard corresponding secretary. Throughout Bowdoin's incumbency the officers of the Academy remained a relatively stable group.

Joseph Willard, the descendant of clergymen going back to the seventeenth century, had been a brilliant classics student at Harvard and had been kept on as a tutor. His subsequent occupancy of a pulpit in Beverly was not distinguished, but during the Revolution he was an ardent patriot. When Samuel Langdon, exhibiting nervous symptoms, resigned the presidency of Harvard in August 1780, weary from the strain of running the university through the Concord exile of the revolutionary years and from confronting obstreperous students when they returned to Cambridge, Willard was chosen in his stead, though not actually inaugurated until 19 December 1781. The Harvard Corporation meeting at which Langdon resigned did not run smoothly; some members opposed the capitulation to student clamor. Bowdoin's skill was enlisted to draft a letter of resignation that would make the transition appear respectable, and he took the initiative in securing from the legislature a grant minutely calculated at 497 pounds, 10 shillings, to enable Langdon to move his family and effects from the college.[23]

Willard was learned in astronomy and mathematics as well as in classics, and he made an ideal corresponding secretary during the formative years of the Academy. Having at one time briefly studied medicine, he was instrumental in founding the medical school at Harvard. He had an imposing physique—for a time he had trained as a seaman—and there were no successful student tumults during his presidency of the university. When Samuel Cooper died at the close of 1783,

22. Academy Records, 1:35.

23. Archives of the Commonwealth: Journal of the House of Representatives (MS), May–Oct. 1780, 1:129 (19 Sept. 1780), 1:181 (3 Oct. 1780). Commonwealth of Massachusetts, *Acts and Resolves of the Province of the Massachusetts Bay* 21 (1779–80) (Boston, 1922), 649–50 (3 Oct. 1780). William Gordon's championship of Langdon had jeopardized the chances of securing financial assistance for him; see MHS, *Collections*, ser. 6.4 (Belknap Papers, 3), 196, John Eliot to Jeremy Belknap, Boston, 11 Sept. 1780.

Willard succeeded him in office, thereby incorporating in his one person the natures of both Harvard and the Academy. In matters of religion he was not quite as latitudinarian as Price and Priestley, but he joined Bowdoin in cementing their relationship with the Americans.

Under Bowdoin's presidency, Ebenezer Storer occupied the post of treasurer as he had at Harvard. The Reverend Caleb Gannett was the first recording secretary and subsequently the perennial keeper of the cabinet. Changes in the composition of the rest of the council responded to the vagaries of State House politics. John Hancock was a councillor until the bitter election of 1785 in which Bowdoin defeated Hancock's stand-in, Thomas Cushing, for the governorship of Massachusetts; from that time Hancock's name vanished from the council rolls. The lawyers John Lowell and Robert Treat Paine, close friends of Bowdoin, stayed on through the decade, and so did the Reverend Edward Wigglesworth of Harvard. Professor John Warren joined "General" James Warren on the council and outlasted him. (James Warren resigned his Fellowship on 1 October 1791, writing to Storer with his accustomed testiness, "I have not attended the meetings of the Academy for several years, & probably never shall again: in this situation the propriety of wishing no longer to be considered as a member may be obvious without giving my particular reasons.")[24] When Samuel Adams and John Adams were back in Boston, they were invited into this inner sanctum of the intellectuals, and John Adams pulled along his brother-in-law Richard Cranch. Samuel Williams, the Hollis Professor at Harvard, was a member of the council before his disgrace, and Benjamin Lincoln, the general who helped Bowdoin quell Shays' Rebellion, appeared on its roster for a time, as did Cotton Tufts, the Reverend Phillips Payson, and Loammi Baldwin, an engineer who as a young man used to walk from Woburn to Cambridge with Benjamin Thompson to hear John Winthrop's lectures at Harvard. Even a casual acquaintance with the political and personal currents of hostility that coursed through the membership of the council leaves the impression that they were not always one happy family; but they appear to have gone about their business with such decorum that hardly a ripple of religious or political controversy breaks the smooth surface of the minute book.

At the time Bowdoin took charge, he held no other public office—a friend referred to his *otium cum dignitate*.[25] It soon became evident who constituted the group that would effectively run the Academy. The president and the council initiated all proposals and the membership generally approved them, a tradition that has been preserved for two centuries. Since there was no official meetinghouse

24. Academy Letters, 1:116, James Warren to Ebenezer Storer, Plymouth, 1 Oct. 1791.

25. MHS, *Collections*, ser. 6.9 (Bowdoin and Temple Papers, 1), 448, Arthur Lee to Bowdoin, Philadelphia, 25 Dec. 1780.

during the first decade, both the governing body and the Academy were mobile. The site of the general meetings alternated between the Philosophical Chamber at Harvard and a building in Boston, at first either the courthouse or the Massachusetts Bank, later a room in the "Manufactory House" that was shared with the Massachusetts Medical Society.[26] Sessions to which the public-at-large were admitted were held in Cooper's Brattle Street Church, the hallowed place where Bowdoin's inaugural had been celebrated and where, after his death, a eulogy would be delivered by John Lowell. The councillors usually met at Bowdoin's house, the Massachusetts Bank, or the courthouse.

The Records of the Academy contain the statutes as adopted on 30 August 1780, in ten chapters; a number of later amendments to the original statutes are either noted in the margin or incorporated into the text in another hand.[27] The model for the statutes, despite the War for Independence, was plainly the Royal Society of London. Americans had been among its members since the seventeenth century, and the legal framework of the two societies was carved from the same pattern. Many parts of the original act and the statutes of the American Academy appear to be translations from the Royal Society Charta Secunda of 22 April 1663. The basic similarities in the order of governance of the two learned societies testify to the continuity of cultural forms between the mother country and the rebel colonials. While they had broken away politically, Americans like Bowdoin still conceived of themselves as bearers of the English intellectual tradition, and looking for inspiration to the charter of the most famous scientific body in the world was not considered shameful, though the fact was unadvertised.

The Royal Society's basic administrative structure of a president, council, and Fellows was preserved and the original Fellows and president pro-tem of the Academy were explicitly named in the Massachusetts Act, by authority of the Commonwealth, as their English counterparts had been in 1662 by authority of the Crown. The act provided "that they and their successors and such other persons as shall be elected in the manner hereafter mentioned shall be & continue a body politic and corporate by the same name forever." The Charter of 1662 had called the Royal Society "one body corporate and politic in fact, deed, and name, really and fully," and stipulated that "by the same name they may have perpetual succession."[28] This was standard language of incorporation under English law. Its charter had awarded the Royal Society a "Common Seal to serve for transacting all causes and affairs whatsoever" and the power to "break, change, and make anew that Seal from time to time." In the act, the Academy

---

26. Commonwealth of Massachusetts, *Laws and Resolves*, 1782–83 (Boston, 1890), 465, Resolution of the legislature acting on a petition of Cotton Tufts et al., 20 Mar. 1783.

27. Academy Records, 1:5–22.

28. Record of the Royal Society of London, 4th ed. (London, 1940), 226.

was granted a seal along with the right to employ it in "whatsoever cause or business shall concern the Academy" and the "power and authority from time to time to break, change, and renew the common seal at their pleasure"—though the republican Academy received no blazons of honor as had the Royal Society. The restriction of the meeting places of the societies was expressed in similar terms, and the provisions for subsequent elections and for oath-taking are almost identical. Close examination of both documents leaves little doubt that whoever drafted the Massachusetts Act had a copy of the Royal Society Charter before him.

The provisions of the Academy statutes are obsessively meticulous; nothing is left to chance, or haphazard. The Massachusetts legislature had given the Fellows great liberty in the selection of future officers and members, though it had designated the first members, had empowered James Bowdoin to convene them, and had provided that the number from Massachusetts should not at any time be more than two hundred or less than forty. From the beginning, a sizable body of Fellows was contemplated, unlike the forty immortals of the French Academy; but the founders had insisted upon a solid Massachusetts base even though the society bore the grand title American. On 31 July 1781, procedures were modified to require the consent of three-fourths rather than two-thirds of the members for election of a new Fellow. The numerical goal of the Academy was in accord with the practice of the contemporary Royal Society of London, which in the period from 1781 to 1785 had an average of 476 ordinary and 95 foreign members.[29]

The friendly rival of the American Academy, the older American Philosophical Society of Philadelphia, had been incorporated in Pennsylvania by a law enacted 15 March 1780, and was recognized as the continuation of a voluntary society that had been founded more than a decade earlier, in 1769. By law the yearly value of the real estate of the Philadelphia society could not exceed that of ten thousand bushels of "good merchantable wheat."[30] The original Philadelphia statutes had been consulted with profit by Benjamin Guild in 1779, even before the Massachusetts bill was introduced into the legislature, though there were structural and ideological differences between the two bodies. The statutes of the Philadelphia society provided for one patron, who should be His Excellency the President of the Supreme Executive Council of the Commonwealth "for the time being," a president, three vice-presidents, four secretaries, three curators, one treasurer. The draftsmen had also inserted a special clause with Quaker overtones that stressed the neutrality of the arts and sciences in times of war:

29. Sir Henry Lyons, *The Royal Society, 1660–1940. A History of its Administration under its Charters* (Cambridge: Cambridge University Press, 1944), 320–43.

30. Philadelphia, American Philosophical Society, *Transactions* 2 (Philadelphia, 1786), Copy of the Act of Incorporation, xiii.

And whereas nations truly civilized (however unhappily at variance on other accounts) will never wage war with the arts and sciences and the common interests of humanity, *Be it further enacted by the authority aforesaid*, That it shall and may be lawful for the said Society, by their proper officers, at all times, whether in peace or war, to correspond with learned societies, as well as individual learned men, of any nation or country, upon matters merely belonging to the business of said Society; such as the mutual communication of their discoveries and proceedings in philosophy and science; the procuring books, apparatus, natural curiosities, and such other articles and intelligence as are usually exchanged between learned bodies for furthering their common pursuite.[31]

When the American Philosophical Society was founded in 1769, the stipulations for selecting papers to be published in its *Transactions* were adopted "from the Rules of that illustrious body the ROYAL SOCIETY of London, whose example the American Philosophical Society think it their honor to follow, in their endeavours for enlarging the Sphere of Knowledge and useful Arts."[32] In 1780, at the height of the Revolutionary War, the American Academy was not publicly proclaiming its dependence on London in any sphere, but its rules in effect derived from both the Philadelphia and the London societies. In language and procedures the London model appears even more prominent in the Boston academy than in the Philadelphia one.

The council of the Academy, meeting in Bowdoin's house, started out with a bang. From the inception of the society there were sanguine members like the Reverend Professor Samuel Williams, who expected to enlist the entire American people as participants in the labors of a body that, though rooted in Massachusetts, would become a national institution. At a council session on 3 January 1781, he proposed that an address be issued to the public "requesting a communication of experiments, observations and productions of Nature or Art to the Academy." Six months later, on 2 May, Bowdoin joined the enthusiasts and signified his intention of emulating the great European academies by publishing memoirs. As an initial step toward that end he recommended that a committee review the "literary communications" to determine their disposition. At the same council meeting a committee composed of three pillars of Harvard, Professors Wigglesworth and Williams and Caleb Gannett, was charged with classifying the subjects to which

31. Ibid., xvi. Suspicion of espionage was averted by spelling out the legitimate subjects of interchange and by adding this clause: "*Provided always*, that such correspondence of the said Society be at all times open to the inspection of the Supreme Executive Council of this Commonwealth."

32. American Philosophical Society, *Transactions* 1, 2d ed. (Philadelphia, 1789; first ed., 1771), Advertisement, iv. The paragraph was included in the second edition of vol. 1, though it had been dropped from vol. 2 (1786), where the Advertisement and 1769 Laws and Regulations were republished.

the Academy might devote itself to best advantage. They cast their net over a wide area and on 29 May presented an outline of activities that encompassed the whole theater of nature physical and human. The ambitious project, though it died aborning, reveals the sense of mission to develop the country's material and cultural resources that animated the Fellows of the Academy in its early days. Beginning with the good earth, the plan progressed in nine stages to the study of language as a human phenomenon, one of the major preoccupations of European intellectuals of the time. For all its comprehensiveness, the design was already marked by a characteristic of American scientific inquiry that endured for almost two centuries—a predilection for the practical and the pragmatic and avoidance of the speculative and the abstract, a preference for statistics over mathematics and for observations over system-building.

The report of the Committee for Arranging Subjects is a testament of the Academy's utopian moment:

1. That one Class examine the various Soils of the Country—what are their respective qualities—which are the most prevalent; the substances best adapted to improve them—what are their natural growths; Also, what have been and are the various methods of culture—which have been found, on experiment, to have the preference—how far rules for European husbandry are applicable to America—In what respects they agree and wherein they differ. Experiments particularly to be made and varied on the Siberian wheat.

2. That a second Class examine the growth of vegetables, and remark the various phaenomena, observable in them through the Seasons; that they collect and preserve the seed, leaf and flower of the various vegetables in the Country, determine their proper names and give a particular description of them, especially of those peculiar to America.

3. That a third Class collect samples of the various minerals and fossils in the Country and describe their situations and the quality of their respective Soiles.

4. That a fourth Class make a chemical analysis of vegetables, minerals & fossils & ascertain their medical & other properties.

5. That a fifth Class examine the various diseases of the Country—what are most prevalent—the causes of disorders peculiar to the Country; the longevity of the Inhabitants—the ratio between births and deaths—the difference of their ratio in Sea-port towns and the Country, in old and new settled parts of the Country, the degree of emigration from different parts of the Country to other parts: the Emigrants, however, are not to be taken into the estimate for determining the ratio between the births and deaths in any particular district.

6. That a sixth Class attend to mathematical disquisitions and astronomical observations; that they particularly make accurate observations of the eclipses of Jupiter's Satellites and determine the latitude of different places; also, that they ascertain the variation of the magnetic needle in different parts of the Country.

7. That a seventh Class make Meteorology their special object; observe the azimuth, meridional height, vertical direction and various phaenomena of the aurora borealis; register the height of the fluid in the barometer and thermometer, the affections of the hygrometer with the weather and winds, noting from time to time the disorders that may appear among the Inhabitants of places, in which such observations are made; that they determine the quantity of fluid, which shall fall in one year on a given surface, and the quantity of evaporation from a similar surface.

8. That an eighth Class examine into the progress of the mechanic arts in America, their present State, & make the improvement of them their special object.

9. That the object of a ninth Class be the rationale of Language, particularly the rationale, genius, idiom and construction of the English language.

Though the committee report was approved for submission to the membership, a year and a half later sober reason prevailed over fantasy and the council reconsidered the impressive scheme. While giving lip-service to the original spirit, they arrived at a simpler, less unwieldy classification for the work of the Academy. After a few false starts the Academy adopted a tripartite division, and has been re-organizing itself at intervals ever since.[33] On 29 January 1783, the Fellows voted to regularize their business under three heads: Mathematical (including astronomical and geographical); Physical (including natural philosophy, natural history, and agriculture); and Medical (medicine, anatomy, and chemistry). Studies that today would be the concern of classes devoted to humanities and the social sciences were somehow bypassed, though there was room for them in the original charter.

Quite early, members of the council worried lest the Academy become a façade with nothing going on behind its walls. Fellows were asked to signify their particular interest to one of the secretaries, though they were not to consider themselves restricted to a subject they had specified, and were at liberty to change it at their pleasure.[34] Committees of three to five members in each recognized category were elected for two years and charged with supervision of its work. To reap a scientific harvest was a Calvinist duty, and every committee member was obliged to produce a paper of his own at least once a year or vacate his post, a rule not rigidly enforced. Willard, Samuel Williams, and Gannett took care of the first category; the second was the province of Theophilus Parsons, Benjamin Lincoln, and Manasseh Cutler; and Holyoke, Dr. John Warren, and Tufts covered the medical discipline. The order was one of descending generality. The committees were charged also with reviewing the papers that had been received from all sources and selecting some judged worthy of publication, final decision being left to the Academy as a whole; it was not found "practicable, amidst the distresses and calamities of the

33. Academy Records, 3:42–43; 1:44–46, 56.
34. Ibid., 46.

war (however desirable it might be) to carry on a regular course of annual Trans-actions in all the various branches of Science"—a rare concession to the reality of the Revolution.[35]

Annual election of officers was a solemn matter to be formally conducted and vigilantly supervised. On the appointed day the president was to take his chair at three o'clock in the afternoon. Three scrutineers were chosen by election, and the balloting, which was secret, was to last until five. If there was no clear choice for an office (presumably a majority), the voting was to continue until one was reached. Each elector was to deliver a folded list of his choices to the scrutineers, who would sit beside the president and check against the roll of the Academy the name of the voting member. When the scrutineers had sorted out the ballots they would communicate the results to the president, whose duty it was to announce the elected officers for the ensuing year. In the event of a tie, the scrutineers had recourse to lots — the statutes had carefully provided for all contingencies.[36]

The short term of its officers notwithstanding, the Academy, founded at a moment when the democratic tide was high, reserved the right of recall in case of neglect of trust or disobedience of its orders. The president had considerable power: he regulat-ed debates, called for reports, preserved decorum, summoned meetings, executed the statutes. If he was absent from the state or died, the vice-president took over. Though the council was conceived of as the body that normally initiated new legislation, this did not preclude individual members from making independent proposals. Financial control was effectively in the hands of the president, treasurer, and council, who had the right to conclude bargains in matters touching academic property. The council directed the correspondence of the secretaries and indicated what papers were to be recorded.[37] The secretaries of the Academy were virtually secretaries to the president and never enjoyed the prestige of a *secrétaire perpétuel* of the French Academy of Sci-ences. Isaac Newton running the Royal Society from the presidency, an autocratic tradition that the contemporary president, Sir Joseph Banks, had maintained, was the ideal to be copied, and Bowdoin played the role with poise and dignity.

With the dismal example of Harvard's tribulations with its former treasurer John Hancock before them, the Academy drafting committee made provision in the fifth chapter of the statutes for their treasurer to give security, for accounts to be audited annually, for the keeping of careful records, and for wary supervi-sion by the whole body over the investment of monies and their disbursement for special projects. Lest financial continuity be disrupted by death, a vice-treasurer

35. Ibid., 56–57. The decision was important enough for Caleb Gannett to inform E. A. Holyoke about it on 5 February 1783 (Salem, Essex Institute: Holyoke Papers, Box 5, Folder 4).

36. Academy Records, 1:5.

37. Ibid., 8.

was added to take over the accounts immediately upon the demise of the treasurer. Mr. Bowdoin was determined to run a tight ship. But it was not only the president's respect for money that dictated orderly practices. Despite the affluence of some of its members, the Academy knew financial stringency in the lean years that followed the war, and slovenliness or waste could not be tolerated. Even the modest annual dues of two dollars for Commonwealth members could be paid in installments; delinquency was a perennial problem; and in May of 1789, a desperate Academy petitioned the General Court to authorize a lottery, lamenting their "weakness arising from the want of funds," while the sphere in which they might be useful was enlarged.[38]

Special attention was paid to the appointment of the keeper of the cabinet, who, in addition to classifying and describing such materials as, it was hoped, would be presented to the Academy, would also serve as librarian. Though they were all deemed honorable men, the objects were to be exhibited only at meetings or in the presence of the keeper. Records of books borrowed by members, including even the president, were to be carefully maintained, with the dates of their return noted.[39] Edward Wigglesworth, the first member to be honored with this office, promptly resigned. One might infer from the resignation a year later of its second occupant, James Winthrop, that the post was fraught with unusually onerous duties — or boredom.[40]

Rules for stated meetings of the Academy and its council were precisely spelled out; nothing was left to whim. As the institution was designed to answer to the intellectual needs of both Boston and Cambridge, it was stipulated that stated meetings in Boston take place on the last Wednesday in January and the day next preceding the last Wednesday in May, and that meetings at the University of Cambridge be set on the Wednesday next preceding the last Tuesday in August and the second Wednesday in November. For men who led regulated lives and had many avocations, it was necessary to fix timetables also for council meetings, twice a year in Boston and twice a year in Cambridge. An exception to this clockwork was allowed for a session at which the president might choose to deliver an inaugural philosophical discourse, in which event he was granted the option of performing in either Cambridge or Boston. And there was fleeting recognition of the dangerous times in which they lived: if it should be unsafe to convene in either Boston or Cambridge, they might meet anywhere else within a thirty-mile radius of Boston, an unhappy prospect that never materialized.[41]

38. Ibid., 12, 101, meeting of 14 Mar. 1787; 124–26 (26, 29 May 1789); 145 (24 May 1791).

39. Ibid., 12, 14, 66 (12 Nov. 1783).

40. Academy Letters, 1:12, James Winthrop to Joseph Willard, Cambridge, 17 Oct. 1781; Academy Records, 1:51 (30 Jan. 1782).

41. Ibid., 16.

The original requirement for an Academy meeting quorum was eleven Fellows, and for the council four in addition to the president.[42] In the light of the difficulties of travel, it is hard to imagine full attendance from the dispersed towns where members resided. Often an Academy meeting was an occasion for some of the Fellows to dine together, an inducement to the men who lived at a distance. Records of those present at general meetings were not kept, but personal diaries show that when a quorum was not reached members who appeared might be compensated for their trouble with a dinner at Bowdoin's mansion. In patent imitation of the Royal Society, which ever since Newton's rule had extended a special welcome to ambassadors and other noble visitors, the American Academy—with a somewhat more democratic penchant—provided: "No person shall be introduced to any meeting of the Academy, but by vote of the Academy, except American and Foreign Ambassadors, Members of Congress, Members of the supreme Legislative and Executive of the State of Massachusetts for the time being, and Members of similar Institutions with this Academy, who may be introduced by any member of the Academy."[43]

The presence of God in the Academy was problematic. In seventeenth-century England, Dissenters had fought valiantly to uphold their right of refusal to take oaths, especially in academic institutions. The Massachusetts act establishing the Academy had provided for the administering of oaths, but the tenth and last chapter of the original statutes appears to have hedged on the issue. It is silent on the matter of a Fellows' oath, though it was specified that the officers "shall each take the following oath, mutatis mutandis: I   A. B. elected to the office of [blank] in the American Academy of Arts and Sciences, do swear, that I will, according to my best judgment and discretion faithfully discharge the duties of the trust reposed in me. So help me God."[44] The *mutatis mutandis* may have left a crack open for either adventitious changes or conscientious objections. Quakers had been elected to the Massachusetts Governor's Council and for them "affirmation" had been accepted in place of oath-taking. The records indicate that while the very first meeting of the Fellows on 30 May 1780 was opened with a prayer by Samuel Langdon, thereafter the practice was discontinued.[45] The present Academy has allowed theology to make its way into the society, bound with philosophy in the same class as a recognized form of knowledge; but prayer is still excluded except in a private capacity.

---

42. Ibid., 16. At the meeting of 28 January 1784 (ibid., 69), it was voted that seven be a quorum for receiving communications and adjourning.

43. Ibid., 16–17.

44. Ibid., 22.

45. Ibid., 35.

As befitted men accustomed to legal procedures, synods, and legislative contests, the framers of the Academy statutes multiplied their rules, regulations, and resolutions. The ideals of the scientific machine, of the orderly Puritan life, and of James Harrington's ballot-ridden *Oceana*, that long-winded utopia whose dullness renders inexplicable its influence on American constitution-makers, all contributed to the legalistic spirit. The rules of governance and the rules of scientific procedure were interwoven to fashion an American learned body in the European image. The punctilio of forms inherited from European courts insinuated itself into civilized American institutions like the Academy, and has endured through the centuries. There were of course other elements in American society to whom this way was repugnant. On more than one occasion they burst through the barriers with religious revivals and anarchic violence, but never in the Academy.

First Fruits

The purposes of the Academy, set forth in the penultimate paragraph of the act, were so general that they were subject to a variety of interpretations among members and well-wishers abroad. An underlying question was whether the Academy should concern itself chiefly with practical problems whose solution would lead to an immediate enhancement of the material prosperity of America, or whether Academicians should devote themselves to the advancement of abstract science. In fact, both lines of activity were pursued.

When John Adams had made his initial proposal for an academy in Boston, he aimed primarily to promote the useful arts through ingenious practical inventions and to foster agriculture, not to support the astronomical, physical, and mathematical sciences, which he considered too remote to occupy a society such as he envisaged. By his own account a Mr. Arnold's display of American birds and insects in Norwalk, Connecticut, and the royal botanical gardens in Paris fascinated him as examples of scientific achievement, and after he retired he indulged in modest agricultural experimentation in the stony fields of Quincy. In a letter from Amsterdam on 5 September 1780, Adams expressed the hope that one of the first objects of the new Academy, as well as of the recently revived Philadelphia society, would be the "formation of botanical Gardens, and Collections of the Birds, Beasts and Fishes as well as Trees, and Plants which are peculiar to that Country in order to a natural History of it. An ample field this." The Reverend Manasseh Cutler, who sat on the Academy's committee for "physical" studies, was of like mind. He worried that "mere science" would deflect the members from what ought to be the first objects of their attention, improvements in the various branches of agriculture and the useful arts that would increase the wealth of the country and the happiness of its citizens. And Ebenezer Hazard and Jeremy Belknap (the latter not yet a Fellow) were in accord that the Academy should elect to its ranks some ingenious business-men and intelligent shipmasters, who could communicate experiments, observations, and curious specimens from abroad to interest the speculative members.[46]

Those less parochial in outlook saw the Academy as committed to the cosmopolitan ideals of the Enlightenment. When Thomas Jefferson was elected to membership in 1787, Corresponding Secretary Willard belatedly forwarded a certificate accompanied by a letter: "The Members were happy, Sir, in having the opportunity of enrolling in their Catalogue the name of a Gentleman so eminent in the philosophic world; and they hope the election will not be unacceptable to you." And in a reply to Eliphalet Pearson, Jefferson alluded to the Academy's mission in straightforward Baconian terms as the "advancement of science."[47] Bowdoin himself characterized the Academy more generally as a "philosophical society."

Many of the American Academicians tended to confine their scientific activities to observing eclipses, collecting plants, insects, mineral curiosities, and animal monstrosities, and compiling meteorological data. Some who had studied with John Winthrop preserved an amateur interest in celestial mechanics. Most of the letters and papers presented to the Academy sound like the run of communications to the Royal Society more than a century before, with the papers of Boyle, Newton, and Hooke omitted — a gaping lacuna, to be sure. But under the direction of James Bowdoin the mathematical and astronomic sciences were always afforded a place of prominence, at least in publications, and theory was not wholly neglected.

The chronicle of the papers presented to the Academy in the first decade of its existence does not lend itself to lively commentary, but like the "begats" in the biblical Book of Chronicles it is to be endured in appreciation of the heroic efforts of the patriot philosophers in their tentative and faltering beginnings.

In the summer of 1780, while the Academy was still in its inchoate stage, the ingenious David Rittenhouse gave to Ebenezer Hazard a piece of asbestos that was promptly forwarded to the Academy. Rittenhouse had used some of the filaments of the asbestos soon after it was taken out of the earth as a wick for a lamp. Hazard also sent pyrites that he had collected at Lancaster, where they were plentiful.

---

46. John Adams, *Correspondence in the Boston Patriot*, 159 ff., Letter 29, Quincy, 31 July 1809, quoting letter to Dumas, Amsterdam, 5 Sept. 1780; also, *Papers*, ser. 3.10, ed. G. L. Lint (Cambridge, Mass.: Belknap Press of Harvard University Press, 1996), 126; Manasseh Cutler, *Life, Journals and Correspondence*, ed. W. P. and J. P. Cutler (Cincinnati, 1888), 2:216, Cutler to General Lincoln, Ipswich, 18 May 1783; MHS, *Collections*, ser. 5.2 (Belknap Papers, 1), 88–89, Belknap to Hazard, Dover, 8 Mar. 1781, and 94, Hazard to Belknap, Jamaica Plain, 17 Apr. 1781.

47. Jefferson, *Papers* 16 (1961), 111–12, Joseph Willard to Jefferson, Cambridge, 16 Jan. 1790, transmitting the certificate of election, dated 29 May 1787 (Academy Records, 1:34). There was a reply from Jefferson to Willard (*Papers* 16:289, New York, 1 Apr. 1790), and another to Eliphalet Pearson (Academy Letters, 1:126, Philadelphia, 22 Dec. 1791).

They contained sulphur, he wrote, and notwithstanding the regularity and polish of some of them, they were in their natural state. He offered to procure other specimens as opportunity arose, and he was as good as his word. On 10 August he despatched a piece of lapis calaminaris with an unusually large proportion of zinc, found in Exeter, New Hampshire; perhaps the Academy could make an important exploration there. For his scientific assiduity Hazard was rewarded by election to the Academy at its first regular meeting on 31 January 1781. Rittenhouse, a stalwart of the American Philosophical Society, became a member of the Academy a year later.[48] By 22 November, a mere fortnight after its official opening, the Academy was already issuing public requests for useful information and products of nature, especially in astronomy and geography, cataloguing replies, and pushing forward the frontiers of knowledge.[49] Ezra Stiles, president of Yale, sent in an essay on making sand-iron by the late Reverend Jared Eliot of Killingworth, obtained by Dr. Benjamin Gale of that town from the Reverend John Devotion of Saybrook—"both which Gentlemen are of a philosophical disposition." But only Gale was elected a Fellow, though at Stiles's behest, Bowdoin had nominated both men for the honor. Stiles himself was chosen at the first official meeting.[50]

Even before it was formally established and its officers installed, the Academy sponsored an important Massachusetts enterprise, though it proved to be an inauspicious entry into the world of science. An eclipse of the sun had been forecast for 27 October 1780, to be totally observed only at Penobscot Bay in an area that had lamentably fallen into enemy hands. The forthcoming event had aroused interest not only as a natural prodigy never before observed since the settlement of the country, but as a means of correcting lunar tables and determining longitudes vital for sacred chronology and for navigation. The theoretical and practical aspects of an expedition to view the eclipse recommended it to the Academy, the more so since it was to be led by Professor Samuel Williams, charter member of the newborn society. James Bowdoin and other "lovers of learning and mankind" joined Harvard in petitioning the legislature for assistance. An appeal to the commander of the British garrison, to allow Williams and his team to encamp on enemy territory for the sake of science and human welfare met with a favorable response — in itself an extraordinary act in the midst of a bitter conflict — and the Massachusetts Board of War handsomely fitted out the state galley with ample

48. Academy Letters, 1:5, 6, Ebenezer Hazard to Bowdoin, Jamaica Plain, 8 July and 10 Aug. 1780. The lapis later turned out to be zinc (ibid., 9, Hazard to Bowdoin, Jamaica Plain, 23 Feb. 1781). See also Academy Records, 1:33, and 40, meeting of 31 Jan. 1781.

49. Ibid., 40, 41.

50. Academy Letters, 1:8, Ezra Stiles to Bowdoin, Yale College (New Haven), 22 Nov. 1780, and Bowdoin to Ezra Stiles, 30 Nov. 1780; Academy Records, 1:33 (22 Aug. 1781), and 32 (31 Jan. 1781).

provisions and accommodations for Williams and his assistants. The mountain labored and produced a mouse. While a few novel phenomena were observed and recorded, the group failed to see the total eclipse, apparently because of Williams's ineptitude: he chose the wrong site, a blunder that wasted a unique opportunity to advance science and enhance the honor of the state. Williams later complained that the American team had been hampered by the unobliging attitude of the British commander at Penobscot—the same Colonel Archibald Campbell who as a prisoner of war had been treated with great civility by James Bowdoin.[51]

But ordinary Americans, perhaps unaware of the episode's sorry outcome or the support given Williams by the Academy, took pride in the new society and flooded its cabinet of curiosities with any materials that might provide clues to the rich resources of their country. One David Watson, who for a number of years had been ditching salt meadows in the town of Wells, dug up a stone that appeared to be a work of art with an animal's head at one end; through the Reverend Daniel Little of Wells the discovery was reported to the Academy. A kind of scientific patriotism was born. Hugh Maxwell sent Bowdoin, "President of the Society for Propagating Usefull Knowledge," his observations on trees as conductors of lightning, along with his reflection that it was "a duty incumbent on every person to offer such communications; and to make such inquiries as may tend to serve the publick."[52] Simple men envisioned vast potentialities in any chance find. In their excited imaginations the Academy took on the character of a body with unlimited means to exploit a new metal found in the earth or a mechanical gadget that an ingenious countryman had put together. The initial enthusiasm did not long endure; but for a while it bred a passion for scientific improvement in the most outlandish places. The prestige and popular acceptance of the Academy are evident in the listing of its officers, councillors, and members in a pocket almanac published in Boston by T. and J. Fleet in the tenth year of American independence.

The repute of the Academy brought it within the ken even of semiliterate correspondents, who fancied that the institution was a powerful force in the moral as well as the intellectual sphere. A moving petition, written in an uneducated scrawl, was

51. Archives of the Commonwealth: Journal of the House (MS), May–Oct. 1780, pp. 98–99, 104, entries for 9, 12 Sept. 1780; Commonwealth of Massachusetts, *Acts and Resolves of the Province of the Massachusetts Bay* 21 (1779–80) (Boston, 1922), 595, chap. 145 (12 Sept. 1780); Robert F. Rothschild, "What went wrong in 1780?" *Harvard Magazine* 83.3 (Jan.–Feb. 1981), 20–27; William Pynchon, *Diary; a picture of Salem life, social and political, a century ago*, ed. F. E. Oliver (Boston, 1890), 81, entry for 8 Dec. 1780; *Boston Gazette*, 13 Nov. 1780. The expedition accidentally made a discovery later appreciated by astronomers: a fine thread of light at the circumference of the sun, partially broken into small drops, was discerned amid "universal gloom and darkness."

52. Academy Letters, 1:8 verso, David Watson to the Academy, Jan. 1781; MHS, Miscellaneous Bound Papers, Hugh Maxwell to Bowdoin, 21 June 1787; Academy Records, 1:106, meeting of 22 August 1787.

addressed to Caleb Gannett in January of 1783, asking that the gentlemen scheduled to meet that month use their influence with the General Assembly to end slavery: "The Negros what haef tha don—what haef tha don to us that we shuld thus inslave them—is freedom the thing we claem and fight for and do we yet hold enosent afarocans in slavery—amaseng ded ouer fathers com hether to flee from slavery and do we practest it . . . hath not God and natur the Congras and ouer Constuesion all sad freedom is the right of every man—."[53] Though Fellows who were jurists were active as individuals in the abolition of slavery under the Massachusetts constitution, the records of the Academy sessions do not reveal any deliberations on moral or metaphysical subjects, taboos inherited from the Royal Society.

The diary of the Reverend Manasseh Cutler (1742–1823), elected to the Academy shortly after its initial organization, is one of the few personal accounts left by a participant that treats in any detail the sessions of the first decade. Like many another Congregationalist pastor, Cutler had tried his hand at a variety of occupations before settling into the ministry. After graduation from Yale in 1769 (an idiosyncrasy that may explain his omission from the original list of Fellows), he taught school in Dedham, practiced law briefly on Martha's Vineyard, and kept shop as a ship's chandler. Finally he turned to the study of theology, and after a trial period struck roots in the Third Church of Christ in Ipswich. Cutler's pastoral duties did not absorb him to the exclusion of other activities. He systematized and catalogued the flora of New England, and as agent for the Ohio Company negotiated for the purchase of land in the Northwest Territory, introducing amendments into the Ordinance of 1787 to provide for education, freedom of religion, and the exclusion of slavery.[54] Cutler's notes on the Academy supplement the bare-bones entries of the official records of the proceedings.

The year 1781 yielded two anonymous letters from "A Poor countryman," one on the aurora borealis, another on the "darkness on the 19th of May 1780," a phenomenon that also brought a communication from Samuel Williams; a letter from the Honorable Arthur Lee on the effect of lightning in Philadelphia, particularly on Dr. Shippen's house, during storms on 26 June and 8 July, with drawings of the house enclosed; and a letter from the Reverend Daniel Little on the time and manner of the first importation of Siberian wheat into America.[55] The meeting of 29 May 1781, with some twenty-two members in attendance, had turned its attention to a paper by "Philomath" on a matter of immediate practical concern: "The new concise method of computing interest at 6 per cent per annum exhibited, as deduced from a larger

53. Academy Letters, 1:17, unsigned letter to Caleb Gannett, Jan. 1783.

54. See Manasseh Cutler, *Life, Journals and Correspondence*, 2 vols.; Janice G. Pulsifer, "The Cutlers of Hamilton," *Essex Institute Historical Collections* 107.4 (Oct. 1971), 333–408; James E. Humphrey, "Botany and Botanists in New England," *New England Magazine* (March, 1896).

55. Academy Records, 1:48, 49, 50.

operation by the double rule of Three, and improved."[56] Relating the weather to the incidence of disease was a perennial preoccupation of the Academy, and the Reverend Manasseh Cutler devoted some effort to enriching the storehouse of knowledge on the subject. He presented a paper correlating the general state of the weather and course of the wind in Ipswich from 1 July 1780 to 28 May 1781, including temperature and barometric pressure, with the diseases most frequent each month in Ipswich, Beverly, and Salem. On the same occasion Cutler made a gift to the society of a sample of sheet-lint from Dr. Spofford, who had contrived a machine for scraping it with great dexterity. "It was much admired."[57] Observations of the solar eclipse of 27 October 1780 brought papers from Ipswich, Providence, and Newport that would batten the slim findings of the Reverend Samuel Williams.[58]

The Commonwealth of Massachusetts sometimes considered the Academy an agency that might be engaged directly in the war. On 6 July 1781, the General Court of Massachusetts, acting upon a memorial from one Benjamin Dudley, resolved to recommend him to the patronage of the Academy. The legislature earmarked for the Academy a sum not to exceed three hundred pounds in order to employ Dudley "in such mechanical arts &c as to them may seem most beneficial to the State" (which turned out to be the manufacture of cannon). Less than £30 was disbursed; Dudley got lost in Philadelphia; and the Academy petitioned to expend the money for another purpose. Dudley surfaced again in November of 1785, with a request to the Academy for assistance in carrying out experiments to improve the manufacture of iron. A committee appointed to correspond with him and ascertain his skill made its report to the membership; but, no longer prodded by the exigencies of war to make a hasty decision, the members sent the report back for additional study, and no further action is recorded. In March of 1787, when he was in the throes of stamping out Shays' Rebellion, Bowdoin as president of the Academy was still pressing its claims before the state, of which he was at that point governor; and by warrant of the governor and council the money was finally dispensed by the Massachusetts treasury.[59] Interlocking directorates were not viewed with alarm in the early years of the Republic.

For its part, the Academy tried to make use of local officials to further its demographic studies. At the meeting of 22 August 1781, it was declared that calculations of the rapid population growth of the United American States and of the longev-

---

56. Ibid., 47.

57. Ibid., 48; see also Cutler, *Life, Journals and Correspondence* 1:85.

58. Academy Records, 1:49, 50.

59. Academy Letters, 1:10, Resolve of the General Court, 6 July 1781; Academy Records, 1:61, 82, 88. See also Commonwealth of Massachusetts, *Laws and Resolves*, 1786–87 (Boston, 1893), 467–68, Resolve of 1 Mar. 1787, when the sum of £132, 12 shillings, 2 pence lawful money was allotted to the Academy, which with £27, 7 shillings, 10 pence already expended was in lieu of £300 "new emision money" granted for Dudley in July 1781.

ity of their inhabitants properly fell within the province of the society and would serve the interests of the several states. The Academy therefore voted to request the secretaries of Massachusetts, New Hampshire, Rhode Island, and the territory called Vermont to furnish the Reverend Edward Wigglesworth, Hollis Professor of Divinity at Harvard, or either of the two Academy secretaries, with the data in their files that Wigglesworth would need for his population researches.[60]

Art, science, and agronomy all occupied the attention of the Academy in the year 1782. In testimony that the judgment of beauty, not only practical inventions and compilations of statistics, was a legitimate concern of the Fellows, paintings and engravings by Mr. John Furnass of Boston were exhibited at the January meeting, and it was voted "That the Academy have viewed with pleasure these specimens of ingenuity and good taste in so young an artist as Mr. Furnass, and cannot but esteem him as deserving the kind notice and encouragement of those who love the Fine Arts, and are disposed to promote the cultivation of a promising Genius, hitherto favoured with but very small advantages for improvement." In harmony with the display, the Academy listened to a letter from the Reverend Samuel West, a charter member, on the making of porcelain.[61]

The Assembly of 28 May heard an important communication from one of the foreign members, Richard Price, announcing William Herschel's discovery of the new planet Uranus.[62] But in November the members returned to earth again with the Reverend Peter Whitney's account of an apple tree in Petersham that bore a singular fruit, and with Cotton Tufts's observations on horn-distemper, a disorder affecting cattle. Instruments of war were never far from the early concerns of the Academy, which received a report by William Hickling on a new method of firing shells, accompanied by drawings of the apparatus.[63]

As the war drew to a close the Reverend Samuel Mather showed his septuagenarian versatility in a letter proposing a seal for the Academy, and also giving an account of the origin and success of inoculation against smallpox in Boston, a report that Dr. Benjamin Waterhouse was permitted to consult in the presence of the recording secretary nearly five years later, long after its author's demise.[64] Dr. Waterhouse himself read his "Observations on Epidemic Disease" to his fellow-Academicians on 27 May 1783. So considerable was the esteem in which the Academy was held that the good doctor obtained permission to advertise this preview

60. Academy Records, 1:49.

61. Ibid., 52, meeting of 30 Jan. 1782.

62. Ibid., 53.

63. Ibid., 55, meeting of 13 Nov. 1782.

64. Academy Letters, 1:18, Samuel Mather to Bowdoin, Boston, 14 Jan. 1783; ibid., 60, Benjamin Waterhouse to the Academy, Cambridge, 20 Oct. 1787; Academy Records, 1:110 (14 Nov. 1787).

when he published his essay, in order to impress potential purchasers.[65] Beyond doubt, the most noteworthy event of the year was the submission of three papers by President James Bowdoin that abandoned practical, everyday concerns for cosmic speculations: one was a critique of Franklin's hypothesis of light; a second, and crucial, communication advanced Bowdoin's theory of how the efflux of light from the sun and fixed stars, which, with the law of gravity, threatened their ultimate extinction, might be countered by the existence of an encompassing orb; the third supported this hypothesis with proofs drawn from natural phenomena and Scripture.[66]

Between the Philosophical Society in Philadelphia, of which Bowdoin had been made a member, and the American Academy of Arts and Sciences in Boston there was a friendly emulation. Though the Philosophical Society had been founded earlier and had achieved some distinction, at this time it was not entertained with fare more illustrious than was the Boston Academy. During the postwar years the star of science did not shine very brightly in either establishment. While the Academy concentrated on tables of morbidity and mortality, drawn up in answer to a questionnaire, and on Bowdoin's hypothesis explaining how the Newtonian universe contained its energy, the Philosophical Society in Philadelphia listened to a harangue from Dr. Smith, vice-president of Princeton, proving philosophically the biblical account of the origin of mankind in a single couple, a refutation of polygenetic theses that had been circulating since Isaac de La Peyrère's scandalous theory about pre-Adamites on other continents. Describing his visit to the Society in November 1785, the Reverend Jeremy Belknap commented that it was neglected by most of its members, and that scarcely ten could be assembled for a meeting except on the rarest occasions. His account of learned exchanges in Boston was no more stirring: "We had nothing of any great consequence at the Academy," he told his friend Hazard in the summer of 1789.[67]

In one respect the Boston society lagged behind its Philadelphia rival. While the Academy was long a homeless waif, the Philadelphians could boast a splendid new two-storied building, seventy by fifty feet. Its cellars and garrets were expected to become sources of revenue that could be used for scientific endeavors. It was anticipated that the very existence of the building would serve as an incentive to philosophical speculation among the members — a notion that has survived in

65. Ibid., 60.

66. Ibid., 59, meeting of 27 May 1783, and 68, meeting of 31 Dec. 1783; see also Academy, *Memoirs* 1.2:187–233. Bowdoin's three papers, plus his inaugural address, were reprinted in 1786; they were also reprinted in *The American Museum* 3.3 (March 1788; 2d ed., Philadelphia, 1789).

67. Manasseh Cutler, *Life, Journals and Correspondence* 2:233, Belknap to Cutler, Dover, 18 Nov. 1785; MHS, *Collections*, ser. 5.3 (Belknap Papers, 2), 160, Belknap to Hazard, Boston, 20 Aug. 1789.

twentieth-century institutes and universities. The public subscriptions to the Philadelphia society were generous, fully one-sixth coming from Englishmen. Franklin gave £200 and lent £500 more. The judgment of one of Bowdoin's Philadelphia correspondents, however, was perhaps more to the point: "In the Philosophical Society nothing has lately been read of consequence, excepting some observations & conjecture of Mr Rittenhouse on the formation of clouds."[68]

Cornwallis was defeated at Yorktown, the Treaty of Peace with Britain was negotiated and signed, rebellion broke out in western Massachusetts, troops shot into a crowd besieging a courthouse and interfering with the functioning of justice. But throughout the tumultuous decade the Academy met at its appointed hours and listened to papers as scheduled. Even in the darkest period of Governor Bowdoin's ordeal during Shays' insurrection the Academy proceeded with its statutory meetings. The rebels succeeded in closing down courthouses, but the portals of science remained open.

Medical prodigies continued to exert their fascination: on 26 January 1785, there was a communication from Dr. John Warren about an uncommon case of hair found in the cavity of the abdomen. In January of 1786 letters were received about the minerals to be found at Gay Head on Martha's Vineyard and about the extraction of fresh water from salt—a subject that kept recurring through the early years. Convening at Harvard on 8 November 1786, the members heard the Reverend Noah Atwater's attempt to account for the tails of comets and the aurora borealis by the different velocities of light, a paper communicated by Samuel Williams; Dr. Leverett Hubbard's description of the case of a person affected with a gangrene of the scrotum, also communicated by Williams; and a letter from General Samuel H. Parsons containing an account of his discoveries in the country bordering the Ohio River, communicated by the Reverend Joseph Willard. Cognizance was then taken of a number of letters addressed to His Excellency the governor of Massachusetts and president of the Academy: from the Reverend Daniel Little, a prolific correspondent, his observations among the Penobscot Indians, with a specimen of their language; from Samuel Freeman, Esquire, an account of a remarkable aurora borealis seen 22 March 1786; from the Reverend Samuel West and Dr. William Baylies, a prominent Dighton physician who was also a Fellow, a report of their observations and discoveries at Gay Head; from John Gardner, Esquire, a drawing of a ferryboat representing an easy method of crossing a river solely by means of the current, and an account of a granary contrived by him for preserving grain from vermin and keeping it ventilated and dry. The patriot philosophers, devoted as they were to science, were not unduly squea-

68. MHS, *Collections*, ser. 7.6 (Bowdoin and Temple Papers, 2), 166, Samuel Vaughan, Jr., to Bowdoin, Philadelphia, 5 Mar. 1787.

mish: on 14 March 1787, Dr. William Gammage of Cambridge exhibited a human foetus at the six-month stage, a demonstration recorded without comment in the minutes of the meeting. At the session on 26 May 1789, the Reverend Isaac Story, smugly touting the virtues of his profession, presented his calculations "showing the advantage which the ministerial profession claims above all other callings, collectively considered, in point of longevity."

The Academy's interest in promoting agriculture became known to a Mr. Crocker of Somerset in England, who in July of 1789 submitted an essay on apple orchards and cider-making. Seemingly aware of divergent tendencies among the Fellows, Crocker placed himself unequivocally in the camp of those who favored the practical arts, to the neglect of theoretical science: "Notwithstanding I hold all due respect for *mathematical* and *philosophical* disquisitions [two important objects of your institution] yet I conceive that the world, in general, desire a principal advantage from the *due* application of the sciences to *the common concerns* of life." Crocker concluded a long exposition of his methods with a heady prediction: "Thus, by the month of June or July, the Cidermaster will be possessed of a sparkling vinous, animating liquor; fit for the best citizens of 'The free and independent States of America' to regale themselves with." There is no evidence that the Academy took the trouble to test his extravagant claim.[69]

A major effort of the Academy's first decade was the raising of subscriptions to defray the cost of publishing its memoirs. The Philosophical Society in Philadelphia had won world renown through its volume printed in 1769. To be a proper academy like the Royal Society or the French Academy of Sciences, the Boston society had to issue a collection of memoirs showing that its members were actively contributing to the corpus of world knowledge. Manasseh Cutler, charged with supervision of the enterprise, approached his task with patriotic earnestness: "As the literary character of this State abroad is greatly concerned in the first publication of the American Academy, papers for this volume ought to be selected with the utmost care and attention."[70] Cutler's sense of how the *Memoirs* might affect the image of the state outside its borders was shared by the Massachusetts representatives to the Congress of the Confederation, Elbridge Gerry and Samuel Osgood, both Fellows of the Academy. The work was still in press when they wrote from Annapolis on 8 March 1784, cannily suggesting that it would be politic to send a bound copy to the delegation of each state for its public library, and to earmark an additional copy for the library of the United States. This generosity

69. Academy Records, 1:77, 86, 96–97, 100, 123; see also Academy Papers, 1:110, Isaac Story to Bowdoin, Marblehead, 20 May 1789, and Academy Records, Miscellaneous Communications.

70. Cutler, *Life, Journals and Correspondence* 2:215–16, Cutler to General Lincoln, Ipswich, 18 May 1783.

would advertise the literary eminence of the Academy and produce a "Disposition in [the recipients] to promote and honor it."[71]

To be *primus inter pares* was the conscious goal of the competitive patriot philosophers for their Academy and their state. There was a feeling, also, that in some way the publication would declare the viability of the American nation as a civilized entity. Despite this solicitude, however, the project seems to have been mismanaged. Long after its scheduled appearance, the *Memoirs* was still in the "brew-tub." Sheets would have to be redone and lists of errata appended—though Cutler consoled himself that they would not exceed those inserted in the Royal Society's *Transactions*.[72] As late as September 1787, Ebenezer Hazard, who had subscribed to the volume, was unable to procure a copy, as were other subscribers he had recruited, and his friend the Reverend Jeremy Belknap complained that the whole matter had been handled injudiciously, since the Academy was in debt, while large numbers of books remained unsold and undistributed.[73] The first volume of the Boston Academy, appearing in 1785 and including papers to the end of 1783, lacked the stylistic polish and scientific worth of the first Philadelphia volume, which Adams had heard praised at Parisian dinner parties. As for its engravings, John Singleton Copley said they were better than he had expected, but betrayed "a total want of the knowledge of Perspective in every part of them."[74] The preface to the volume, written by Bowdoin, had the tone of an apologia. It explained deficiencies in the work of the Academy by the want of such leisure and affluence as could be found in similar European institutions. But notwithstanding the impediments, a burden of responsibility to the nation had to be shouldered. Bowdoin issued a clarion call to the Fellows: "It is the part of a patriot philosopher to pursue every hint—to cultivate every enquiry, which may eventually tend to the security and welfare of his fellow citizens, the extension of their commerce, and the improvement of those arts, which adorn and embellish life. Nor can such traces and vestiges, as may occur, of the manners and resources of its aboriginal inhabitants, be unworthy the collection."[75]

71. Academy Letters, 1:22, E. Gerry and Samuel Osgood to Benjamin Guild, Annapolis, 8 Mar. 1784.

72. Cutler, *Life, Journals and Correspondence* 2:236, Cutler to Belknap, Ipswich, 10 Feb. 1786.

73. MHS, *Collections*, ser. 5.2 (Belknap Papers, 1 [1877]), 441, 490–91, Hazard to Belknap, New York, 25 July 1786, and 25 Sept. 1787; 494, Belknap to Hazard, Boston, 30 Sept. 1787. A copy was finally delivered personally to Hazard by Cutler on a visit to New York (ibid., 496, Hazard to Belknap, New York, 17 Nov. 1787).

74. Academy Letters, 1:57–58, John Adams to Bowdoin, London, 15 Oct. 1786, transmitting letter from Copley to Adams, London, 15 Oct.; Adams, then minister to St. James, had lent Copley his copy. See also Walter Muir Whitehill, "Learned Societies in Boston and Vicinity," loc. cit., 151–73. Despite his low opinion of American artistic talent, Copley accepted membership in the Academy (Academy Letters, 2:5, Copley to Eliphalet Pearson, London, 20 Feb. 1792).

75. Academy, *Memoirs* 1:viii. Despite its shortcomings, the members voted on 29 May 1787 to

For all its errata, the first volume of the Academy's *Memoirs* was a substantial tome in quarto of almost six hundred pages, adorned with a number of engravings. The astronomical and mathematical outweighed the botanical and technological pieces, as might have been expected from a society over which Bowdoin presided. His own three "physical papers" ran to forty-six pages, in addition to which his contributions included the preface and a reprint of his *Philosophical Discourse* (with the omission of a few acidulous remarks about the British). It was seen fit to introduce into the preliminary matter of the volume a description of the corporate seal — one of the lesser artistic endeavors of the Academy — and its allegorical interpretation. The central figure was Minerva, flanked on the right by a field of Indian corn, bounded by an oak-crowned hill sloping toward the outskirts of a town. Agricultural implements lay at the goddess's feet. On her left were a quadrant and a telescope, a ship at sea heading toward the town, and a sun risen above a cloud. The whole was surmounted by the motto *Sub Libertate Florent*. Though the symbolism was obvious, an explanatory passage underscored its meaning: "The device represents the situation of a new country, depending principally on agriculture, but attending at the same time to arms, commerce, and the sciences. The sun above the cloud represents, not only our political state in 1780, when the Academy was first incorporated, but also the rising state of *America*, in regard to empire, and the arts and sciences. The motto conveys the general idea that arts and sciences flourish best in free States."[76]

The papers printed by the Boston Academy sounded quaint and were rather behind the times. Articles in the Philadelphia *Transactions* on the transit of Venus had provided information useful to European astronomers and natural philosophers. Bowdoin's hypothesis about a hollow sphere of an undefined substance encasing the sun's planetary system may well have aroused chuckles in private, even when it received formal congratulations in public;[77] and his scientific-theological argument that the perfection of the Newtonian system demonstrated divine omniscience was beginning to be hackneyed in more sophisticated scientific circles. In the early years of the Academy the promoters of science were more prominent than its practitioners. With Winthrop dead, Franklin away, Rumford not yet a

---

send the *Memoirs* to the various academies and societies of Europe and the United States (Academy Records, 1:103).

76. Academy, *Memoirs* 1:xix. In 1954 Rudolf Ruzicka re-drew the seal, which, as Walter Whitehill commented, had deteriorated into a black glob. The Academy unfortunately has not availed itself of its legal right under the Act of Incorporation to update its symbol. For a description of the Academy bookplate attributed to Joseph Callender and almost identical to the seal, see Boston Athenaeum, *Athenaeum Items, A Library Letter* 88 (Jan. 1988), 5–6.

77. Yet Richard Price took the papers seriously and responded to their arguments, noting his agreement with Bowdoin's observations on light, but criticizing the theory of the encompassing orb (MHS, *Collections*, ser. 7.6 [Bowdoin and Temple Papers, 2], 78–80, Price to Bowdoin, Newington-Green, 25 Oct. 1785).

member, and Oliver too tainted by his Tory associations to assume a leading role, there was no one in the society but Bowdoin to hold aloft the torch of scientific innovation, a dim and flickering light. His three papers on Newtonian cosmology published in the Academy *Memoirs* at least aroused controversy. They were entitled "Observations upon an Hypothesis for solving the Phenomena of Light: with incidental Observations, tending to shew the Heterogeneousness of Light, and of the electric Fluid, by their Intermixture, or Union, with each other"; "Observations on Light, and the Waste of Matter in the Sun and fixt Stars, occasioned by the constant Efflux of Light from them: with a Conjecture, proposed by Way of query, and suggesting a Mean, by which their several Systems might be preserved from the Disorder and final Ruin, to which they seem liable by the Waste of matter, and by the Law of Gravitation"; and "Observations tending to prove, by Phaenomena and Scripture, the Existence of an Orb, which surrounds the whole visible material System; and which may be necessary to preserve it from the Ruin, to which, without such a Counterbalance, it seems liable by that universal Principle in Matter, Gravitation."

Ever since early manhood James Bowdoin had been preoccupied with one of the oldest problems of the Newtonian system. Was not the universe destined to run down, revealing some inadequacy in the perfection of the original creation? Was Newton committed to a view of the globe that envisaged the probability of its annihilation? Would other planets be inhabited after the destruction of the earth? Newton's contemporaries and disciples conjectured that there had been at least a near-miss when the comet of 1680 passed close to the earth. William Whiston, once a favorite disciple of Newton's, had demonstrated to the satisfaction of many religious Newtonians that the Deluge was a natural event caused by the passing of a similar comet. The perfection of the universe implied stability, and Bowdoin could not live at peace with the prospect, however remote, of the destruction of the earth, or the planetary system, or the whole universe. And yet, as a convinced Newtonian, he was aware that the emanation of light from the sun could lead to an attenuation and imbalance in the system, ultimately dooming it. Franklin's electrical experiments and his observations on the force of lightning seemed to bring the whole question to the fore again.

The climax of Bowdoin's scientific achievement had been the presentation to the Academy of his grand hypothesis, meant to solve the problem of a universe apparently subject to deceleration and dissolution. In his first paper Bowdoin approached with great diffidence Franklin's queries concerning the nature of light, and as introduction to his own cosmological theories set forth a number of strictures on Franklin's views. He was fully confident, he was careful to note, that "our celebrated countryman, whose happy genius has contributed so largely to the advancement of philosophic knowledge, will be pleased with any attempt for that purpose, whether successful or not, even though it should be upon principles, that may not perfectly harmonize with some of his own."[78]

Cadwallader Colden had reasoned in his *Principles of Action in Matter* (1751) that the solar system was doomed to dissolution by the gradual diminution of the sun's energy through radiation. Bowdoin's hypothesis was intended to counter this prospect, though he did not deny the power of God to destroy the system if He so willed it. The absolute volition of the Calvinist God was in no wise diminished, while at the same time the perfection of the existing system was sustained. Bowdoin posited the existence of a complex mechanism devised by an omniscient Creator, a web of hollow, concave spheres or orbs, with walls of varying thickness, enclosing the solar system, the several planetary systems comprising the heavens, and the whole system of systems. An interchange of rays among the sources of light in each system, which could not pass beyond the inner surface of the sphere, would be the means of restoring to each system the quantity of light it emitted, and would thereby prevent the waste of its matter. Not only would the systems be preserved by their encasement, but their mutual gravities would be so regulated as to keep them at the distance assigned to them. If the Creator had not set such an arrangement in operation, would not the "whole choir of systems" have crashed toward their common center of gravity?

Bowdoin drew positive evidence for his theory of an orb surrounding the whole visible material system from the existence of the Milky Way, "the luminous girdle in the blue expanse," and from the expanse itself. He supposed the girdle to be reflected from the concave surface of a far distant orb and propelled from the numerous systems enfolded by the orb. But Bowdoin was not content to rely on astronomy alone. He rejoiced at the "happy co-incidence between phenomena and scripture," agreeing and elucidating each other, and he embellished his third essay with copious citations from Genesis, Amos, Job, and Psalms respecting the stories God built in the heavens and the lights of the firmament.[79] With scholarly scrupulousness, Bowdoin admitted that, knowing no Hebrew, he referred to the meanings of Old Testament passages "by information only." The nominal Hebrew language study to which he had been subjected at Harvard left no lasting imprint and he relied on a standard compendium of exegetical treatises.

Just as Isaac Newton failed to divorce completely the book of nature from the book of Scripture, so James Bowdoin the devout Newtonian opened himself to the charge of a similar transgression: though theological questions had been banned from the Academy, he called upon the prophets of the Old Testament to sustain the grandiose cosmological theory he had designed to rout the unbelievers and vindicate God and Newton in one final hypothesis. The separation of the two books

78. Academy, *Memoirs* 1.2:188.
79. Ibid., 222, 230.

appeared to be preserved, however, if Scripture was invoked merely to give greater credibility to scientific conclusions that accorded with statements and phrases in the Bible. The biblical usage of terms like heaven, heaven of heavens, and heavens of heavens confirmed Bowdoin in his vision of a series of concentric orbs each containing its own system of stars and planets. The three terms were plainly distinguished one from the other, "which must imply some essential difference between them. To suppose the contrary is to confound language, and involve it in uncertainty. It would be to suppose those expressions void of meaning; and would be treating scripture with the indecency, to which no other book, appearing to be dictated merely by common sense, would be entitled."[80] Proofs from "Phaenomena and Scriptures" raised more than an occasional scientific eyebrow even among Bowdoin's friends, but no refutation appeared in print. No more than the revered Newton could Bowdoin completely shuffle off his theological coils, despite dogmatic adherence to the principle of the separation of the two books — as sacred a tenet in the scientific world as the separation of powers in the political world.

The momentum of his own reveries carried Bowdoin along. A great, embracing orb might, "like Saturn's ring, be provided on both sides of it, with ample means of making it a suitable place for habitation: the habitation of myriads of millions of animate beings, equal or superior to those, which people our planetary system." And beyond that great orb, he envisioned other concentric orbs, inhabited and including within them innumerable planetary systems resembling the solar system, and like that system, "animated, and adorning the infinite expanse."[81]

The conjuring up of the glorious spectacle of a universe throbbing with life harbored an implicit threat. Like Newton himself, Bowdoin saw the moral and the physical order as related domains. The very irregularities of the planetary system, such as the passing of a comet close to the earth and raising the Deluge, exemplified a perfectly timed interplay between the physical and moral worlds. The moral corruption of the generation of the Flood was predestined in Calvin's sense, and God had also predetermined the passing of the comet that would cause the annihilation of the wicked. Thus what appeared to be physical irregularities were not fortuitous and served a moral purpose in the universe. The depravity of men could lead to the God-willed destruction of the earth and its replacement by a better planet peopled with superior beings.

In due time these observations of Bowdoin's went through the normal procedures that had been set up for the selection of papers worthy of publication; not even a president of the Academy was immune from peer criticism. The Reverend Manasseh Cutler, charged with sending the papers around for review, transmitted

---

80. Ibid., 228.
81. Ibid., 204–05.

Bowdoin's treatise to Andrew Oliver, Jr., in Salem, who had been added to the committee for examining "physical," including "philosophical," papers. Oliver was independently wealthy and lived a retired life of scientific contemplation. Five years Bowdoin's junior, he too had studied with John Winthrop at Harvard. Oliver's proficiency in mathematics was well known, and he had been elected a member of the American Philosophical Society in 1773. His *New Theory of Lightning and Thunder Storms* was later published in their *Transactions* (1786), and an *Essay on Comets in Two Parts* (1772), dedicated to Winthrop, which explained the direction of the comet's tail as a consequence of the sun's atmospheric pressure, had been translated into French by no less an authority than the astronomer Jean-Sylvain Bailly. Despite his unfortunate Tory connections, Oliver was sufficiently respected to have been chosen a charter member of the American Academy. His response to Bowdoin, a well-informed and carefully argued analysis, was evidently addressed solely to the second paper, and thus makes no reference to Bowdoin's scriptural citations in support of his theory.

Bowdoin's hypothesis was derived in part from William Whiston's *A New Theory of the Earth, from its Original to the Consummation of All Things, Wherein the Creation of the World in Six Days, the Universal Deluge, and the General Conflagration, as Laid Down in Holy Scriptures, Are Shewn to be Perfectly Agreeable to Reason and Philosophy* (1696). The work had been accepted by John Winthrop in his *Two Lectures on Comets, Read in the Chapel of Harvard College* (1759), but was disputed in Andrew Oliver's *Essay on Comets*. Oliver doubted whether the comet's tail could deluge the earth with water as Whiston had supposed, and he found it absurd to imagine that God had created comets to serve as sources of punishment for moral evils on planets. The world-system was perfect in itself and did not require such eccentric interventions. Bowdoin's adaptation of the *physica sacra* of the previous century to allow for divine punishment on earth clearly ran counter to Oliver's convictions.[82]

To judge Bowdoin's theory must have placed a man of science in an uncomfortable predicament; for though the treatise had a rationalist structure, it was in essence the desperate dream of a visionary unable to countenance the nothingness of universal destruction, or even to entertain the idea of partial destruction as a geological event without theological implications. On 15 March 1784, Oliver wrote to Bowdoin with courtesy, "The Perusal gave me great Pleasure: But it contains an Hypothesis, which, with all due Deference, I beg the Liberty to observe upon, as it is offered for the Consideration of the Society." He could not accept the supposition that a concave sphere consisting of matter sui generis surrounded

82. See John C. Greene, "Some Aspects of American Astronomy, 1750–1815," in Brooke Hindle, ed., *Early American Science* (New York, 1976).

each planetary system or each collection of systems or the whole system of systems comprehending the visible creation. Oliver had read Newton's *Principia* and understood the problem that troubled Bowdoin: the continual operation of the Newtonian law of gravity throughout the planetary systems of the universe in the end had to bring about its dissolution. In fact Bowdoin had been full of wonderment as to why this prospect had not materialized long before. Oliver quoted Bowdoin verbatim: "'It has (as you say) been observed by Philosophers, (Sir I Newton demonstrates it in his Principia) that a Body placed any where within a hollow Sphere, which is homogeneous, and every where of the same thickness, will have no Gravity, wheresoever it be placed; the opposite Gravities always precisely destroying each other.' But you think *that* Observation cannot be applied to the hollow Sphere above described; for, 'by the Description it is not homogeneous nor need it be of equal thickness.'" The Bowdoin who as a young man had piously reiterated the tenets of Baconian experimental science had allowed himself to go wild with this hypothesis. Oliver accepted its conditions and then demolished it on Newtonian principles. The same mentality that a century before would have exercised itself on refinements of theology now turned to the world of science with equal absorption.

Bowdoin had been disturbed at the thought that his omniscient God should create a universe deficient enough in one respect to lead to chaos. Oliver did not have to confront this eventuality. If God was infinite and perfect in every sense of the word, no limits could be placed upon His powers that would in any way derogate from the perfection of that infinite Intelligence. God's essence must be supposed to be immense. Oliver quoted Sir Isaac's phrase to the effect that infinite space was the sensorium of the Deity (a phrase that Newton profoundly regretted once Leibniz got hold of it and began to mock his rival as guilty of an anthropomorphic analogy). If God was immense in His essence, Oliver contended, He must be equally so in His productions and operations. The telescope gave assurance that the stars were innumerable and that what was perceived was but a small part of the immensity of the universe: more and more "luminaries" were being discovered as the magnifying powers of telescopes increased, and this led to the rational presumption that such stars existed throughout the universal extension and that the essence of the Deity was co-extended with them, an article of both the Christian and the philosophic creeds. Oliver saw no reason, then, why all the primary globes in the universe might not have been so disposed as to retain their relative situation to one another through indefinite periods—he did not quite say infinite time. Since there was thus no common center of gravity throughout το παν (the universe), hypotheses such as Bowdoin's were unnecessary to demonstrate the perfection of the divine creation.

A fortnight after receiving Oliver's letter, Bowdoin sent him a rebuttal of sorts.

He voiced his disappointment that Oliver had not considered all three papers at the same time, and then proceeded with some general reflections intended to undermine Oliver's stance. Bowdoin took him to task for ignoring the "uniformity of nature," which postulated that, as the earth had its center of gravity, so did every other system, and so did all of them together share a common center of gravity. On the other hand, to Oliver's argument that the world created by the Deity had to replicate His own greatness in all its parts, Bowdoin rejoined that such a notion was "derogatory to the character & dignity of the Supreme Author" and would "degrade him below some" of his own productions. After a few limp attempts to buttress his concave sphere embracing all of creation, Bowdoin abruptly ended his ruminations. At the outset of his letter he had bluntly reminded Oliver that as an Academy committee member he had access to the other two papers and could favor their author with his comments. It was clear that, until then, Bowdoin would confine himself to an interim response.[83]

But this was not the end of James Bowdoin's scientific tribulations. He had hardly been relieved of his gubernatorial office after Shays' Rebellion when Pelatiah Webster of Philadelphia, a Yale man born in Connecticut in 1726 (the year of Bowdoin's birth as well), an ordained pastor, an unsuccessful merchant, a teacher, and a political and economic pamphleteer, took up the hypothesis published in the Academy *Memoirs* and drew from it conclusions that were the opposite of what James Bowdoin had expected. It appears that Bowdoin had invited trouble gratuitously by sending his papers to Webster, who excused the delay in acknowledging them with an unkind reference to the disorders in the state of Massachusetts that he inferred had engrossed all of Bowdoin's attention and would have left him no leisure to reply to scholarly criticism. After conventional flattery of the author's genius, Webster attacked him with no holds barred.

How could such a stupendous piece of the creation as a hollow sphere, which had to take the form of a solid boundary of that part of the universe that came within human ken, exist without some kind of substantial proof of its reality? Was not this hollow sphere more an extravagance of imagination than a philosophic principle? Pelatiah Webster did not for a moment doubt that the Almighty, if He had had occasion to resort to such a concave sphere, had the power to create one as easily as He could make a balloon; but Webster wondered whether it was "quite decent in us to ascribe to him such amazing Efforts of omnipotence" without real evidence of the entity's existence. Even if there were such a sphere, Webster was unable to concede that it could have solved the problem for which it was originally introduced. If the concave sphere was of uniform thickness in all of its parts and a

---

83. MHS, Bowdoin and Temple Papers, Andrew Oliver to James Bowdoin, Salem, 15 Mar. 1784; Winthrop Papers, James Bowdoin to Andrew Oliver, 13 Apr. 1784.

globe of matter was placed in its center, the equality of attraction in every direction would keep it stationary, deprived of all motion. If, however, a diameter should be drawn through the center and the planetary globe were placed somewhere in one quarter of the delimited space it would be three times more distant from one side of the sphere than the other. The attraction to the near side would be nine times greater than that toward the farther side, and all balance of attraction would be lost. The planet would then be drawn from its position and come into contact with the side of the sphere that was nearest to it.

After building a succession of other hypotheses on top of Bowdoin's hypothesis, Pelatiah Webster found that in some of its aspects it violated the "very Common Maxim among Philosophers, viz. that Nature does Every thing in the Easiest way." He left for the end a strenuous objection that was bound to hurt the pious Bowdoin, a charge that the hypothesis, running counter to a fundamental principle of philosophers since the "Reformation of Newton," was deliberately calculated to remove from the internal constitution of the material universe the seeds of death and the necessary tendency toward dissolution. This contradicted the received and established opinion of all good divines, as well as good philosophers, that the universe would have—and had to have—an end. The world was not designed by its Creator to be of infinite duration. While Newton did not express himself with the consistency and authority imputed to him by Pelatiah Webster on the inevitability of a catastrophe that would destroy the earth and its inhabitants, there are many texts (and manuscripts he could not have seen) that might support Webster's affirmation. Pelatiah Webster then delivered a smashing blow: "Errors in Philosophy even in the first Character are venial, but to be a bad Christian must be dolefull indeed!" Throughout his life derogatory epithets had been hurled at Bowdoin by British officials, rival politicians, and Shaysite rebels, but never before had he been called a bad Christian.

Pelatiah Webster concluded with a condescending half-apology:

> I hope, Sir, You will not be offended by the freedom of my Remarks. Wilst Rapt in pursuit of Your flight of tho't, I have too much forgot Your dignity of Character, & address'd You more with the freedom of a Classmate than perhaps I ought. I have only to say in Excuse that Philosophy knows no Compliments or distinctions. *Ardua Tentare* Enobles the mind, wilst it requires Strength of Genius to be Capable of it, & I hope Your Vast Extent of Enquiry & investigation will not be Checked because I Stumble by the way & cannot keep pace with You—I am pleased with the Richness of Your mind & Your Turn to Philosophick researches, & sho.ᵈ think myself very happy to be in the neighborhood of a Gentleman of like Genius & Taste, with whom I might now & then Spend an Evening or Liesure hour in that kind of mental Improvement, & Your communications will Ever be very acceptable to me.[84]

84. Ibid., Pelatiah Webster to James Bowdoin, Philadelphia, 16 Nov. 1787. At a meeting of the Massachusetts Historical Society in 1889 (see their *Proceedings*, ser. 2.4 [1887–89], 66) an "extract"

Bowdoin's feelings were not assuaged by the elaborate compliments.

Webster's sharply critical estimate of Bowdoin's hypothesis was not widely circulated and did not bring him into great repute. Nevertheless, on 12 December 1787, Bowdoin answered his arguments at length and with meticulous care. He conceded that if there were not sufficient reason to demonstrate a hypothesis or to render it at least probable, it had to fall like any other baseless structure. However, although it might not have as solid a foundation as Pelatiah Webster required, Bowdoin was clearly outraged by its condemnation as a mere "extravagance of imagination." After all, he argued, men were limited in judging the reality of such an idea by what was known from analogy, from the phenomena, and from Scripture. Bowdoin refuted through internal analysis the hypothetical instances of planetary placement Webster had described, but was far more disturbed by the theological implications of the criticism. He refused to consider the physical aspects of God's creation by themselves. While the charter of the Academy had carefully omitted theology from its province following the precedent the Royal Society had firmly established, in practice Bowdoin, like Newton before him, was incapable of preserving an absolute separation between the book of nature and the book of Scripture. The consequence of Bowdoin's hypothesis was a mixing of science and theology after the manner of some Newtonian divines and of the textbook from which John Winthrop had taught him.

The irregularities and interferences in any particular cosmic system, Bowdoin surmised, might well have been part of the original divine plan. When such irregularities occurred they served a moral purpose. They were meant to correct or extirpate the moral irregularities of the planet's inhabitants, "and like purposes, without disturbing the general economy of nature, they may, in future, be intended to answer." In this perfect order the system had been so arranged that irregularities in nature took place at the precise moment when moral chastisement had to be administered to sinners. Such corrections were anything but faults in the original creation, and did not betray a want of wisdom or of power in God's contriving the system. On the contrary, they were the completest demonstration of both. Bowdoin's conception appears to have been derived from the work of John Woodward, *An Essay toward a Natural History of the Earth* (1695), and William Whiston's *New Theory of the Earth* (1696). In grand excursions of *physica sacra*, they had contended that mountains and valleys, deep oceans, and anything else that detracted from the perfect rotundity of the earth could be accounted for

---

was read from Webster's letter (actually, a pamphlet enclosure) refuting arguments against adoption of the federal constitution; on this subject the two men would have been in accord. Webster was a self-pitying ne'er-do-well who called himself "the Tennis ball of Fortune," but had some intellectual prowess, and completed studies of currency and finance said to be of great value to the U.S. government; see Ezra Stiles, *Extracts from the Itineraries and other Miscellanies. . .* (New Haven: Yale University Press, 1916), 579–80.

by the Flood, which was necessary for the punishment of Noah's wicked generation, and proved that the physical world was subservient to the moral. The Flood had been brought about either by a comet's approaching too closely to the earth or by some other strange planetary movement. None of these events, however, were haphazard; they demonstrated God's supreme wisdom and power. God was unknowable, but Bowdoin was nonetheless preoccupied with showing His perfection.

Bowdoin had recently read the theory of William Herschel that the stars now in clusters were at the moment of creation spread evenly through the heavens, and had been drawn into the clusters from the operation of universal gravitation. As a result some parts of the heavens were relatively unpopulated with stars. From his reading of this theory Bowdoin jumped to the conclusion that Herschel believed the universe or the visible part of it had been and was in rapid progress toward dissolution. But such a doctrine Bowdoin could not bring himself to accept. So far as he was concerned, the Scripture account of an apocalyptic end was confined to this earth and its atmosphere alone, just as was the Mosaic history of the creation "according to the interpretation of good philosophers and good divines too." There might be tendencies to dissolution in the earth's system, Bowdoin reluctantly admitted for the sake of argument, but he could not infer the dissolution of the whole from this circumstance. Compared with the immense aggregate of matter in the universe, our planetary system was but an atom. Might not those tendencies to dissolution be imaginary and never produce or issue in what was apprehended? Or, if real, might not the seeds of death operate like partial evils to effect a greater or a general good? Might not the intended irregularities and interferences have been foreordained by an omniscient God in order to achieve moral consequences such as divine punishment? Bowdoin categorically rejected Webster's assertion that the material universe carried in its very stamina the causes of its end and the principles of its dissolution.

Having answered, at least to his own satisfaction, Webster's scientific objections and having repudiated his eschatology, Bowdoin could not refrain from a sarcastic peroration: "I agree with you 'that errors in philosophy are venial; but to be a bad christian must be doleful indeed!'—From y.ᵉ former part of this declaration, I fully depend on your pardon of my philosophical errors; and with respect to the latter part of it, to convince you, that I am no bad christian, I beg leave to assure you that I am with christian Sincerity & with Sentiments of the most christian regard, dear Sir y.ʳ m.º hble. Serv.ᵗ"[85]

No further animadversions came from Pelatiah Webster to impugn Bowdoin's philosophical reputation and to question his emendations of the Newtonian system by the introduction of concave spheres.

85. MHS, Bowdoin and Temple Papers, Bowdoin to Pelatiah Webster, 12 Dec. 1787 (in a secretary's hand).

In 1787, while he was still harassed by the Shaysites and worried about the outcome of the gubernatorial election, Bowdoin nevertheless took the trouble to send to Dr. Benjamin Waterhouse, Hersey Professor of the Theory and Practice of Physics, Dr. Benjamin Rush's oration before the American Philosophical Society on the influence of physical causes on the moral faculty. Rush was especially interested in the application of medical principles to the interpretation of diseases and remedies mentioned in the Bible. Waterhouse scathingly denounced this attempt on the part of a fellow physician—whom he disparaged as a "Chemist"—to combine materialism and Revelation without discovering the *tertium quid* to make the mixture homogeneous. Rush, he declared, was no more illustrious in theology than a theologian would have been in medicine. He derided the notion that "the figurative expression of *full of Idleness* & *full of bread* meant the repletion of the bowels & vessels of the human machine"; or that Isaiah was prescribing in the area of dietetic medicine when he prophesied, "Butter and honey shall everyone eat that is left in the land"; or that Moses forced the benighted Jews to drink hepar sulphuris (whose smell Waterhouse likened to a rotten egg's), so that when they thought of their idolatry, by an association of ideas they would vomit with abhorrence.[86] Bowdoin could no more bring amity to these two embattled physicians than he could put a checkrein on the disturbances that led to Shays' Rebellion.

During the year of Bowdoin's death communications to the Academy continued as usual: at the January meeting of 1790, an accurate history of a locked jaw consequent upon a wounded membrane and another examination of the comparative longevity of the clergy with other people;[87] at the May meeting, an enquiry into the physical influence of education on health, beauty, and disposition, along with a paper on the semicircular shapes of rainbows and another defending metempsychosis in a limited sense, a subject that a decade earlier might have been derided as sheer superstition.[88] The August meeting featured once again a letter on the extraction of fresh water from salt by Jacob Isaacs, a member of the Newport Jewish community who had been vainly soliciting financial aid for his project.[89]

The impression is inescapable that after an effective, if self-conscious, entrance into the world of learning, the Academy lost much of its lustre and tended to plod along in routine, unimaginative fashion. Bowdoin's ten-year rule had started out with more fanfare than it ended: the broad-based academy contemplated at the outset, with active members from other states and relations with members abroad,

---

86. MHS, Bowdoin and Temple Papers, Benjamin Waterhouse to Bowdoin, 1787. Rush, who was in fact professor of chemistry at the University of Pennsylvania, had presented his paper on 27 February 1786.

87. Academy Records, 1:132, meeting of 27 Jan. 1790.

88. Ibid., 134, meeting of 25 May 1790.

89. Ibid., 138, meeting of 25 August 1790; see also Academy Papers, 2:10, Bowdoin to Jacob Isaacs, 19 June 1790.

by the time of his death had been trimmed to the dimensions of a provincial society. Some of the more critical members, at least, mocked the solemnity with
which patent absurdities were presented and referred to committees for further
study. The Reverend Jeremy Belknap, writing to Ebenezer Hazard in February
1789, observed that the Academy sometimes had "very droll communications,"
among which he listed a Moravian missionary's account, sent from Ohio by member Winthrop Sargent, of a wingless, locust-shaped insect that planted itself in the
earth and shot up into a vegetable, with stalk, leaves, and flowers. The story of this
transmogrification "raised, not a *laugh* (for that would have been unbecoming a
philosophical body), but a *smile*; and some whispers were circulated: 'This is a fine
Ohioism.' [So much for New England condescension to the hinterland.] . . . But
what is more laughable, if possible, is that committees are sometimes chosen to
consider and report upon such communications. Great men have their weaknesses
as well as little!"

The life of the flowering locust was prolonged by the ministrations of the president himself. Perhaps to offset the cool reception of Sargent's tale and any offense
to his intellectual aspirations, Bowdoin wrote him on 21 April that the Moravian's
account was extraordinary, and added that in an effort to convince the members
of its credibility he had related to them an instance of the union of animal and
vegetable natures that he had beheld twenty years earlier: he had received from
one of the British sugar islands the gift of an insect, dead but well preserved, that
was half-caterpillar and half-wood. The skeptical Belknap had obviously been unmoved by Bowdoin's recital, for the following December, when he mentioned to
Sargent that a new volume of Academy *Memoirs* was contemplated, he earnestly
advised him "as a friend . . . to say nothing more about the vegetable-insect," as
the information he had received must have been erroneous. The matter was not
dropped as promptly as Belknap would have wished, for on 30 July 1790 he again
wrote Sargent, expressing his annoyance that Bowdoin had ever communicated
the story to the Academy, and quoting an ingenious theory of Manasseh Cutler's,
perhaps with tongue in cheek, that an insect might have swallowed a seed, which
then germinated in its bowels and sprang forth a flower after its insect-host had
died![90]

Often a quorum was lacking for Academy meetings. In 1789 the Reverend
Manasseh Cutler complained that the *vis inertiae* prevailed even among the sec-

---

90. MHS, *Collections*, ser. 5.3 (Belknap Papers, 2 [1877]), 103–04, Belknap to Ebenezer Hazard,
Boston, 12 Feb. 1789. See also ibid., 160, letter of 20 Aug. 1789; MHS, Winthrop Sargent Papers,
Bowdoin to Sargent, 21 Apr. 1789; ibid., Belknap to Sargent, Boston, 8 Dec. 1789; ibid., Belknap to
Sargent, Boston, 30 July 1790. In 1794 the Academy was still preoccupied with the problem of a "veg-
etable insect"; see Academy Papers, 2:20.

retaries, who sometimes allowed as much as four years to elapse before informing new members of their election, a tardiness that persuaded Cutler to take matters into his own hands and forward the certificates to his friends.[91] The secretaries were occasionally remiss in other respects as well: when an anonymous communication was read at a meeting, Caleb Gannett inadvertently supplied the author's name in an account he gave to the press, for which he hastened to write a letter to Dr. Holyoke begging his pardon for the violation of confidence.[92] The Academy of Arts and Sciences was not the only Massachusetts institution to have fallen upon dullish days—perhaps an inevitable letdown after the heroic period of protest and war against the British. A letter of 20 March 1789, from Nathaniel Appleton to Dr. Holyoke described the difficulties encountered by the Academy of Medicine in getting papers for its sessions. One detects an undercurrent of nostalgia for the good old days of fevers and plagues, as the writer laments that now, "a time of general Health—the publick mind seems absorbed in Politicks."[93]

World Renown

Despite its mediocre performance, the Academy acquired friends and repute in foreign parts. The election of a European member often elicited a reply accepting the honor with thanks, while expressing regret that illness, old age, or other concerns prevented the new Fellow from participating actively in the work of the Academy. Well-wishers of America—and no others were chosen until Count Rumford's perplexing appearance on the rolls in 1789—took the opportunity to hail the Republic and to foretell a brilliant future for the new nation. Thomas Brand Hollis sent an enthusiastic acceptance from England shortly before the Treaty of Paris formally ended hostilities: "Happily time has proved that a magnanimous and free people even in the midst of calamity and oppression are equal to any just enterprise. . . . The European societies are too much contracted, but the liberal minds of the Americans will see things in a more extensive view, and their societies like their governments be generous commonwealths, under which only, true science can flourish."[94] With such comparisons, designed to flatter the self-esteem of the new nation, Brand Hollis showed himself no less a partisan of America than his patron Thomas Hollis, Harvard's great benefactor, had been.

Joseph Priestley wrote Corresponding Secretary Willard from Birmingham on 23 June 1785, "I rejoice that, after so noble and successful a struggle for your *liber-*

---

91. MHS, Winthrop Sargent Papers, Cutler to Winthrop Sargent, Ipswich, 28 Sept. 1789.

92. Salem, Essex Institute: Holyoke Papers, Box 5, Folder 2, Gannett to Holyoke, 12 Sept. 1789.

93. Ibid., Folder 1.

94. MHS, *Proceedings* 43 (1909–10), 612–13, T. B. Hollis to Joseph Willard, The Hide, 15 Aug. and 3 Sept. 1783.

ties, you are now, in times of peace, attending to matters of *science*. I hope you will have the same success in your exertions in this way."[95] Priestley had been extravagantly admired by Winthrop, Franklin, and Bowdoin, and in 1773 they had tried to rescue him from grave financial straits by settling him in an American college. But Winthrop agreed with Franklin that even if a post could be found, Priestley's "religious principles would hardly be thought orthodox enough."[96] Nearly a decade had passed, a war had been fought, and the Academy under James Bowdoin was far less restrictive than the colleges: Priestley was warmly welcomed into the ranks of membership.[97] However alarming his religious principles might have been, he was in any event a staunch Establishment man when it came to ideas of social justice. "The poor," he wrote in his catechism published in Salem in 1785, "should be content with their low situation in life, and by frugality and industry endeavour to make their circumstances as easy as they can. And the rich should be humble and thankful to God for all they enjoy, and endeavour to do as much good to others as possible."[98]

Unsolicited letters were occasionally received from foreigners, begging the privilege of membership and enumerating their own works. Some lovers of liberty saw affiliation with the Academy as a declaration of faith in the new nation; others, as a testimony to their personal distinction. Laurent van Santen of Leyden, in a letter of 21 November 1780, described himself as a student of Greek and Roman literature who was zealous for the cause of liberty and full of reverence for all forms of knowledge that enlightened the mind and purified the heart. He inquired about the progress of classical studies in the new republic, said that he was sending the Academy some of his books, and tactfully suggested that it would give him great pleasure if he could be of use to the American savants.[99]

A Baron J.G.A. de Hüpsch de Lontzen from Cologne, member of the Imperial Academy of St. Petersburg and a dozen other learned societies, enclosed with his request for election to honorary membership a two-page fly-sheet on flora and fauna. A man of many parts, he also sent along a pamphlet on resuscitating apparently deceased persons.[100] Hüpsch was eager to be put in touch with people who could supply him with animal skins and other American curiosities. Though prodded by the corresponding secretary of the Academy, Professor Eliphalet Pear-

95. Ibid., 619, Priestley to Joseph Willard, Birmingham, 23 June 1785.

96. Franklin, *Papers* 20:90–91, John Winthrop to Franklin, Cambridge, 4 Mar. 1773.

97. Academy Records, 1:33, 51, meeting of 30 Jan. 1782.

98. Joseph Priestley, *Extracts from his catechism* (Salem, 1785).

99. MHS, Bowdoin and Temple Papers, Laurent van Santen to Bowdoin, Leyden, 21 Nov. 1780. Van Santen had a number of publications, including translations, to his credit.

100. Academy Letters, 1:75, Baron de Hüpsch to the Academy, Cologne, 23 Apr. 1789; Academy Records, 1:130, meeting of 11 Nov. 1789.

son, Manasseh Cutler was unimpressed. He had no inclination to initiate a correspondence with the baron, and disdained his proposal to exchange samples of the
natural productions of their respective countries. His object, wrote Cutler, with all
the haughtiness of an authentic naturalist toward an amateur, "seems to be to load
the shelves of his museum with ye subjects of natural history, without any view to
ye Science. These papers seem to give him the air of a *Show-man*, rather than a
philosopher." But on second thought, since the baron was exceedingly polite and a
foreigner of some standing in his own country, Cutler was prepared to send along
a few specimens of small value when he had time, lest Hüpsch think Americans
were ignorant of their own antiquities. Hüpsch's *Nouvelles Découvertes de quelques
Testacés pétrifiés rares et inconnus* was not worth translating, though it might "fill up a
few pages in a Magazine which would otherwise probably be occupied with something of as small merit." That was Cutler's patronizing verdict on 28 December
1789.[101] But what was good enough for European érudits proved good enough for
the Fellows of the Academy, and Hüpsch was elected to membership the following
month.[102]

The writer of a letter in a sensitive hand was a French physician who had published a work on optics, *Mémoires académiques, ou nouvelles découvertes sur la lumière
relative aux points les plus importans de l'optique* (1788)—one Dr. Jean-Paul Marat.
Scorned by official French scientists, Marat appealed to the American Academy in
the hope that he would win from them the recognition that had been denied him
at home. He addressed its president from the rue du vieux Colombier in Paris on
8 February 1788:

> I hope you will receive this work in the Academy over which you preside. The author,
> devoted to the search for useful truths, believes that he has discovered a number that
> are of the greatest import because of their effect on the construction of optical, as-
> tronomic, and naval instruments and on the study of Science, which the new findings
> make shorter and easier. I beg you, Sir, to engage the Society in examining my book
> rigorously, to name commissioners who would repeat the new experiments it contains
> to verify the results that I have deduced, and to approve the doctrine that follows from
> them, insofar as I have succeeded in raising a corner of the veil of Nature.

The book was presented to the Academy by Bowdoin at its meeting of 12 November 1788, and thanks were voted to the author. A committee consisting of
Vice-President Willard, Caleb Gannett, and Eliphalet Pearson—none of them
particularly qualified for the task—was appointed to test Dr. Marat's principles,
but the Academic wheels revolved slowly and Marat lay dead, murdered in his tub,
without the committee's having discharged its obligation. Whatever the merits of

---

101. Academy Letters, 1:87, Manasseh Cutler to Eliphalet Pearson, Ipswich, 28 Dec. 1789.
102. Academy Records, 1:25, 133, meeting of 27 Jan. 1790.

his optical discoveries, today more appreciated by historians of science than they used to be, he was not elected a Fellow, though other strange Europeans were.[103]

Spanish noblemen, foreign publicists, British men of science, and French royal emissaries, who had all befriended the nation in its darkest days, were co-opted for the new Academy, as well as future leaders of the French Revolution.[104] Jacques-Pierre Brissot de Warville, elected in 1785, announced to Bowdoin two years before the French Revolution the formation of a Société Gallo-Américaine whose object was to refute the calumnies about America that were rife in most of the European periodicals and to make American institutions better known on the Continent. Brissot promised to send his treatise *De la France et des Etats-Unis* as soon as it was published, and offered to recruit French teachers for the University and for Boston in general. A subsequent visit to the new land enhanced Brissot's enthusiasm, and at the close of 1788 he dashed off a hasty note to Bowdoin from New York, imparting to him a great secret: he was embarking for Europe at once and would return with his family in six or eight months. But the French Revolution, which he ardently supported, made his plans obsolete and claimed his life in 1793.[105] Brissot was not the only foreign member to toy with the idea of emigrating. As Europe was beset increasingly by political turmoil and the threat of war, America loomed as a haven to intellectuals, for whom the Academy was proof that a high state of civilization had been attained in the new land. Dr. Richard Price wrote to Corresponding Secretary Willard in October of 1787, "We are here at present trembling under the apprehensions of another war with *France*. . . . Should peace and liberty and science flourish in the united states and a wise and efficient plan of federal government be there established, we shall here know where to go when calamities come, and it will be of less consequence what happens in Europe."[106] The sentence recalls Gibbon's famous chapter 38 of the *Decline and Fall* published half a dozen years earlier, where he held out hope to his fellow-Europeans that if their world could not withstand the pressure of renewed barbarian invasions, the survivors could flee in ten thousand vessels to a European-civilization-in-America.

In September 1780, Samuel Cooper, vice-president of the Academy, had apparently offered membership to an officer of the French expedition in Newport. Coo-

---

103. Academy, *Memoirs* 2.2 (Charlestown, 1804), list of donations, including Marat's *Nouvelles découvertes*. See also Academy Letters, 1:63, Marat to Bowdoin, Paris, 8 Feb. 1788, and Academy Records, 1:119, 120, meeting of 12 Nov. 1788.

104. MHS, Bowdoin and Temple Papers, Bowdoin to General Knox, 24 Nov. 1788: Bowdoin declared his willingness to propose the two Spanish noblemen for admission to the Academy and asked for their titles and "literary character"; on 29 May 1789, the Duke de Almodovar and the Marquis de Santa Cruz were elected (Academy Records, 1:25).

105. MHS, Bowdoin and Temple Papers, Brissot de Warville to Bowdoin, Paris, 1 Feb. 1787, and New York, 4 Dec. 1788.

106. MHS, *Proceedings* 43: 626–27, Richard Price to Joseph Willard, Hackney, 10 Oct. 1787.

per was gregarious, and when he became expansive with company he might have promised anything. A letter in French from a M. de Corny, who on Lafayette's recommendation had been made *fournisseur* of the troops, accepted the honor that had been extended to him by Cooper. (M. de Corny conflated Harvard and the Academy, a comprehensible error.)

> You have had the goodness to offer me the title of associate of the Society of Arts, Sciences, and Belles-lettres of the university of Cambridge. I am very much touched by this honor, and the more so because it will forge another bond attaching me to you. I beg you, then, dear Doctor, to send me that certificate which I shall bring back with pleasure to my country as a testimonial of your esteem and friendship. Send it to me as soon as you can, for I plan to go to France for the winter and return in Spring with the second division. I will gather up my various works which I will have the honor to send you, as a gift to your learned society.[107]

Dominique Louis Ethis de Corny (originally Ethis de Novéan) was a run-of-the-mill member of the Paris Parlement, a barrister and public prosecutor until his resignation in 1789, and either wiser counsel prevailed in the Academy or Cooper forgot about the whole matter: the name does not appear on the membership rolls. The "various works" to which his letter alluded seem to have been fictitious. M. de Corny left America in February 1781; his compatriot Claude Blanchard described him as a rapacious intriguer whose brief sojourn in America had been costly and of little help to the French army, while it did no harm at all to his fortune.[108]

Though occasionally peculiar figures of dubious repute slipped in, on the whole the foreign members of the Academy elected in the first decade of its existence were an eminent group of scientists, men like D'Alembert, Condorcet, Euler, William Herschel, Buffon, Lalande. One of the more esoteric foreigners who early became a member was Antoine Court de Gébelin, who did much to spread its renown in Paris. It is not quite clear how relations were first established between the Academy and Court de Gébelin, a Protestant érudit living in Paris who in his day was known for a scholarly extravaganza entitled *Monde primitif analysé et comparé avec le monde moderne considéré dans son génie allégorique et dans les allégories auxquelles conduisit ce génie précédé du plan général des diverses parties qui composèrent ce monde primitif*, nine large quarto volumes published from 1773 to 1782. Possibly John Adams mentioned the Harvard Hebraist Stephen Sewall and Court de Gébelin to each other in the course of his shuttling between Boston and Paris. In any case,

---

107. San Marino, Cal., Huntington Library, de Corny to Cooper, Newport, 27 Sept. 1780, postscript.

108. Claude Blanchard, *Guerre d'Amérique*, 36, 63. Though de Corny wrote a few slim works on administration, nothing was published earlier than 1789.

Adams was the intermediary between Harvard and Court, who entrusted Adams with a gift to the university of the first six volumes of his chef d'oeuvre.[109]

The son of a famous Protestant émigré preacher, Court de Gébelin had been dispatched from Lausanne on a mission to help alleviate the disabilities of his Huguenot co-religionists. His attempt to purchase Protestant "liberties" from the French Crown was not a success. Protestant communities would agree neither upon the proposals of their delegate nor upon his person. At the time of the Calas affair he wrote *Les Toulousaines*, a passionate defense of the persecuted, which he later withdrew when Voltaire, the absolute monarch of the condemned, found fault with it. This rare bird, a Protestant man of learning in Paris, enjoyed a social triumph among intellectuals who were sponsoring new causes like the war of the American insurgents and the right of Huguenots to a legal status in France. A friend of Benjamin Franklin—who was not above making fun of Court's learned lucubrations[110]—John Adams, and the *philosophes*, he was received everywhere, a living reminder of the iniquities perpetrated by the revocation of the Edict of Nantes. Though his religion was an obstacle to his becoming a member of the Académie des Inscriptions et Belles-Lettres, whose more sober érudits considered him a fantast, he was consoled by an appointment as a royal censor, one of the curious anomalies of the last days of the *ancien régime*.

Court de Gébelin saw in Stephen Sewall the sort of helpmate from afar that obsessive scholars are forever seeking to lend support to their theories. As Hancock Professor of Hebrew and other Oriental Languages at Harvard, Sewall knew Hebrew, Aramaic, and Arabic; living on the borderlands of Indian country, he also had access to American Indian tongues. Court de Gébelin made a valiant effort to rouse him to scholarly action in a letter of 3 March 1780: if only Sewall pursued his studies of Indian and Hebrew etymology he would soon be able to prove that these languages were but variants of an original primitive tongue, as he, Court de Gébelin, had already deduced from his study of Greek and Latin etymologies. Court flooded Sewall with letters, a few of which, surviving sea voyages that took months and even years, are still extant.[111] Sewall was of course not ready to embrace any such ambitious theories. He was a cautious critic of the Bible who availed himself of the contemporary findings of English and Dutch scholarship without falling into enthusiasms, religious or erudite.

109. San Marino, Cal., Huntington Library, Court de Gébelin to the President and Fellows of the Harvard Corporation, Paris, 2 Mar. 1780; the letter was written in English.

110. Court de Gébelin figures a number of times in Franklin's correspondence; see his *Writings*, ed. Smyth, 1:85, 199; 7:43, n. 2, and 436; 8:246–48.

111. Letters from Court de Gébelin to Sewall have been inserted into volume 1 of Sewall's "Lectures on Hebrew and Oriental Literature delivered in Harvard College between the years 1765 and 1782" (MS), housed in the Harvard University Archives.

The Marquis François de Barbé Marbois, first councillor of the French embassy in America and an Academy member, was enlisted to provide Court de Gébelin with materials. In turn, Marbois tried to get help from the bibliophile Benjamin Guild, who noted in his diary his efforts to secure a dictionary of the Indian language for a French gentleman — unmistakably Court — trying to prove that all languages derived from one.[112] Though only part of a network of scholars to whom Court de Gébelin appealed for evidence to sustain his theory, Sewall had produced the prize exhibit, a copy of the inscriptions on Dighton Rock on the east bank of the Taunton River, forty miles south of Boston. In the *Monde primitif*, Court cited Sewall's communications telling of an expedition in September of 1768, in which he was joined by Thomas Danforth, William Baylies, Seth Williams, and David Cobb.[113] The markings on the rock had been noticed for half a century or more, and various theories had been advanced about their origin. Some thought they were Phoenician, an idea that Court had seized upon, others imagined that the incisions were not in an alphabetic, but in a hieroglyphic, language, either Chinese or Japanese. On the basis of the inscriptions and "other evidence" Court de Gébelin concluded that the original peoples of the Boston area were all of a "race Orientale," probably Phoenician, and that the languages of America from the North to the South Pole were the same as the original speech of the "primitive world." In his wildly romantic interpretation every figure and notation acquired meaning. Dighton Rock became the record of Carthaginian seamen who for a time had lived peacefully with the Indians but eventually sailed home, after consulting their oracle and receiving assurances of a safe return. Court de Gébelin graciously thanked in print the learned North American correspondents who had sent him sketches, from which he had an engraving of the rock made for binding with his text. "One will there see that it is most likely, we should say almost self-evident, that this is a Phoenician monument and doubtless a Carthaginian one divided into three scenes, one past, one present, one future."[114]

Court de Gébelin was blissfully unaware of the opinion of Dighton Rock that Sewall had expressed in a letter to Ezra Stiles in January of 1768: "I confess I have no faith in the significancy of the characters. There is indeed in some of the figures an appearance of design. But the strokes in general appear to be mere *lusus Indorum* [Indian doodles]."[115] Stiles, who continued to be fascinated by Dighton Rock and similar inscriptions in Connecticut, ended by believing that they were carved in Hebrew. He thought he could make out the names of Adam and Abraham, rein-

---

112. MHS, Diary of Benjamin Guild, 1 Sept. 1774–1 Nov. 1779 (MS), entry for 24 Sept. 1779.

113. Court de Gébelin, *Monde Primitif* 8 (Paris, 1781), 58–59, 561–68.

114. Ibid., 561–68, and Plate 1, no. 1.

115. Sewall to Stiles, January 1768, cited in E. B. Delabarre, *Dighton Rock. A Study of the Written Rocks of New England* (New York: Walter Neale, 1928), 55–56.

forcing the old notion that the Indians were in fact dispersed Israelites. Stiles was aware that his theories might be greeted with incredulity. As he wrote to his fellow epigrapher Sewall, "I know I expose myself to be considered as carryed away into imagination & conjecture. But I am willing to risque this imputation, if I could stir up a general Inquiry & Examination on Rocks & Stones &c. &c. illustrative of the Antiquities of America."[116] Recent conjectures tend to view the Dighton Rock incisions as a disconnected series extending over time: the name of the explorer Miguel Cortereal, with the date 1511, as well as that of one Thacher, have been isolated; the rest are now believed to be later Indian jottings and pictures with no identifiable meaning.[117] Despite Sewall's skepticism, Dighton Rock continued to attract the attention of the Academy. Both volume 2 (1793) and volume 3 (1809) of its *Memoirs* included articles attempting to decipher the inscriptions on the rock and calculate its antiquity.

When notified by Sewall in February 1781 about the founding of the Academy, Court de Gébelin expressed his amazement that this event took place amid the ravages of war, and predicted that it would have favorable consequences for the nation's prosperity and the uncovering of America's remote origins.[118] In his conclusion to the eighth volume of the *Monde primitif* (1781) he reported the formation in America of a "society of sciences and arts," one of whose purposes was to assemble everything of note on the early history of the continent. He waxed eloquent over the prospects of the Academy: "What may we not expect from so numerous and well constituted a body?"[119] As for Dighton Rock, he earnestly advised efforts at conservation, since the rising waters of the river were likely to erode the inscriptions and thus wipe away the witness of this most illustrious monument of the ancient world.

Court's blandishments fell on receptive ears, and on 22 August 1781, upon the nomination of Stephen Sewall, he was elected a Fellow of the American Academy.[120] It was his hope that close ties would be established between the American learned society and a recently founded literary society named the Musée de Paris, or Société de Sciences, lettres & beaux Arts, of which he was president. Franklin

116. Academy Letters, 1:97, Sewall to Bowdoin, Cambridge, 12 July 1790, transmitting an extract from Stiles's letter, and his memoir. Stiles's absorption with the problem became widely known, and elicited a letter about the inscription on a rock in western Connecticut from a wealthy Amsterdam Jew of dubious repute, Isaac Pinto, who, incidentally, had predicted the defeat of the American colonies (Academy Papers, 1:125, Pinto to Stiles, New York, 14 Apr. 1790; Academy Records, 1:137, meeting of 25 Aug. 1790).

117. See Delabarre, *Dighton Rock*.

118. Harvard University Archives: Sewall Lectures, vol. 1, Court to Sewall, Paris, Aug. 1781 (received 18 Nov. 1783).

119. Court de Gébelin, *Monde Primitif* 8:567.

120. Academy Records, 1:46, 48.

was a member of the French group and had promised to cement relations between
the two bodies. Court had ambitious plans for publishing the work of members
of the Musée, and he invited Academicians to send him their communications, offering to print them along with the French memoirs if their authors so desired.[121]
When hostilities between England and America ceased—though the Treaty of
Peace was still many months away—the Musée de Paris held a brilliant celebration that Franklin honored with his presence. On 14 March 1783, Court de Gébelin sent Stephen Sewall a detailed account of the festivities that had taken place
on the sixth. Recitations in verse and prose began shortly after five, followed by a
concert that lasted from seven or eight until ten. The elites of the academic world
and of the city of Paris were present at this assembly, which was graced by no
less than four hundred beautiful ladies. The celebrants drank to the health of the
United States of America and the Boston "literary society," to which Dr. Franklin
replied in a manner that excited widespread admiration.

The two societies were virtually twins, the Musée de Paris having been formed
by a few friends in November 1780, the time of the Academy's official inauguration. The French group had multiplied so rapidly that it was obliged to rent a large
mansion and to build a superb auditorium holding four hundred persons as an ad-
junct. An intimate association and constant correspondence with the Academy was
their most ardent wish. Science, like commerce, could spread only through the exchange of products between one country and another: "The knowledge acquired
in one land is generally lost to others, a great misfortune. We shall neglect nothing to prevent this from happening."[122] The enthusiastic welcome of the French
intellectuals led by Court de Gébelin more than compensated for the iciness with
which Sir Joseph Banks of the Royal Society had received the new American star
in the firmament of science.

The publication of the first volume of *Memoirs* in 1785 aroused a certain amount
of interest in France and England. Bowdoin's friend Michel-Guillaume-Saint Jean
de Crèvecoeur wrote him from Paris on 21 October 1786 that the volume was
awaited with impatience by several persons devoted to the progress of practical
science throughout the world. He took occasion to thank Bowdoin for the copy of
his inaugural address at the Academy and, with sublime indifference to chronology, expressed wonderment at the capacity of this governor of a great state to find
the leisure and acquire the learning demanded by the subjects covered in his elo-

121. Harvard University Archives: Sewall Lectures, vol. 1, Court de Gébelin to Sewall, Paris, Apr.
1781. Though the letter was not received until 18 November 1783, the Fellows at their meeting of 28
May 1782 had already voted to accept Court's invitation "to establish an intimate confederation and
correspondence with the Museum of Paris" (Academy Records, 1:54).

122. Harvard University Archives: Sewall Lectures, vol. 1, Court de Gébelin to Sewall, 14 Mar.
1783.

quent discourse (which had been delivered, of course, more than four years before Bowdoin became governor of Massachusetts). Agriculturist Crèvecoeur, author of *Letters from an American Farmer* (1782), proposed a practical goal for the Academy: the introduction into France of American agricultural products of better quality than the wretched stuff hitherto received. He hoped that the Academy would publish instructions on how to improve American butter, cheese, hams, and gammons, and offer prizes that would open the people's eyes and stimulate their industriousness.[123] When Crèvecoeur received the first volume of the *Memoirs*, filled with a discussion of the Newtonian system, he tendered his hearty thanks without comment—theoretical physics was not his forte—and in return dispatched a book printed on newly invented paper made from the bark of a species of linden tree, along with specimens of other papers.[124] Richard Price declared that the volume of *Memoirs* contained much important information. Sir Joseph Banks, president of the Royal Society of London, who got a copy from Dr. Price, responded in his customary spirit of denigration: it included curious matter. No copy had been sent directly to the Royal Society—small wonder after its president's cold indifference to the Academy's initial notice—and Sir Joseph, ever haughty, expressed the hope that future volumes would reach the Society without benefit of intermediary.[125]

The publication of the *Memoirs* drew criticism as well as faint praise from foreign readers. On 30 October 1786, the Reverend Manasseh Cutler replied at length to a set of objections from Dr. Jonathan Stokes, a distinguished English botanist, whose attachment to the United States did not inhibit his strictures against its newborn cultural institution. Stokes found the name of the American Academy distasteful because it savored too much of French titles and was inappropriate for a private philosophical society. Cutler explained that he had had nothing to do with the naming since he was a latecomer, but that the choice was defensible. Since Britain in 1780 was an enemy and France a generous ally, the founders wished to avoid any echo of the Royal Society, as well as to distinguish the Academy from the Philadelphia Society. As for defects in the volume, Cutler was fully aware of them, and called the publication a mere experiment. He launched into a tale of woe detailing the many difficulties encountered in producing a book of such magnitude. The members were inexperienced; the whole venture was run by a committee that had not coordinated its efforts. The printers were young and zealous and had contracted for too low a price; to keep them from bankruptcy a special subsidy had

123. MHS, *Proceedings* 13 (1873–75), 238–39, Michel-Guillaume-Jean de Crèvecoeur to Bowdoin, Paris, 21 Oct 1786.

124. Ibid., 239, Crèvecoeur to Bowdoin, Paris, 3 Feb. 1787.

125. MHS, Bowdoin and Temple Papers, Richard Price to Bowdoin, Newington-Green, 24 July 1786. Nevertheless, Sir Joseph accepted membership in the Academy on 30 April 1788 (Academy Records, 1:34).

to be raised; even so it was necessary to omit the index. Having read the statutes of the Academy, the English critic found that an aristocratic spirit pervaded them, since the council had to approve nominations before they were presented to the body of the membership. Cutler was taken aback, once again pleaded innocence on the ground that the statutes were passed before his own election, and lamely offered as the excuse for the objectionable provision "certain local circumstances." The oath of office was justified on the ground that atheists surely could have no objection to an oath as a political formality, and a mere affirmation was always accepted as a Quaker's oath in America.[126] If Stokes wounded the pride of the Academy, it was to the credit of the Fellows that their dedication to scientific inquiry transcended amour-propre: Stokes was elected to membership on 20 August 1788, an honor that he graciously accepted half a year later.[127]

Subsequent volumes of Academy *Memoirs*, slimmer than the first grandiose publication, did not appear with any regularity or frequency: the second, in two parts, came after intervals of eight and eleven years; part 1 of the third volume five years later, and part 2 after another lapse of six years. The great expectations of annual or biennial harvests of science were not fulfilled.

A Short-Lived Competitor

The stately sessions of the American Academy failed to satisfy the literary appetites of all Bostonians. Wit, poetry, and random philosophical imaginings found no place in an institution that cultivated the "barebones" style of the Royal Society of London. There was nothing to amuse the ladies; neither love nor adventure was ever mentioned, and matters of religion were excluded, at least in principle. Small wonder that the Academy soon witnessed the sprouting of a rival, a monthly review that called itself *The Boston Magazine* and was published by a Society for the Publication of *The Boston Magazine*. The Society comprised about a dozen local intellectuals, who voted in new members with the solemnity of a proper literary academy. The enterprise endured from late 1783 through 1786, and at one point worried the Reverend Jeremy Belknap, who feared that it was stealing the Academy's thunder by translating its learned disquisitions into popular language.

The editors of *The Boston Magazine* shamelessly confessed that only one third of its pieces were original, the rest being excerpts from European reviews or filler composed of meteorological information and brief notices from home and

126. Cutler, *Life, Journals and Correspondence* 2:267–71; Stokes had written him on 17 August 1785.

127. Academy Records, 1:34; Academy Letters, 1:72, Stokes to Joseph Willard, Kiddeminster, 9 Mar. 1789.

abroad—"as much as can be expected from a new country," they added by way of excuse, "just emerging from the calamities of war, in the dawn of public literature, and amidst a variety of scenes fitted to engage the attention of people, many of whom, at a season of greater leisure, might employ their pens upon literary subjects, and afford speculations equally instructive and amusing."

When the Society for the Publication of *The Boston Magazine* was founded at a meeting on 25 November 1783, only Benjamin Guild and the Reverend John Clarke enjoyed dual membership in the new venture and in the American Academy. (George Richards Minot and Dr. Joseph Warren, literary lights, were later additions to the rolls of the Academy.) Generally the Academy drew upon the older, more serious members of the Boston establishment, while the *Magazine* attracted wild and daring youth eager to open new pathways.

Among the first articles approved for publication by the Society were an essay on the nature of time and another on the free exercise of conscience in religious matters, along with "Dr. Doddridge's to his wife's bosom," pieces on humanity and chronology, criticism of contemporary English writers, a celebration of conjugal happiness, and a monody on the death of Dr. Samuel Cooper. There were also rejections, notably "To a Lady with a penknife." Usually the select committee of the Society was eclectic in its choices: "A Fable on Love, Beauty and Prudence"; "Observations on education"; "Verses on a young attorney"; "On happiness"; "On contentment"; "On justice"; descriptions of the Amsterdam exchange and of Niagara Falls; "On taste and Genius"; "On vanity"; an "Epigram on a lady who squinted." Audacious questions were broached, such as "Has the discovery of America been useful or hurtful to mankind?" When copy was running short, an injunction was laid upon members of the Society to produce material themselves by the next meeting. This yielded an account of a singular species of monkey and the narrative of a shipwreck off Cape Breton Island.

For a time the creative juices flowed freely in Boston, stimulated by the exaltation of victory. But the promise of a rich intellectual life was not always realized either in the Academy or in *The Boston Magazine*. The harsh reality of a postwar social and economic crisis soon put an end to the euphoria. While it lasted, however, *The Boston Magazine* provided eastern men of letters with matter that the Academy would not have risked. In the July 1784 issue there was a full-page engraving of the late Monsieur Voltaire, accompanied by a critical estimate of his life and works. It was judicious, carefully weighing his vices and his virtues, but outspoken:

> The Pucelle, or Maid of Orleans, ought to be hid in a privy on the summit of Parnassus. . . . He was not a profound philosopher, and yet he was far from being ignorant in the sciences; he was a tolerable metaphysician of the second class. . . . His opposition to christianity was not only indecent and disingenuous, but was moreover, carried on

with a degree of acrimony, spite, bitterness and bigotry which has not been perceivable in the writings of any deist, known to us, in the present age. In natural religion though he seemed sometimes wavering, undetermined and inconsistent, yet he never appears to have contracted the stupid frenzy of atheism.[128]

The Boston Magazine ended its life with a rather lengthy and boring account of the proceedings of the General Court on 14 October 1786, when Shays' Rebellion was in full furor. In the literary area, as elsewhere, the rebellion cast its ominous shadow. Though the Society had managed to include a costly engraving of the ascent of Mongolfier's "Aerial Balloon," poetical essays yielded to darker subjects such as the condition of laborers and methods of punishing criminals in Rome.[129] The economy of Boston (a settlement of 2,100 houses, according to the Magazine's estimate) could not support a literary journal in the midst of an uprising. The American Academy survived, nourished by dinner invitations from Boston merchants and prosperous lawyers during the worst of times.

128. The Boston Magazine 1:362–63.
129. Ibid., 434.

8

SHAYS' UNNATURAL REBELLION
The Academy Fellows Go to War

⟨Ͼ❋Ͽ⟩

THE RECORDS of the Academy give no hint of the trials endured by its leading members in the mid-1780s, at the time of the agrarian uprising that shook the market towns of inner Massachusetts, though the president as governor of the Commonwealth and the lawyers and judges and legislators and merchants who figured prominently on the roster of the Academy were actively involved in suppressing the rebellion. The geographic distribution of the members reveals at a glance that the Academy was predominantly an establishment of "eastern gentlemen"—professional men and traders who enjoyed a similar style of life in coastal towns and the areas contiguous to them. There were a few Fellows from Worcester, Northampton, and Stockbridge, but it is doubtful that they attended sessions regularly, if at all; the journey from the western towns was so long and expensive that many of them even neglected to send representatives to the legislature in Boston. Wealth, learning, and professional skill were concentrated in the eastern counties. The coastal towns and the rural areas of the interior were so markedly different from each other that some recent historians have been moved to write about them as two cultures.

Eastern Philosophers Against Western Countrymen

The inhabitants of Massachusetts were almost all of British stock, English or Scotch-Irish; they were nurtured on the same Bible and, with the exception of a sprinkling of Baptists and isolated Quakers, they attended Congregational churches. The Episcopal churches were alien impositions that had been patronized by the royal governors and during the Revolution had been suspect as Tory havens; regaining respectability was a slow process. Episcopalians were not readily welcomed into the Academy, and those who were admitted had to be latitudinarians who betrayed no leanings toward the establishment of an episcopacy, the bogey of the patriots. Yet for all the homogeneity of national origin and religious belief there was a deep cleavage between the rationalist Christianity of the Boston clergy and their wealthy parishioners on one side, and on the other the emotional piety and conversion experiences of those who had responded to the Great Awakening and to the millennial expectations aroused by a radical evangelicalism. The passion of yeomen and husbandmen expressed in total surrender to Christ during a revival that departed from the staid order of meetinghouse observance could later drive them to rebel against the Commonwealth's courts of law, with their complex procedures derived from British royal justice and their rigid insistence on rules that ignored the plight of farmers in the western part of the state.

The rural counties were settled with family homesteads virtually self-sufficient in fulfilling their needs for food, shelter, and clothing. At harvesttime independent yeomen exchanged labor with their fellows without written agreements, and the artisans' products they required were paid for in kind with the surplus of their freeholds. Even the rare ministrations of a doctor were recompensed with goods and services. To facilitate exchange and to supply a few special products like glass, needles, and medicines, market towns grew up, with shops that depended for their stock upon the eastern merchants, whose prosperity was tied in considerable part to sales abroad and, in return, the importation of foreign luxuries.

Two years before Shays' Rebellion broke out, the historian George Richards Minot (later a judge and member of the Academy) confided to his journal astute psychological observations about the behavior of social collectives in Massachusetts, though he refrained from using the term "class." He distinguished between the attitude of merchants and traders in the maritime towns, who could readily convert their stock to money and were accustomed to sudden reversals of fortune in either direction, and that of countrymen, always more tenacious of their property, their land, whose possession gave them prestige and gratified their pride and spirit of independence. Minot understood their different reactions to the collection of taxes. Unlike the merchants, the yeomen could not readily dispose of portions of their property to discharge debts; entire farms were now in jeopardy, and Minot sensed how deep would be the wounds inflicted by any measures that threatened loss of ownership. When he came to write an account of the rebellion shortly after the events occurred, he adopted something of the moralizing manner of the classical Roman historians, but his social analysis was keen and he was praised for his balanced presentation of the bitter partisan strife.

Minot presented *The History of the Insurrections in Massachusetts* to his friend Governor Bowdoin in November of 1788—a sketch of the preliminaries had appeared in *The Boston Magazine*—and perhaps on the strength of it was elected to the Academy at its next session, 28 January 1789. It was Minot's opinion that during the latter part of the eighteenth century, as the demand for imported goods had risen in rural areas, the inhabitants were drawn more and more into a market economy that bound them to the vicissitudes of the overseas trade of the coast. More significant perhaps was the rise in taxes, or their more aggressive collection, after the Revolutionary War. The once nearly self-sufficient yeomen became debtors, and as debtors were at the mercy of a legal system that could throw them into jail to rot. The small independent domains on which they lived with their families as free men were subject to invasion by tax collectors, who seized their animals and, the ultimate tragedy, put up freeholds for sale because of tax delinquency. Tenancy, the desperate resort of the dispossessed husbandman, was equated with slavery. The rousing Leveller rhetoric of the English civil war, with its bitter denunciation of lawyers as the minions of Satan and demands for a measure of economic as well as political equality, resounded in the protests of the Massachusetts farmers. The grand declarations of the lawyers and merchants of the American Revolution were translated into a new rough speech peppered with curses and adapted to radical purposes.[1]

The coastal towns had flourished during the wars of the British against the French in Canada, campaigns the Calvinist Bostonians had supported with a fervor born of their hatred of papism. In the decades of conflict with the British Crown the Boston artisans, who were dependent upon expanding commerce, had backed their merchant and lawyer leaders and heeded their Harvard-educated preachers, as new doctrines were popularized that invoked natural law theory and proclaimed the right of self-preservation when the Crown levied its vexatious taxes. When the Revolution drew to a close, coastal merchants excluded by Britain from the profitable West Indian trade and unable to pay for the goods they had imported on credit from British mercantile houses were caught. There were bankruptcies on both sides of the Atlantic. During the war the paper certificates issued by the Congress had kept economic life moving, while men like James Bowdoin cannily made efforts to convert their paper money into goods. When Bowdoin had lost ships and had difficulty collecting rents from his tenants, he had lodged a formal plea for tax abatement with the town of Boston; but as governor he showed little sympathy for the harassed farmers whose tax payments were in arrears. Other

---

1. MHS, Journal of George Richards Minot, 1784–1791, entry for 13 Sept. 1784; Minot, *The History of the insurrections, in Massachusetts, in the year MDCCLXXXVI, and the rebellion consequent thereon* (Worcester, Mass., 1788), esp. p. 13. See also Academy Letters, 1:67, Minot to Bowdoin, 1 Nov. 1788; Academy Records, 1:34; and Worcester, American Antiquarian Society: Minot, "History of the insurrections" (MS), 33–34. In this original manuscript Minot included passages on the hostility to lawyers that were omitted or toned down in the printed version. A section that was later dropped endeavored to explain how ill-will toward members of the bar fed a rebellious spirit: "Whether the choice was owing to accident or design, the cry against the practitioners at the bar, was the most favourable means that could have been adopted for introducing the future commotions that took place in the Commonwealth. Ambitious and envious men felt a mortification at the share of fame, which was given to some characters of the law in the late revolution, and at the style of life which many of them afterwards adopted. . . . And men of intrigue anticipated with pleasure those vacancies at the elections, which might be occupied by themselves and their friends."

Boston merchants pressed the shopkeepers of the western towns to whom they had sold "luxuries" on credit, and the shopkeepers in their turn filed suit against their yeoman debtors.

The animus of eastern merchants against the farmers may well have had in it something of vengefulness aroused by reports of their hoarding and profiteering during the war. A Salemite wrote bitterly in 1779, "Thay (the Farmers) dont consider the suffring sea ports. I believe in General they have no feeling for us, but want all our money, goods, houses, & then our Selves to be there Servants."[2] And John Eliot, pastor of the New North Church, in a letter of 29 March 1780, described the poverty of Boston, with its many widowed families, and deplored the greed of country people who had extorted all the town's money in exchange for desperately needed fuel.[3]

Though two years earlier Bowdoin had professed his unwillingness to stand for election—"It does not comport with my inclination to be the only slave in the State, a slave to the humours and caprices of the multitude as he must be who wishes for an office dependent on their Suffrages"[4]—he was a candidate in the gubernatorial race of 1785. Hancock, too ill to run again, had favored Thomas Cushing in order to keep the door open for himself at a later election—that was James Warren's acerb comment in a letter to John Adams in Paris. But Hancock could not transfer his personal popularity to his supporter; the patriots united against Cushing; and the failure of any candidate to win a clear majority threw the election into the legislature. Bowdoin, the tall, pale, intellectual merchant with the dignified air, was the choice of both houses, and on the surface all was "Peace, Tranquillity and Satisfaction."[5] Yet Warren was too shrewd not to perceive that trouble was in the offing. The drain of specie to make remittances for "baubles" imported from England had created an extreme scarcity of hard money. Commerce had been ruined by the war, and agriculture and industry were declining. People were unable to pay their debts, bankruptcies were common, and taxes could not be collected. If moderation did not prevail, Warren warned, anarchy would be the outcome.[6] But moderation was not

---

2. "Revolutionary Letters Written to Colonel Timothy Pickering," in Essex Historical Institute (Salem), *Historical Collections* 44 (1908), 314, George Williams to Pickering, Salem, 3 July 1779.

3. MHS, *Collections*, ser. 6.4 (Belknap Papers, 3), 177–78, John Eliot to Jeremy Belknap, Boston, 29 Mar. 1780.

4. MHS, Bowdoin and Temple Papers, Letter Book, 247, Bowdoin to George Erving, 13 Nov. 1783. He had in fact declined election to the General Court as representative from Boston in May 1782.

5. MHS, *Collections* 43 (Warren-Adams Letters, 2), 262, James Warren to John Adams, Milton, 4 Sept. 1785.

6. Ibid., 272, Warren to Adams, Milton, 30 Apr. 1786. A year before, his wife in a letter to Adams had decried the Americans' increasing avidity for pleasure (ibid., 252, Mercy Warren to Adams, Milton, 27 Apr. 1785).

the way of James Bowdoin when other men defaulted in their business obligations. The stern Calvinist spirit that had been relaxed in his religious views reasserted itself and demanded adherence to the letter of the law in contractual relations.

Minot wrote his history of the rebellion in the spirit of the doctrine that history was *magistra vitae*. Civil commotions required investigation, in order that principles might be deduced for preserving the future tranquillity of the Commonwealth. Others might wish to bury the painful events in oblivion, but Minot insisted on facing them and vindicating the public reputation of those who had suppressed the uprising. According to his *History*, during the long years of the War of Independence, ordinary men had become well acquainted with the science of the rights of mankind, but had acquired no equivalent insight into the mazes of finance. They had come out of the war with "honest prejudices" against impost and excise duties, associated in their minds with monarchy and tyranny. While the value of the paper currency that had been issued was falling, Massachusetts levied a tax of 5 percent to help pay the foreign debt of the nation and resorted to further levies to discharge the interest on its own state debt. Payments of taxes, suspended during the war, were in arrears even when people were allowed to use depreciated certificates. The landed interests and the merchants tended to divide on economic policy: the owners of real estate attacked imported luxuries as the direct cause of the depreciation of the currency. What remained of puritanical values, as well as the ascetic morality that Montesquieu had identified with republics, required the sacrifice of luxuries, which were linked with political evil. Prosperity was based upon hard manual labor, and it was sinful to encourage the vices and indolence of the people by supplying them with an abundance of imported "gew-gaws."

As if echoing Bowdoin's inaugural speech before the Academy, Minot deplored the sinking of maritime towns into a voluptuousness fed by the precarious wealth of naval adventurers. Massachusetts was on the road to perdition. Men of fortune vied with one another in the display of their riches. In turn they were aped by the less opulent citizens, and the townspeople lost the old Puritan virtues of diligence and thriftiness. Republics could thrive only when they were frugal, but the yeomen who had signed up in the revolutionary army had latterly been seduced into evil dissipated ways. Foreign manufactures had flooded the state, and so great was the reputation abroad of American merchants that individuals had been granted much more credit than they could sustain. Massachusetts towns, to read Minot, were turning into little Sodoms. Not much attention was devoted to the expansion of exports. The fisheries that had been the mines of Massachusetts were neglected during the war, and Nantucket whaling, which had once occupied 2,500 men and employed 150 boats, now counted only 19 vessels.

Unlike Minot, Benjamin Rush attributed the popular unrest to a frame of mind he called *anarchia*, rather than to economic distress. It was generated, he maintained, by an excess of the passion for liberty and a wild exhilaration that followed upon the successful outcome of the war. In consequence, neither opinions nor behavior were amenable to the dictates of reason or the restraints imposed by government. Rush, however, was not notable for his political discernment. At the very time the rebellion was gaining momentum, in October of 1786, he wrote smugly to Dr. Richard Price from Philadelphia, which was comfortably distant from the scene of action, "The commotions in New England have happily subsided without the loss of a life, or the effusion of one drop of kindred blood."[7]

Landed interests had hoped to place virtually the whole burden of taxation upon trade. The merchant class countered that this would not stave off economic catastrophe, for high excises would only favor the merchants of neighboring states, whose goods, at lower prices, would be smuggled into Massachusetts. The merchants asked for an equal distribution of the burden between agriculture and commerce. In 1785 there was a re-evaluation of property, and as new property that came into the market was assessed and the old re-assessed at a higher rate, grumbling was rife, especially in the counties of Hampshire and Berkshire.

The Agony of Governor Bowdoin

The new governor entered upon his duties with the odds against him. Not only was he confronted by a rickety financial and commercial structure in the state, but he had to refute preposterous charges that he had been ambivalent in his loyalties during the Revolution and was still under foreign influence.[8] From afar, the Marquis of Buckingham voiced his misgivings about Bowdoin's political future in a prescient letter to his kinsman Sir John Temple: "Although I am happy to see that State in which your connections lie, more immediately in the hands of a character so respectable as Mr. Bowdoin's, yet perhaps I may for his sake wish that he had suffered another year to pass over; as I am convinced that nothing but experience can bring back the mind of America to cool reflection from the intoxication which her independence has given to her." Like Dr. Benjamin Rush, the marquis saw psychological rather than economic disarray as threatening disaster. But no such apprehensions tempered the enthusiasm of other friends of the new governor. Dr. Richard Price sent Bowdoin

7. George Rosen, "Emotion and Sensibility in Ages of Anxiety," loc. cit., 744, quoting Rush, "Account of the Influence of the Military and Political Events of the American Revolution upon the Human Body," in his *Medical Inquiries and Observations*, 2d American ed. (Philadelphia, 1794), 1:263–78; MHS, *Proceedings*, ser. 2.17 (1903), 353, Rush to Price, Philadelphia, 27 Oct. 1786.

8. MHS, *Collections*, ser. 7.6 (Bowdoin and Temple Papers, 2), 47, Bowdoin's address to the General Court, 27 May 1785, refuting rumors of British influence. See also MHS, Bowdoin and Temple Papers, Bowdoin's draft of reply to *Columbian Centinel* article doubting his patriotism during the Revolution.

warm congratulations and declared that his election was a far greater honor than the accession to power, merely by descent, of a French or British monarch.[9]

Bowdoin had the hearty good wishes of the merchants of Massachusetts. In the time of troubles that had come upon them, they could rely on him to protect their interests, which they identified with the security and prosperity of the state. Sixty-nine merchants and traders of Boston in their congratulatory address offered assistance with good will and alacrity: "Our finances are deranged, our commerce exposed, and our government has not yet acquired that degree of energy and of dignity which is essentially necessary to our national happiness. . . . But we esteem it a peculiar felicity that in the present alarming state of our commerce, we have for our Governor a gentleman who cannot fail to sympathize with us at the gloomy prospect of our declining trade, and who we doubt not will chearfully make every exertion in his power to render us again respectable as a commercial people." Letters in the same vein arrived from manufacturers and tradesmen of Boston, and also from the inhabitants of Newburyport, whose message was presented by three Fellows of the Academy—Tristram Dalton, Theophilus Parsons, and Nathaniel Tracy. Like their Boston counterparts, the good citizens of Newburyport deplored the critical state of their commerce and the crushing burden of public debt, but took comfort that they had "by the Blessing of Heaven a Governor whose abilities, integrity & unremitted attention to the interests of the People, will provide every remedy in the power of the supreme executive authority of this Commonwealth." They promised to further the benevolent design of the government through unflinching adherence to the principles of piety, religion, and morality—as though a treasury of virtue could have impact on the sorry state of the Massachusetts exchequer.[10]

Bowdoin satisfied their expectations in sufficient measure to win re-election in the spring of 1786. On 31 May 1785, in his first full-length address to the General Court after taking office, he had dealt with the monetary crisis, and thereafter sent to the legislature a stream of messages on economic questions. He deplored the excessive importation of foreign goods, but was enough of a laissez-faire advocate to believe the situation would work its own cure when high prices dried up the market.[11] He sought to increase demand for Massachusetts goods by trying to persuade the governors of other states to enter into reciprocal arrangements for

9. MHS, *Proceedings* 9 (1866–67), 70, Buckingham to Temple, Margate, 8 July 1785; MHS, *Collections*, ser. 7.6 (Bowdoin and Temple Papers, 2), 80, Richard Price to Bowdoin, Newington-Green, 25 Oct. 1785.

10. Ibid., 50 (4 June 1785); 52–53 (7 June 1785); 56 (7 July 1785); John J. Currier, *History of Newburyport, Mass. 1764–1905* (Newburyport, 1906), 82–83.

11. Commonwealth of Massachusetts, *Laws and Resolves*, 1784–85 (n.p., n.d.), 708–09 ff.; MHS, *Collections*, ser. 7.6 (Bowdoin and Temple Papers, 2), 60, reply to the citizens of Newburyport, 22 July 1785.

eliminating the duties on interstate trade.[12] His exertions on behalf of the merchants induced the French to grant concessions on the admission of whale oil shipped in American bottoms.[13] And he secured the passage of an act to regulate navigation and commerce and impose retaliatory restrictions on British shipping (a move rendered largely ineffective when Connecticut opened its ports to foreign products). Referring to the Massachusetts act as a temporary expedient against Great Britain until such time as Congress was vested with power to regulate trade, he appealed to his fellow-governors to adopt similar measures in order to foil the unjust designs of foreigners.[14]

Bowdoin's efforts at retrenchment and his long-range plans to promote manufactures, trade, and commerce testify to his concern for putting the economy of the state on a sound footing. But when it came to taking immediate steps to make the tax systems more equitable and otherwise alleviate the mounting distress of farmers and small rural shopkeepers, he had tunnel vision. He lacked sympathetic understanding of their condition and of the bitter resentment exacerbated by his seeming indifference and his elegant style of life. At the inception of his first term, on 8 June 1785, he had responded to the clamors for relief of near-destitute citizens with a *Proclamation for the Encouragement of Piety, Virtue, Education and Manners, and for the Suppression of Vice*—an implicit rebuke to the ordinary men of Massachusetts for over-enjoying the fruits of victory and thereby bringing calamity upon their heads.[15] By enforcing the Sabbath laws and the rules against drunkenness, blaspheming, and gambling, he sought to elevate the moral tone of the Commonwealth, to discourage luxuriousness, and to prepare the people for the sacrifices that lay ahead. But the flow of righteous rhetoric did not answer to their economic needs; and Bowdoin's determination to fill the coffers of the state's treasury with the revenues lawfully due it, whatever the consequences, was at the very least rash and obtuse.

When financial stringencies grew acute and the discontent that had been festering for a number of years came to a head late in the summer of 1786, provoking armed attempts to disrupt the courts, followed by sporadic acts of terror against individuals, Bowdoin had already been re-elected for a second term; lawyers and

12. Ibid., 62, Bowdoin to the governor of Connecticut, 27 July 1785; 63, to the governor of Maryland, 28 July 1785; 76, to Patrick Henry, governor of Virginia, 18 Oct. 1785.

13. See Jefferson, *Papers* 8 (1953), 662–63, James Bowdoin to Thomas Jefferson, 23 Oct. 1785; 9 (1954), 262, Jefferson to Bowdoin, Paris, 8 Feb. 1786; see also MHS, *Collections*, ser. 7.6 (Bowdoin and Temple Papers, 2), 87, Bowdoin to John Adams, 12 Jan. 1786.

14. See, for example, his circular to the governor of Maryland, 28 July 1785, transmitting the Massachusetts Act (ibid., 63).

15. *A Proclamation for the Encouragement of Piety, Virtue, Education and Manners, and for the Suppression of Vice . . . the eighth Day of June, A.D. 1785* (Boston, 1785).

judges who were members of the Academy, such as David Sewall and Nathaniel Sargeant of the State Supreme Judicial Court, were on the firing-line; and legislators led by Samuel Adams—many of the Senators were Academy Fellows[16]—had the responsibility of aiding the governor in his defense of the Commonwealth against subversion. The old revolutionaries donned new uniforms. The only militia units that could be raised were from the coastal areas, and Fellows of the Academy reported for duty—the western part of the state generally ignored the summons. Bostonians and other seaport merchants among the Academy members voluntarily subscribed to a fund for provisioning the militia, with the expectation that they would later be reimbursed by the legislature or at least profit from army procurement contracts. Bowdoin headed the list with a "loan" of £250; John Hancock's name was conspicuously absent.[17]

Throughout the turbulent period of Shays' Rebellion, Sam Adams and Bowdoin concerted together as once they had against the royal governors. Though Adams refused to become a councillor, his activity in the Senate in Bowdoin's behalf was crucial, and he was regularly invited to the meetings at which response to the insurgents was planned. Samuel Phillips, Thomas Cushing, and other Academy members in the Senate and outside the legislature generally backed the governor, demanding stern measures such as the temporary suspension of habeas corpus and the raising of the militia. The Assembly at first dragged its feet. John Hancock and James Warren stood on the sidelines of the fray.

In the eleventh year of the independence of the United States, on Tuesday, 29 August 1786, began the agony of James Bowdoin. A large concourse of people, armed with guns, swords, and other deadly weapons, to the beating of drums and the playing of fifes, took possession of the courthouse at Northampton in the county of Hampshire on the day appointed for the sitting of the courts. Insurgency spread quickly to other counties and disrupted the orderly administration of justice, which would have entailed dispossessions for non-payment of debts. At first the rebels attacked the civil courts to halt creditors' suits; soon they marched against the criminal courts to protect their comrades accused of riot.

Governor Bowdoin from his council chamber issued a proclamation that he had revised twice in his own hand, strengthening the language as he rewrote the document. If the rebels prevailed, he warned, universal riot, anarchy, and confusion would ensue. He knew from reading political theorists that anarchy would likely

16. In 1787, Academicians who were Massachusetts senators included Samuel Adams, Caleb Strong, Cotton Tufts, Tristram Dalton, Richard Cranch, and Samuel Phillips, Jr. (president of the Senate).

17. Archives of the Commonwealth: Massachusetts Archives, 189:64–66, Subscription lists; 288 r and v, list of officers paid by the Commonwealth.

terminate in despotism and that the American dream, fairest prospect of political happiness, would be destroyed. Since the Devil could no longer be blamed as the active agent in this attempt to subvert law and government, Bowdoin denounced in his stead the machinations of human domestic enemies who had treacherously assumed the character of the best and most zealous friends of the people. The image of the people as naturally pure and innocent was preserved, while the finger of accusation was pointed at ringleaders and their abettors, a category into which British polemicists had once thrust colonial insurgents like Bowdoin himself.[18]

Instead of invoking Thomas Jefferson's "decent respect for the opinion of mankind," Bowdoin's proclamation cited the threat to America of loss of credit and a good name—Puritan attributes—and of becoming contemptible in the eyes of other nations. Men who had helped to establish freedom in the sight of God and the world would now wantonly dash the hopes of people everywhere. Life, liberty, and the pursuit of happiness, which echoed the sensate morality of the *philosophes*, gave way in Bowdoin's proclamation to life, liberty, and property, the old Lockian trinity. Bowdoin set up sharp distinctions between "good people" and hostile, unlawful, traitorous combinations. He conjured up the horrors of a civil war. The dire prophecies of his inaugural address to the Academy were being fulfilled far more speedily than he could have imagined. The president of an academy for the promotion of arts and sciences reverted to the role of a prophet admonishing the idolaters with the voice of an angry God. A new Moses, he felt it his duty to punish the wayward Israelites who had broken the covenant. For a moment it seemed as though the Puritan theocracy were resurrected.

In some townships citizens assembled to bear witness that the restiveness of the people was not altogether unjustified. When Bowdoin had sat on the council of the royal governors he had laid the onus for the merchants' uneasiness and unhappiness upon the acts of the British Crown. Now for many he was himself the source of popular distress. Some men formed mediating committees to plead for leniency and an understanding of the anguish of the disaffected. Their language was moderate, their collective action often spontaneous. They hoped to prevent the shedding of blood in a fratricidal encounter. Even the conservative Salem lawyer William Pynchon, repeating in a diary entry for 9 September 1786 a wild rumor that Bowdoin himself would march to Concord at the head of companies of artillery and militia from Suffolk and Middlesex, questioned the wisdom of a military display against desperate farmers burdened with heavy taxes and debts.[19]

But by 11 September the freeholders and other inhabitants of the town of Boston were exhibiting uneasiness of their own, fear that the constitutional security

18. Ibid., 1–4, Proclamation of 2 Sept. 1786.
19. William Pynchon, *Diary*, 248, entry for 9 Sept. 1786.

of their lives, liberties, and property was in danger. Though they talked about the restoration of harmony as their object, their speeches no longer masked growing bitterness and apprehension: the freeholders assembled in Faneuil Hall to address Governor Bowdoin demanded direct action against the rebels. In his reply the governor thanked the Bostonians for their patriotic zeal, while he rebuked the men of unnamed counties for withholding assistance from the sheriffs who tried to keep the courts open. There was an implicit threat even to the inhabitants of Boston in Bowdoin's rhetorical question: Would reluctant citizens have anything to blame but their own supineness and indifference, if their persons and property were exposed to the "violent and fraudful attempts of wicked and designing men, who being freed from all restraint of law will be encouraged to make such attempts?"[20] The very prospect would chill the minds and hearts of his audience and strengthen their determination to support orderly, constitutional government. Eventually £5,000 in lawful money was raised by subscription to arm and equip 4,200 men, and the whole town of Boston assumed a military appearance.[21]

Noah Webster, though he believed the rebels had a legitimate grievance in the manner of funding the domestic debt, was unalterably opposed to their recourse to arms, and reflected the mounting alarm of intellectuals in his correspondence with Timothy Pickering. On 10 August 1786, he had remarked on the political ferment in the state, observing drily that the common people were spending their money on rum and tea instead of saving it to pay their taxes. A month afterward he was even more apprehensive: "The mob is headed by some desperate fellows, without property or principle."[22] Six weeks later Pickering, in Philadelphia, received a letter in the same vein from his brother John, a charter Fellow of the Academy, who was in Salem: "The unhappy insurrections in several parts of the Massachusetts & obstructions to the Courts of law have filled the minds of the thinking members with anxious concern. Our general court met in consequence of these tumults & are now sitting. A very small part of the inhabitants of Essex appear to countenance the conduct of their western brethren."[23] Timothy Pickering had earlier been apprised of imminent danger by his brother-in-law and fellow-Academician Nathaniel Peaslee Sargeant in a letter of 10 August, the same day Noah Webster had chosen to write him, that described the contagion of the court closings and advanced the theory of a Tory conspiracy to exploit the economic distress of Mas-

20. MHS, *Collections*, ser. 7.6 (Bowdoin and Temple Papers, 2), 111–12.

21. MHS, *Collections*, ser. 6.4 (Belknap Papers, 3), 325, Jeremy Belknap to his wife, Boston, 14 Jan. 1787.

22. MHS, *Proceedings* 43:130, 132, Noah Webster to Timothy Pickering, Salem, 10 Aug. 1786, and Boston, 13 Sept. 1786.

23. MHS, Pickering Papers, John Pickering to Timothy Pickering, Salem, 27 Oct. 1786.

sachusetts citizens in order to overturn the government: "The aspect of our public affairs is truly alarming. I could write you a volume on ye Subject, but suppose ye Newspapers will carry you bad news fast enough—Northhampton & Worcester common Pleas are stopt—This week I suppose Concord, Taunton & Berkshire courts will stop. ye next week I expect our court [the Supreme Judicial Court] at Worcester & so in succession at Springfield, Great Barrington & Taunton will share ye same fate—The flagitious Tories, taking advantage of the Pressure of honest debts, high Taxes, & scarcity of money, have stirred up a true Catalinarian Conspiracy against ye Government—God only knows if they will not go nigh to succeed."[24] Artemas Ward, a general during the Revolution, a judge at Shrewsbury, and a signer of the Academy bill, also blamed the troubles on the machinations of British agents, not a wholly outlandish notion since the newly reappointed Canadian governor, Sir Guy Carleton, Lord Dorchester, was flirting with the insurgents.[25] William Cushing, one of the original Fellows of the Academy and a judge of the Massachusetts Supreme Judicial Court, saw tyranny and dictatorship lurking in the shadows: evil-minded persons, leaders of the insurgents, were plotting "to bring the whole government and all good people of this state, if not continent, under absolute command and subjugation to one or two ignorant, unprincipled, bankrupt, desperate individuals."[26]

The militant opposition of Academy members to Shays and his men was not limited to expressions of indignation, or financial support for military expeditions into the disaffected counties. General Benjamin Lincoln, later a member of the Academy council, was commander of the troops.[27] The erratic James Winthrop, though usually opposed to strong, centralized government, enlisted in the militia and fought under General Lincoln against the insurgents. Oliver Prescott was another charter member of the Academy who served as a general. David Cobb, an incorporated Fellow, member of the Society of the Cincinnati, store owner, surgeon in the revolutionary army, judge of the Bristol County Court of Common Pleas sitting in Taunton, and major general of the Fifth Division of the Massachusetts Militia, also joined the governor's forces. Cobb was called the "warrior judge," and is credited with an indomitable spirit, as well as an uninhibited flow of curses, that

24. MHS, Pickering Papers, N. P. Sargeant to Timothy Pickering, 10 Aug. 1786.

25. Archives of the Commonwealth: Massachusetts Archives, 190:252, General Artemas Ward to Bowdoin, Shrewsbury, 12 Sept. 1786.

26. *Hampshire Gazette*, 6 June 1787.

27. Lincoln had had a heroic military career. Wounded and taken prisoner during the War of Independence, he was released and fought at the Battle of Yorktown. In October of 1781 he was made secretary of war by Congress, resigned after the treaty of peace was signed, and subsequently became a member of the Constitutional Convention, lieutenant-governor of Massachusetts, and collector of the Port of Boston.

kept the rebels at bay. His famous utterance, "I will hold this Court if I hold it in blood; I will sit as a judge or I will die as a general," may well be apocryphal, but his combined shrewdness and courage in dealing with the insurgents are unquestioned. On 30 October 1786, when the Supreme Court was sitting in Taunton, he recounted to Bowdoin how he had dispersed the rebels: "That fire and rage with which they had alarmed the county for some days past appear'd to have vanished, and the sight of government in force made them as peaceable a sett of rioters, as ever, with so much impudence, advanced so near their enemy."[28]

The turn of events had rattled even the steady Manasseh Cutler. He wrote from Ipswich on 6 October 1786, "We are in this Commonwealth on ye very borders of complete anarchy. A most infamous insurrection has taken place, within a few weeks, in all ye western & one of ye southern Counties, viz. Worcester, Middlesex, Hampshire, Berkshire & Bristol. The minds of ye people are thrown into a most violent ferment & their passion all aflote." The same spirit had infected Rhode Island, where officials had cravenly capitulated to the rebels, and New Hampshire, whose entire General Assembly had been made prisoner. After describing the attack on the courts, listing the complaints of the rebels, and summing up their intent as the revision of the state's constitution and the annihilation of its government, Cutler fell to musing on the broader philosophical implications of the insurrection. The stubborn rebelliousness of the Shaysites bred fear in the minds of Academy members and a certain disenchantment about the universal preparedness of Americans to exercise all the rights that naturally appertained to the human condition. After the euphoria of the Revolution with its faith in a benign human nature, Calvinist ministers were reverting to doctrines of depravity:

> It seems to be more problematical then ever, whether mankind are in a state for enjoying all ye natural rights of humanity, & are possessed of virtue sufficient for ye support of a purely republican Government. Equal liberty in civil Community appears finely on paper, but ye question is, can it be realized? America is the first nation, on earth, who have had an opportunity for making a fair experiment, & will ere long decide one of ye most important questions in ye philosophical world. You will perhaps begin to think me a tory.—I wish for liberty—but not at ye expence of Govt—The new States I hope, when they come to form Constitutions, will guard against ye evils in ye Old—& realize that coercive Government is as necessary for ye existence of civil society, as ye soul for ye existence of ye body—but not to dwell on this subject—One thing I am persuaded of—that these commotions will tend to promote our plan & incline well disposed persons to become adventurers—for who would wish to live under a Government subject to such tumults & convulsions.

---

28. Colonial Society of Massachusetts, *Collections* 36, "The Early Life of David Cobb," 448; see also Archives of the Commonwealth: Massachusetts Archives, 190:295.

Earlier correspondence makes clear that "our plan" and "adventurers" refer to the settlement of the Ohio territory, of which Cutler was a leading proponent, and the recruitment of emigrants among those eager to flee the turbulence of Massachusetts.[29]

Samuel Dexter, the aged friend and devoted admirer of Bowdoin, introduced new distinctions into political speech. The Massachusetts constitution was excellently devised for good Christians and philosophers, but it was far too "democratical" for the ignorant and unprincipled multitude. Dexter became the advocate of force—he knew the damned when he saw them, degenerate sons of worthy ancestors. Cajolery in dealing with them could serve no good purpose, and giving way in any degree was dangerous.[30] From afar Richard Price consoled Bowdoin that it was perhaps the design of Providence to pass the states through the school of errors and sufferings in order that in the end they might be an example for mankind such as the friends of liberty and virtue hoped for.[31]

Bowdoin's daughter, Elizabeth, who dearly loved and revered her father, was beset by worry. She knew that the pressure of public business kept his mind in a state of constant agitation, and she had lived in England long enough to recognize the spirit of the Levellers, to put on the same plane those that had property and those that had none. The people were restless, she fretted, and would not be satisfied even if the Angel Gabriel appeared on earth with laws written by the Almighty. If only her father were in private life! Men of his abilities were too good for so despicable a race of mortals. Time and again Elizabeth lashed out impetuously against the barbarous people. Her father's conduct was generally approved by right-thinking citizens, but she thought his troubles with the rash, ungovernable ones were increasing. Yet family letters indicate that during the months of Shays' Rebellion Bowdoin's state of health was unimpaired; the challenge and activity energized him. Elizabeth thanked God that after six months of anxiety and ceaseless conflict her father was indeed extremely well.[32]

As the insurrection gathered strength, Hancock's men intrigued against the beleaguered governor. Peter Thacher, the forthright, often blunt, pastor who succeeded Samuel Cooper at the Brattle Street Church, has left a circumstantial analysis of their conduct at the time of the crisis. In a letter of 15 September 1786, addressed to Hancock's crony Thomas Cushing, Thacher was sympathetic to the governor and critical of the machinations of the Hancock party:

29. MHS, Winthrop Sargent Papers, Cutler to Sargent, Ipswich, 6 Oct. 1786, and 24 Mar. 1786.

30. MHS, *Collections*, ser. 7.6 (Bowdoin and Temple Papers, 2), 115–16, Samuel Dexter to Bowdoin, Roxbury, 3 Oct. 1786.

31. Ibid., 131, Richard Price to Bowdoin, Newington-Green, 22 Jan. 1787.

32. MHS, Bowdoin and Temple Papers, Elizabeth Temple to her mother, New York, 3 Oct. 1786, 6 Nov. 1786, and 19 Feb. 1787.

Those, who a week before, had censured the proclamation [of the governor] as being too gentle & lenient, & who thought that government could not exist, unless its energy was exerted, *now* deprecated bloodshed and thought it best to temporize with the people & give way to their humour. They censured the governor severely and Mr. H-'s friends improved the opportunity with all their industry: they trumpeted it around that had *he* been governor, this difficulty would not have taken place. . . . Mr. B had too great notions of the dignity of government, & was not capable of guiding the vessel in a storm, as Mr. H had done. . . .

You cannot imagine what high spirits this matter has given to friend H-k. He is gone to Connecticut in a one horse chaise to shew his humility & hopes, I doubt not, to come in fully the next year. Adams has behaved well. The lawyers hang aloof (except Sullivan who has done well) and appear to be waiting for an opportunity to secure themselves, or to unite in the dissolution of the government.[33]

Bowdoin had offered to support the judges and keep the courts open by force, no matter how unpopular such a course might be, but there were judges who vacillated, and the legislature was dilatory. William Pynchon, who was well informed on the political atmosphere in Boston, recorded the divisions in the legislature, some of the members arguing for vigorous measures and suspension of habeas corpus, others pleading for a redress of the insurgents' grievances.[34] General William North deplored the fickleness of the General Court and predicted that at its next session it would give a triumph to the insurgents.[35] It was even said that some of the officers of the Springfield Court of Common Pleas had sat down to dinner with notorious rebels.[36]

"Every Phylosopher is not a Politician"

Bowdoin's address to the General Court on 28 September 1786 rang with prissy rectitude: "If at present, or in any future time, there should be any real grievances subsisting, they ought to be, and there is a moral certainty they will be, redressed: for no tax or burthen, of any kind, can be laid upon the people, that does not equally affect, the persons, who lay them; and if, through inadvertence, mistake, or any other cause, their Acts are productive of any grievous or unsalutary effect, they themselves must feel it; and therefore will be prompted, not only from a principle of duty to their constituents,

33. MHS, Cushing Papers, Peter Thacher to Thomas Cushing, Boston, 15 Sept. 1786.
34. Pynchon, *Diary*, 252, entry for 6 Oct. 1786.
35. MHS, *Proceedings* 90 (1978), 171–72, Adj. Gen. William North to Baron von Steuben, 23 Nov. 1786.
36. MHS, *Collections*, ser. 7.6 (Bowdoin and Temple Papers, 2), 126, Levi Shephard to Bowdoin, Northampton, 28 Dec. 1786.

but from their own feelings, to repeal or alter the obnoxious Act." [37] All this was held to be self-evident, derived from the excellence of the Massachusetts constitution. Bowdoin viewed the government of Massachusetts as he did the governance of the world: both were self-regulating. The energy of the sun was preserved within the planetary system by a sphere that contained it, and the same principle held true in the government of men. If grievances should arise, men of the Commonwealth would move to rectify them by natural self-restraint, thus preventing anarchic eruption. In the end, after the rebels had been subdued, it was the perspicacious and sharp-tongued James Warren who voiced his disappointment in Bowdoin with the wry comment, "Every Phylosopher is not a Politician." The government of men was not analogous to the order of the universe. Warren made a snide reference to one of Bowdoin's papers published in the Academy *Memoirs* two years earlier: "The surrounding solid orb in the Heavens may restore the scattered rays of Light to the Sun and prevent the waste of that Body by an endless diffusion. But no Government can be supported but on its own principles." [38] Invoking extraordinary measures such as suspension of habeas corpus in order to preserve the government was traducing the very principles on which that government had been founded and would thus destroy its reason for existence.

The position on Shays' Rebellion adopted by James Warren and his wife was at variance with that of most of the Academy members. The Warrens were caught between the forces of anarchy in the mass of the people and the clandestine projects of those who would pollute their small-town republican ideal with notions of aristocracy and of monarchical central power. On 22 October 1786, James Warren grimly announced to his friend John Adams, "We are now in a State of Anarchy and Confusion bordering on a Civil War." [39] Two months later, in a letter to Adams written from Milton, where the Warrens occupied a mansion formerly belonging to Governor Hutchinson, Mercy described the polarization engendered by the rebellion and, with a certain detachment, compared America to an unruly youth: "In this country, lately armed for opposition to regal despotism, there seems to be on the one side a boldness of spirit that sets at defiance all authority, government, and order, and on the other, not a secret wish only, but an open avowal of a necessity for drawing the reins of power much too tight for republicanism, or even for a wise and limited monarchy. Perhaps America is in the predicament of an adventurous youth, who has disengaged himself from parental authority, before the period of maturity that might have taught him to make a proper use of his freedom." [40]

37. Archives of the Commonwealth: Massachusetts Archives, 190:270; address printed in Commonwealth of Massachusetts, *Laws and Resolves*, 1786–87, p. 929.

38. MHS, *Collections* 73 (Warren-Adams Letters, 2), 293, James Warren to John Adams, Milton, 18 May 1787.

39. Ibid., 278, Warren to Adams, Milton, 22 Oct. 1786.

40. MHS, *Proceedings* 64 (1930–32), 160, Mercy Warren to John Adams, Milton, Dec. 1786.

Since James Warren would have no truck with either party he was maligned by both. His wife later wrote admiringly of him, "He bears and has borne the unprovoked abuse with the Dignity of conscious rectitude, and that Philippic calmness which is never the companion of *insurgency, Anarchy* or *Fraud*." [41] John Adams, while no less censorious than the Warrens of the loose living of his compatriots, had a more patronizing attitude. Their fellow-countrymen, he reminded Warren, had never exhibited very exalted virtue, and had always run after "foreign manners and Fashions." [42] For the sake of orderly government, it was necessary to concentrate effective power in the hands of the first magistrate—a position that the Warrens, suspicious of incipient despotism, had to reject.

Ugly rumors were abroad that members of the Warren family were Shaysite sympathizers, and after the fracas was over, in a letter of 7 May 1789 to John Adams, Mercy Warren refuted the calumnies that her son Winslow had joined a "rebellion against a government which his family were so instrumental in establishing." [43] When Winslow, in financial straits, had failed to secure appointment as consul in Lisbon, the Warrens unfairly turned on James Bowdoin for abandoning old friends and not supporting his application. [44] (In fact, both Bowdoin and Adams wrote to Thomas Jefferson in behalf of Winslow.) [45] The family was the Warrens' unit of emotional existence, a bastion of virtue against a corrupt world, and the township was as broad a unit of government as they could tolerate with ease. The rigid standards of their "old Roman" Calvinism in a New England landscape were not readily accepted by others. In despair, Mercy Warren dreamed of an isolated refuge for her family, away from the tumult of politics. James Warren, the Cato of the Revolution, retired from the fray, and one day even stopped paying his dues to the Academy—he owed nobody a reason. Bowdoin and John Adams, now turned federalist, were no longer his political allies.

While Bowdoin pigheadedly tried to apply the sound practices of a private commercial establishment to the economy of a state deeply scarred by the war and its aftermath, insurgent "countrymen" asserted defiantly that they would not pay taxes. Either taxes would be lowered or the town houses of the rich would be pulled down about their ears, an anonymous letter-writer threatened: "Blood shall be spilt Country men will not be imposed on We fought for liberty as well as you did. They shant keep their women in such fine dresses. I want to know what is

41. MHS, *Collections* 73 (Warren-Adams Letters, 2), 312, Mercy Warren to John Adams, Plymouth, 7 May 1789.

42. Ibid., 280, John Adams to James Warren, London, 9 Jan. 1787.

43. Ibid., 312, Mercy Warren to John Adams, Plymouth, 7 May 1789.

44. Ibid., 267, James Warren to Elbridge Gerry, Milton, 9 Oct. 1785.

45. See Jefferson, *Papers* 8:601; 9:97, 189, 263, during the period October 1785 through February 1786.

Become of all the money that has Been Raised hear this ten years past. they must Let us now Before we pay them." The grievances of a farmer in the Salem area, described by William Pynchon, had the same ring: "One was the cursed bank of money in Boston, where they let none of it go into the country. . . . Another was the governor's salary, when he could find several [who] would serve as governor for half a crown a day. Then the women of the governor's family lived without work, when they should go to work as well as *his* wife and daughters."[46] For all his confidence that he could read the common mind, Bowdoin knew not how to calculate the rancor of poverty-stricken farmers to whom his lofty elegance was an outrage: when the legislature voted in January of 1787 to cut his salary, he promptly had the bill withdrawn, claiming that his assent would violate the constitution and penalize any less affluent successors.

On 17 November 1786, members of the General Court tried to placate the rebels with an agreement condemning the diffusion of a taste for "foreign Frippery, Dress, & Extravagance" that was robbing the Commonwealth of hard specie and discouraging native manufactures, and promising to form associations that would promote remedial measures in the towns they represented.[47] But the demands for tax relief on the part of those who had borne the hardships of the war and were now in distress went largely unheeded, while the government sought to frighten the Shaysites into submission by throwing them into prison without trial. By an act of 10 November 1786, suspending the privilege of the writ of habeas corpus, the governor was empowered to commit to jail "any person or persons whom the Governor and Council shall deem the safety of the Commonwealth requires should be restrained of their personal liberty or whose enlargement is dangerous thereto." On 7 December 1786, the *Post Rider* reported that leaders of the insurgents met in Patch's Tavern in Worcester, where they resolved at a council of war to move on Boston and release their confined fellows. And a week later it was said that in the county of Hampshire 970 rebels would march under the direction of Daniel Shays, the generalissimo himself.[48] General Artemas Ward estimated 1,500 as the whole force of the insurgents and advised maintaining great superiority in the numbers of the militia in order to cow the opposition without shedding blood.[49] The rebels put a price on Bowdoin's head and called him a Tory.

46. Pynchon, *Diary*, 249–50, entry for 18 Sept. 1786.

47. "Solemn Agreement and Association" (drawn up in the handwriting of James Bowdoin III), in MHS, *Proceedings*, ser. 2.8:496. In the meantime Bowdoin had issued a proclamation, 26 October 1786, threatening to evict squatters on government lands in the eastern counties (Bowdoin College, Hawthorne-Longfellow Library, Bowdoin Family Papers).

48. MHS, *Collections*, ser. 7.6 (Bowdoin and Temple Papers, 2), 117, estimate by Major William Shepard.

49. Ibid., 118, General Artemas Ward to Bowdoin, Shrewsbury, 16 Dec. 1786.

In a retrospective moment four years after the events, Bowdoin's friend John Lowell reviewed the gravity of the crisis: "These combinations were extensive and formidable, and perhaps there was a time in which it was uncertain, whether even a majority of the people were not at least in a disposition not to *oppose* the progress of insurgency. Like causes of uneasiness, in a greater or less degree, existed in most of the confederated states: The contagion appeared to spread and unless the progress of their success had been suddenly arrested, the flame which was already kindled, would probably have caught the combustibles scattered throughout the states, and have raged with irresistible fury."[50] In the winter of 1786–87 the threat posed by Shays and his men led to proposals from Bowdoin and his supporters for the intervention of federal troops; but at a time when states jealously guarded their autonomy from any national encroachment, there was reluctance to resort to so drastic and unpopular a measure, and pious wishes were expressed that the good sense of the citizenry and the efforts of local governments would eventually prevail.[51]

The minutes of the Massachusetts Council from 27 November to 27 December 1786 attest to Bowdoin's firmness in the use of the military to keep the insurgents from effecting the total breakdown of the courts. Suddenly thrust into the role of commander-in-chief, he issued succinct orders to officers of the militia and arranged for the provisioning of the troops. At the same time that he was engaged with military and financial problems, he played the part of the great judge who decided on the right of the imprisoned to be liberated on bail.

When caught, insurgents often lost their enthusiasm for the cause. They petitioned for freedom, pleading the advance of the season and their need to attend to their farming, solemnly promising to conduct themselves as peaceable, quiet, and good citizens, and to use their best endeavors for the apprehension of anyone still in opposition to the government. Letters poured in from local selectmen testifying to the character of captured rebels, their industriousness and frugality; they were good commonwealthsmen who had always paid their taxes. Prisoners themselves lamented that their eyes were now open, but alas, too late; they had been misled by the artifices and frauds of ruthless men. Petitions were submitted on behalf of citizens with impeccable records who had defended the government and had been

---

50. John Lowell, *An Eulogy on Hon. James Bowdoin, LL.D. before the American Academy of Arts and Sciences, delivered January 26, 1791* (Boston, 1791), 16–17.

51. See MHS, *Collections*, ser. 7.6 (Bowdoin and Temple Papers, 2), 167, 169–70, Bowdoin to Rufus King and Nathan Dane (delegates to the Congress of the Confederation), 6, 11 Mar. 1787. Both Jefferson and Lafayette concurred in the opinion that federal troops should not be employed. See their letters from Paris to Colonel William S. Smith on 20 December 1786 and 16 January 1787, respectively. Lafayette was especially concerned that such a measure might "arm the people against federal ideas"; see Louis B. Gottschalk, *Lafayette Between the American and French Revolution, 1783–1789* (Chicago: University of Chicago Press, 1950), 283–84.

mistakenly jailed. Leafing through these documents one sometimes feels that the confusion of French revolutionary arrests is in rehearsal.

Releases frequently followed pleas, but only when Governor Bowdoin issued a direct order. He had the power to incarcerate and to set free. He personally examined the tearful petitions of the condemned and their families and handed down the verdicts. Under sentence of death, Henry McCulloch of Pelham confessed to his grief and shame at the foolish, wicked words he had uttered, but those that knew him would testify that his heart was humane. Though he cut a fine figure on a horse, which encouraged him to pose as an officer, he held no such position in the rebel army. He had left his home unarmed, and had picked up an old cutlass before the attack on the Springfield arsenal in January of 1787 only for show. If he could not persuade the governor to pardon him, he begged for at least a long stay of execution in order to prepare for the awful doom awaiting him.[52] The wife of one of the prisoners lamented that their children, "attentive to the manafest anguish of their Mother, catch the immotions of her heart, and mingle their instinctive tears of sympathy, which flow with little interruption, and add new pangs to the aganies of grief occasioned by the malancholy prospect before her. . . ."[53] Aged parents laid bare their wretchedness and their blasted hopes:

> Permit us to say that we have brought up a large Family of Children and attended to their Education with all the Tenderness of parental Affection, Supported them in Infancy & submitted to a great Variety of Disquietudes & Fatigues on their Account, hoping to derive Consolation from them in the decline of Life.

> We have seen some of them in Danger Anxiety & Pain, in Sorrow Sickness & Death whereby we have been called to spend wearisome Days & wakeful Nights. But we can now say with mournful lament that we never before had seen Affliction.[54]

On 24 January 1787, armed with the awesome authority granted by the suspension of habeas corpus, Bowdoin ordered the sheriff of Worcester County to arrest Lieutenant Colonel Joseph Sargent of Princeton, Aaron Broad of Holden, James Freeland of Sutton, physician, Daniel Baird of Worcester, yeoman, and Aaron Smith of Shrewsbury, gentleman. These men could hardly be designated as rabble. Yet a brief report sent from the area three days later shows that the rebels got no quarter from those in the field charged with suppressing the rebellion:

> I am left here to Victual the Troops under Maj Gen Warner, who now commands here, I am in Want of N E Rum, I have heard from Mr Ruggles who now I suppose to be at Springfield With Gen Lincoln,—Gen Sheppard has fired on the Rebels, killd a

---

52. Archives of the Commonwealth: Massachusetts Archives, 189:303.
53. Ibid., 409.
54. Ibid., 399.

number & wounded more, I have this minute left head Quarters, we suppose Shays to have got into the wood, Some of his Men have deserted to Gen Sheppard, others have returnd home to the Town of Ward ashamed.—We are in high spirits & things go on tollerable well.—The chief of the provisions I have on hand, is ordered on to Springfield therefore I must have more soon.[55]

Ruggles himself, writing from the commissary in Pittsfield on 11 February 1787, interspersed his request for victuals with vengeful language in which satire, mixed metaphors, and the biblical utopia were intermingled: "Never I believe in any Rebellion was there so many Turn Coats as at the present—all. all. Seem Freinds. Staunch Freinds of Government.—However we trust the Names and the Characters of those Wretches who have so long disturbed our Israel will be known. . . . The Goodly Temple of Liberty Raisd in this Country at the Expence of much Blood and Treasure, shall not be attempted to be trodden down, without Sacrificing the unhallow'd Hands that dare attempt it." To the selectmen of the towns of western Massachusetts, to whom he asked for expeditious delivery of rum and other commodities, he repeated that the army was engaged in the support of "*Legal, Constitutional authority* against the attacks of the most lawless and abandoned of mankind."[56]

Pacification was sustained by bread and rum—augmented as the war dragged on by brandy, pork, candles, soap. Bowdoin's carefully laid plans for a peaceful settlement had gone awry when General Lincoln's men shot to death Shaysites who had advanced in defiance of the government's formal orders. Those who shed the blood of their countrymen sealed the political fate of the Huguenot governor James Bowdoin II.

Of necessity Bowdoin became aware of the limitations of a confederacy. On 19 January he had ordered the sheriff of Hampshire County to arrest seventeen men in his bailiwick, including Shays, but Massachusetts troops could not cross state lines in hot pursuit and the rebels had found safe havens in New York, Connecticut, and Vermont as if they were foreign nations.[57] With the support of people in the adjacent counties they were able to make forays into Massachusetts from a protected area. After New York belatedly agreed to cooperate with her neighbor, the rebellion was contained and then crushed. But as late as 8 May 1787, Bowdoin complained to his brother-in-law in England, "The insurrectious disposition

55. Ibid., 83–85, Robert Pope, Report from the commissary at Worcester to Richard Devens, Commissary General, 27 Jan. 1787.

56. Ibid., 134, Joseph Ruggles to Richard Devens; see also Worcester, American Antiquarian Society: Shays' Rebellion Collection, 1786–87, Order Book (photostat), p. 22, Joseph Ruggles to the selectmen of Northfield, Northampton, 9 Feb. 1787.

57. Archives of the Commonwealth: Massachusetts Archives, 189:81–82.

of our Western Counties has found me so much employment, that I have had scarcely time to attend to anything else. [It is in a fair way of being quelled: and wd ere now have been effectually so, could our militia have followed the Insurgents beyond the boundaries of the State]."[58] Frustrated by the ease with which the rebels could elude his militia, Bowdoin tried to coax them into submission with offers of leniency. When his policy failed to break the resistance of the diehards, who imputed it to the government's incapacity to defend itself, in exasperation he fell back on the language of honor and duty and a rigid Calvinism that relentlessly bifurcated mankind into the elect and the damned.

No Neutral Characters Allowed

The Governor's address of 3 February 1787 to the General Court was in the spirit of Joshua at Jericho: "Art thou for us or for our adversaries?" (5.13). After detailing the measures he had taken to keep the courts open, Bowdoin summoned the legislators to adopt a criterion—the word was his—for discriminating between good citizens and insurgents, "that each might be regarded according to their characters: the former as their Country's friends and to be protected; and the latter as public enemies, & to be effectually suppressed." The mark of virtue or of vice was to be emblazoned on each man's forehead. Only a few years before, Bowdoin himself had been high among the insurgents—the term that the *philosophes* of France had used positively to describe the rebel American colonials whose cause they espoused. Now the word insurgent had become pejorative. The Bowdoins of the land were in power, and the rabble—Shays' men and their sympathizers—were declared public enemies. In his sermon-message to the General Court (not an unusual form for American official pronouncements) Bowdoin demanded that every man show his colors. Solon had denounced those who refused to take sides in a contest. A latter-day lawgiver, Bowdoin had read his Plutarch, and his preaching was an amalgam of the ancient pagan morality with the language of the Old Testament. "No neutral characters should be allowed, nor any one suffered to vibrate between the two," he told the General Court. Only vigorous, decisive action to support the militia would prevent a civil war that could finally engulf the whole Confederacy.[59]

The Shaysites, a motley crew, claimed that they were as good as the prominent citizens of Boston, that they had sacrificed as much for liberty as any others. For

58. MHS, Bowdoin and Temple Papers, Letter Book, 269, Bowdoin to George Erving, 8 May 1787; see also Bowdoin's letters to governors of New York, Connecticut, and Vermont in the spring of 1787 (MHS, *Collections*, ser. 7.6 [Bowdoin and Temple Papers, 2], 169, 171, 185–86).

59. Commonwealth of Massachusetts, *Laws and Resolves*, 1786–87, p. 962, Bowdoin, Address to the General Court, 3 Feb. 1787.

Bowdoin, post-revolutionary society had to be based upon sound principles of property, and the ultimate sanction was force. The insurrection was "unnatural," he declared, using an adjective to which his eighteenth-century hearers would have resonated with indignation. In his stilted oratory, the antonyms of liberty and slavery were replaced by the alternatives of liberty and license. Many of the arguments that Burke five or six years later would muster against the French Revolution were prefigured in Bowdoin's addresses to the General Court during Shays' Rebellion.

On 4 February 1787, the House and the Senate, led by Sam Adams, declared that a "rebellion exists within this Commonwealth." They supported the governor in all his endeavors and adopted his language: "It is to be expected that Vigour, Decision & Energy, under the direction & blessing of Heaven, will soon terminate this unnatural, unprovoked rebellion; prevent the effusion of blood, and the fatal consequences to be dreaded from a civil war: and it is the determination of this Court, to establish a criterion, for discriminating between good citizens & others, that each may be regarded according to their characters & deserts." The Senate and House congratulated the governor on the success with which Providence had been "pleased hitherto to bless the wise, spirited & prudent measures" he had undertaken. They urged upon him further constitutional action that would destroy the seed of rebellion, quiet the minds of the good people of the Commonwealth, and re-establish the authority and dignity of government.[60] The Calvinist rhetoric of the elect and the damned was resurrected in an amended form, and the religious discrimination between "the good" and "others" was mixed with the Enlightenment distinction between what was "natural" and what was "unnatural." Almighty God was called upon to be the Arbiter.

Following the governor's lead the legislators denied that the obduracy of the insurgents was to be ascribed to misapprehension, or animosity provoked by circumstances they had mistakenly viewed as grievances, or misguided zeal to promote the public happiness. Such apologias for their conduct could no longer be entertained, since all the motives of government had been carefully explained to them, and the government had announced that it was prepared to act with leniency. (The commissioners who conducted a post-rebellion inquiry with a view to granting indemnity nevertheless felt it their duty to the "community" to point out that members of the General Court had not set forth the reasons for the resolves and actions taken by the government.) For those who "may not have considered the evil nature and tendency of their crime," the General Court on 4 February 1787 offered clemency if they surrendered their arms and took an oath of allegiance to the Commonwealth.[61] Slowly but surely old religious forms crept back;

---

60. Ibid., 424–26, Legislative action of 4 Feb. 1787.
61. Ibid., 423–24.

"evil" was again becoming a legal concept. The oath, necessary for admittance to communion, was now transferred from the congregation to the Commonwealth.

On 7 and 8 February, despite the conciliatory phrases in official statements, the General Court with the approval of Governor Bowdoin rejected a petition calling for "reconciliation" signed by one Francis Stone as "Chairman of a Committee of certain officers from the Counties of Worcester, Hampshire, Middlesex & Berkshire." Stone's 30 January petition to the Court had been moderate, even humble, in tone. It begged for a pardon and promised that the insurgents would lay down their arms and return to their respective homes. The legislators were angered, however, by Stone's threats of a great effusion of blood if they failed to make peace. They impugned the representativeness and good faith of the petitioners, and scoffed at their reference to the rebellion as an "error" and a "failing." The members of the Court were affronted by the rebels' assumption that they were on an equal plane with the legislature.[62] The old war-horses of the Revolution were now in power, and memory of the caucuses and network of committees of correspondence and safety was wiped out: Sam Adams demanded that the rebels express a due sense of their crime and make public confessions. Governor Bowdoin issued a proclamation on 9 February for the apprehension of Daniel Shays, Luke Day, Adam Wheeler, and Eli Parsons, and warned of the penalties that would be incurred by those who harbored the leaders of this "unnatural, unprovoked, and wicked Rebellion." A £150 reward was offered for Shays, £100 for the others — prizes calculated to activate the patriotic energies of naturally virtuous citizens.[63] Nudged by its elder statesman Franklin, who was president of the state at the time, Pennsylvania declared support for its sister state by proclaiming additional rewards for the capture of the four miscreants.[64]

Throughout the fall of 1786 and the first months of 1787, a steady flow of petitions from the towns of Massachusetts had reached the General Court. Their tone was often querulous, sometimes apprehensive, but all were animated by deep discontent and a bitter sense of injustice. Financial distress was universal: "money seems to have taken its flight to some other Country"; "men's bodies are taken for debt." But other grievances, too, were laid before the legislature. Men who had not actively defended their country now unfairly occupied posts of honor and profit; bounties were not set aside for the encouragement of fisheries, husbandry, and manufactures; the mode of taxation operated unequally between landed and mercantile interests; there were too many justices of the peace and too large a Senate and House of Representatives.

62. Ibid., 434.

63. Archives of the Commonwealth: Massachusetts Archives, 189:121, Proclamation of 9 Feb. 1787.

64. MHS, *Proceedings* 3 (1859), 179–80, Benjamin Franklin to Bowdoin, Philadelphia, 23 Mar. 1787, enclosing an act of the Pennsylvania legislature and a proclamation of its council (in response to letter of 10 Feb. from Bowdoin) relating to the additional rewards.

The present administration had created "general uneasiness" among the people, for the government of laws had given way to a government of men in which legislators performed dual functions as judicial officers. Many of the towns complained of the high salaries of the governor and other public servants, and several demanded that the General Court be moved from Boston: "considering the depravity of human nature," they feared that the members were unduly responsive to Boston's concerns, and that they would attend to their own affairs, especially their merchant speculations, at the expense of government business, which would be delayed, protracted, and more costly. The writers affirmed their detestation of mobs and riots: not one man in town had "gon forth Either with Swords or Staves to oppose the authority of the Commonwealth." But they called for reform and an act of indemnity or free pardon for the erstwhile rebels who had laid down their arms and sworn their allegiance to the government. A letter from Lunenberg with homely eloquence rebuked Bowdoin's administration for its shallow and unsympathetic attitude: "A military Force may kill, capture or disperse the Body in Arms against Government; but will it restore their alienated Affections? Chains may restrain a Madman from Acts of Violence & Outrage; but they will not remove the Cause of his Insanity."

A committee of both legislative houses appointed to consider the petitions was dismayed that pardons had been asked for the atrocious offenders who had treated with contempt the offer of the General Court and had been "pointing their weapons of destruction against the very vitals of government." The committee rejected out of hand the notion of a general indemnity and gave short shrift to most of the complaints lodged by the towns; but in a report on 22 February 1787 they made three grudging admissions: payment of interest due on public securities had not been provided for; the state treasurer had not been properly restricted in drawing orders; the governor's salary was unreasonably high.[65] The elaborate bills of particulars submitted by the towns had been drained of their substance and compressed to almost nothing.

At the time that bellicose pronouncements were issuing from the governor's chamber and the legislature, the rebellion was already crumbling. General Lincoln had surprised the main body of the insurgents under Shays at Sheffield, killed 30, taken 150 prisoners, and dispersed the rest. Shays had offered by letter to surrender his arms and those of his followers on condition of a general pardon, and requested Lincoln to desist from further hostilities until the General Court had responded to the petition currently before it.[66] Elizabeth Temple, in a letter to her mother on

65. Worcester, American Antiquarian Society: Shays' Rebellion Collection, e.g., Petitions to the General Court, Dracut, 29 Sept. 1786; Winchendon, 21 Dec. 1786; Western, 18 Jan. 1787; Grafton, 27 Jan. 1787; Lunenberg, 19 Feb. 1787.

66. Archives of the Commonwealth: Massachusetts Archives, 190:335, Daniel Shays to General Lincoln, Pelham, 30 Jan. 1787.

19 February 1787, reported that her father's last speech, which did "honor both to his head, and heart," was much approved in New York political circles, and she rejoiced at the happy prospect that the rebellion would now be subdued.[67] On 26 March 1787, William Short, Thomas Jefferson's secretary, summarized for Jefferson, then away from Paris, the dispatches in recently arrived newspapers. He wrote disparagingly of the Massachusetts governor's severity: "Govr. Bowdoin in his speech to the house convened the 3d. of Febry. advises vigorous measures, although there was nothing in fact to be apprehended; he founds his advice on the insurgents having treated with contempt the late mild offer held out to them by the acts of the former session. It appears on the whole that if Government will only be mild and at the same time firm, the whole affair is at an end. I am more certain of their firmness than their mildness."[68] Bowdoin himself in a letter of 15 March to the governor of New York betrayed a certain smug pride in the success of the Massachusetts militia, which he conjectured had secured New York, and perhaps the whole United States, from the dread consequences of a more extensive rebellion.[69] Nevertheless, the complacency of the more prosperous citizens of Massachusetts had sustained a severe blow, and apprehensions among them died slowly. Writing to Bowdoin from Westfield on 14 March 1787, General William Shepard dissociated himself from the optimism of General Lincoln and pressed his view that the spirit of rebellion had subsided temporarily, but remained uncrushed. A hard-liner, Shepard condemned the policy of pardoning the Shaysites, which would only allow them to reassemble in Vermont and renew their attacks. And in May of 1787 the Reverend Jeremy Belknap nervously reported, "It is said our insurgents are mustering again, either to rescue those culprits ordered for execution, or commit predatory mischief."[70]

When called upon to quell the rebellion, Bowdoin the upright servant of God had demanded that each man stand up and be counted. But the biblical image of the avenging angel of the Lord may have to be emended. Once victory was certain, concepts and rules of conduct born of the Enlightenment and alien to the absolutism of the seventeenth-century theocracy came into play. Montesquieu's ideal of leniency was also an integral part of Bowdoin's moral order; though he judged and condemned, he was not without mercy, so long as a formal confession of guilt had been made and ceremonial words of repentance had been uttered. In the exercise of leniency he was

67. MHS, Bowdoin and Temple Papers, Elizabeth Temple to her mother, New York, 19 Feb. 1787.

68. Jefferson, *Papers* 11 (1955), 240–41, William Short to Jefferson, Paris, 26 Mar. 1787.

69. MHS, *Collections*, ser. 7.6 (Bowdoin and Temple Papers, 2), 171, Bowdoin to Gov. George Clinton, 15 Mar. 1787.

70. Archives of the Commonwealth: Massachusetts Archives, 319:53; MHS, *Collections*, ser. 5.2 (Belknap Papers, 1), 480, Belknap to Ebenezer Hazard, Boston, 18 May 1787.

seconded by General Lincoln himself. When the back of the rebellion had been broken and it was clear that tranquillity would soon be restored to the western counties, Bowdoin in a message of 26 April to the General Court congratulated its members on the success of the government's measures, and thanked them for their "cordial & spirited co-operation with the executive in those measures: which were planned & executed, pursuant to your recommendations; & have been honoured with your repeated approbation"—clearly he was quite ready to share with them the opprobrium he had to bear for the manner of subduing the insurgents, as well as any plaudits that might come his way. Bowdoin declared his faith in liberty without "licentiousness, and its natural consequent,—despotism," in property, and in the promotion of public happiness; and he censured those politicians who believed that a republican government founded on the principles of "equal liberty" could not long survive.[71] Four days later, on 30 April 1787, he signed pardons for some of those who had supplicated his grace and favor. The commissioners appointed to examine the cases of prisoners— Benjamin Lincoln, Samuel Phillips, Jr., and Samuel A. Otis—required that in every instance two or more persons of known attachment to the government certify that the felon was duly penitent of his crime. Some 790 men on a blacklist lodged with the office of the secretary of the Commonwealth gave guarantees of their future loyalty, and most received a promise of amnesty without reservation; a small number suffered restrictions and disqualifications. Of fourteen who had been convicted and sentenced to death, Bowdoin pardoned eight and reprieved the rest, who were later pardoned when Hancock took office. According to Judge Minot, reprieves were granted in a cruel manner dictated by policy: in the county of Hampshire, only after the condemned had arrived at the gallows and all preparations for execution had been completed was the sheriff allowed to open his instructions. Thus the power of the government to carry out the death sentence was dramatically declared, and its clemency advertised.[72]

Repudiation of the Commander-in-Chief

Bowdoin's measures were praised elsewhere in the nation, but not by many in Massachusetts. By the time the insurrection spent its force and Shays fled to New York, there to end his days at the age of eighty-five as a respectable citizen of Sparta, Bowdoin had been repudiated by the voters, and Hancock, his hands unstained by the blood of his fellow-citizens, had ejected his old rival from the governor's chair. Mercy Warren later wrote that no man could have acted with greater firmness, precision, and judgment than Governor Bowdoin. Yet for all his virtuous conduct,

71. Commonwealth of Massachusetts, *Laws and Resolves*, 1786–87, p. 981.

72. Archives of the Commonwealth: Massachusetts Archives, 189:265; Minot, *History of the Insurrection*, 171–88; Barry, *History of Massachusetts* 3:255; Fiske, *Critical Period*, 183, 184.

the popular current set against him and carried Hancock once again to the headship of the state—though, Mrs. Warren was quick to add, he was wise enough not to contravene the measures of his predecessor, and by coercive or lenient action, as required, he calmed the fractious citizenry.[73]

Bowdoin made a not ungraceful exit from the local political scene. In his final message to the legislature he deftly turned defeat into the realization of his own ardent desire to resume life as a private citizen, a course that would otherwise have been construed as abandonment. He contemplated his role in the nation's history with the detachment of a true patriot philosopher:

> It has been my lot to pass through the several grades of political life, during a period the most interesting, that *America* ever saw: and it is with real satisfaction, I can take a review of it in the solitary hour of reflection. As I have been so long versant in it, & have had so large a share of the honours of my Country, it is certainly decent to wish for retirement, that younger men, & of more ability, might succeed to the chair of Government. I am happy, that with this wish the voice of the people co-incides; as in the contrary case, I could not have indulged it, without the imputation of deserting them in the present critical situation of affairs.[74]

While no written denunciation of Hancock from the hand of Bowdoin is preserved, his daughter, Elizabeth, in a letter of 15 April 1787 to her sister-in-law, reacted like a tigress to the political defeat. At a time when the state needed judicious leaders at its helm, the people chased after a miserable "shackle headed" animal who had been a pest to the country for years. It would have been fortunate if he had never been born or "had lost his empty pate on one of those glorious expeditions during the war when he turned out with a greater number of aids than ever the Great Frederic had." During the election contest Hancock had traveled through the countryside in a plain two-wheeled carriage to point up the contrast with her father, a man with whom neither he nor anyone in his retinue was fit to break bread. Hancock's plan was "to vain" all who owned property. Seizure of her father's and grandfather's holdings was not the least of his objectives. A Cassandra, Lady Elizabeth—her husband, John Temple, had succeeded to a baronetcy the previous December and become His Majesty's resident and consul general in the United States—prophesied that before six months had elapsed paper money and Shays would be triumphant. She worked herself up into a merciless attack on Hancock, dragging the death of his young son into the tirade: "Poor wretch will nothing drive from his head that Bubble Popularity. Not the Death of an only Child—nor viewing that poor immatiated body that resemble the discription of Death in the Revelations. the first I shou'd think would

73. Mercy Otis Warren, *History of the American Revolution* 3:354.

74. Commonwealth of Massachusetts, *Laws and Resolves*, 1786–87, p. 981, James Bowdoin to the Massachusetts General Court, Boston, 26 Apr. 1787.

Check it for a few Months at least—that the Bubble will break I have no doubt—and that he will even sink lower than the poor deluded wretches who have blown it up—I have almost worked my self to be as Nervous as my Mother."[75] Her father had been humiliated by Hancock and her rage was boundless.

Bowdoin could draw consolation from the approval of right-thinking people, who congratulated him on his successful quelling of the rebellion. Crèvecoeur wrote him on 26 August 1788, long after the furor had subsided and Bowdoin was out of office, in admiration of the prudence, firmness, and energy he had displayed. He trusted the experience of Massachusetts to convince people that society could not be organized by reason alone without a forceful government and that abuse of freedom could degenerate into outrageous license.[76] Samuel Vaughan, Jr., of Philadelphia struck an Enlightenment posture. The people had been deluded. Since they had the misfortune to have been educated under a corrupt British government, the citizens had not yet learned to distinguish liberty from license. Perhaps they would have to await a new generation born in liberty, he consoled his friend. Everything was so novel that bewilderment prevailed even among the legislators. Philadelphia men of public spirit, Vaughan reported, thought the only recourse was to found a Society for Political Enquiries that would come forth with principles clearly defining the limits of conduct for individuals and the state; perhaps the Society would inspire other groups to form similar organizations.[77] Montesquieu had been lying on the shelves for a long time; now the moment had arrived to apply his counsel. Citizens concerned with the public weal might have forgotten his prescriptions for the security of the individual and the security of the state, but at least they remembered his questions, and they were hearing more and more about a new science from Scotland, where solutions to the prickly dilemmas might be discovered. Salvation through political economy was to be the new panacea.

Letters to Thomas Jefferson, who had kept in close touch with the course of the rebellion, not unexpectedly rejoiced in the government victory and generally praised Governor Bowdoin's conduct under duress. James Madison discounted anxieties that the return of good weather would encourage the rebels to reform their ranks, but worried that they would exert their strength in the legislature, whose composition had been changed in the recent elections, and that Hancock, "an idolater of popularity," would be seduced into "dishonorable compliances."[78] John Jay had similar

75. MHS, Bowdoin and Temple Papers, Elizabeth Temple to Sarah Bowdoin, New York, 15 Apr. 1787.

76. MHS, *Proceedings* 13 (1873–75), 239–40, Crèvecoeur to Bowdoin, New York, 26 Aug. 1788.

77. MHS, *Collections*, ser. 7.6 (Bowdoin and Temple Papers, 2), 165, Samuel Vaughan, Jr., to Bowdoin, Philadelphia, Mar. 5, 1787.

78. Jefferson, *Papers* 11:307, Madison to Jefferson, [s.l.], 23 Apr. 1787.

forebodings: he thought that Bowdoin had acted in an upright manner, supported by the legislature, but since many of the delegates in both houses had been defeated at the polls along with the governor, he was apprehensive of changes that might undermine authority.[79] Benjamin Franklin gave a different significance to the elections. He insisted that a great majority of the people had been in favor of Bowdoin's actions to quell the rebellion, but that Hancock had always been more popular and once he was a candidate could be assured of easy victory. He then added that Bowdoin's opposition to the bill reducing the governor's salary had contributed to his defeat.[80] The businessman's predominant concern with money reckonings blinded Bowdoin to political realities and precipitated his downfall.

During his terms as governor, Bowdoin was occasionally obliged to turn his attention to problems other than the near-bankruptcy of the state and Shays' Rebellion. In addition to his intercessions for the merchants, he acted to obtain the release of a seaman taken prisoner by the British who somehow ended up in a French jail. He tirelessly introduced young Americans who had business abroad to diplomats who might be of assistance to them, carefully chose delegates to the Annapolis convention on the state of American trade, and corresponded frequently with John Adams in London about commercial and diplomatic affairs. He placed before the Massachusetts General Court and the Congress the celebrated Stanhope case.[81] But however effective or irreproachable his conduct in such matters, it counted for nothing on the political tally-sheet. Scorned once again by the Massachusetts electorate, in the three years of life remaining to him Bowdoin continued to fulfill the functions of his calling as a businessman and as president of the American Academy. Though some of the old vigor was gone, he interested himself actively in family affairs, embarked on new commercial ventures, and continued to play a significant role in the political life of the state and the nation.

The Aging Revolutionaries

James Bowdoin and John Adams had together striven to win American independence, to draft a constitution for Massachusetts, to establish an American Academy. In the mid-seventeen-eighties, the two former revolutionary leaders were invested with political power—Bowdoin as governor of a commonwealth that behaved as a quasi-

79. Ibid., 313, John Jay to Jefferson, New York, 24 Apr. 1787.

80. Ibid., 301, Franklin to Jefferson, Philadelphia, 19 Apr. 1787.

81. See ibid. 8:516, Elbridge Gerry to Jefferson, New York, 12 Sept. 1785; 653–54, Abigail Adams to Jefferson, London, 19 Oct. 1785; 9 (1954), 6, Jefferson's account, undated; 16, Jefferson to William Carmichael, Paris, 4 Nov. 1785; 10 (1954), 70, Adams to Jefferson, London, 26 June 1786; 160, Bowdoin to Jefferson, 22 July 1786; 162, Abigail Adams to Jefferson, London, 23 July 1786.

sovereign state, Adams as minister plenipotentiary to the Court of St. James. But exalted office brought few satisfactions to either man and bred in them a disenchanted
realism. Bowdoin's tribulations and disappointments were borne with stoical fortitude,
as was his custom, a posture easier to maintain since the vicissitudes of his political
career at least left his fortune and style of life intact. Adams, never a wealthy man and
according to his own testimony all but impoverished by the demands of his diplomatic
station, was not one to endure silently his financial distress or emotional anguish.

Adams's mood in this period was openly revealed in a letter of condolence written
in May of 1786 to Mercy Warren on the death of her son. After a few lines of com-
miseration, Adams quickly shifted to a recitation of his own woes: the ingratitude
of the people, who lavished adoration on the ostentatious while ignoring those who
served them quietly and well; the adversities he had encountered in public life and
the impediments that still bedeviled him. He made an effort to combat his bitterness
and near-despair with philosophical reflections on the way of the world:

> You speak of honors, Madam; but what honors have been decreed to me? Do you sup-
> pose I am honored in this Country? . . . . You speak of affluence too. If I were my own
> master and could I spend what is allowed me as I should choose, I should live in affluence
> indeed; but when you consider that I have a Rank to support here that I hold in trust
> for others, and that this Rank cannot be let down, without betraying that trust, you may
> depend upon it, I am driven to my wits' ends for means. . . . Our Country will do like all
> others—play their affairs into the Hands of a few cunning fellows, and leave their faith-
> ful servants to close their long glories with a sigh to find the unwilling Gratitude of base
> Mankind. Yet I don't wholly approve this sentiment. Human nature is not ungrateful.
> But while many rate their merits higher than the truth, it is almost impossible that the
> public mind should be exactly informed to whom they are really obliged.[82]

In the exchanges between Adams and Bowdoin, which usually involved official
business, the manner adopted was generally formal as befitted their new dignity; but
on occasion the reserve gave way to confidences, familiar phraseology, and candid
observations. While both men were confronted by serious problems in the discharge
of their duties, more often advice and counsel flowed from Bowdoin to Adams than
in the opposite direction; during his years abroad, Massachusetts politics had become
too distant from Adams to arouse his active interest and encourage his intervention.

The signing of the Treaty of Paris did not halt overt hostility on the part of Americans toward British naval officers who chanced to land at their seaport towns. In one
such incident a Captain Stanhope of the *Mercury* was accosted by a former American
prisoner of war, Jesse Dunbar, who had been repeatedly flogged for refusing to work
on the British ship under Stanhope's command. Though Dunbar swung at Stanhope,

---

82. MHS, Adams Papers, John Adams to Mercy Warren, London, 24 May 1786 (Adams Letter
Book); printed in *Collections* 73 (Warren-Adams Papers, 2), 275–76.

no actual injury was inflicted, but the captain insisted on immediate redress from Governor Bowdoin for the riotous conduct of a Massachusetts citizen. In keeping with the prestige of his office, Bowdoin coolly explained that not all ex-combatants could be expected to return to their prewar "good humour," and suggested that the courts were open to the captain if he felt himself ill-used and wished to institute formal proceedings. After an extravagant and insolent reply from Stanhope, further communication between the two men was limited to curt, harsh notes. In his report, accompanied by letters and depositions, to Adams in London on 10 August 1785, Bowdoin took the opportunity to proffer some advice on dealing with balky foreigners: "In our transactions with foreigners, especially british, it is necessary they should be made sensible, we have a spirit of resentment, & that it will be shown when occasions offer." En passant, he enclosed "Memoirs, taken from a Volume of our American Academy, now printing here," which he hoped might afford Adams half an hour's amusement.[83] Bowdoin did not forget that he was at once governor of the Commonwealth and president of the Academy. Adams, too, occupied himself with Academy business amid his other cares. He was often the intermediary between members residing in England and the officers of the Academy or Harvard, transmitting their letters and gifts of books, and he arranged for a regular exchange of the Academy's *Memoirs* with the Royal Society's *Philosophical Transactions*.

An abiding concern of both men was the economic crisis in America, which British trade policy was seriously exacerbating. Bowdoin spelled out in detail the arguments Adams might advance to convince the British that their restrictions on American trade were irrational and would ultimately prove disastrous to themselves. Adams agreed with the analysis, but confessed that he was exasperated by British obduracy in pursuing a course detrimental to themselves and to the United States. Since Bowdoin's letter of 12 January 1786 was to be delivered by an American merchant in whom he had confidence, he skipped diplomatic niceties and used more colloquial speech in writing about the blind prejudices of the British. If they refused to listen to reason, "the old lady must be left to her fate, & abandoned as incurable."[84] Bowdoin was making strenuous exertions to persuade the French to take American (i.e., Massachusetts) whale oil and looked to expanding commercial relationships with France to replace the old ties to Great Britain, which threatened loss of the American market to the manufactures of the former mother country. Adams was skeptical about the willingness of the British to face up to the consequences of their own shortsightedness:

> The great revolution in trade which you mention ought to be promoted by every friend of America, and it must take place. I have made use of all these considerations.—But if

83. MHS, Bowdoin and Temple Papers, Bowdoin to John Adams, 10 Aug. 1785.

84. MHS, *Collections*, ser. 7.6 (Bowdoin and Temple Papers, 2), 87, Bowdoin to John Adams, 12 Jan. 1786.

an angel from Heaven should declare to this Nation that our States will unite, retaliate, prohibit or trade with France, they would not believe it. There is not one man in this nation, who pretends to believe it and if he did he would be treated with scorn.

Let me intreat you, Sir, and every other Citizen of the United States to extinguish all hopes of relief to their trade from this country.

Adams and Bowdoin consulted with each other about matters besides commercial treaties and the state of the economy, or the affairs of individual Americans and Englishmen. Adams acknowledged to Bowdoin his anxiety over a whole series of diplomatic problems ranging from the possibility of buying peace from Turkey to the revolts in South America: "This is all confidential between you and me and a few discreet friends." Adams was full of apprehension: "God bless our Country, but I still tremble for its safety."[85]

While Adams fretted over the hazards of America's international position, Bowdoin had to meet the challenge of armed rebellion against his authority and the governmental institutions of the state. At this point in their lives both men were harassed and frustrated in their attempts to build a strong, stable, and prosperous nation according to their own lights. Their outlook on American prospects was shaped by discouraging events and was inevitably bleak. An upsurge of spirits, however, followed the ratification of the federal constitution and the transition from a weak confederation to a union of states that could fortify one another and deal effectively with foreign powers, friendly or hostile. When Adams was elected to the vice-presidency, Bowdoin sent him a message on 10 April 1789, expressing his "real pleasure," and he lost no time in making recommendations for appointments to the Revenue Department and to the federal judiciary. His most pressing plea grew out of a political cabal that he felt duty-bound to expose. A few unnamed individuals had been scheming to secure a federal judgeship for Chief Justice Cushing of Massachusetts, with the sole aim of gaining possession of the State Supreme Court through this "laudable" manoeuvre, as Bowdoin sarcastically described it. In order to thwart their despicable plot, Cushing should be left on the Massachusetts bench and the federal office tendered to Bowdoin's friend John Lowell.[86] Though James Warren might denigrate his skills and abhor his methods, the philosopher Bowdoin, recovered from the blows of Shays' Rebellion and his electoral defeat, was once again dabbling in local politics—on this occasion to no avail.

85. Ibid., 96–97, John Adams to Bowdoin, London, 9 May 1786.
86. MHS, Bowdoin and Temple Papers, Bowdoin to John Adams, 10 Apr. 1789. A letter from George Washington, New York, 9 May 1789, politely declining to discuss Bowdoin's nominees for public office in his letters of 18 February and 24 April, is further testimony of Bowdoin's renewed interest in politics (Collections, ser. 7.6 [Bowdoin and Temple Papers, 2], 192–93).

9

THE CLOSE OF AN EPOCH

ᚖᚖ

FOR ELEVEN years a Boston clockmaker named Joseph Pope was at work on a gigantic orrery, six and a half feet in height and six and a half feet in diameter. When completed it was covered with a glass dome. The signs of the zodiac were painted on the side panels, and a hexagonal frame of mahogany in Chippendale style supported the structure. Its corners were decorated with effigies of three figures, Benjamin Franklin, James Bowdoin, and Sir Isaac Newton, each repeated four times. Paul Revere is said to have cast the statuettes in bronze from wood carvings by Simeon Skillin, a noted local craftsman. When Pope's house caught fire in 1787, the year the orrery was completed, Governor Bowdoin, understandably anxious about a work so flattering to his status as a scientist, sent a squad of six men to rescue the masterpiece. With Bowdoin's blessing, the subject of the orrery was introduced into the Academy. A committee appointed to examine it declared itself much satisfied and impressed, and its inventor was rewarded with election to Fellowship—a signal honor for an artisan, even one who dabbled in theoretical science and who justified the Academy's high estimate of him by submitting "Remarks on Attraction and Impulsion."[1] After the failure of an attempt to purchase his chef d'oeuvre of science and art through private subscription, the General Court of Massachusetts allowed a lottery to raise the necessary funds, and the orrery ended up at Harvard, a complex piece of apparatus widely appreciated.

In 1789, when Pope sailed for Europe, he carried with him a letter from Bowdoin warmly recommending him to the Marquis de Lafayette as a fellow-Bostonian who had distinguished himself by his

> Genius in the mechanical department. Among other proofs of it, he has constructed an elegant Orrery, or Planetarium, exhibiting upon a large scale the planetary motions within our Solar System. It is now ye property of our University at Cambridge, having been purchased for about £350 Sterling; and far surpasses everything of that kind in America. As Mr. Pope is going to France by way of England, it is his wish to render himself useful to Gentlemen that may have occasion to employ him in the line

---

1. Academy Records, 1:106, meeting of 22 Aug. 1787; 112–13, meeting of 30 Apr. 1788, report of committee; 34, election of Pope, 20 Aug. 1788; Academy Letters, 1:62, Pope to Bowdoin, Boston, 22 Jan. 1788.

of his business and I believe it is in his power to give them entire satisfaction—Not only his ingenuity but the real honesty of his character will recommend him.

Bowdoin was ready to extend himself for those in his entourage whose performance had won his respect. Another letter of introduction, with almost identical phraseology—this one addressed to the secretary of the Royal Society—also recommended Pope for his honesty and ingenuity.[2]

Joseph Pope's vision of a universe of science in which Franklin, Bowdoin, and Newton were set on the same plane was not idiosyncratic.[3] The Boston *Columbian Centinel* recognized in James Bowdoin a New England Newton. The association of Franklin with Newton goes back to Joseph Priestley's judgment of Franklin's papers as "expressive of the true principles of electricity; just as the Newtonian philosophy is of the true system of nature in general."[4] The presence of James Bowdoin in this august company is witness to the quaint parochialism of Boston science in the revolutionary period. There are of course more occult connections among the three: Newton's death followed closely upon Bowdoin's birth, and Bowdoin and Franklin both died in 1790.

The Exercise of His Callings

Though defeated at the polls by the ebullient, unbeatable Hancock, Bowdoin's head remained unbowed; in contrast with James Warren, he was not visibly embittered by the loss of political office. He was still surrounded by family and friends whose affection cushioned him against the jolts of public life; and to some degree he was inured to repudiation by the electorate. However unpopular his measures had been with large segments of the voters, he could at least congratulate himself that the Shaysites had been worsted and order restored to Massachusetts. Even Hancock tacitly acknowledged the salutary effect of his predecessor's conduct, since, according to Mercy Warren, he did not expunge from the record books Bowdoin's regulations, but by judiciously applying them when they were needed helped to keep the state on an even keel.

Bowdoin's personal, commercial, and intellectual interests had a continuity that was barely interrupted by the storms of his two terms in the governor's chair. As president of the Academy he held meetings, kept the learned communications flowing

2. MHS, Bowdoin and Temple Papers, Bowdoin to Lafayette, 4 June 1789 (draft); MHS, *Collections*, ser. 7.6 (Bowdoin and Temple Papers, 2), 194, Bowdoin to the Reverend Charles P. Layard, 4 June 1789.

3. See Frederick E. Brasch, "The Royal Society of London and its influence upon scientific thought in the American Colonies," *The Scientific Monthly* 33 (Nov. 1931), 461–63.

4. Joseph Priestley, *The history and present state of electricity, with original experiments*, quoted in I. Bernard Cohen, *Franklin and Newton* (Philadelphia: American Philosophical Society, 1956), 37.

—albeit somewhat sluggishly—and corresponded with scholars, scientists, and literati in the United States and abroad. In July of 1788 he was elected to membership in the Royal Society, eloquent testimony to his prestige in the scientific world. As paterfamilias, he had the comfort of seeing the fortunes of his children well secured. James, his close business collaborator, was treading in his father's footsteps, though lightly and at a distance. He was a merchant, a public official, and a gentleman farmer with accomplishments in the field of animal husbandry that made his election to the Academy in 1786 not wholly an act of nepotism.[5] James was married to his cousin Sarah Bowdoin, wealthy in her own right. Elizabeth, Lady Temple, was handsomely installed in New York with her husband and children. The Reverend Manasseh Cutler dined with the Temples in July of 1787, and left in his diary a rapturous account of the visit. He dilated on their spacious home, adorned with fine sculpture and paintings by European masters; the liveried servants who attended them; the plentiful dinner and excellent wines. His most glowing phrases were reserved for Lady Temple, the greatest beauty he had ever seen. The good minister was intoxicated by her well-proportioned figure, fresh skin, regularity of features—charms enhanced by good sense, sociability, and a gentle though majestic air. Her smiles alone "could not fail of producing the softest sensibility in the fiercest savage." Her six-year-old daughter, Augusta, was a "perfect prodigy." Sir John was dismissed with a briefer notice: he was a complete gentleman, deaf, and more interested in wine than in the poultry and roast beef served at his table.[6]

The older daughter of the Temples, Elizabeth, raised by the Bowdoins in the absence abroad of her parents, had grown into a captivating sixteen-year-old whose charms had smitten the Marquis de Chastellux. When Thomas Winthrop, a wealthy and intelligent suitor, sought her hand, he first applied to her grandfather, who found this scion of the distinguished Winthrop family altogether acceptable. But Bowdoin was too tactful to usurp openly the prerogative of a father. In November of 1785 he wrote his son-in-law congratulating him on his safe arrival, with his wife and little girl, in New York, and informing him that Thomas Winthrop had for some time been paying his addresses to daughter Betsy. Winthrop had asked the Bowdoins for Betsy's hand, but while they had no objection to the match, since the suitor was of "good character, good family & good circumstances," they told him that her "disposal" rested with her parents. Young Winthrop would therefore shortly call on them in New York to ask their consent.[7] With their blessing, the couple were wed by Peter Thacher of the Brattle Street Church in July of 1786, a union that finally joined the

---

5. Academy Records, 1:34 (23 Aug. 1786).

6. Manasseh Cutler, *Life, Journals and Correspondence* 1:234–35.

7. MHS, Bowdoin and Temple Papers, Bowdoin to John Temple, 28 Nov. 1785; L. S. Mayo, *The Winthrop Family in America* (Boston, 1948), 212–13.

House of Bowdoin with the clan of the founding father of the colony. Thomas Winthrop in his turn became a Fellow of the Academy of Arts and Sciences. Bowdoin's family affections remained intense as his life neared its end. Unable to accept an invitation from the Temples in the spring of 1790 because, he wrote, he was engaged in settling the details of his father-in-law's estate, he urged them instead to visit the Bowdoins in Boston, for he longed to see Sir John, Betsy, and "the little Prattler."[8]

Bowdoin's zest for profit-making had not waned with age, nor had ill-health robbed him of acuity. In his customary methodical manner he settled the estate of his late father-in-law, Captain Erving. And in 1789, less than two years before his death, he initiated a bold trading venture, investing his money and keeping a vigilant eye on the details of the new enterprise. He instructed his London agents to insure the *Astrea*, a 350-ton vessel embarking on a round trip between Salem and Canton, and entrusted its master, James Magee, and supercargo, Thomas Handasyd Perkins, with four thousand Spanish milled dollars for the purchase of tea and other goods. Describing those in command of the ship as sober, sensible men whose families were known in Boston—Perkins later became Boston's leading China merchant—Bowdoin declared that their unexceptionable characters and the fast, strong, well-equipped boat had induced him to become a shipper again, and, he supposed, would favorably affect the insurance premiums for which he was liable.[9] He wrote also to a correspondent in Canton informing him of his interest in the *Astrea* and recommending Thomas Perkins, his agent in the matter, as a man of integrity, business sense, and sobriety. (In passing he raised the possibility of sending another trading vessel to India.)[10] Success crowned this venture, as it had many of Bowdoin's other investments. The *Astrea* entered Salem Harbor at the end of May 1790 with a rich cargo of tea and cotton whose worth netted Bowdoin a profit of some 18 percent. Unfortunately he fell ill in August, before he could personally collect the monies that would have accrued from the sale of the goods.[11]

At the same time that family and business matters engaged him, Bowdoin closely followed the course of public affairs domestic and foreign. In June of 1789 he wrote to Lafayette in sanguine mood about the constitutions of their respective nations; he was confident that the American constitution would have happy consequences, and hoped that the French constitution was already in operation, bringing glory to France and honor to its initiators.[12] In October Bowdoin sent his son-in-law, Sir

8. MHS, Bowdoin and Temple Papers, Bowdoin to John Temple, 22 Apr. 1790.

9. Ibid., Letter Book, 277, Bowdoin to Lane, Son, and Fraser, 31 Jan. 1789.

10. Ibid., 278, Bowdoin to Edward Dowse, 3 Feb. 1789.

11. Kershaw, *Bowdoin, Patriot and Man of the Enlightenment*, 275–78, 284–85; MHS, *Collections*, ser. 5.3 (Belknap Papers, 2), 232, Belknap to Hazard, Boston, 27 Aug. 1790.

12. MHS, Bowdoin and Temple Papers, Bowdoin to Lafayette, 4 June 1789 (draft).

John Temple, a letter about events in France that approached banality in its cautious avoidance of commitment in any direction: "The Revolution in France is a most extraordinary one; and from it will result very important consequences, some of which it may be conjectured will not be very advantageous to G. Britain; but however that may be, if it should terminate in a Government founded on just principles of liberty, it will be the era of political happiness to the French nation."[13] Bowdoin's advocacy of good government was not likely to give offense to any party.

Bowdoin's chief political concern was the fate of the new United States Constitution, and here his stand was unequivocal. He had declined to attend the Constitutional Convention of 1787, to the dismay of his daughter, who thought he belonged in such a distinguished assemblage and wanted him out of the state when that "Puppy," Hancock, took the reins of office.[14] But in early 1788 he consented to be a member, along with his son, of the Massachusetts convention to ratify the federal constitution, and to chair the committee on proposed amendments. Bowdoin is credited with using his powers of persuasion, often exercised during fine dinners at his mansion, to secure adoption of the Constitution by rather reluctant delegates.[15] George Richards Minot was as incisive in analyzing their divergent attitudes toward the Constitution as he had been in narrating the outbreak of Shays' Rebellion. In his journal for 1788 he noted the striking division of the convention members: "Those of the learned professions and the men of property were almost unanimously in favour of the constitution. But the great body of middling land holders were opposed to it. The contest was therefore extremely unequal. All the learning and eloquence was on one side, while the plain dictates of common sense suffered from want of powers of expression on the other."[16]

Bowdoin's experience with the Shaysites and his mercantile interests converged to make him an ardent spokesman for a strong central government. In congratulating Washington on his nomination to the Convention, the only counsel he had ventured to give turned on forging a union powerful enough to secure commercial advantages from the countries of Europe. In his view the survival of the new nation, beset by domestic and external difficulties, demanded a forceful government to settle differences among the states and to represent them collectively in dealing with foreign powers. A federal congress had to levy taxes and duties to pay off foreign and domestic debts. Otherwise, the trade and navigation of the states (especially Massachusetts), Bowdoin warned his fellow-delegates, would have to bear the whole burden, affecting merchants

13. MHS, *Collections*, ser. 7.6 (Bowdoin and Temple Papers, 2), 196, Bowdoin to Temple, 10 Oct. 1789.

14. MHS, Bowdoin and Temple Papers, Elizabeth Temple to her mother, New York, 30 May 1787.

15. See, for example, the Reverend Jeremy Belknap's notes on the Massachusetts convention for ratifying the federal Constitution (MHS, *Proceedings* 3, especially p. 304).

16. MHS, Journal of George Richards Minot, 1784–91, entry for Jan., Feb., 1788.

and all other segments of the population. Unless Congress were authorized to regulate trade, the United States would have no effective means of retaliation if other nations took measures against them at their ports; interstate rivalries would make them prey to the malevolent schemes of foreign foes: "The power of Congress, both in the legislative and executive line, is the power of the people, collected, through a certain medium, to a focal point; at all times ready to be exerted for the general benefit."

Bowdoin invoked Solon and Montesquieu indiscriminately in his appeal to those who feared a concentration of power as the prelude to tyranny. Apart from the high moral character of those who made the laws, a guarantee of their excellence was the fact that they would personally affect the law-makers themselves. The remote possibility of abuse was hardly a valid reason for withholding the authority required to promote the prosperity and happiness of the entire nation. Bowdoin ended with a muddy metaphor that nevertheless bears witness to his earnest enthusiasm for the Constitution and the vital importance he attached to its acceptance. It would "complete the temple of American Liberty; and like the key stone of a grand and magnificent arch, be the bond of union to keep all the parts firm, and compacted together."[17]

Massachusetts ratified the federal Constitution in February 1788 by a vote of 187 to 168. In May Bowdoin jubilantly wrote Benjamin Franklin that the adoption of the Constitution was almost completed and that he expected to congratulate him on the felicities arising from it before the year was out, as well as a century later—another of Bowdoin's playful references to his friendship with Franklin in the hereafter.[18] To his brother-in-law George Erving, who had emigrated to England, Bowdoin observed in August that the Constitution had already been approved by eleven of the states, and would probably be in operation by the following March: "If it be well administered I believe ye States will be very happy under it. Having long experienced the evils arising from inefficiency, they will the more readily submit to a firm and efficient government, to which from choice as well as necessity they will be strongly attached: though it is easily conceivable that some individuals, whose views and wishes cannot be realized under good government, will endeavor to disrest the mind of the people. . . ." He concluded with a prediction of American prosperity, spiked with a few aspersions cast at Great Britain for its continued harassment of American trade:

It is imagined here, that after a few years experience, which will determine what alterations are eligible, the federal constitution will become fixt; that good government being firmly established, a great number of people, and many of the better sort will

17. *Debates, Resolutions and other Proceedings of the Convention of the Commonwealth of Massachusetts, January 9, 1788–February 7, 1788, to ratify the Constitution recommended by the Grand Federal Convention* (Boston, 1808), 116–17, 121.

18. MHS, *Proceedings*, ser. 2.4:302–03, Bowdoin to Franklin, ca. 1 May 1788.

emigrate hither from different parts of Europe, and that ye United States from that circumstance, as well as by natural Encrease will in a short time be viewed in a respectable light, even by the Ministry & Polititians of Great Britain: whose System of Politicks in regard to American Commerce will probably be somewhat if not greatly altered, when Congress, under ye new Constitution will have the power of regulating it within ye Ports of ye United States.[19]

While old fellow-patriots like the Warrens were put off by Bowdoin's federalism, and suspected monarchical tendencies in those who pled for centralized authority, Bowdoin and John Adams were ranged on the same side. A letter of 11 June 1789 to Bowdoin from Adams, now vice-president of the United States, confided to him his feelings about the burdens of the new administration: "We proceed Slowly; but in digesting Plans so new, so extensive and so important, it is impossible to bring Bodies of Men to a clear Comprehension of Things and a mutual Satisfaction without long deliberation and debate."[20]

Though in 1787 Hancock had wrested the governor's chair from him, and for the second time in a popular election he had swallowed the bitter pill of defeat administered by a detested rival, Bowdoin enjoyed a compensatory triumph in another sphere. When George Washington, the newly inaugurated president of the United States, came to Boston on a ceremonial visit in October 1789, he stood upon his personal and official dignity and refused to call upon Governor Hancock before the governor had paid his respects at the presidential lodgings. All of Hancock's cajolery, entreaties, pleas of physical incapacity availed him nothing; not until he turned up with presumably gout-swollen legs swathed in red flannel did Washington condescend to drink tea at his mansion one evening—and on the way back, he stopped off to see his old friend Bowdoin. The president had little in common with the volatile, tricky Hancock, and naturally gravitated toward Bowdoin, in whom he had confided during the most trying days of the war. In the diary of his Boston sojourn, Washington noted that he went to Sunday services at the Episcopal and Congregational churches, both times attended by Mr. Bowdoin; that Bowdoin was a member of his retinue when he toured the college at Cambridge; and that he was a guest at a large dinner party in Bowdoin's house.[21] Such marks of favor did not go unobserved. There was comment in the press that Washington preferred Bowdoin's company to that of the governor—balm for Bowdoin's political wounds.[22]

19. Ibid., ser. 2.11:178, Bowdoin to George Erving, 12 Aug. 1788.

20. MHS, Bowdoin and Temple Papers, John Adams to Bowdoin, New York, 11 June 1789.

21. George Washington, *Diaries*, ed. Donald Jackson and Dorothy Twohig (Charlottesville: University Press of Virginia), 5 (1979), 476–81 passim.

22. *Columbian Centinel*, 14 Nov. 1789; MHS, Mercy Warren Papers, Letter Book, 477, Mercy Warren to Henry Knox, Oct. 1789.

An Ethereal Voyage

The last exchange of letters between Benjamin Franklin and James Bowdoin looked to future worlds, Franklin's to scientific discovery and a new theory of the earth, Bowdoin's to a heavenly sphere in which they would be united. On 31 May 1788, Franklin wrote Bowdoin from Philadelphia asking whether the American Academy of Arts and Sciences—which both men persisted in calling "the Philosophical Society"—had a copy of a French work "Sur les Arts et les Métiers" (Henri-Louis Duhamel du Monceau's *Descriptions des Arts et Métiers*, in thirty-two folio volumes, published 1761–89). If not, he proposed to bequeath it to them in his will, and indeed he did so. Then Franklin made one of those intellectual leaps of which he was capable even in his eighty-second year. He drew up a long list of scientific questions similar, *mutatis mutandis*, to Newton's queries at the end of the *Optics*, and sent them along to his friend. He wanted to relive the olden days of their first acquaintance, when he was forty-four and Bowdoin a mere twenty-four. Now that both were no longer burdened with the cares of political office, the time was auspicious for them to begin anew: "Our ancient correspondence us'd to have something philosophical in it. As you are now more free from public cares, and I expect to be so in a few months, why may we not resume that kind of correspondence? Our much regretted friend Winthrop once made me the compliment that I was good at starting game for philosophers; let me try if I can start a little for you."

A swarm of scientific problems was let loose from Franklin's box, many of them still unresolved. How did the earth acquire its magnetism in the first place? Did iron ore exist when the globe was formed or was it produced in the course of time? Was it not possible that ages elapsed before the earth was endowed with magnetic polarity? If, Franklin reasoned, iron ore could exist without this polarity and might obtain it from an external cause, could the earth have received its magnetism from some such cause? His questions were a springboard for a hypothesis on universal magnetism: "In short, may not a magnetic power exist throughout our system, perhaps thro' all systems, so that if men could make a voyage in the starry regions a compass might be of use? And may not such universal magnetism with its uniform direction be serviceable in keeping the diurnal revolution of a planet more steady to the same axis?"

Franklin's new theory of the earth offered answers to questions about the Deluge that had preoccupied Western thinkers since Woodward and Newton, especially after reports of seashells high in the mountains of the northern zone had become frequent. One of Franklin's suppositions led to another. Did not the discovery of seashells and the bones of tropical animals in cold high places suggest that the magnetic poles of the earth had shifted? If the poles had been changed by some external force, the Deluge could be explained as a natural phenomenon and the perennial difficulty confronted by biblical commentators of how the waters were disposed of after it was over could be surmounted. With marvelous simplicity Franklin rolled the globe around and let the waters of the oceans flow from one part to another, with measurable consequences: "If the poles were again to be changed and plac'd in the present equator the sea would fall there about 15 miles in height, and rise as much in the present polar regions."

Since the seventeenth century, geological theorists had been perplexed by the "wrack of the surface of this globe," the mountain ridges and rocky strata. Franklin would put their minds to rest by positing the existence of a fluid, internal mass at the center of the earth so dense that the heaviest of substances could float upon it. This internal globe would be extremely sensitive to any change in the earth's axis; its form would be subject to alteration; and parts of it could burst the shell of the earth and rise about it, creating "deranged" strata and thus accounting for the roughness of the earth's surface. Franklin in his homely manner compared the earth to an egg. If one altered the position of the fluid it contained and placed its longer diameter where the shorter one was, the liquid would have to burst through the shell. If a wave of Franklin's dense internal fluid were somehow set in motion, might it not pierce the shell of the earth in some places and not in others? Franklin was clearly thinking of earthquakes, about whose course he had had a circumstantial report from a "very ingenious Peruvian" he met in Paris. The recent earthquake in Peru appeared to bear out his wave theory. Its disorders had been accompanied by a wave of rumbling sound that at first was distant, then increased in volume at the point of eruption, and gradually receded. After an inquiry, South Americans had been able to chart the path of the subterranean noise from a place some degrees north of Lima all the way down to Buenos Aires.

The scientific excursion ended, Franklin's valedictory was tender: "I am ever, my very dear Friend, yours most affectionately." [23]

Bowdoin's response to Franklin's new theory of the earth was graced with a touch of gentle humor. He was clearly not up to grappling with the long list of problems Franklin had posed. When they had shuffled off the material of the body, Bowdoin replied, their souls would have ample leisure to fly about among the planets in special machines and discuss Franklin's questions:

> I observe you expect to be free from publick cares in a few months. You certainly have a right to be so, considering the long and important services you have rendered your Country: but I fancy they will find, especially at this crisis of their publick affairs; more business, and not less important than the past, for a Gentleman, who knows

23. MHS, *Collections*, ser. 7.6 (Bowdoin and Temple Papers, 2), 189–92, Franklin to Bowdoin, Philadelphia, 31 May 1788. The series to which Franklin alluded is now on deposit at the Boston Athenaeum; see *Athenaeum Items. A Library Letter*, no. 88 (Jan. 1988), 4.

so well how to execute it. If however you choose to receed from Politicks, it will be a happy circumstance in a philosophical view, as we may expect many advantages to be derived from it to philosophy.—I have read, and repeatedly read, your ingenious queries concerning the cause of yᵉ Earth's magnetism and polarity, and those relating to the theory of the Earth. By the former you seem to suppose, that a similar magnetism and polarity may take place not only throughout yᵉ whole Solar system, but all other systems, so that, a compass might be useful, if a voyage in yᵉ starry regions were practicable. I thank you for this noble and highly pleasurable suggestion, and have already enjoyed it. I have pleased myself with the idea, that when we drop this heavy, earth attracted body, we shall assume an aetherial one; and in some vehicle, proper for the purpose, perform voyages from planet to planet with the utmost ease and expedition; and with much less uncertainty than voyages are performed on our ocean from port to port. I shall then be very happy in making such excursions with you: when we shall be better qualified to investigate causes by discerning with more clearness and precision their effects. In the meantime, my dear friend, until that happy period arrives, I hope your attention to the subject of your queries will be productive of discoveries useful & important, such as will intitle you to a higher Compliment than was paid to Newton by Pope, in the character of his Superior Beings: with this difference however, that it be paid by those Beings themselves.[24]

Isaac Newton once wrote of his belief that the children of the Resurrection would fly freely through space in happy converse with one another. Freeman Dyson has recorded his dream of flying among the galaxies with his beloved son. James Bowdoin was not a great physicist—probably he was no physicist at all—but he had the glorious fantasies of one.

Last Days

Within a year, Bowdoin fell ill once again, this time mortally. For the last ten days of his life he was immersed almost constantly in a warm bath, sometimes for unbroken periods of forty or fifty hours. It was reported that he was calm, perfectly resigned, and in command of his reason to the very end.[25] Only a fortnight earlier, he had accepted the dedication of a book of poetry, *Ouâbi: or the Virtues of Nature*, by his friend Mrs. Perez Morton, mingling his praise with suggestions that the author abandon her nom de plume, "Philenia," and that she expand the contents of the little volume with a few additional pieces from her treasury.[26] In deathbed

24. MHS, Bowdoin and Temple Papers, James Bowdoin to Benjamin Franklin, 28 June 1788.

25. MHS, Knox Papers, Henry Jackson to General Knox, Boston, 7 Nov. 1790.

26. [Sarah Wentworth Apthorp Morton], *Ouâbi: Or the Virtues of Nature. An Indian Tale, In Four Cantos*. By Philenia, a Lady of Boston (Boston, 1790). See the author's note and Bowdoin's letter of 16 October 1790, appended to the text.

addresses to his family and servants Bowdoin recommended religion as the only foundation of peace and happiness. At four o'clock on the morning of 6 November 1790, two days short of the tenth anniversary of his inauguration as president of the American Academy of Arts and Sciences, James Bowdoin died of what was diagnosed as a putrid fever and dysentery. Peter Thacher preached at his funeral, taking as his text 2 Samuel 3:38, "And the King said unto his servants, know ye not that there is a prince and a great man fallen this day in Israel?" Thacher recalled Bowdoin's conscientious fulfillment of his duties toward family, friends, and church, and celebrated his "rational, uniform, and energetick" religion.[27] He was buried in the family plot in the Old Granary cemetery on Tremont Street, not far from the mansion where he lived and died, and the State House that was the scene of his political triumphs and defeats. A terse entry for 10 November in the diary of Margaret Holyoke, the doctor's daughter and a master of the laconic, reads, "Pleasant. Mr Bowdoin Interred. Military Honors."[28]

Bowdoin was praised in private letters, public addresses, and the press. John Jay called him "that excellent citizen," Washington "that worthy character."[29] Benjamin Rush cherished among his many admirable traits his "open profession of religion."[30] His émigré brother-in-law George Erving wrote his sister from England, "At this sad and awful moment, what comfort can I, who stand so much in need of comfort, attempt to administer to you!" Her husband had been exalted to the heaven that "his mind as a philosopher and a Christian hath often contemplated with wonder and adoration."[31] The *Federal Register* of the town of Worcester, only four years earlier a hotbed of rebellion, carried an obituary fashioned of superlatives—Bowdoin epitomized every virtue and accomplishment: "No man was more known to the Literati in all parts of the world:—Few men have contributed more to the general knowledge and improvement of his country."[32]

On 26 January 1791, it was announced at a meeting of the Academy, held in the Brattle Street Church, that Bowdoin had left them one hundred pounds—the

27. Peter Thacher, *A Sermon . . . Occasioned by the Death of the Hon. James Bowdoin, Esq. LL.D. F.R.S. Lately Governor of the Commonwealth of Massachusetts; preached November 14, 1790* (Boston, 1791), 4.

28. Salem, Essex Institute: Holyoke Papers, Box 22, Folder 6, Diaries of Margaret Holyoke.

29. Academy Letters, 1:114, John Jay to Eliphalet Pearson, New York, 19 Sept. 1791; 123, George Washington to Eliphalet Pearson, Philadelphia, 14 Nov. 1791 (published in Washington, *Writings* 31 [1939], 416–17). Washington's letter was read at the Academy meeting of 29 February 1792 (Academy Records, 2:8).

30. MHS, *Collections*, ser. 6.4 (Belknap Papers, 3), 473, Benjamin Rush to Jeremy Belknap, Philadelphia, 19 Nov. 1790.

31. MHS, Bowdoin and Temple Papers, George Erving to Elizabeth Bowdoin, Froyle, 26 Dec. 1790.

32. *Federal Register*, Worcester, 11 Nov. 1790.

same legacy he had bequeathed to his granddaughter—and a library of more than twelve hundred volumes, which they could retain or dispose of, using the proceeds to acquire other books.[33] (Four hundred pounds had been left to Harvard to be invested in sound and profitable loans, the interest applied to the advancement of "useful and polite literature.") On the same occasion, John Lowell delivered a formal eulogy of the late president that thoroughly confused his ancestry, but was otherwise a creditable attempt to present a just evaluation of the man in the manner of a French Academician. Lowell reflected on the habits of orderliness that had allowed Bowdoin to pursue effectively a multiplicity of interests, on his Christian faith, "not ostentatious, enthusiastic, or intolerant," on his steadiness of character, and on his resistance to the dissipation to which young men of his class and wealth so often succumbed. He revealed Bowdoin's youthful fling at writing poetry, but hastened to assure his listeners that this penchant was swiftly banished by more serious pursuits. He denied him extraordinary gifts or brilliance of mind, but that was to the good, Lowell observed; great geniuses were usually deficient in judgment and unable to restrain their romantic and impious proclivities, often injuring the world more than they benefited it. Lowell referred briefly to Bowdoin's Huguenot forebears in dilating upon his role as a patriot conspicuously engaged in treasonable acts against the British Crown: "He was a lover of peace, but he did not inherit from his ancestors, nor had he imbibed from any other source the principles of passive obedience and passive resistance."[34]

In appraising Bowdoin's scientific achievements Lowell was more gingerly. He reflected on Bowdoin's integrity in criticizing Franklin's hypothesis on the nature of light as opposed to Newton's, despite his reverence and friendship for Franklin. But Lowell had to admit that the theory of a sphere encircling the planetary system to counteract the waste of light from the sun and fixed stars and to explain certain luminous phenomena in the heavens might be open to some objections. A cautious lawyer, Lowell adroitly switched from the questionable hypothesis to the qualities of mind of its proponent. Bowdoin was not one of those learned scientists too timid to venture on new and unexplored paths. What if his idea was visionary? Some of the most useful and important discoveries in the world had grown out of defective theories advanced by bold and imaginative thinkers. Lowell laid Bowdoin to rest by the side of Plato, Pliny, and Aristotle, Bacon, Descartes, Whiston, and Burnet.

Manasseh Cutler attended the memorial meeting and described its solemnities in his diary: "We walked in procession from the Hall of the Bank to Mr. Thatcher's

---

33. Volz, *Governor Bowdoin & His Family*, 9. See also Academy Letters, 1:100 verso and 101, extract of Bowdoin's will, and letter from James III to Joseph Willard, 17 Jan. 1791.

34. John Lowell, *An Eulogy on Hon. James Bowdoin, LL.D. before the American Academy of Arts and Sciences, delivered January 26, 1791*, 10. See also Academy Records, 1:139.

Meeting House [the Brattle Street Church], where the Hon. Mr Lowell delivered a most elegant oration in honor of our late President, Governor Bowdoin. Very full assembly. We returned in procession. Dined at Dr. Dexter's. Drank tea at Mrs. Bowdoin's."[35]

As long as Hancock was alive and governor of Massachusetts, the question of founding a college in memory of James Bowdoin was debated without conclusion in the General Court of Massachusetts. James Bowdoin III had warned that the very mention of his father's name would foil the establishment of the institution.[36] Bowdoin's death had not ended the hostility between the two rival patriots, and Hancock would never sign a bill honoring his archenemy. But after Hancock died in October of 1793 and Bowdoin's son promised financial support, the General Court on 24 June 1794 passed, and Governor Samuel Adams signed, an act to establish a college in Brunswick, Maine. In a display of filial piety, young James three days later offered the college a thousand dollars in specie and a thousand acres of land in the town of Bowdoin, to be disposed of as the Board of Overseers and Corporation saw fit; his gift was accepted the following December. He also gave them a note he held against Brigadier General Samuel Thompson, interest from which was to fund a professorship of mathematics and of natural and experimental philosophy. And he made bequests to the college of some three thousand books, his collection of scientific instruments, and all his works of art except the family portraits (which eventually came to the college through his widow, Sarah Bowdoin Dearborn). Under the terms of his will, the president of Bowdoin College received £50 sterling, as did the poor of the Brattle Street Church and its minister.[37] The college was the monument raised to James Bowdoin's pre-eminence as an intellectual leader in the early days of the American republic. James Bowdoin III, diplomat and gentleman farmer, made secular institutions such as Harvard University, the American Academy of Arts and Sciences, and Bowdoin College the objects of his largesse, allowing them to overshadow the church, though not completely to displace it. The heavenly afterlife of his father's soul—and his own—was neglected, while James Bowdoin II's earthly immortality was secured in Bowdoin College. John Adams grieved that James III had turned Republican, spurning the federal faith of his father, and had become atheistical to boot.

35. Cutler, *Life, Journals and Correspondence* 1:464–65.

36. Volz, *Governor Bowdoin & His Family*, 3.

37. Ibid., 4–5, 40–41; MHS, *Collections*, ser.7.6 (Bowdoin and Temple Papers, 2), 210–11, James Bowdoin III to the Overseers and Corporation of Bowdoin College, Boston, 27 June 1794; 211–12, Committee of the Overseers of Bowdoin College to James Bowdoin III, Portland, Me., 27 Dec. 1794. There is a copy of the will, dated 4 June 1811, at the Massachusetts Historical Society.

Changing of the Guard

It was not until 24 May 1791, more than six months after James Bowdoin's death, that the Academy proceeded to the election of a new president. The honor fell to His Excellency John Adams, LL.D., vice-president of the United States. Some of the stalwarts of Bowdoin's day at first remained in power under the new administration: Joseph Willard was chosen vice-president, and Samuel Adams, Loammi Baldwin, Richard Cranch, Francis Dana, Caleb Gannett, Benjamin Lincoln, John Lowell, Robert Treat Paine, Dr. Cotton Tufts, and Dr. John Warren, councillors. Since it was presumed that John Adams would be absent from Massachusetts, the statutes were amended to provide that his duties be carried out by the vice-president of the Academy. When Adams was further elevated to the presidency of the United States, a grandiloquent exchange of patriotic sentiments took place between the body over which he presided in name only and the new chief executive of the nation. The congratulatory address was presented by a committee composed of Judge Lowell, the Reverend Dr. Thacher, and Dr. Warren—symbolizing the lawyer, the clergyman, and the doctor, a trinity that constituted the soul of the august body.

In their address the members of the Academy recalled that their institution had been founded at a moment when the country was struggling for its freedom and independence, and they evoked Adams's exertions that had contributed mightily to the establishment of a nation where the rights of men were respected and supported. In passing, the Fellows reaffirmed their devotion to the goals to which the Academy had been dedicated: "Their pursuits are literary. They wish to add to the knowledge which their country already possesses, and to use their correspondence with foreigners engaged in the same pursuits, so as to answer this valuable purpose." They then turned to a glowing portrayal of their country, proclaimed themselves a chosen people, and extolled John Adams as the embodiment of the virtues of their society. The high point of their pledge of allegiance was a promise that Fellows of the Academy, while committed to the advancement of knowledge, would add their mite to strengthen the political order that sustained them:

> They cannot, however, be indifferent to the peace and happiness of the land in which they live, nor to the preservation of those invaluable constitutions of government, which distinguish it from all other nations. They know that these constitutions will not answer the important purposes for which they were formed, unless they are well administered. With pleasure they find their President, whom they have so long known and so highly esteemed, called by the free suffrages of his fellow-citizens, to the arduous task of guiding the counsels, preserving the honour, and supporting the prosperity of the United States, in succession to the man whose distinguished integrity and disinterested patriotism his fellow citizens have so universally attested. Their

aid in accomplishing these desirable purposes cannot be greatly effective; but you may be assured that their influence will always be exerted to promote the measures of a government founded on the basis of true liberty and administered with wisdom and firmness. They feel high satisfaction when they find these virtues marked on the measures which you have hitherto adopted; and they ardently pray that the Infinite Source of Light, and of Power may always direct you, and crown with success your efforts to promote the welfare of your country, and the happiness of mankind.

Adams delivered himself of a gracious reply. He reminded the Fellows that the commands of the public had obliged him to reside in foreign countries and in "distant States" for almost the whole period of the Academy's existence; but no part of any time had been spent with more genuine satisfaction than the "few hours" he had been allowed to pass in their midst. He regretted that "indispensable avocations" had prevented him from sharing in the glory of their success in adding to the knowledge of their country and in the improvement of the useful arts; but he rejoiced in the unanimity with which the Academy, Harvard, and the whole body of the clergy of the Commonwealth, "all so happily connected together," were attached to the federal administration. His eloquence hailed the rising generation of Americans as the most promising and perhaps most important youth that the human species could boast. This new generation of Americans, educated in the principles represented by the Academy, Harvard, and the clergy, could not fail to meet the high expectations the world had formed of their future wisdom, virtues, and energies. After declaring how arduous a task it was to succeed the great Washington, a sacred presence referred to but not named, Adams concluded with an expression of gratitude for the Academy's approval and "explicit sanction" of his policies.[38]

The history of the Academy both during Adams's absentee presidency and after his return to Quincy is hardly brilliant. The minute book drones on with the record of the election of new members, their stereotyped acceptances, the annual selection of officers, and the donation of books to the library. Acknowledgment of the Rumford gift was a principal event. Thirteen years after the signing of the Treaty of Paris, the patriot philosophers were not averse to receiving a benefaction in the form of stocks valued at five thousand dollars from the Tory scientist whose depredations in the towns of Long Island had made him notorious among the Americans.[39] (The Rumford Prize for discoveries on heat or light is still being awarded by the Academy.)

A sample of communications presented to the Academy offers few surprises; for the most part the pabulum of the late Bowdoin epoch continued to nourish the Fellows. Observations of the aurora borealis and records of morbidity and

38. Academy Records, 2:46, meeting of 23 Aug. 1797; 47–49, address and reply.
39. Academy Letters, 2:50, Rumford to John Adams, London, 12 July 1796.

mortality, along with additions to the mineralogical cabinet, were a mainstay. Such esoterica as studies of the effect of human saliva on the lamprey eel, Oliver Fiske's report on a mouse found enclosed in a fossil substance, an account of wild rice in upper Canada, statistics on the lives of Harvard graduates, and animadversions on the dangerous practice of sleeping on damp ground, provided some diversity. A rare example of a foreign communication was a paper by Fr. Adr. Van Der Kemp, a Fellow from Holland, on the theories of Buffon and Jefferson. Dighton Rock continued to fascinate some of the members as it had thirty years before, and at the Academy's expense two hundred copies of the scratchings were run off. A piece by Dr. A. Fothergill introduced on 9 August 1809 arrests the attention of a twenty-first-century browser among the Academy letters and records of the Adams epoch: "An Essay on the art of aërostation, with a view towards rendering aërial voyages not only more useful and interesting to the community but more safe to aëronauts. With hints to inexperienced adventurers on the possibility of steering the balloon, and of evading the danger to which they are occasionally exposed."[40] The most noteworthy figure to make an appearance in the Academy during this dreary period was Nathaniel Bowditch, a self-educated astronomer and mathematician elected in 1799. His numerous papers published in the *Memoirs* and his translation, with commentary, of Laplace's *Mécanique céleste* achieved world renown.

The business of the Academy was usually conducted by a succession of corresponding secretaries, but when Adams was back in Quincy, he occasionally intervened in controversies involving moral questions. In 1804 he firmly upheld the principle of the validity of scientific expression irrespective of its sources. He defended the right to be heard of one George Baron, an Englishman residing in New York, who had criticized James Winthrop's mathematical papers. On 11 April Adams wrote to Judge John Davis, "I know neither the Person nor the Character but it seems to me that a demonstration will not be the less mathematical for the Nation or Morals of the Author. The Academy can not know the Manners of all their correspondents, and if the Cause of Truth is really promoted by a bad Man even whom they know to be Such, I cannot see reason to reject his Labours."[41]

Annually the members of the Academy went through the motions of choosing John Adams as their president, and he regularly accepted the honor. The close of an epoch was signaled when on 4 June 1813, after being duly re-elected once again, Adams finally resigned. He pled his advanced age and the sicknesses and misfortunes in his numerous and dispersed family. Attendance at the meetings of the Academy had become impossible for him. In a moment of candor, he confessed to the members that he ought not to have continued so many years in the presi-

---

40. Academy Records, 2:103, 149–50.
41. Academy Letters, 3:11, Adams to Judge John Davis, Quincy, 11 Apr. 1804.

dency. His farewell letter was a touching reminder of his long association with the Academy and a tribute to its members: "An Election to the Chair of that learned and Reverend and Honourable and every way respectable Society, I have ever esteemed, the highest honour and most precious reward of my Life. And so great and invariable has been the pleasure I have found in the company and conversation of the Members that nothing but necessity would induce me to decline it."[42]

The reins of office were turned over in May of 1814 to the octogenarian Dr. Edward Augustus Holyoke, one of the few incorporating Fellows still alive. Holyoke lasted as president only four of the fifteen years still remaining to him. On 25 May 1818, he wrote a letter of resignation in a shaky hand, pleading his infirmities, and offered the Academy a theodolite, a surveying instrument imported from London, as a parting gift.[43] The next man elected president, the Honorable Christopher Gore, LL.D., simply declined to serve.

Later in the century the Academy made a more felicitous choice. The eminent and versatile physician Dr. Jacob Bigelow, who became a Fellow in 1812 while Adams was still president of the institution, ascended to its highest office in 1846. Bigelow happily lacked the solemnity of James Bowdoin and John Adams, though he was a conscientious and effective president for seventeen years, and contributed to the *Memoirs* several papers ranging from the life of Count Rumford to the death of Pliny the Elder. In an address before the Academy on 27 October 1852, Bigelow surveyed the development of the society from its beginnings in the dark days of the Revolution to its newly flourishing condition. While he paid tribute to the "constellation of worthies" enrolled as the first members and to their heroic efforts to build an edifice of learning amid the constraints and ravages of war, he poked good-natured fun at some of their early preoccupations, not excluding the astronomic hypotheses of the first president. But to forestall any denigration of the Academy in its formative years, he recalled the equally bizarre investigations undertaken by the Royal Society of London in its initial period. He admonished his hearers not to disparage the achievements of their Academic predecessors, whose inquisitiveness and even credulity had kept their minds open to knowledge from whatever source it emanated.

After decades when the Academy had languished in provincial obscurity, Bigelow hailed in purple prose the advent of a new vitality in its enterprises, nourished by the growth of population and the increase of wealth available to support science in its numerous and varied branches. Encapsulating the years of doldrums in a

42. Ibid., 100, Adams to John Farrar (corresponding secretary of the Academy), Quincy, 4 June 1813; Academy Records, 2:173–75.

43. Ibid., 178, meeting of 24 May 1814; Academy Letters, 3:126, Holyoke to the Academy, 25 May 1818; Academy Records, 2:211–12, 217.

metaphor, he conceded that the light of the Academy had not often been overfed with fuel or tended with unremitting vigilance. But, he was quick to add, "it has at least never been suffered to go wholly out; and, after glimmering with uncertain, yet increasing rays, for two thirds of a century, it has at length grown to be an acknowledged beacon in science, a light to the philosophic of our own country, a western star, to whose unshadowed brilliancy and true monitions the European world now looks with interest and respect."[44]

44. Jacob Bigelow, "Address Delivered Before the American Academy of Arts and Sciences," in *Modern Inquiries: Classical, Professional, and Miscellaneous* (Boston, 1867), 339–40; see also MHS, *Proceedings* 17 (1879–80), 457 ff.

APPENDIX 1
Act of Incorporation of the American Academy of Arts and Sciences

An Act to incorporate and establish a Society for the cultivation and promotion of Arts and Sciences

As the Arts and Sciences are the foundation and support of agriculture, manufactures, and commerce; as they are necessary to the wealth, peace, independence and happiness of a people; as they essentially promote the honor and dignity of the government which patronises them; and as they are most effectually cultivated, and diffused through a State, by the forming and incorporating of men of genius and learning into public societies: For these beneficial purposes,

Be it therefore enacted by the Council and House of Representatives in General Court assembled, and by the authority of the same, That the Hon. Samuel Adams, Esq; Hon. John Adams, Esq; John Bacon, Esq; Hon. James Bowdoin, Esq; Rev. Charles Chauncy, D. D. Rev. John Clark, David Cobb, Esq; Rev. Samuel Cooper, D. D. Hon. Thomas Cushing, Esq; Hon. Nathan Cushing, Esq; Hon. William Cushing, Esq; Tristram Dalton, Esq; Hon. Francis Dana, Esq; Rev. Samuel Deane, Rev. Perez Fobes, Rev. Caleb Gannett, Hon. Henry Gardner, Esq; Mr. Benjamin Guild, Hon. John Hancock, Esq; Hon. Joseph Hawley, Esq; Edward Augustus Holyoke, Esq; Dr. Ebenezer Hunt, Jonathan Jackson, Esq; Dr. Charles Jarvis, Rev. Samuel Langdon, D. D. Hon. Levi Lincoln, Esq; Rev. Daniel Little, Rev. Elijah Lothrop, John Lowell, Esq; Rev. Samuel Mather, D. D. Samuel Moody, Esq; Hon. Andrew Oliver, Esq; Dr. Joseph Orne, Dr. Theodore Parsons, Hon. George Partridge, Esq; Hon. Robert Treat Paine, Esq; Rev. Phillips Payson, Samuel Phillips, jun. Esq; Hon. John Pickering, Esq; Hon. Oliver Prescot, Esq; Rev. Zedekiah Sanger, Hon. Nathaniel Peaslee Sergeant, Esq; Micajah Sawyer, Esq; Theodore Sedgwick, Esq; Hon. William Sever, Esq; Stephen Sewall, Esq; Hon. David Sewall, Esq; John Sprague, Esq; Ebenezer Storer, Esq; Caleb Strong, Esq; Hon. James Sullivan, Esq; Dr. John Bernard Sweat, Mr. Nathaniel Tracy, Cotton Tufts, Esq; Hon. James Warren, Esq; Rev. Samuel West, Rev. Edward Wigglesworth, Rev. Joseph Willard, Rev. Samuel Williams, Rev. Abraham Williams, Rev. Nehemiah Williams, and Mr. James Winthrop, be, and they hereby are formed into, constituted and made a Body Politic and Corporate, by the name of THE AMERICAN ACADEMY OF ARTS AND SCIENCES; and that they and their successors, and such other persons as shall be elected in the manner hereafter mentioned, shall be, and continue a Body Politic and Corporate, by the same name forever.

And be it further enacted by the authority aforesaid, That the Fellows of the said Academy may from time to time elect a President, one or more Vice Presidents, one or more Secretaries, and such other Officers of the said Academy, as they shall judge necessary or convenient; and they shall have full power and authority from time to time to determine and establish the names, number and duties, of their several officers, and the tenure or estate they shall respectively have in their offices; and also to authorize and impower their President, or some other Fellow of the Academy, at their pleasure, to administer such oaths to such officers as they shall appoint and determine, for the well ordering and good government of the said Academy: provided the same be not repugnant to the laws of this State.

And be it further enacted by the authority aforesaid, That the Fellows of the said Academy shall have one common seal, which they may make use of in whatsoever cause or business shall concern the Academy, or be relative to the end and design of its institution; and shall have power and authority from time to time to break, change, and renew the common seal, at their pleasure; and that they may sue and be sued in all actions, real, personal and mixed, and prosecute and defend the same unto final judgment and execution, by the name of, The President and Fellows of the American Academy of Arts and Sciences.

And be it further enacted by the authority aforesaid, That the Fellows of the said Academy may from time to time elect such persons to be Fellows thereof, as they shall judge proper; and that they shall have full power and authority from time to time, to suspend, expel or disfranchise, any Fellow of the said Academy, who shall by his conduct render himself unworthy of a place in that body, in the judgment of the Academy; and also to settle and establish the rules, forms and conditions of election, suspension, expulsion and disfranchisement. Provided, That the number of the said Academy, who are inhabitants of this State, shall not, at any one time, be more than two hundred, nor less than forty.

And be it further enacted by the authority aforesaid, That the Fellows of the said Academy shall have full power and authority from time to time, to make and enact such reasonable rules, orders and bye-laws, not repugnant to the laws of this State, as shall be necessary or convenient for the well ordering and good government of the said Academy; and to annex reasonable pecuniary fines and penalties to the breach of them, not exceeding the sum of twenty pounds, to be sued for and recovered in any Court of record within this State, in the name and for the use of the President and Fellows of the said Academy; and the same rules, orders and bye-laws to repeal at their pleasure: And also to settle and establish the times, places, and manner of convening the Fellows of the said Academy: And also to determine the number of Fellows which shall be present, to constitute a meeting of the said Academy. Provided, That the Fellows of the said Academy shall meet twice in a year at the least; and that the place of their meeting shall never be more than thirty miles distant from the town of Boston.

And be it further enacted by the authority aforesaid, That the Fellows of the said Academy may, and shall forever hereafter be deemed capable in the law of having, holding, and taking in fee-simple, or any less estate, by gift, grant, devise or otherwise, any lands, tenements, or other estate, real and personal: Provided, That the annual income, of the said real estate, shall not exceed the sum of five hundred pounds, and the annual income or interest of the said personal estate shall not exceed the sum of two thousand pounds. All the sums aforementioned in this act to be valued in silver, at the rate of six shillings and eight-pence by the ounce. And the annual interest and income of the said real and personal estate, together with the fines and penalties aforesaid, shall be appropriated for premiums to encourage improvements and discoveries in agriculture, arts and manufactures, or for other purposes, consistent with the end and design of the institution of the said Academy, as the Fellows thereof shall determine.

And be it further enacted by the authority aforesaid, That the end and design of the institution of the said Academy is, to promote and encourage the knowledge of the antiquities of America, and of the natural history of the country, and to determine the uses to which the various natural productions of the country may be applied; to promote and encourage medical discoveries, mathematical disquisitions, philosophical enquiries, and experiments; astronomical, meteorological and geographical observations; and improvements in agriculture, arts, manufactures and commerce; and in fine, to cultivate every art and science, which may tend to advance the interest, honor, dignity and happiness of a free, independent and virtuous people.

And it is further enacted, that the place where the first meeting of the Fellows of the said Academy shall be held, shall be the Philosophy Chamber in the University of Cambridge; and that the Honorable James Bowdoin, Esq; be, and he hereby is authorised and empowered to fix the time for holding the said meeting, and to notify the same to the Fellows of the Academy.

APPENDIX 2
Philosophical Attacks on Bowdoin's Cosmology and His Defense

(Massachusetts Historical Society: Bowdoin and Temple Papers; Winthrop Papers)

1.

Hon[d] & dear Sir: Salem 15 March 1784

Having the honour to be chosen one of the Committee for inspecting &c. the Philosophical Papers, communicated to the American Academy; I received, some time since, a large Packet from the Rev'd Mr Cutler, containing a Number of such Papers. Among these is one containing Observations on Light &c. communicated by your Honōr to the Society. The Perusal gave me great Pleasure: But it contains an Hypothesis, which, with all due Deference, I beg the Liberty to observe upon, as it is offered for the Consideration of the Society.

What I refer to is the concave sphere you suppose, "consisting of Matter *sui generis*, surrounding each System, or each Collection of Systems, or the whole System of Systems, comprehending the whole visible Creation, and acting by the Power of Gravity."

This, Sir, you offer as a Remedy against the Effects of the Newtonian Law of Gravitation, the continual Operation of which, throughout the various Systems of the Universe, would finally bring on a Dissolution of the Whole: Indeed you justly query whether it would not long ago have brought it on? "It has (as you say) been observed by Philosophers, (Sir I Newton demonstrates it in his Principia) that a Body placed any where within a hollow Sphere, which is homogeneous, and every where of the same thickness, will have no Gravity, wheresoever it be placed; the opposite Gravities always precisely destroying each other." But you think *that* Observation cannot be applied to the hollow Sphere above described; for, "by the Description it is not homogeneous nor need it be of equal thickness."

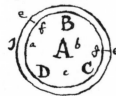

Upon which, Sir, you will give me leave to make one or two Observations.

Let there be an hollow Sphere ABCD,[+] concave towards A, and homogeneous throughout, both in Matter and Thickness, (as at cf, ef &c). A heavenly Body placed at a,

---

[+] To represent the immense Sphere in the Hypothesis

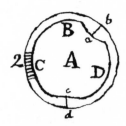

b, or c will be attracted equally towards every Part of the concave Surface, and remain at rest, wherever plac'd within it; as I now take for granted. But if that Sphere should be either thicker in any Part, the Density remaining the same, (as at a b or cd*), or denser with the same Thickness, as at C; any Globes within that Sphere, however near to, or remote from the concave surface of the Sphere, would lose their Indifference to every Part of the same, and tend to the thicker or denser Part; where they would, at length unite in one Mass, approaching such Part with an accelerating Velocity till they finally formed one huge heap of chaotick Worlds.

On the other Hand, were this Sphere homogeneous thro'out; any two or more Bodies placed within it would also in Time, come together in their common Center of Gravity, which would in Effect be the same as if no such Concave Sphere existed.

As our Apprehensions of the supreme Author of the Universe, however inadequate finite Minds may be to the Idea; are, that he is infinite in every sense of the Word, wherein Perfection of any kind is implied; and as prescribing any Limits whatever may be deemed derogatory to the Perfections of that infinite Intelligence which presides over all; his Essence must necessarily be supposed immense. Sir I. Newton calls infinite Space "*the Sensorium of the Deity.*" If immense in his Essence, he must be equally so in his Productions** and Operations. Our Glasses assure us that, innumerable as the Stars appear to unassisted Sight, it is but a small Part that we see without their Aid; and the higher their magnifying Powers arise, the more of those Luminaries are discovered: Which affords us a rational Presumption that they are disseminated through out universal Extension, with which, if the Essence of the Deity be coextended, which is an Article both in the Christian's and Philosopher's Creed; all the primary Globes in the Universe may be so disposed as to retain their relative situations to each other thro' indefinite Periods; there being, in that Case no Common Center of Gravity thro'out the TO ΠAN.

I hope Hon^d Sir you will pardon the freedom herein taken, nor can I doubt when I know your Candour to be equal to your Judgment; in Confidence whereof I subscribe myself Hon^d Sir

Your most respectful & obed^t Servt

A. Oliver

Honble James Bowdoin Esq.

---

* Fig. 2
** For in what Space can his great Fiat fail?—Dr Young

2.

Andrew Oliver, Esq.
    At Salem   Boston, April 13, 1784
    Sir,

I am greatly obliged to you for the favour of your letter of ye 15th ult^e wch I did not receive until ye 30th, and my engagements since have prevented an earlier reply. As you are one of the Com^{tee} of ye American Academy for inspecting &c. the philosophical papers communicated to that Society, you will have an opportunity of seeing the two other papers I laid before them on the same Subject with the one, which has been honoured with your observations on some parts of it. I wish it had so happened that all ye three could have been under your inspection at ye same time, that I might have had ye benefit & pleasure of your criticisms upon them: for which I should have been, and if you will please to favour me with them, I shall be further obliged to you. In expectation of that favour I shall be the shorter on the Subject of your letter.

I agree with you in your several observations on ye hollow sphere, excepting one: wherein you say that "any globes within the hetrogenous Sphere you have described, however near to, or remote from ye concave Surface of the Sphere, would lose their indifference to every part of ye same, and tend to ye thicker or denser part, where they would at length unite in one mass." This effect might be expected, if there were only one part of ye Sphere denser than ye rest, or those globes had no gravitation towards each other to balance their gravitation or tendency to the thicker or denser parts of ye Sphere. But if those denser parts were duely adjusted in regard to number & situation as well as density; and there took place between the globes a mutual gravitation, to which ye gravitation between them and those denser were proportioned & adjusted parts of ye Sphere, in all which adjustments situation & distance would be considered, would not those globes in that case retain their places, and of course be prevented from uniting in one mass, either at the common centre of gravity, or at any one of the denser parts of the sphere?

All these circumstances are included in, and make a part of ye hypothesis, contained in ye paper, to wch your letter refers: as you will observe by recurring to it again. But, if I mistake not, they are not all attended to, in your observations on that hypothesis.

To set aside ye hypothesis you advance an argument drawn from ye immensity or infinity of the author of ye universe, and a supposed necessarily consequent infinity of his productions: from which you infer "that ye heavenly bodies are disseminated thro' universal extension, and may be so disposed as to retain their relative situations to each other thro' indefinite periods, or (as ye argument seems to require) thro' infinite Space: there being in that case no common centre of gravity throughout the ΤΟ ΠΑΝ :" and therefore (by implication) no gravitation or tendency to such a centre.

This conclusion is not supported by phaenomena. On ye contrary, phaenomena, so far at least as they respect our System, prove that there is a centre of gravity. The earth has its centre of gravity: the other planets respectively, theirs: and ye whole System its common centre in ye Sun. Hence, by analogy, & ye uniformity of nature, it may be inferred, that every other System has its centre; and all of them together a common centre.

But it is objected those Systems being disseminated through universal Space there can be no common centre: and that they are so disseminated, you think is so proved. "If ye author of ye Universe be immense in his essence (wch is granted) he <u>must</u> be equally so in his productions and operations." that is, his productions must be immense or infinite. — Here it is supposed, that his productions are ye effect of necessity. If this necessity flows from his essence, as it seems it must do, if it exists at all, must it not be coeval, as well as co-extended, with his essence? and in that case, must not his productions if (being the effect of necessity) they can properly be called his, be like his essence, not only immense or infinite, but eternal and unchangeable, & be, at least in those respects, on an equality with himself? and would not this be derogatory to the character & dignity of their Supreme author? Does not this necessity destroy every idea of choice or free agency with regard to those productions; and degrade him below some of them, if choice or free agency denotes dignity, and belongs to any of his creatures?

These queries among others that might be offered, make me doubtful of ye justness of ye conclusion, that because the author of ye universe is immense in his essence, he must be equally so in his productions. This conclusion you seem to propose is strengthened by ye discoveries made with the assistance of glasses. It is true, as you observe, that ye higher their magnifying powers rise, the greater is ye number of stars discovered: which affords a proof they are very numerous, and beyond our ken aided by the best glasses: but can it properly be adduced in support of a conclusion, which may appear not to follow from the preceeding premises?

These hasty observations I beg leave to submit to your candid correction, and am with great esteem, Dr Sir,

Y^r M^o obt. hbl^e Servt
James Bowdoin

3.

Philadelphia 16 Nov.ʳ 1787

Dear Sir

I duly received your fav.ʳ inclosing your Philosophick Treatise, replete with Literature, usefull Observations, & much Ingenuity of Conjecture—

You may perhaps think that I wanted Taste to relish your Ideas properly, or Gratitude for the fav.ʳ of your Communication, that I have neglected acknologing the rec.ᵗ of it so Long, but I am not willing to admit either of these for the True Reasons. I think I have a better. I was struck with Some of your tho'ts which were new to me, & tho't it best to take time to Examine them, before I troubled you with any remarks, which run me up to that period, when the Troubles & disorders of your States in that Time of your Government wou.ᵈ Effectually Engross all your attention & Leave you little Liesure to consider my Remarks. Since Which sundry avocations of my own have delayed the Matter 'till Now.

The principle which Engaged me most was your hypothesis of an hollow Sphere in Which the heavenly bodies Exist either moving or Stationary, on which I beg leave to make my remarks with all the respect due to Genius, & at the Same time with all the freedom of a Philosopher.

1. It appears to me that an hypothesis of Such a Stupendious piece of Creation as Such an hollow Sphere must be existing as a Solid Boundary of that part of the Universe which falls under our notice, without Some kind of Solid proof of its real entity, is rather an Extravagance of Imagination, than a Philosophick Principle—I don't doubt indeed but the Almighty if he had occasion for such a Vast Sphere, cou'd Create one as Easy as he cou.ᵈ make a balloon: but I cant think it quite decent in us to ascribe to him such amazing Efforts of omnipotence, 'till he Shall give us Some Sort of indications of their real Existence—But

2. if Such a Sphere does Exist, I dont see how it can Solve the Phenomena for which 'tis introduced,—if Such a Sphere existed of Equal thickness or Solidity in Every part & a globe of Matter was placed in its Center, the Equality of Attraction to Every part w.ᵈ keep it stationary, but if a Diameter sho.ᵈ be drawn thro' the Center, and the Planet sho.ᵈ be placed on one fourth part of the said Diameter, 'tis plain that it w.ᵈ be at three times greater distance from one Side of the Sphere than from the other, & of Course (according to the known Laws of Attraction which are in Reciprocal proportion of the Square of the distance) the attraction to the nearest Side wou'd be much Greater (9 times greater) than towards the further Side, & of Consequence all ballance of attraction w.ᵈ be Lost, & the planet w.ᵈ be drawn directly from its Station, into contact with the Side of the Sphere which is nearest to it.—again Suppose Two Semi Diameters of the Sphere sho.ᵈ be drawn meeting Each other at the Center in any given Angle (say 30°) & on the Same Center a Circle sho.ᵈ be drawn whose periphery sho.ᵈ Cut the said Semi-diameters into Two

Equal parts & on the point of intersection of Each, Two planets sho.^{d} be placed i.e. one on Each: now I Say if we cou'd get over the above objections, & the power of Attraction of the Surrounding sphere sho.^{d} keep them both at rest. Yet Nothing could prevent their being drawn by their mutual attraction towards Each other till they w.^{d} come into contact with Each other, for the Powers of Attraction of the Surrounding sphere operating on the Two planets must be perfectly Equal from Every part in order to keep them Stationary, & their mutual attraction towards Each other w.^{d} destroy that ball^{ce} in the direction of its action & of Course draw them towards Each other till they came in Contact.

—Again suppose the hollow Sphere Sho.^{d} be Cut by a plane passing thro' the Center of a Star placed in the middle of one of the Semi-Diameters of the Sphere & perpendicular to the Semi-Diameter, Then let innumerable right lines be drawn from one side of the Sphere thro' the Center of the Star & in that place intersecting the said plane in Every possible Angle, 'tis plain

1. that each of these right lines would be Cut by the plane in the Center of the Star into two unequal parts, 2. that the Attraction of the Star towards the Sphere at each End of Said line, w.^{d} be reciprocally in the Ratio of the Squares of the Said Two Unequal parts of Said line, & therefore, 3. The Attraction w.^{d} be Much Stronger towards the Side of the Sphere at the End of the Shortest line than towards that part w^c is placed at the End of the Longest line, & 4. that Superior Attraction w.^{d} unavoidably draw the Star from its first Station Towards that part of the Sphere w^c was nearest to it. These reasonings are all Grounded on the Supposition of an hollow Sphere, the whole Superficies of w^c is homogeneous, (having every Equal Section composed of Equal Q^{ty} of matter & Equally Shaped & situated) & demonstrate the Error of the received opinion, which you refer to, viz "that a body placed any where within a hollow Sphere w^c is homogeneous will have no Gravity"—Again if we Suppose a Sphere whose Periphery is not homogeneous Let the Irregularity be little or much, it cannot be Capable of more than one point for its Center of Gravity, therefore, 1. if any body at rest gets any how jostled one foot out of that point, its rest is Lost nor can it ever recover its Station & 2. any revolving body within Such a Sphere can never preserve the Same orbit, but must be perpetually varying its Track as long as it continues to move at all—as to the white spots in the heavens being apertures in the sphere thro' which the Stars of an exterior story of the heavens appear to us I think it plain if there were any such appertures they w.^{d} appear to us *Opake* not *bright* Spots, because the rays of the interior Story would pass thro' those apertures and of Course cou.^{d} not be reflected back to us but must be Lost in the vast Expanse beyound them —.to obviate this by Supposing that the Region *beyound* the first arc is vastly more luminous than that *within* it, and of course shines thro the apertures with more or Stronger Rays than are reflected to us from the Interior Surfaces of our Sphere, appears to me

contrary to a very Common Maxim among Philosophers, viz that Nature does Every thing in the Easiest way, and I think it w.^d be much Easier to Suppose (if Such a Sphere really Existed) that the Luminous Spots, Milky Way &c were Occasion'd by the Great reflection of Light which might be made from Some parts of the Interior Surface of the Sphere being better Polish.^d than the rest made of Glass or in some other way Qualified to reflect light more copiously than the other parts of it.—But my worst objection still remains. Your hypothesis is purposely calculated to remove all Seeds of Death & Tendency to dissolution from the internal Constitution of the Material Universe, but tis the received & Establish.^d Opinion of all Good divines, that it must & will have an end, & was not Ever design'd by its creator to be of Infinite Duration & all Good Philosophers Since the Reformation of Newton have as constantly maintain'd that the Whole System carries in the very Stamina of it the very causes of its end, the very principles of Dissolution whose constant & natural operations tend to & must unavoidably end in its final catastrophy & produce at least the ruin of the System, if not the annihilation of its materials.—Errors in philosophy even in the first Character are venial, but to be a bad Christian must be dolefull indeed!—

I hope, Sir, You will not be offended by the freedom of my Remarks. Wilst Rapt in pursuit of Your flight of tho't, I have too much forgot your dignity of Character, & address'd You more with the freedom of a Classmate than perhaps I ought. I have only to say in Excuse that Philosophy knows no Compliments or distinctions. *Ardua Tentare* Enobles the mind, wilst it requires Strength of Genius to be capable of it, & I hope Your Vast Extent of Enquiry & investigation will not be Checked because I Stumble by the way & cannot keep pace with You—I am pleased with the Richness of Your mind & Your Turn to Philosophick researches, and sho.^d think myself very happy to be in the neighborhood of a Gentleman of like Genius & Taste, with whom I might now & then Spend an Evening or Liesure hour in that kind of mental Improvement, & Your comunications will Ever be very acceptable to me.—

I presume to inclose you Two of my Late political pamphlets, which may perhaps amuse you for half an hour, not by any novelty of the tho'ts or power of the Reasonings but because they contain a kind of history of the objections & answers which prevail here, relative to the new Constitution which now Engrosses the Attention of all the United States, & is really of the most Essential consequence to us all.

I have the honour to be with Every Sentiment of Esteem & Respect

Sir,
Your Most Obed.^t
hum.^e Servt
Pela Webster

The hon.^{ble} James Bowdoin Esqr.

4.

Mr. Pelatiah Webster at Philadelphia   Boston Dec.ʳ 12.ᵗʰ 1787

Sir,

With your very obliging & acceptable letter of y.ᵉ 16.ᵗʰ of Nov.ʳ I received your two Pamphlets on the Subject of the proposed Federal Constitution. They contain very just observations on that constitution and the objections, which have been made to it; and I hope they will be of public utility.

I take this opportunity of thanking you for them, and also for the remarks, with which you have honoured a memoir of mine, published with the memoirs of the American Academy.

It seems the hypothesis contained in it of a hollow Sphere, in which the heavenly bodies are supposed to exist, does not meet with your approbation. What gave occasion to the hypothesis, and the reasons on which it is founded, will appear by the memoir: But if they are not sufficient to support it, or to render it in any degree probable, it must like any other baseless fabrick, fall to the ground. It is natural however for the builder to hope, that although it may want the "solid" foundation you require, it may not be so deficient in that respect, as to be deemed a mere "extravagance of imagination": especially when it is considered that upon the idea of its reality, we should probably have no other proof of it than we can now obtain, whether arising from analogy, phaenomena, Scripture or in any other way. "But if such a Sphere does exist, you do not see how it can solve the phaenomena, for (the solution of) which it is introduced": and in proof that it cannot you state several cases of one planet, and of several planets placed within a homogeneous hollow sphere and having reasoned on the cases you say, that "these reasonings demonstrate the error of the received opinion to which I refer, viz, that a body placed any where within a hollow sphere, which is homogeneous and every where of the same thickness will have no gravity, the opposite gravities always precisely destroying each other."—Though the hypothesis be in part founded on the idea, that the hollow sphere is not homogeneous, yet the gravitating principle, as it respects a homogeneous sphere, and the described heterogeneous sphere, being the same; and the operation of it in both producing a balance of the opposite gravities, according to the different combinations and situation of the gravitating matter, it is needful to hint to you some mistakes in your reasonings on the subject.—In the first case you have stated of a planet placed in the centre of such a homogeneous sphere, you observe very justly, that from the equality of attraction, the planet would be stationary but it is necessary further to observe that on removing it from the centre, although a stronger attraction would take place between the planet, and y.ᵉ part of the sphere, towards which it is moved, yet there would be an equally strong counteracting gravitation, arising from a greater portion of the sphere in that case acting on the planet in the counter direction, than acted upon it before the change of its central position; and these opposite gravities will be found to balance each other. With respect to that greater portion of the sphere, notwithstanding the attraction of its parts will be diminished by placing the planet at a greater distance from the centre, yet by that encreased distance its dimensions and consequently its counter gravitation being proportionably encreased, it will, taken all together, possess a power exactly adequate to the annihilating of the opposite attracting power: by which means the planet in its new position, and in every possible position within the sphere, will be stationary. This circumstance seems to have escaped your notice: which being a very important one, and entering into the essence of y.ᵉ question, I am led to doubt your conclusion: viz: "that the attraction to the nearest side of the Sphere would be greater, than towards the further Side; that all balance of attraction would be lost; and that the planet would be drawn from its Station, into contact with the nearest side of the Sphere."

Your next stated case will not be controverted. The two planets mentioned or any number of planets, placed within the described Sphere, would without a projectile or some other force impressed upon them, coalesce; or by their mutual gravitation be drawn into one mass. But this does not affect the hypothesis in question, which is formed upon the idea of a hollow sphere, that is heterogeneous, or of different densities in different parts, and thereby possessing different powers of gravitation, according as the distribution of the several included planetary systems might require: the Systems, considered in relation to each other, and in connection with the Sphere, forming one grand harmonious whole, whose mutual gravitation being duely balanced, would preserve it in an indissoluble union, notwithstanding any interferences, or occasional irregularities in some of its parts.

With regard to such irregularities or interferences as may remarkably injure any particular planet or system, they may be a part of the original plan, intended to correct or extirpate the moral irregularities of its rational inhabitants: the former happening pursuant to the established order & course of things, and at that precise period, when the matter required correction or extirpation; So that instead of being blemishes in the creation, or arguing a want of wisdom or power in contriving and affecting it, they may be the compleatest demonstration of both: the natural world, in the original constitution of it, being made subservient to the moral; and both together further demonstrating the absolute perfection and Supreme excellence of that wisdom and power. —To answer such moral, among other, purposes, Comets seem well adapted. By one of them the general deluge was probably occasioned; and this in consequence of the established laws of gravitation; and at the very period, when correction and extirpation became necessary: and like purposes, without disturbing the general economy of nature, they may, in future, be intended to answer.

It is conceivable then, that your two planets or any given number of planets might retain the stations assigned them, or might revolve round their respective principals without a possibility of interfering with each other, or of being disturbed by any other bodies of the System, further than was originally intended: their orbits, compounded of the gravitating and projectile forces, being uniformly, or with little variation the same.

If the foregoing observations be well founded, of which no Gentleman can form a better judgment than M.ʳ Webster, you will readily determine, whether they do not furnish an answer, not only to your remarks above quoted, but also the remarks contained in the other two cases stated in your letter.

With regard to the luminous Spots in the heavens, I made such use of them as I thought the quoted observations of former Astronomers would justify. But Mr. Hershalle [sic], whose extraordinary magnifiers qualify him to judge better concerning them than preceding astronomers, supposes them to be clusters of stars, that exhibit those appearances.—Having lately read very cursorily what he has published on the subject in the transactions of the royal Society, I can say but little about them, or in particular about his theory respecting the starry heavens. From that hasty reading however, I recollect that his theory would not be subject to what you call your worst objection: for it is not calculated, as you say mine is, to remove from the material universe all seeds of death & tendency to dissolution; and therefore does not militate with y.ᵉ established opinion of all good divines & good philosophers, that it must and will have an end.

According to that theory, the stars, that are now in clusters, were at their creation spread equally through the starry region, but have from y.ᵉ operation of the universal principle of gravitation, been drawn into those clusters; which has occasioned some parts of the heavens to be comparatively destitute of stars. Though I do not recollect he infers from that operation the dissolution of the Universe, it is however very evident from his theory, if he is not mistaken, that the universe or the visible part of it has been, and is, in a rapid progress towards dissolution; which I cannot bring myself into a disposition to believe: and being at present an unbeliever in that doctrine, I am induced to think, that the Scripture account respecting it, to which you refer, is confined to our earth and its atmosphere, especially as the Scripture account given by Moses, of y.ᵉ creation, does not, according to the interpretation of good philosophers, and good divines too, extend any further.

With regard to y.ᵉ Seeds of death disseminated through y.ᵉ Universe or y.ᵉ whole aggregate of material Being & which will produce its dissolution, what proof the philosophers you refer to, have exhibited of it, I do not know: but admitting, and further it is difficult to admit, that there are some tendencies to dissolution in our System, which compared with the immense aggregate is but an atom, is it just to infer from them y.ᵉ dissolution of the whole? Or may not those tendencies be imaginary, and never produce or issue in the apprehended dissolution? Or if real, may they not operate like partial evils to effect a greater, or a general good? Or may they not be the result of the intended irregularities, and occasional interferences above mentioned? And if there be any room for these queries, is the opinion of those divines & philosophers, a certain and incontrovertable truth: "that y.ᵉ whole material universe carries in y.ᵉ very stamina of it y.ᵉ causes of its end, & y.ᵉ principles of dissolution, whose constant & natural operation must unavoidably end in its final catastrophe; and produce at least the ruin of y.ᵉ System, if not the annihilation of its materials"?

Thanking you for the very polite conclusion of your letter, and hoping for your further communications I shall add but a word more.

I agree with you "that errors in philosophy are venial; but to be a bad christian must be doleful indeed!"—From y.ᵉ former part of this declaration, I fully depend on your pardon of my philosophical errors; and with respect to the latter part of it, to convince you, that I am no bad christian, I beg leave to assure you that I am with christian Sincerity & with Sentiments of the most christian regard, dear Sir y.ʳ m.ᵒ ob.ᵗ hble. Serv.ᵗ

James Bowdoin

INDEX